OSSAN IDOL! 05

MANGA ◆ ICHIKA KINO
ORIGINAL STORY ◆
MOCHIKO MOCHIDA
CHARACTER DESIGN ◆
MIZUKI SAKAKIBARA

STORY

MIROKU, A 270 LB UNEMPLOYED SHUT-IN WAS SPURRED ON BY THE POPULARITY OF HIS "LET'S TRY DANCING!" VIDEO, JOINED A GYM, GOT IN SHAPE, AND TRANSFORMED INTO A MIDDLE-AGED HUNK IN NO TIME! ALONG WITH YOICHI AND SHIJU, HE CAUGHT THE EYE OF A FAMOUS PRODUCER, MR. LAVENDER, AND THE THREE MEN SUCCESSFULLY DEBUTED AS MIYOSHI! THE EVENTS THEY PARTICIPATED IN WERE ALL HUGE SUCCESSES TOO. BUT KIRA, A MEMBER OF THE YOUNG AND SUPER-POPULAR IDOL GROUP TENKA, VIEWS MIROKU AS HIS ENEMY!

CHARACTERS

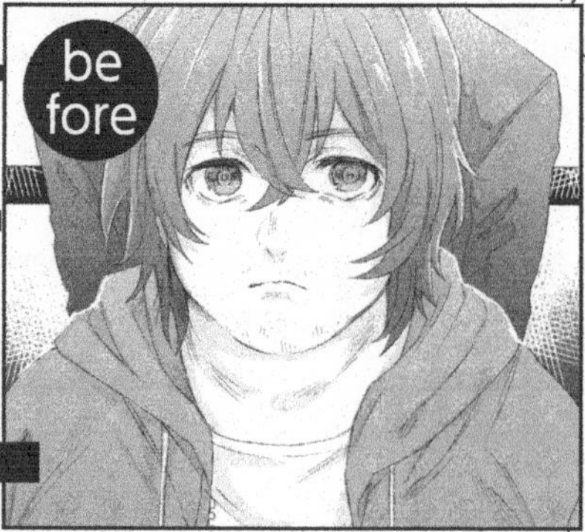
be
fore

MIROKU (36)

MIROKU OSAKI

UNEMPLOYED. SHUT-IN. VIRGIN INTERNET ADDICT. WEIGHS 270 LBS. GIVES OFF PHEROMONES UNCONSCIOUSLY

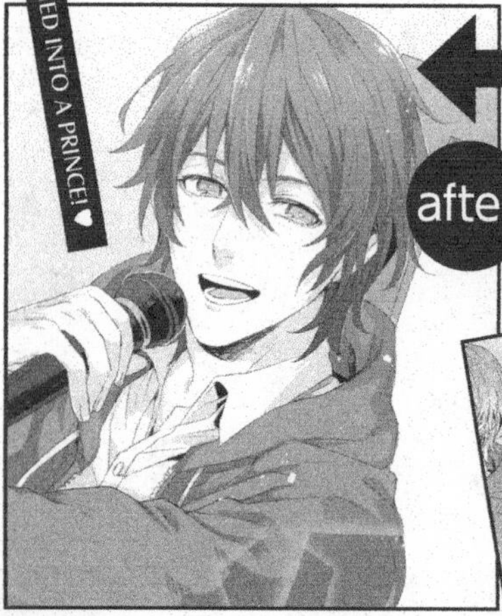
TURNED INTO A PRINCE!♥
after

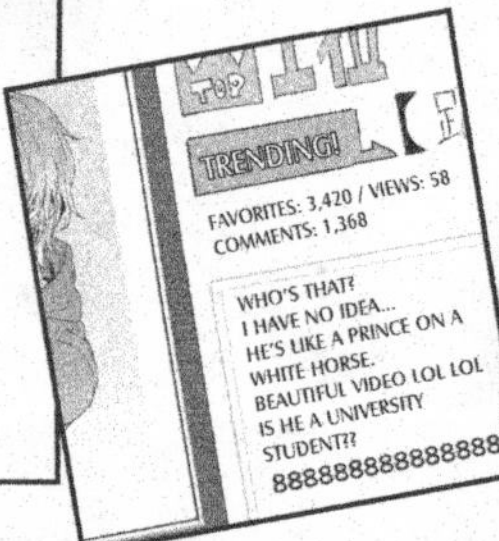
TRENDING!
FAVORITES: 3,420 / VIEWS: 58
COMMENTS: 1,368
WHO'S THAT?
I HAVE NO IDEA...
HE'S LIKE A PRINCE ON A WHITE HORSE.
BEAUTIFUL VIDEO LOL LOL
IS HE A UNIVERSITY STUDENT??
888888888888888

HE PRESSED "UPLOAD" BY MISTAKE AND HIS "LET'S TRY DANCING!" VIDEO WENT VIRAL!

FUMI'S HERO, THE MAN WHO SAVED HER FROM A TROUBLESOME CUSTOMER, WAS ACTUALLY MIROKU BACK WHEN HE WAS CHUBBY!

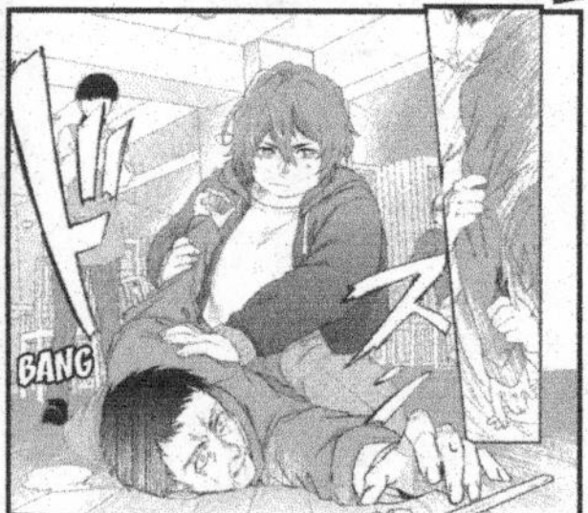
BANG

FUMI

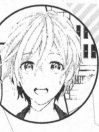

FUMI KISARAGI

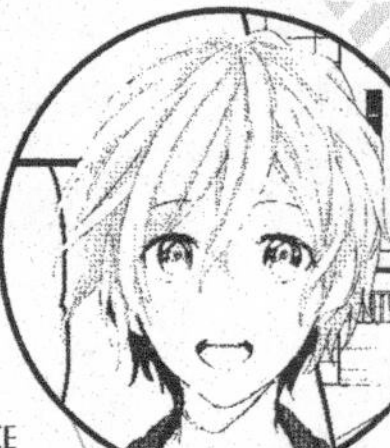

YOICHI'S BUBBLY NIECE WHO WORKS AT HIS OFFICE. SHE ALWAYS PUTS HER ALL INTO HER WORK.

YOICHI (41)

YOICHI KISARAGI

YOICHI IS THE CEO OF A SMALL ENTERTAINMENT COMPANY. HE AND MIROKU MET AT THE GYM. HE USED TO BE AN IDOL FOR THE SHINEEZ TALENT AGENCY.

SHIJU (40)

SHIJU ONOHARA

A FORMER DANCER AND HOST, NOW UNEMPLOYED AND LEADING A LIFE ON THE EDGE. HE WAS THE ONE WHO SUGGESTED THAT MIROKU TAKE PART IN THE DANCE COMPETITION.

▪▪▪▪▪ TENKA ▪▪▪▪▪

ROU   KIRA   ZOU

KAMO LAVENDER

PRODUCER EXTRAORDINAIRE OF NATIONALLY TREASURED IDOL GROUPS SUCH AS UGUISUDANI SEVEN.

MIHACHI OSAKI

MIROKU'S OLDER SISTER WHO WAS YOICHI'S BIGGEST FAN IN HIS IDOL DAYS AND LOVES HIM EVEN NOW.

OSSAN IDOL

CONTENTS

Chapter 24

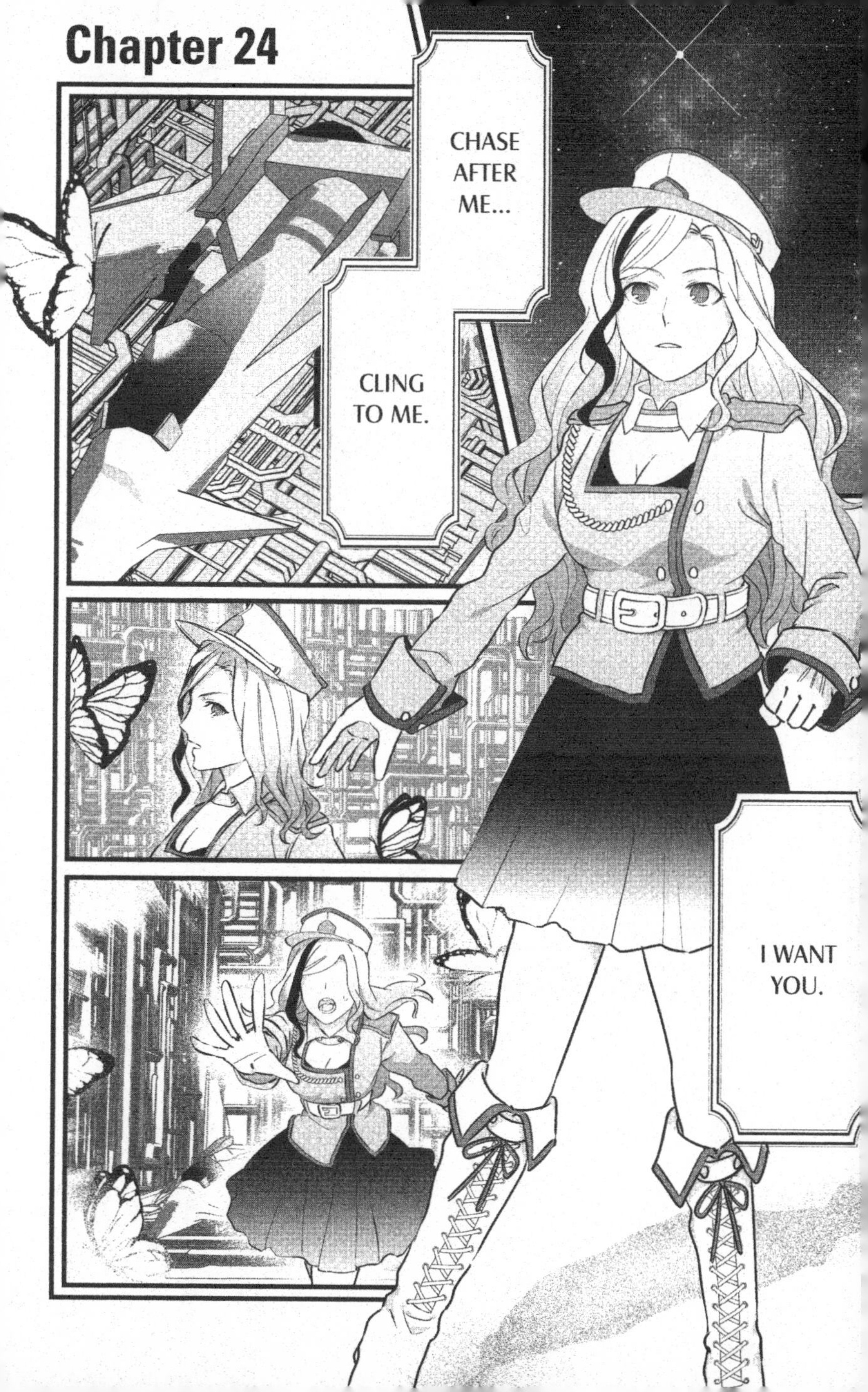
CHASE AFTER ME...
CLING TO ME.
I WANT YOU.

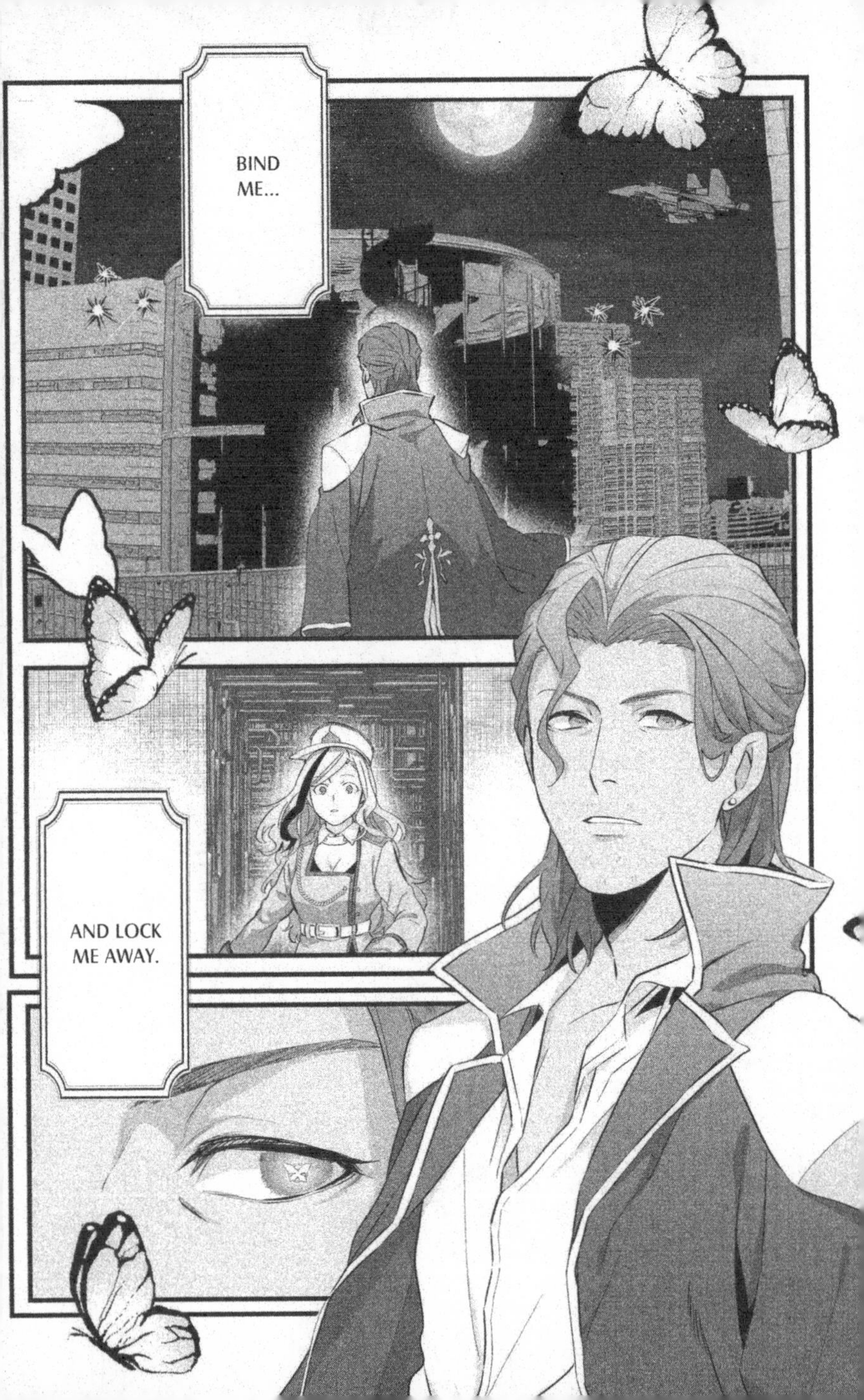
BIND ME...
AND LOCK ME AWAY.

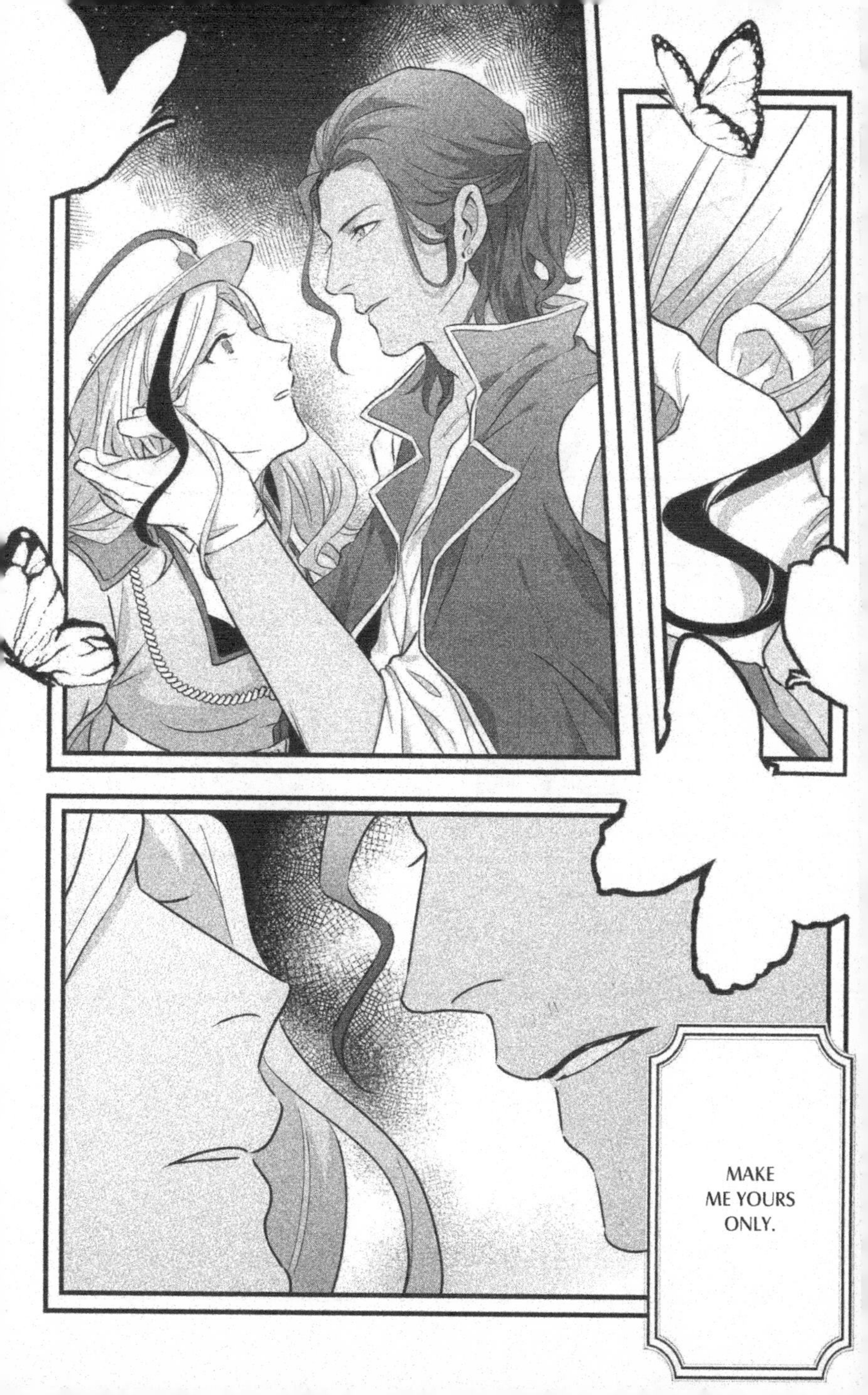
MAKE
ME YOURS
ONLY.

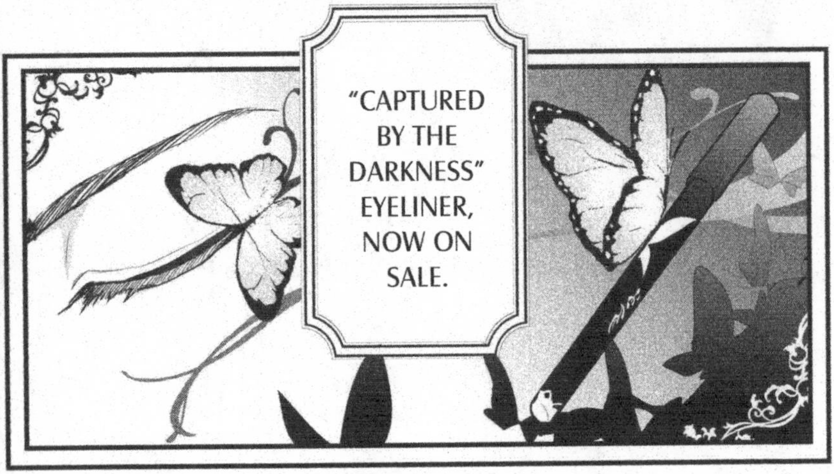
"CAPTURED BY THE DARKNESS" EYELINER, NOW ON SALE.

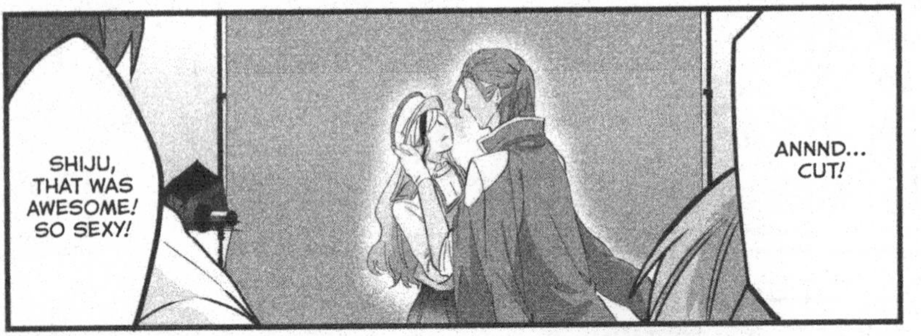
ANNND... CUT!
SHIJU, THAT WAS AWESOME! SO SEXY!

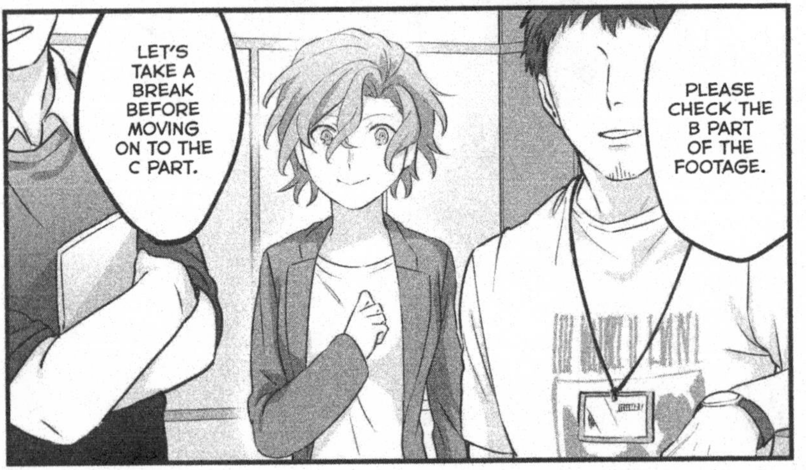
PLEASE CHECK THE B PART OF THE FOOTAGE.
LET'S TAKE A BREAK BEFORE MOVING ON TO THE C PART.

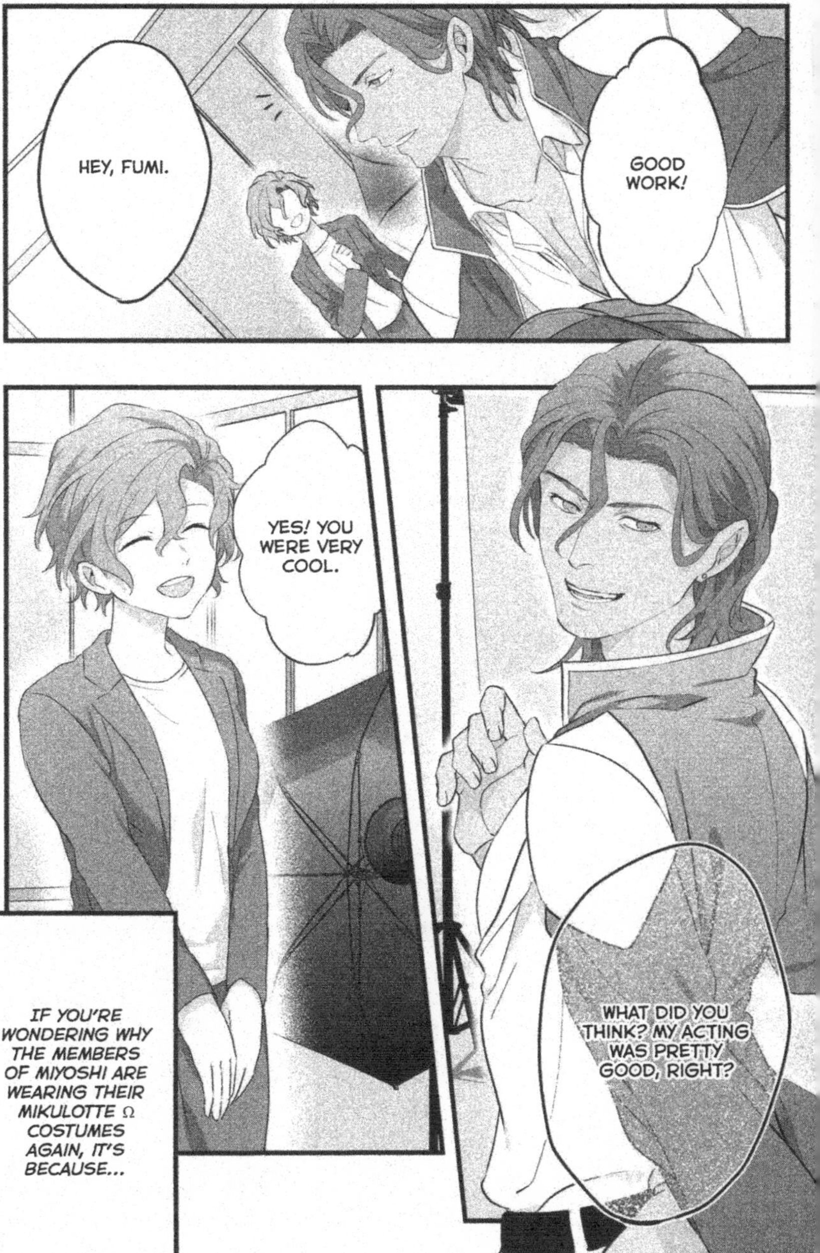
GOOD WORK!
HEY, FUMI.
WHAT DID YOU THINK? MY ACTING WAS PRETTY GOOD, RIGHT?
YES! YOU WERE VERY COOL.
IF YOU'RE WONDERING WHY THE MEMBERS OF MIYOSHI ARE WEARING THEIR MIKULOTTE Ω COSTUMES AGAIN, IT'S BECAUSE...

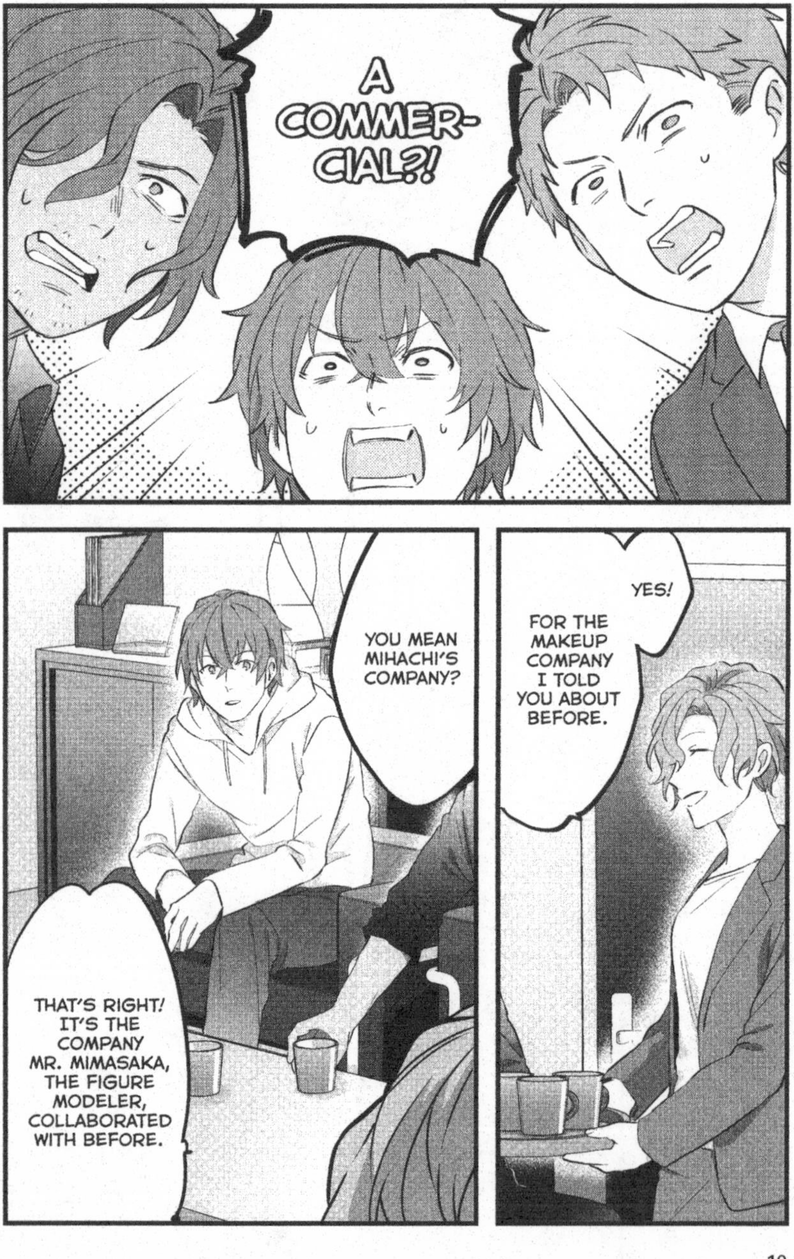
A COMMERCIAL?!
YES!
FOR THE MAKEUP COMPANY I TOLD YOU ABOUT BEFORE.
YOU MEAN MIHACHI'S COMPANY?
THAT'S RIGHT! IT'S THE COMPANY MR. MIMASAKA, THE FIGURE MODELER, COLLABORATED WITH BEFORE.

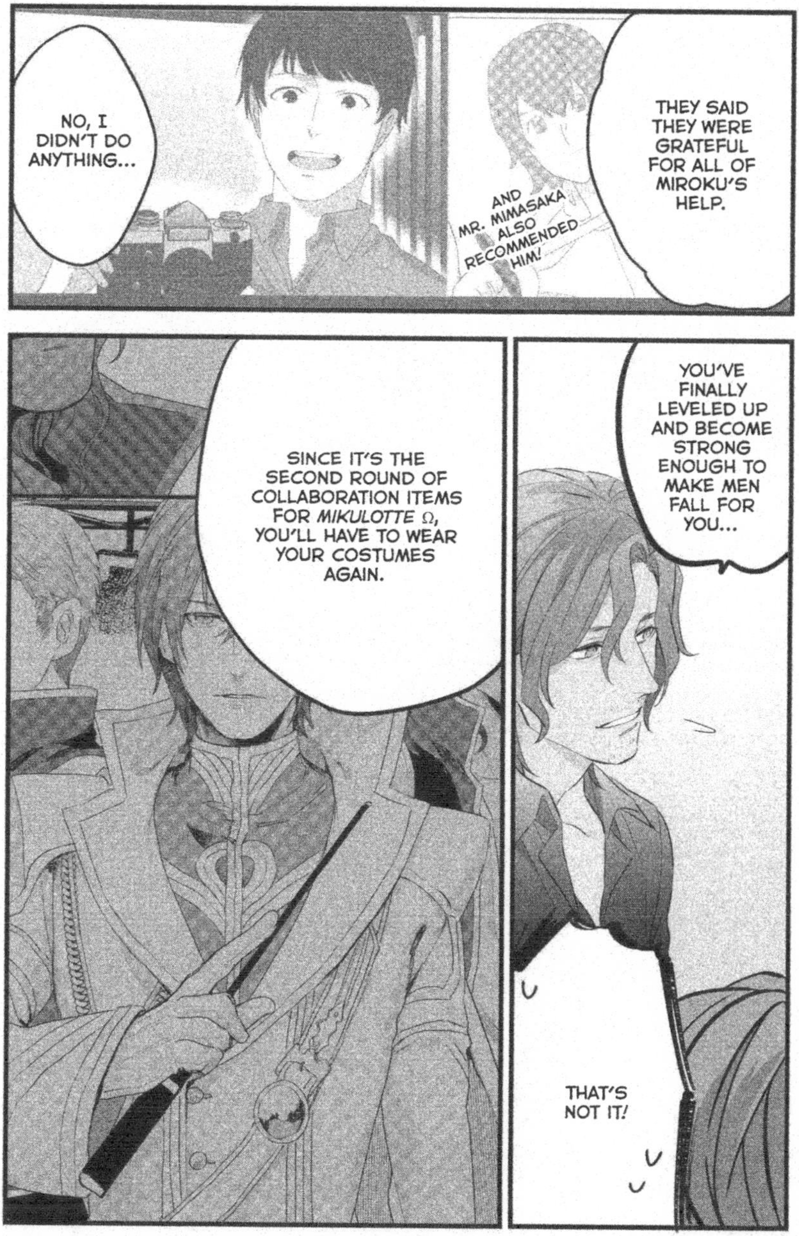

THEY SAID THEY WERE GRATEFUL FOR ALL OF MIROKU'S HELP.
AND MR. MIMASAKA ALSO RECOMMENDED HIM!
NO, I DIDN'T DO ANYTHING...
YOU'VE FINALLY LEVELED UP AND BECOME STRONG ENOUGH TO MAKE MEN FALL FOR YOU...
THAT'S NOT IT!
SINCE IT'S THE SECOND ROUND OF COLLABORATION ITEMS FOR *MIKULOTTE* Ω, YOU'LL HAVE TO WEAR YOUR COSTUMES AGAIN.

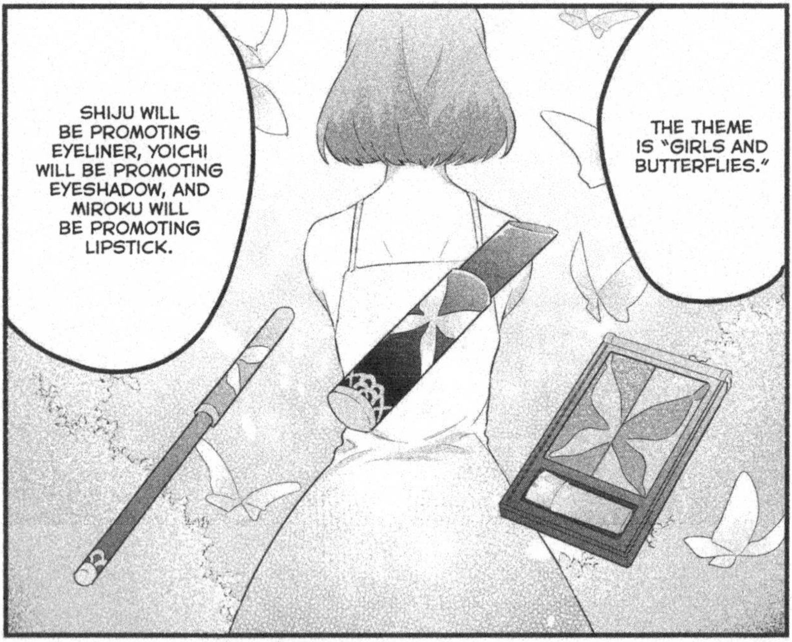
THE THEME IS "GIRLS AND BUTTERFLIES."
SHIJU WILL BE PROMOTING EYELINER, YOICHI WILL BE PROMOTING EYESHADOW, AND MIROKU WILL BE PROMOTING LIPSTICK.

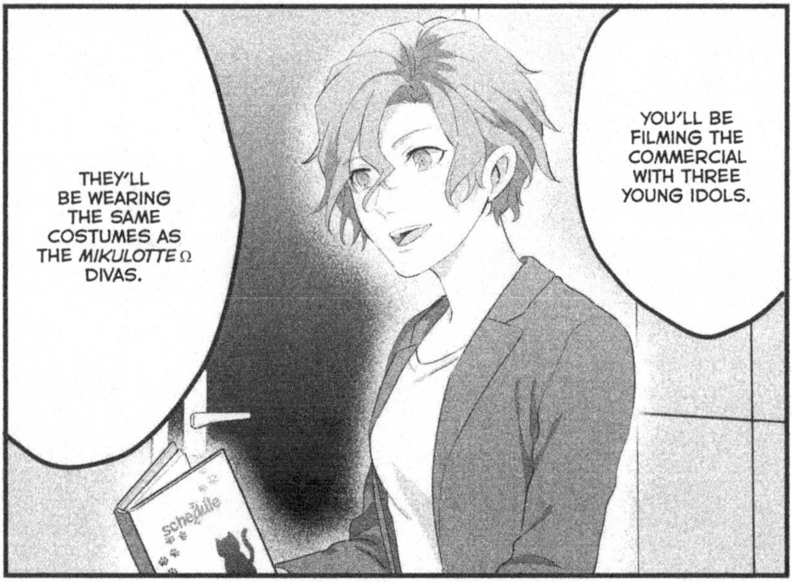
YOU'LL BE FILMING THE COMMERCIAL WITH THREE YOUNG IDOLS.
THEY'LL BE WEARING THE SAME COSTUMES AS THE *MIKULOTTE* Ω DIVAS.
schedule

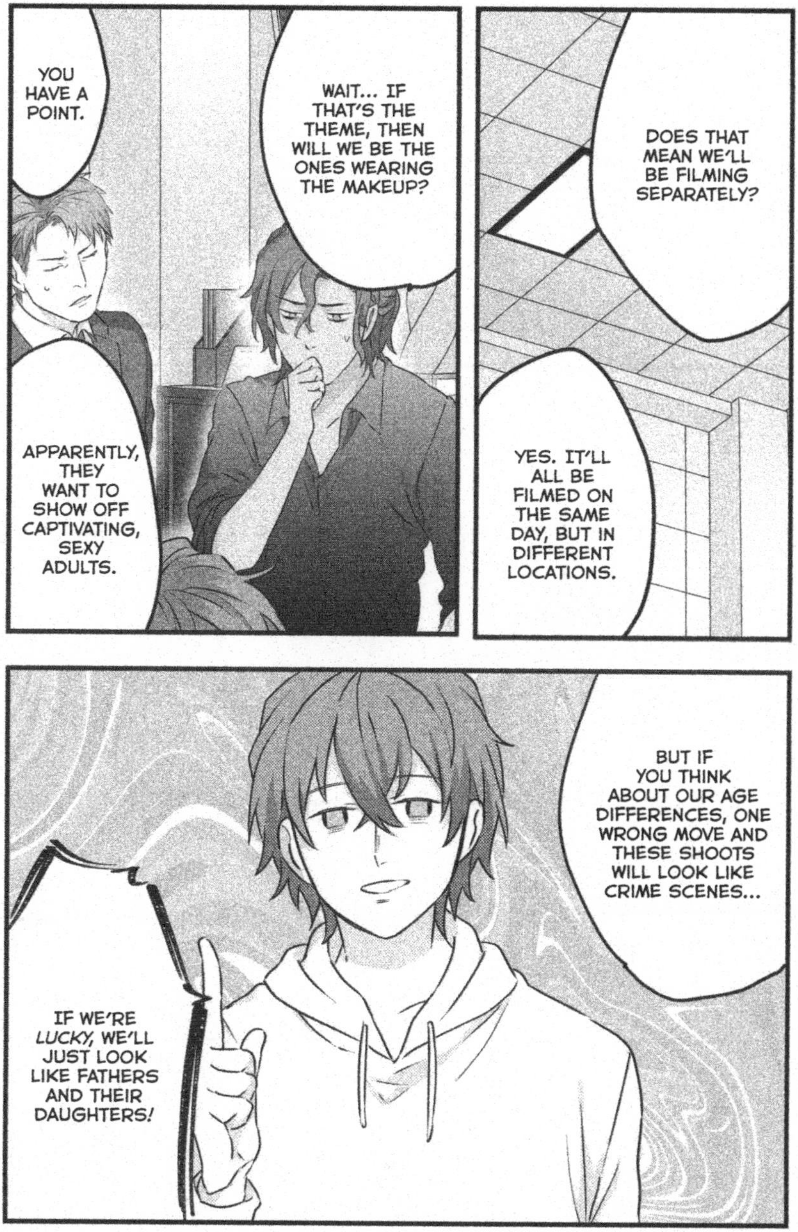
DOES THAT MEAN WE'LL BE FILMING SEPARATELY?
YES. IT'LL ALL BE FILMED ON THE SAME DAY, BUT IN DIFFERENT LOCATIONS.
WAIT... IF THAT'S THE THEME, THEN WILL WE BE THE ONES WEARING THE MAKEUP?
YOU HAVE A POINT.
APPARENTLY, THEY WANT TO SHOW OFF CAPTIVATING, SEXY ADULTS.
BUT IF YOU THINK ABOUT OUR AGE DIFFERENCES, ONE WRONG MOVE AND THESE SHOOTS WILL LOOK LIKE CRIME SCENES...
IF WE'RE *LUCKY*, WE'LL JUST LOOK LIKE FATHERS AND THEIR DAUGHTERS!

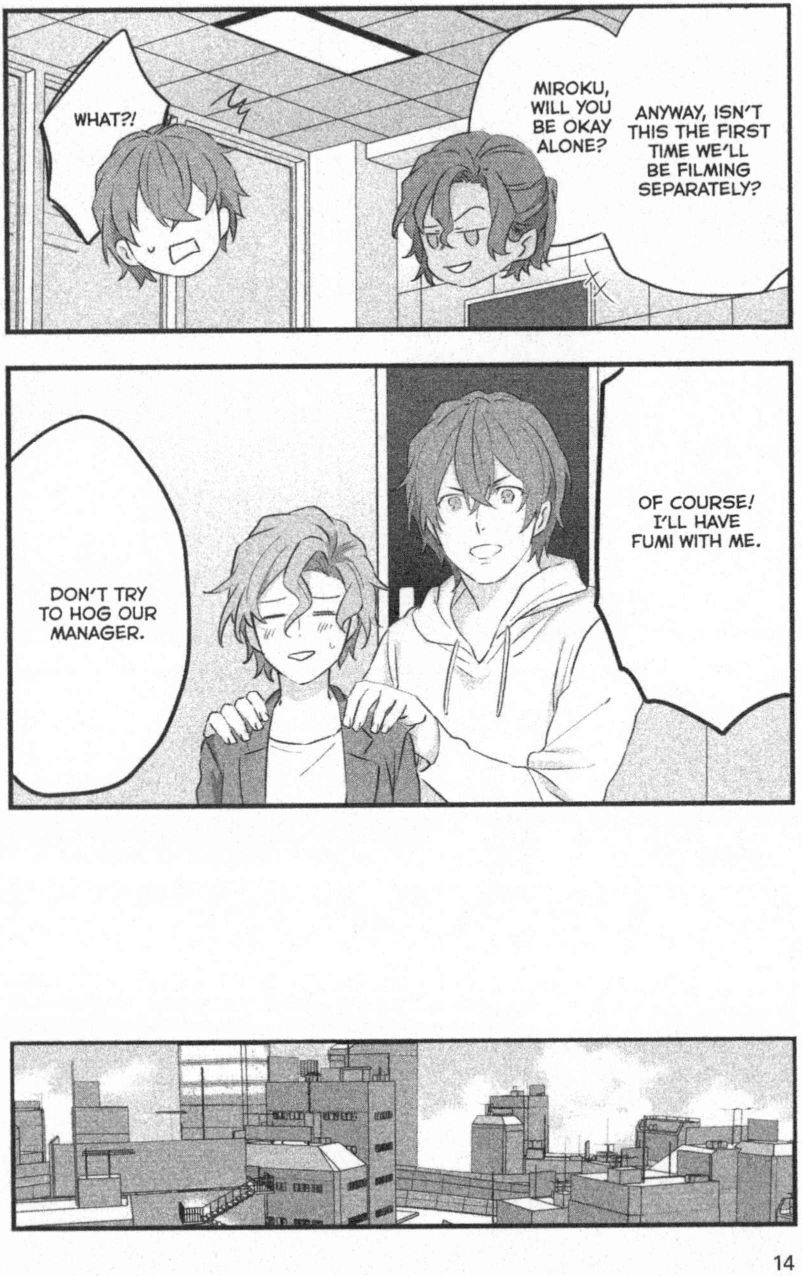
ANYWAY, ISN'T THIS THE FIRST TIME WE'LL BE FILMING SEPARATELY?
MIROKU, WILL YOU BE OKAY ALONE?
WHAT?!
OF COURSE! I'LL HAVE FUMI WITH ME.
DON'T TRY TO HOG OUR MANAGER.

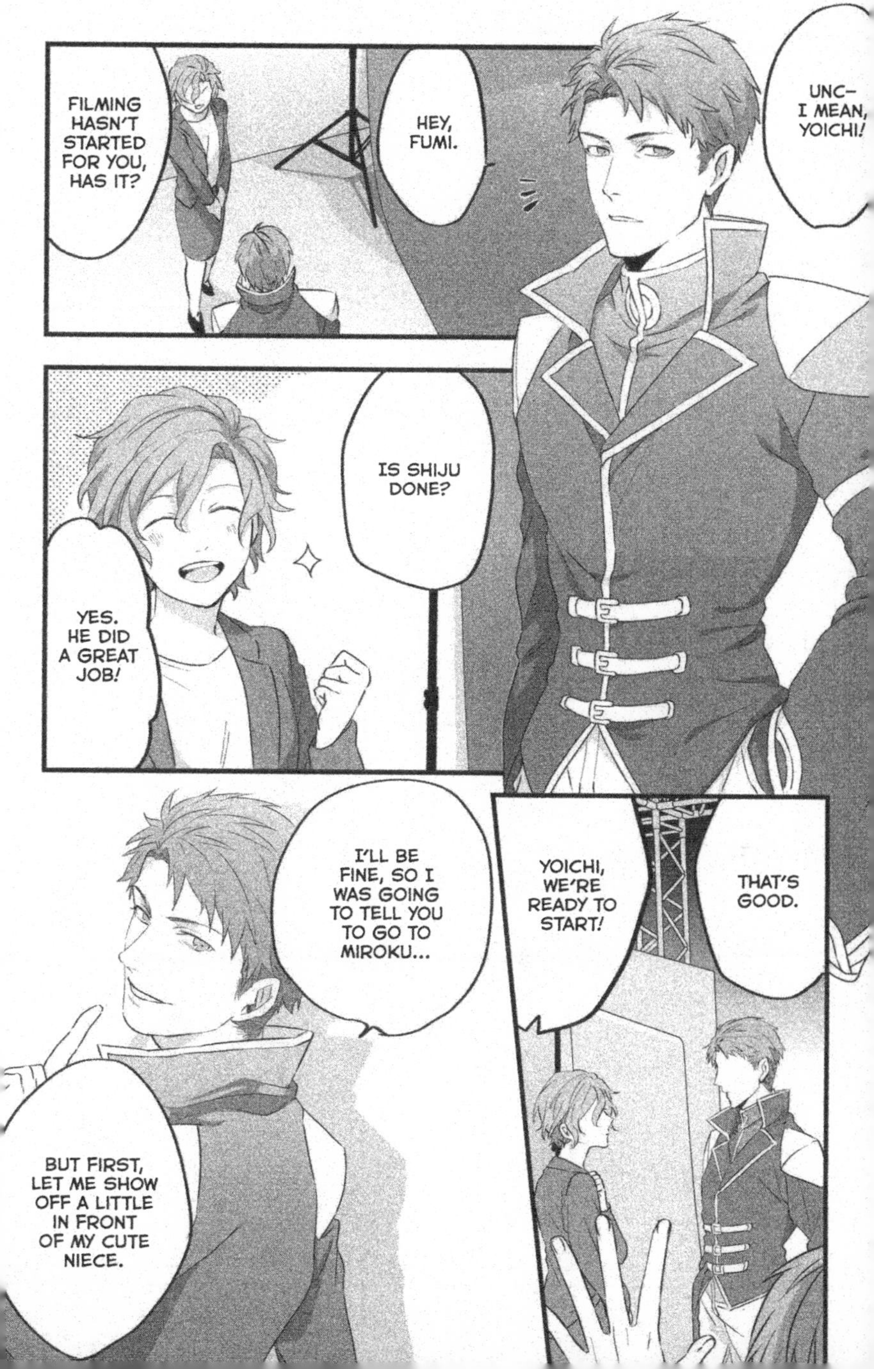
UNC— I MEAN, YOICHI!
HEY, FUMI.
FILMING HASN'T STARTED FOR YOU, HAS IT?
IS SHIJU DONE?
YES. HE DID A GREAT JOB!
THAT'S GOOD.
YOICHI, WE'RE READY TO START!
I'LL BE FINE, SO I WAS GOING TO TELL YOU TO GO TO MIROKU...
BUT FIRST, LET ME SHOW OFF A LITTLE IN FRONT OF MY CUTE NIECE.

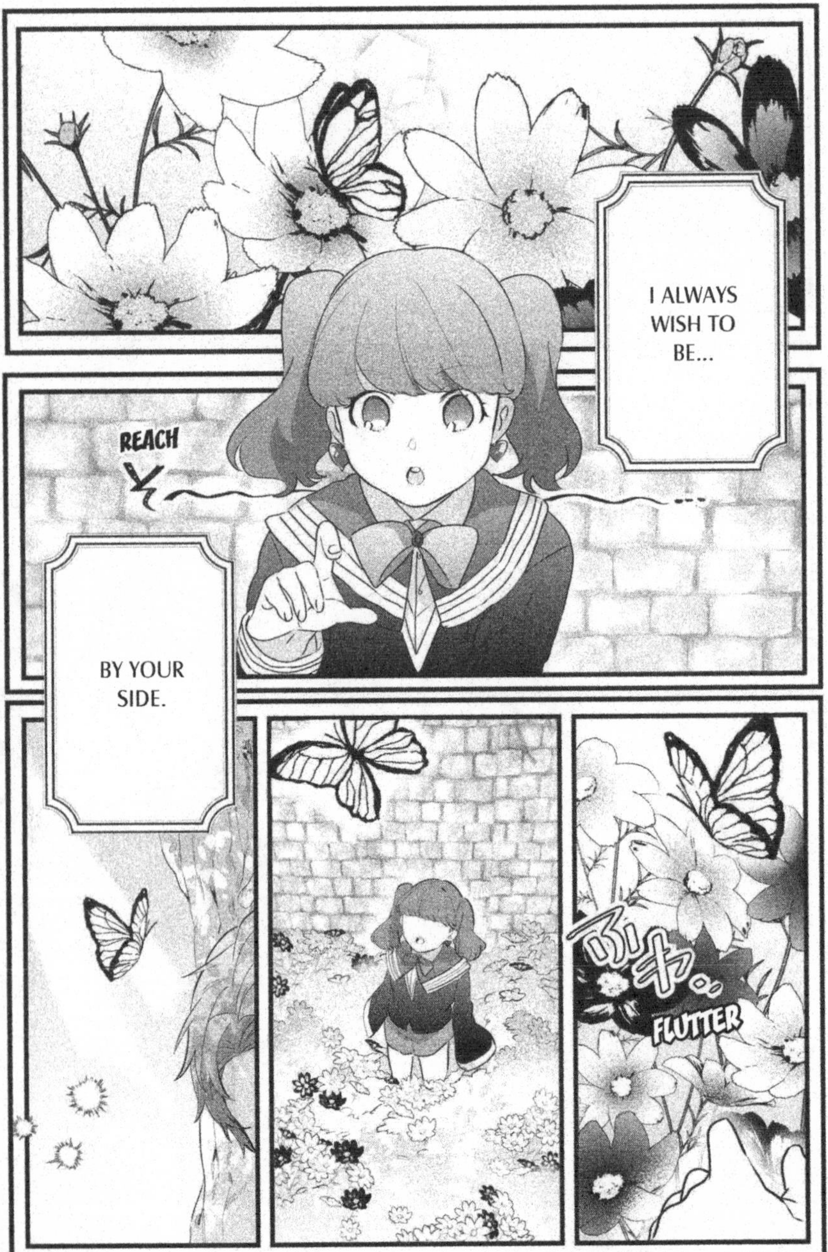

I ALWAYS WISH TO BE...
REACH
BY YOUR SIDE.
FLUTTER

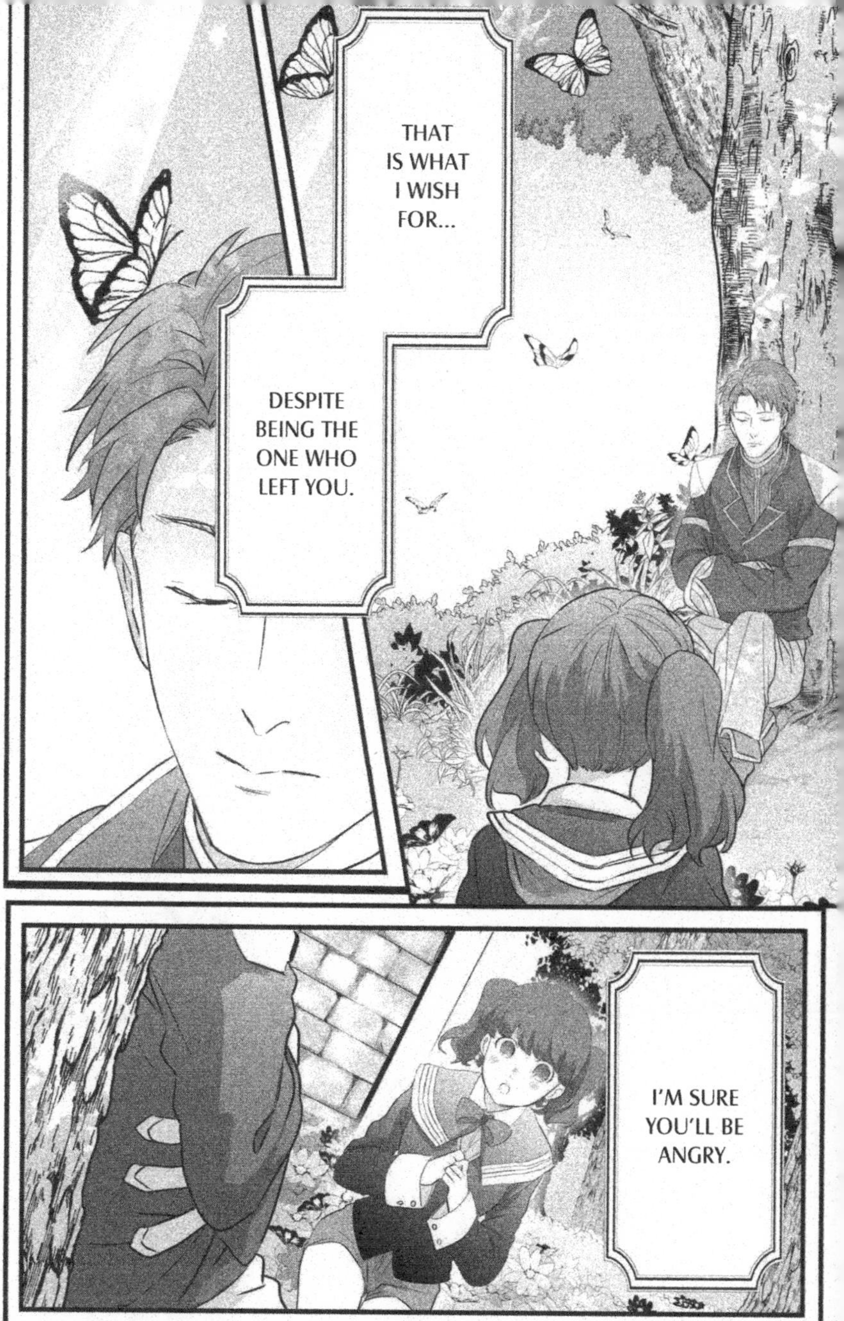
THAT IS WHAT I WISH FOR...
DESPITE BEING THE ONE WHO LEFT YOU.
I'M SURE YOU'LL BE ANGRY.

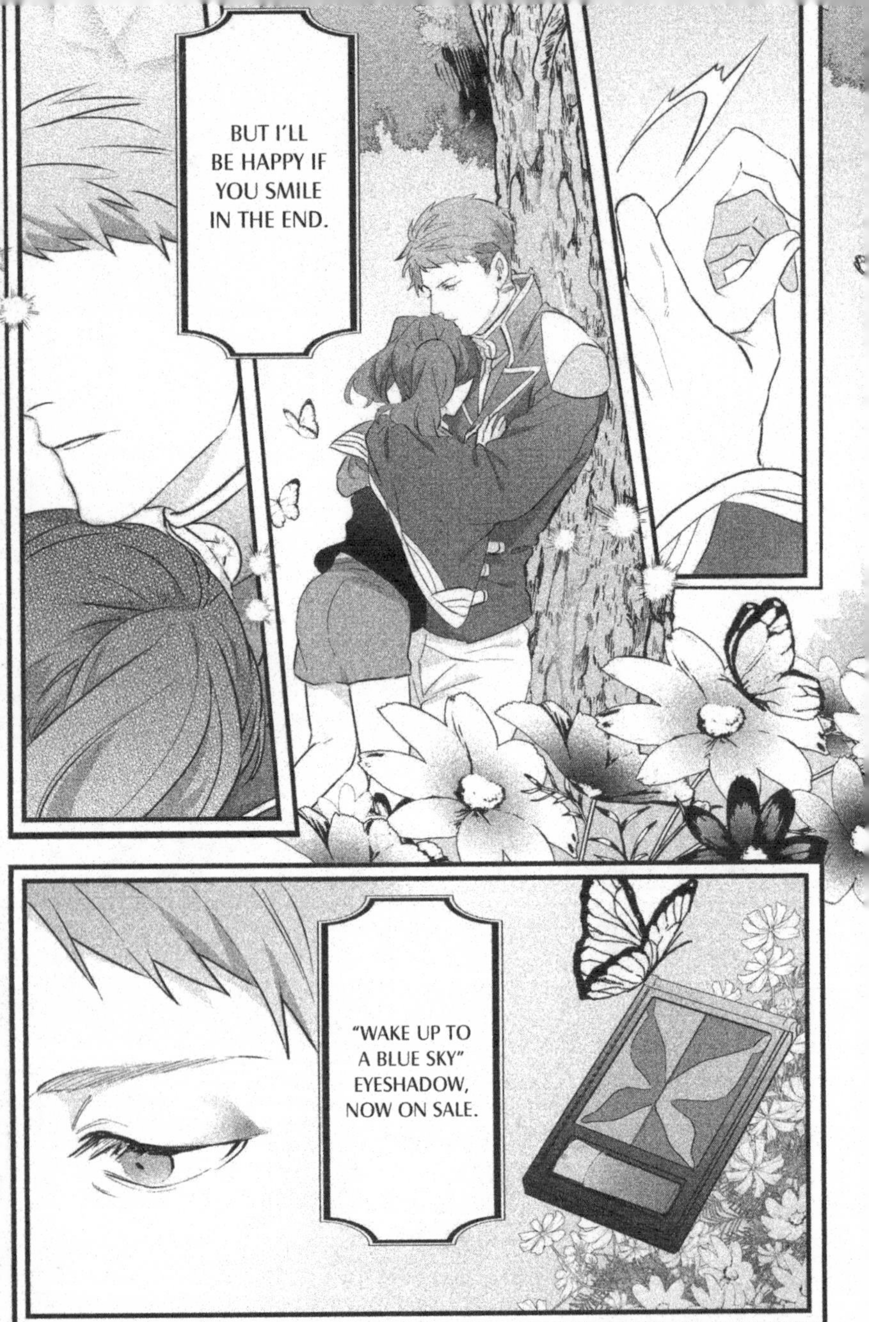
BUT I'LL BE HAPPY IF YOU SMILE IN THE END.
"WAKE UP TO A BLUE SKY" EYESHADOW, NOW ON SALE.

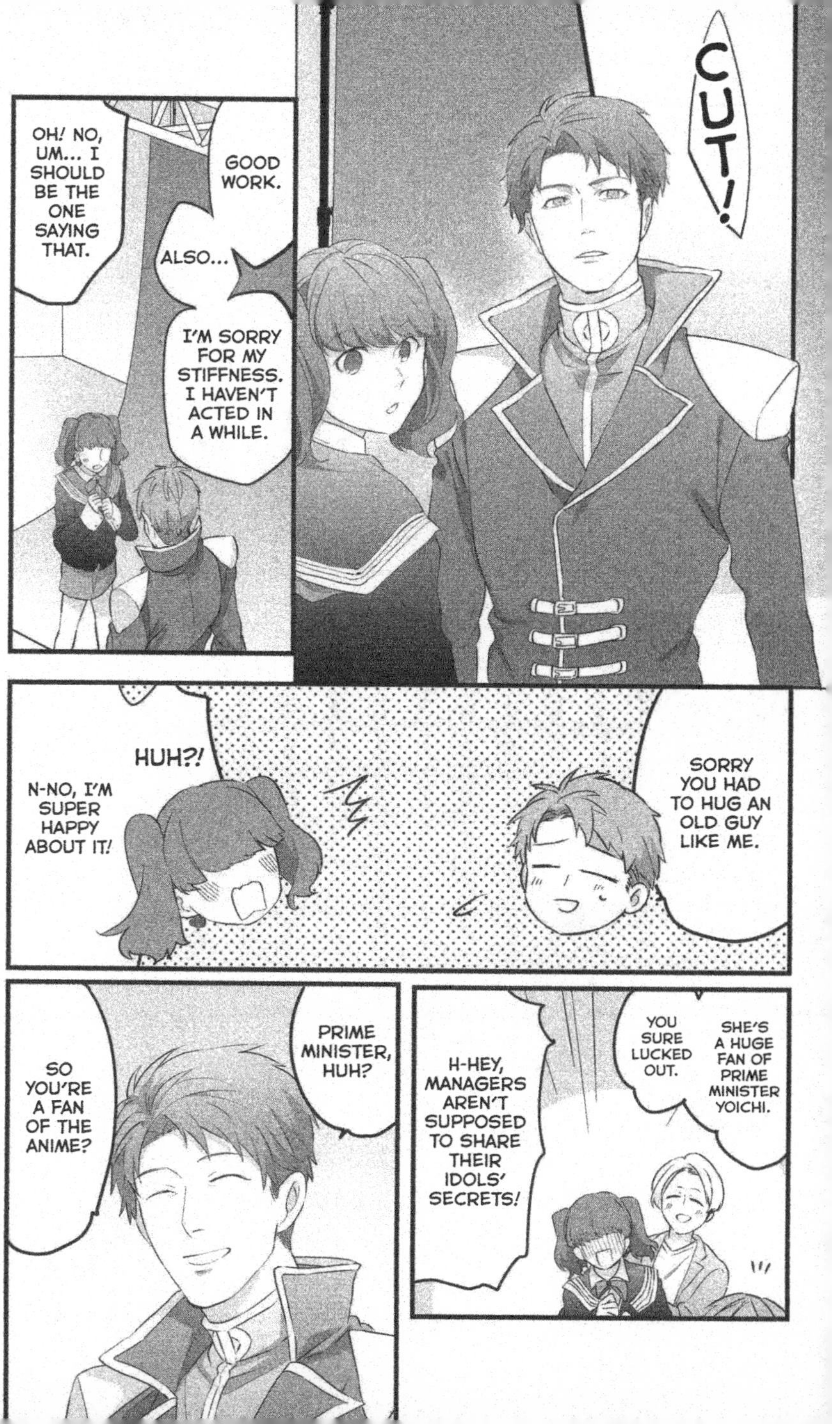
CUT!
GOOD WORK.
OH! NO, UM... I SHOULD BE THE ONE SAYING THAT.
ALSO...
I'M SORRY FOR MY STIFFNESS. I HAVEN'T ACTED IN A WHILE.
SORRY YOU HAD TO HUG AN OLD GUY LIKE ME.
HUH?!
N-NO, I'M SUPER HAPPY ABOUT IT!
SHE'S A HUGE FAN OF PRIME MINISTER YOICHI.
YOU SURE LUCKED OUT.
H-HEY, MANAGERS AREN'T SUPPOSED TO SHARE THEIR IDOLS' SECRETS!
PRIME MINISTER, HUH?
SO YOU'RE A FAN OF THE ANIME?

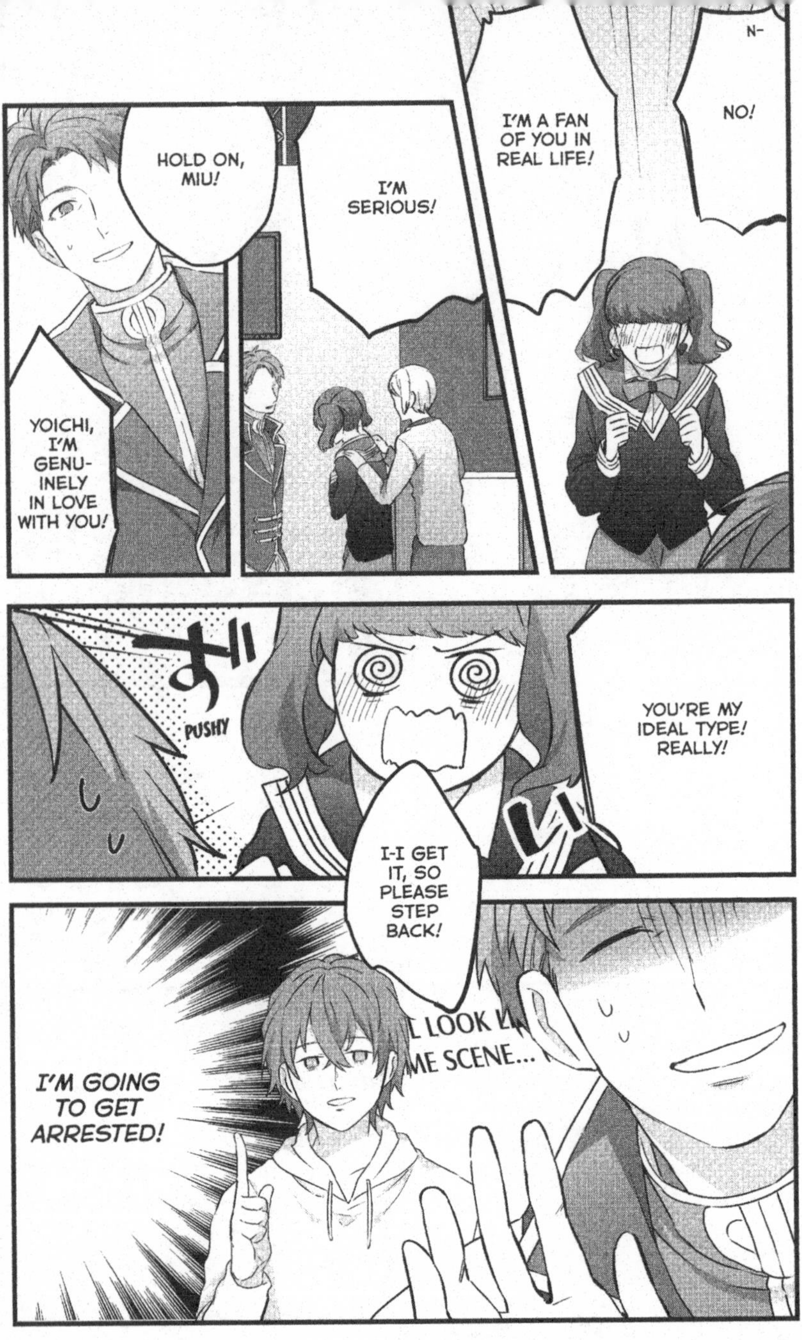
N-
NO!
I'M A FAN OF YOU IN REAL LIFE!
I'M SERIOUS!
HOLD ON, MIU!
YOICHI, I'M GENU-INELY IN LOVE WITH YOU!
YOU'RE MY IDEAL TYPE! REALLY!
PUSHY
I-I GET IT, SO PLEASE STEP BACK!
I'M GOING TO GET ARRESTED!

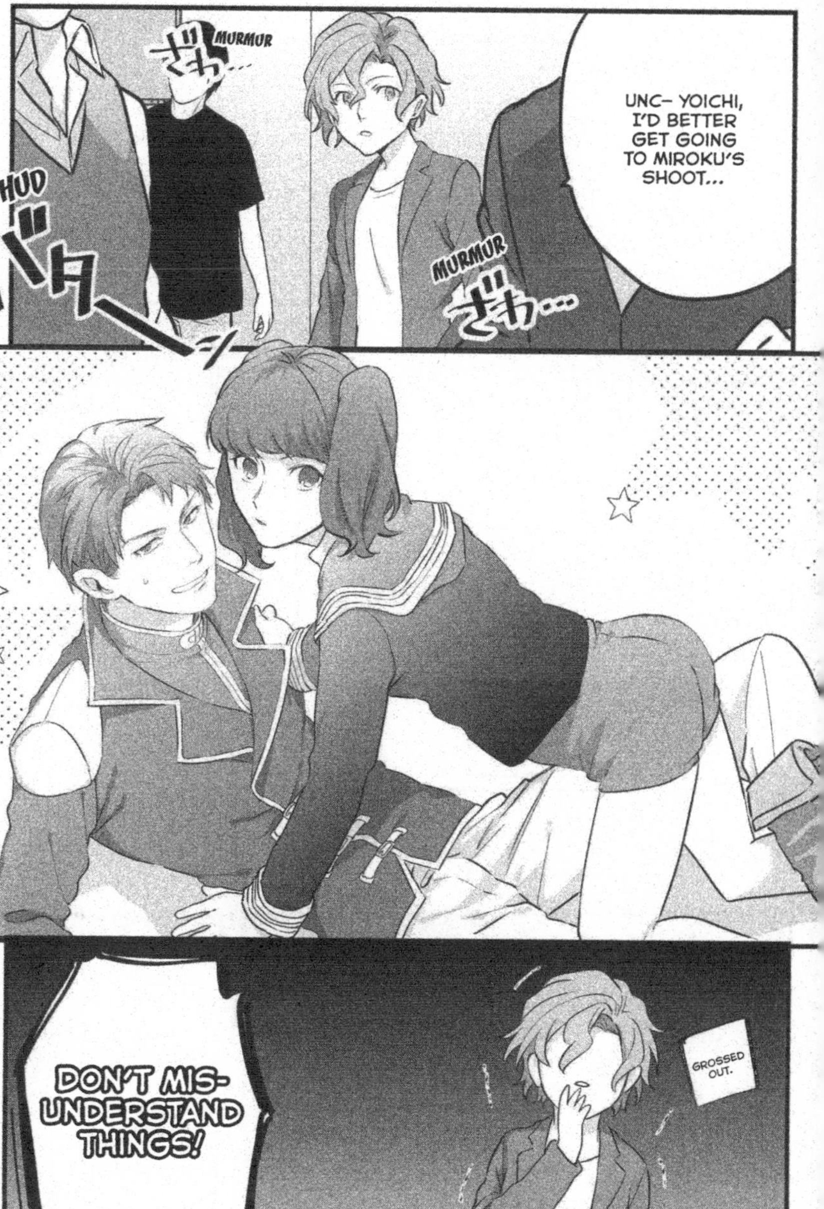
UNC– YOICHI, I'D BETTER GET GOING TO MIROKU'S SHOOT...
MURMUR
ざわ…
MURMUR
ざわ…
THUD
バターン
GROSSED OUT.
DON'T MIS-UNDERSTAND THINGS!

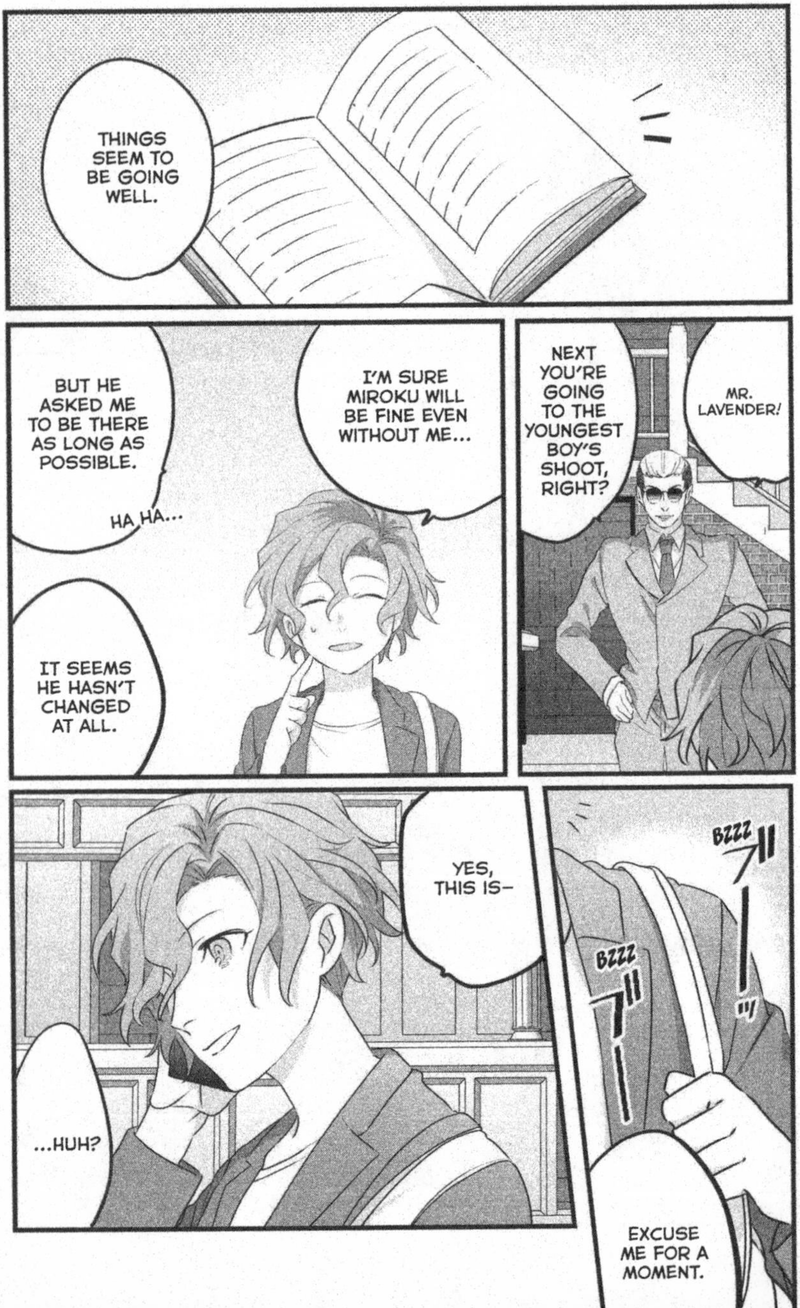
THINGS SEEM TO BE GOING WELL.
MR. LAVENDER!
NEXT YOU'RE GOING TO THE YOUNGEST BOY'S SHOOT, RIGHT?
I'M SURE MIROKU WILL BE FINE EVEN WITHOUT ME...
BUT HE ASKED ME TO BE THERE AS LONG AS POSSIBLE.
HA HA...
IT SEEMS HE HASN'T CHANGED AT ALL.
BZZZ
BZZZ
EXCUSE ME FOR A MOMENT.
YES, THIS IS–
...HUH?

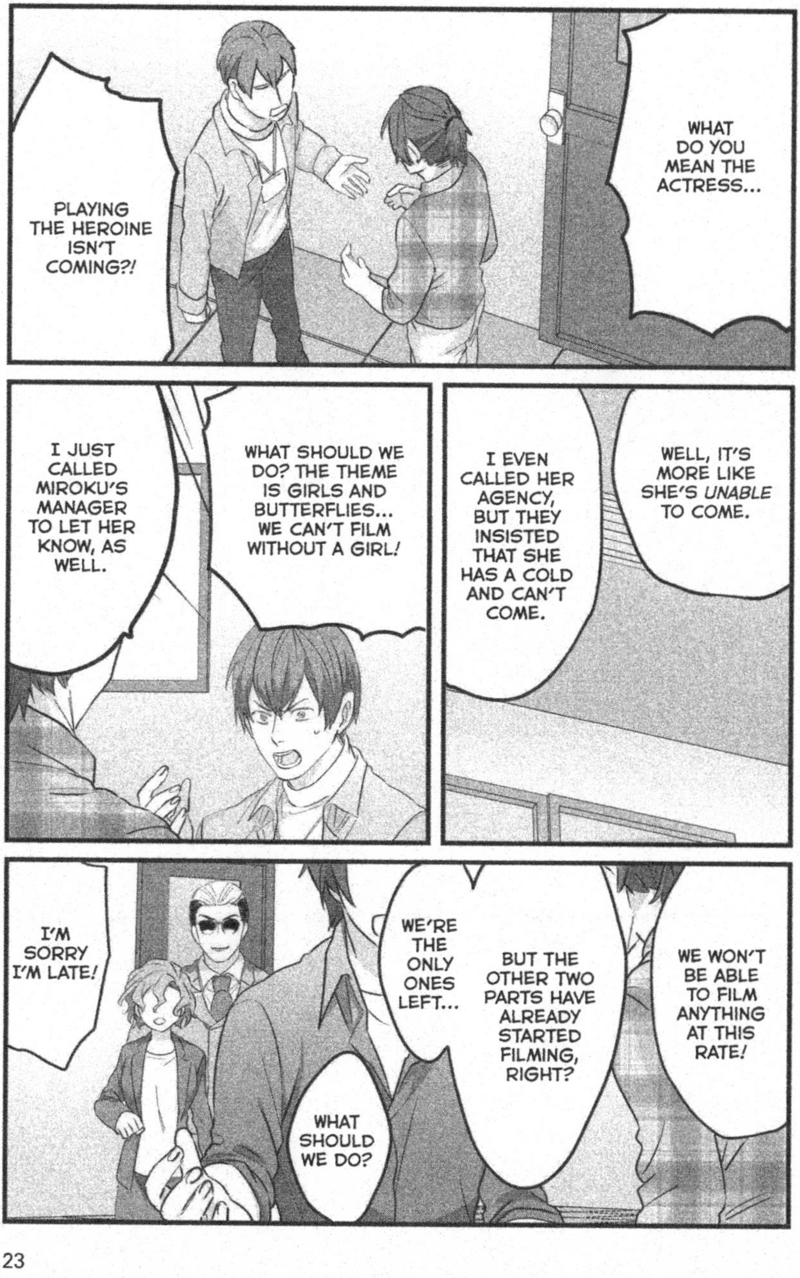
WHAT DO YOU MEAN THE ACTRESS...
PLAYING THE HEROINE ISN'T COMING?!
WELL, IT'S MORE LIKE SHE'S *UNABLE* TO COME.
I EVEN CALLED HER AGENCY, BUT THEY INSISTED THAT SHE HAS A COLD AND CAN'T COME.
WHAT SHOULD WE DO? THE THEME IS GIRLS AND BUTTERFLIES... WE CAN'T FILM WITHOUT A GIRL!
I JUST CALLED MIROKU'S MANAGER TO LET HER KNOW, AS WELL.
WE WON'T BE ABLE TO FILM ANYTHING AT THIS RATE!
BUT THE OTHER TWO PARTS HAVE ALREADY STARTED FILMING, RIGHT?
WE'RE THE ONLY ONES LEFT...
WHAT SHOULD WE DO?
I'M SORRY I'M LATE!

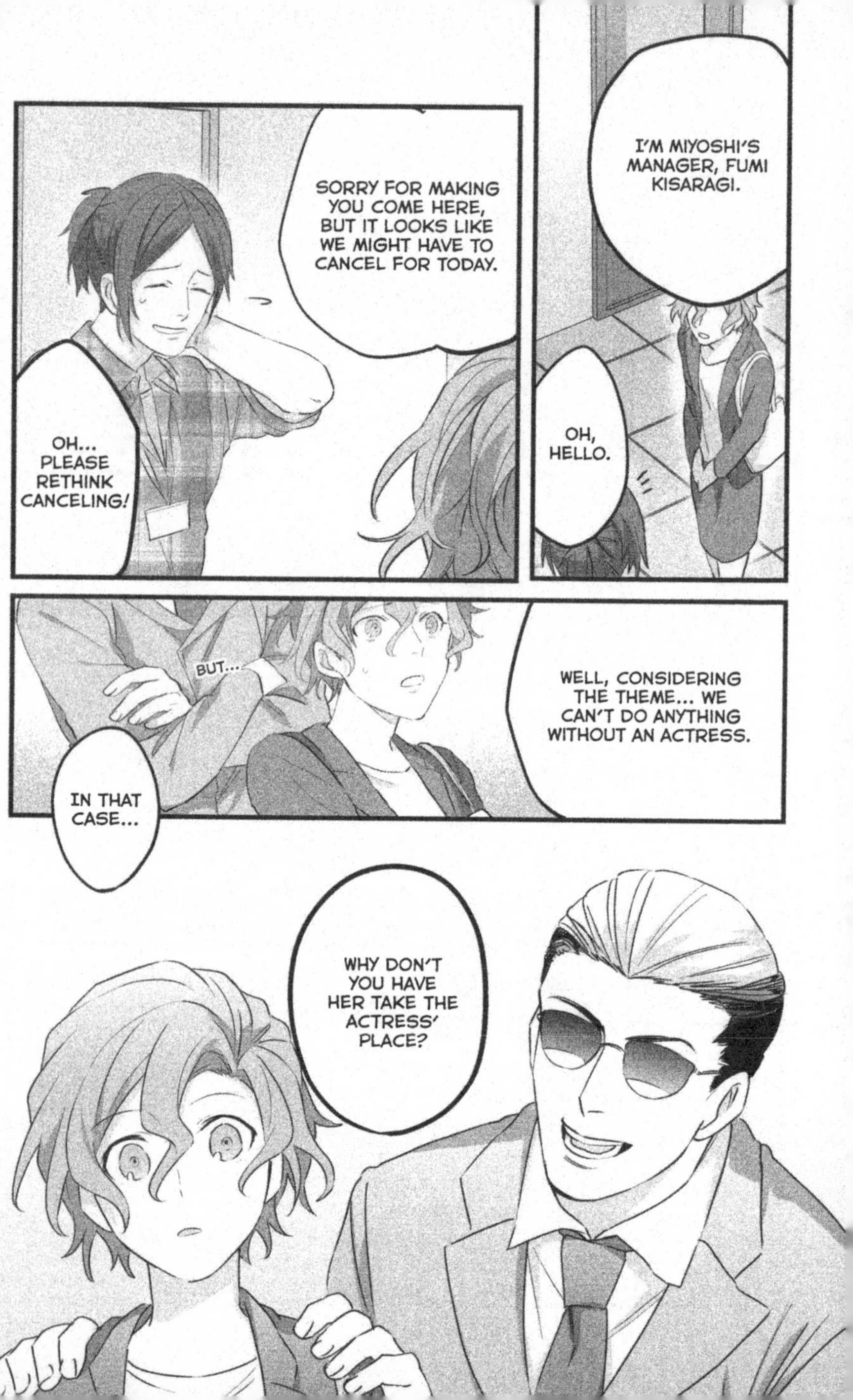
I'M MIYOSHI'S MANAGER, FUMI KISARAGI.
OH, HELLO.
SORRY FOR MAKING YOU COME HERE, BUT IT LOOKS LIKE WE MIGHT HAVE TO CANCEL FOR TODAY.
OH... PLEASE RETHINK CANCELING!
WELL, CONSIDERING THE THEME... WE CAN'T DO ANYTHING WITHOUT AN ACTRESS.
BUT...
IN THAT CASE...
WHY DON'T YOU HAVE HER TAKE THE ACTRESS' PLACE?

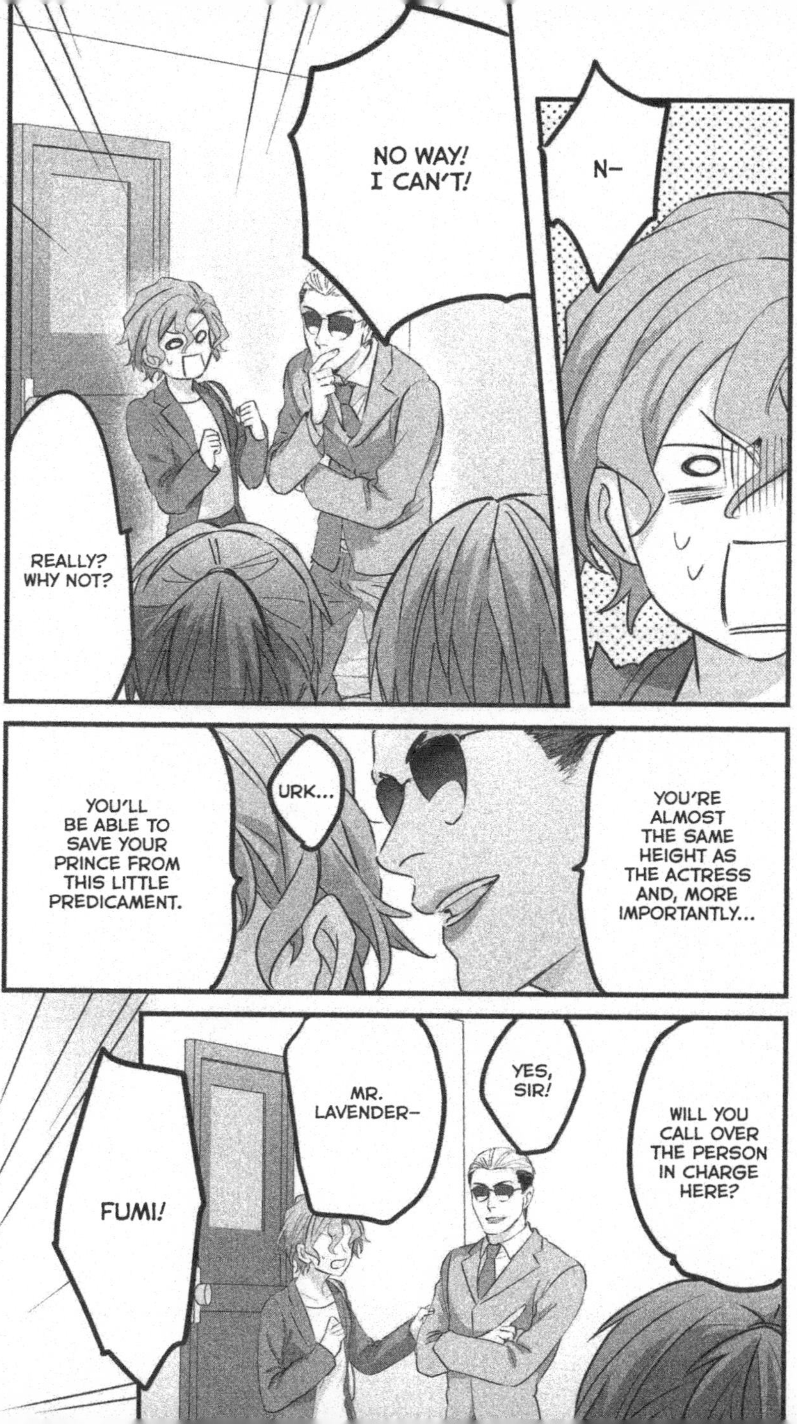
N–
NO WAY! I CAN'T!
REALLY? WHY NOT?
YOU'RE ALMOST THE SAME HEIGHT AS THE ACTRESS AND, MORE IMPORTANTLY...
URK...
YOU'LL BE ABLE TO SAVE YOUR PRINCE FROM THIS LITTLE PREDICAMENT.
WILL YOU CALL OVER THE PERSON IN CHARGE HERE?
YES, SIR!
MR. LAVENDER–
FUMI!

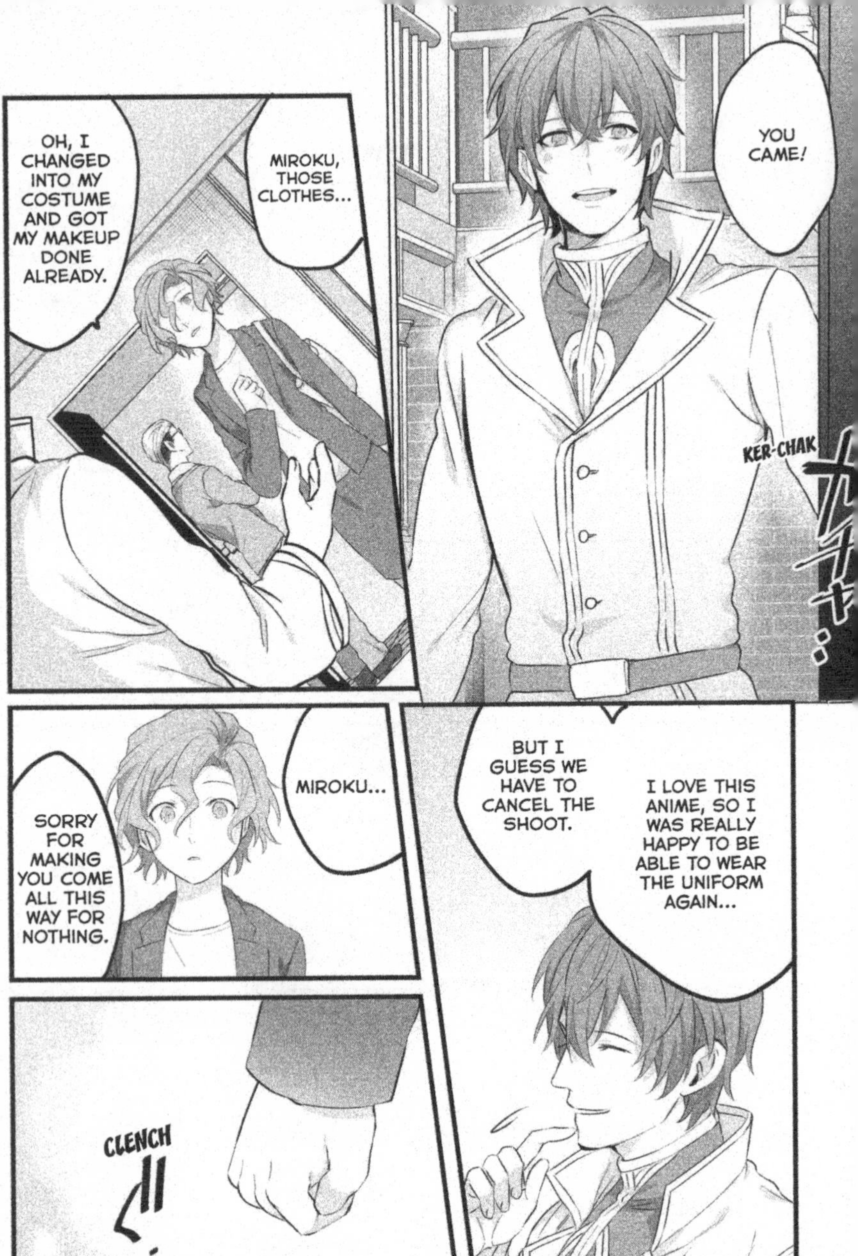
YOU CAME!
KER-CHAK
MIROKU, THOSE CLOTHES...
OH, I CHANGED INTO MY COSTUME AND GOT MY MAKEUP DONE ALREADY.
I LOVE THIS ANIME, SO I WAS REALLY HAPPY TO BE ABLE TO WEAR THE UNIFORM AGAIN...
BUT I GUESS WE HAVE TO CANCEL THE SHOOT.
MIROKU...
SORRY FOR MAKING YOU COME ALL THIS WAY FOR NOTHING.
CLENCH

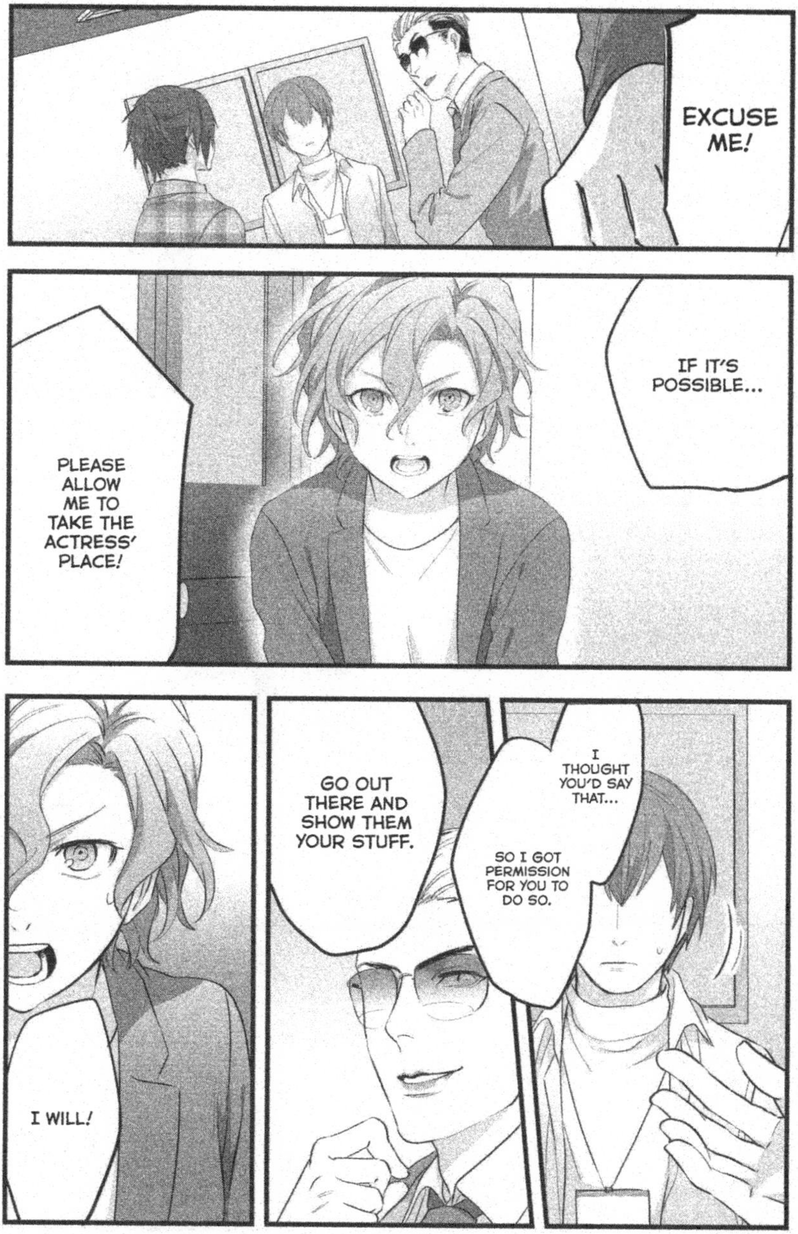
EXCUSE ME!
IF IT'S POSSIBLE...
PLEASE ALLOW ME TO TAKE THE ACTRESS' PLACE!
I THOUGHT YOU'D SAY THAT...
SO I GOT PERMISSION FOR YOU TO DO SO.
GO OUT THERE AND SHOW THEM YOUR STUFF.
I WILL!

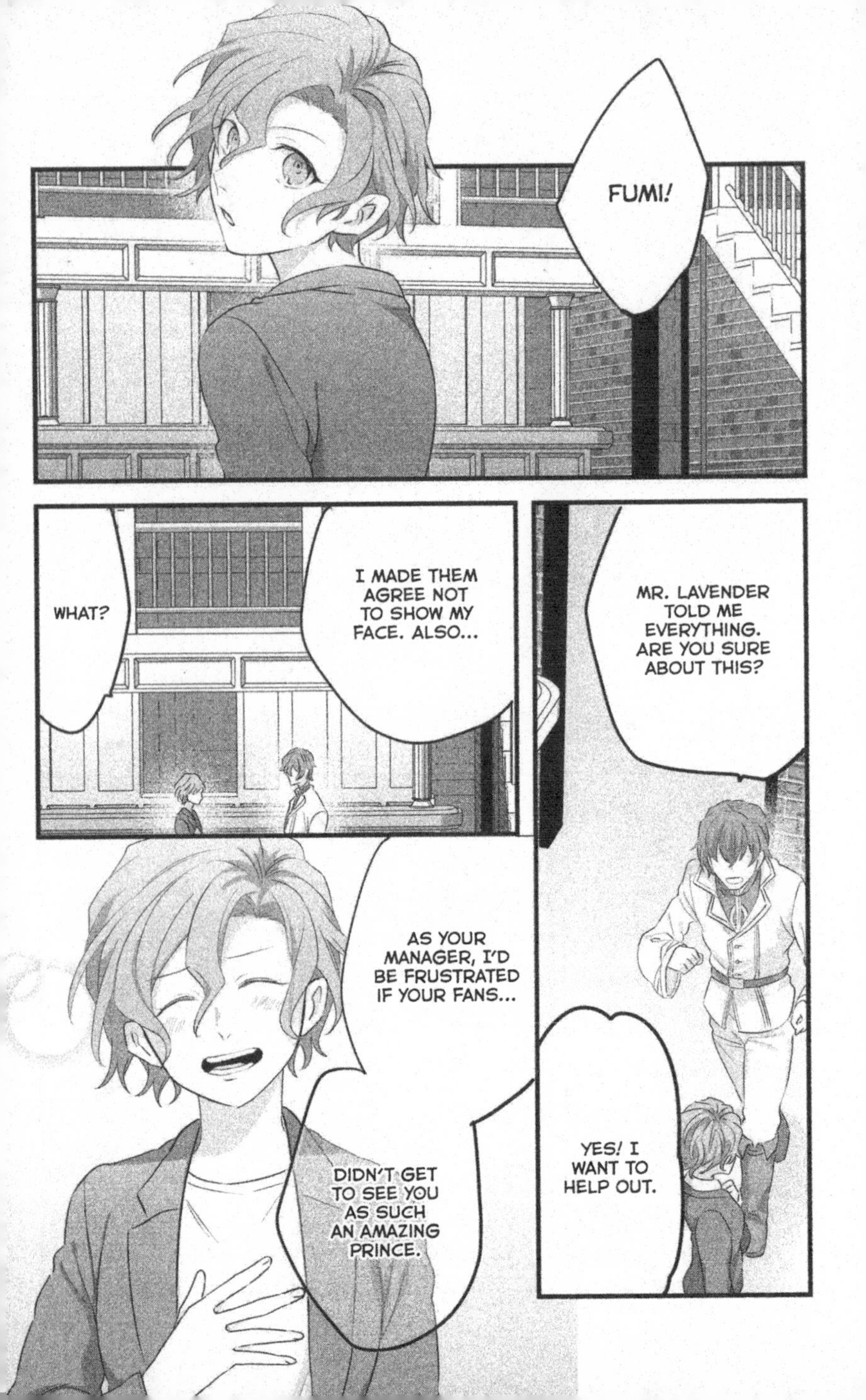
FUMI!
MR. LAVENDER TOLD ME EVERYTHING. ARE YOU SURE ABOUT THIS?
YES! I WANT TO HELP OUT.
I MADE THEM AGREE NOT TO SHOW MY FACE. ALSO...
WHAT?
AS YOUR MANAGER, I'D BE FRUSTRATED IF YOUR FANS...
DIDN'T GET TO SEE YOU AS SUCH AN AMAZING PRINCE.

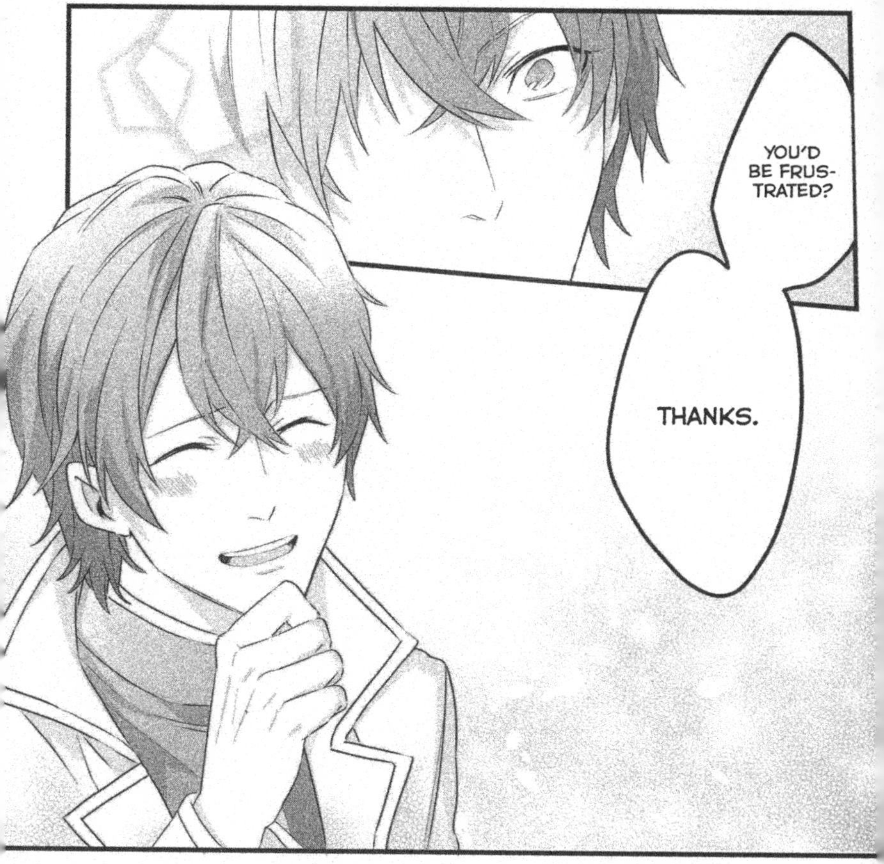
YOU'D BE FRUS-TRATED?
THANKS.

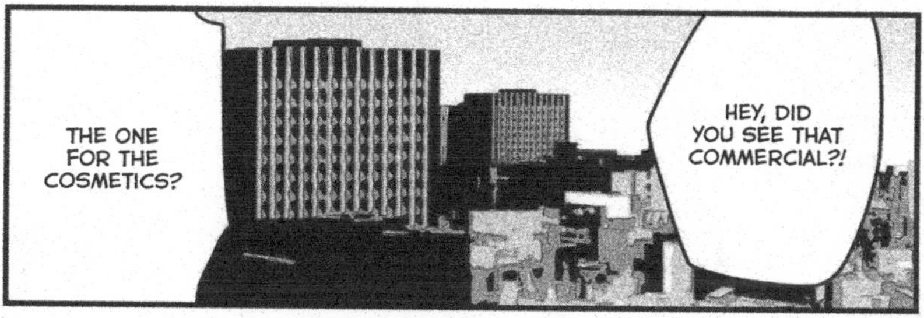
HEY, DID YOU SEE THAT COMMERCIAL?!
THE ONE FOR THE COSMETICS?

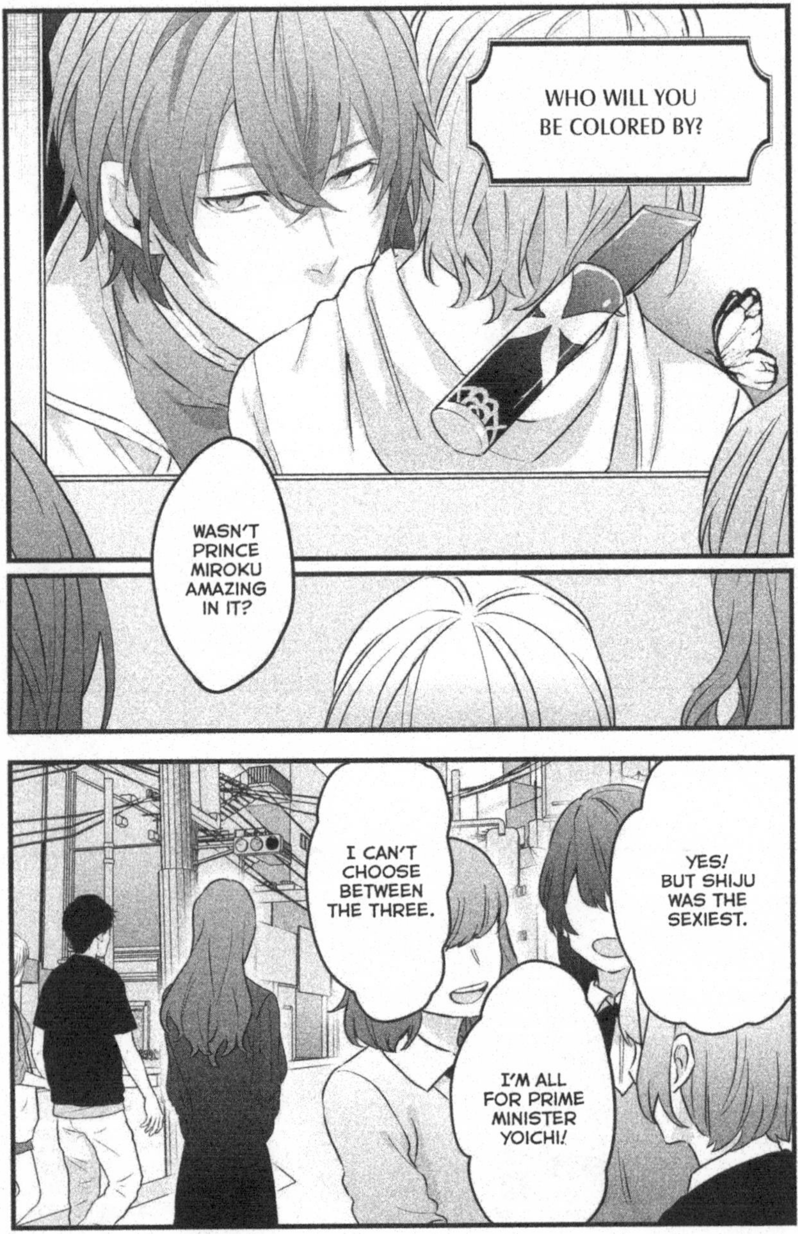
WHO WILL YOU BE COLORED BY?
WASN'T PRINCE MIROKU AMAZING IN IT?
YES! BUT SHIJU WAS THE SEXIEST.
I CAN'T CHOOSE BETWEEN THE THREE.
I'M ALL FOR PRIME MINISTER YOICHI!

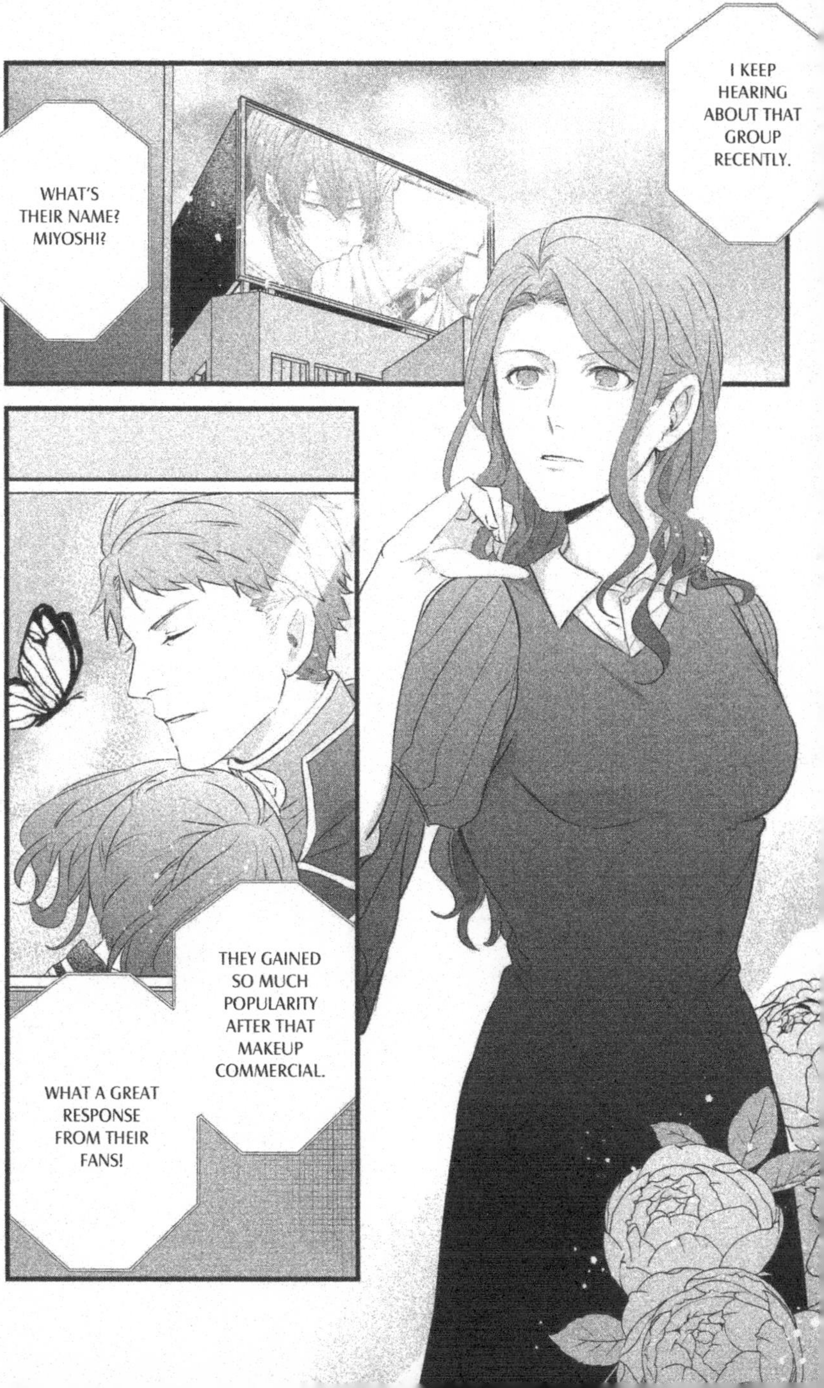
I KEEP HEARING ABOUT THAT GROUP RECENTLY.
WHAT'S THEIR NAME? MIYOSHI?
THEY GAINED SO MUCH POPULARITY AFTER THAT MAKEUP COMMERCIAL.
WHAT A GREAT RESPONSE FROM THEIR FANS!

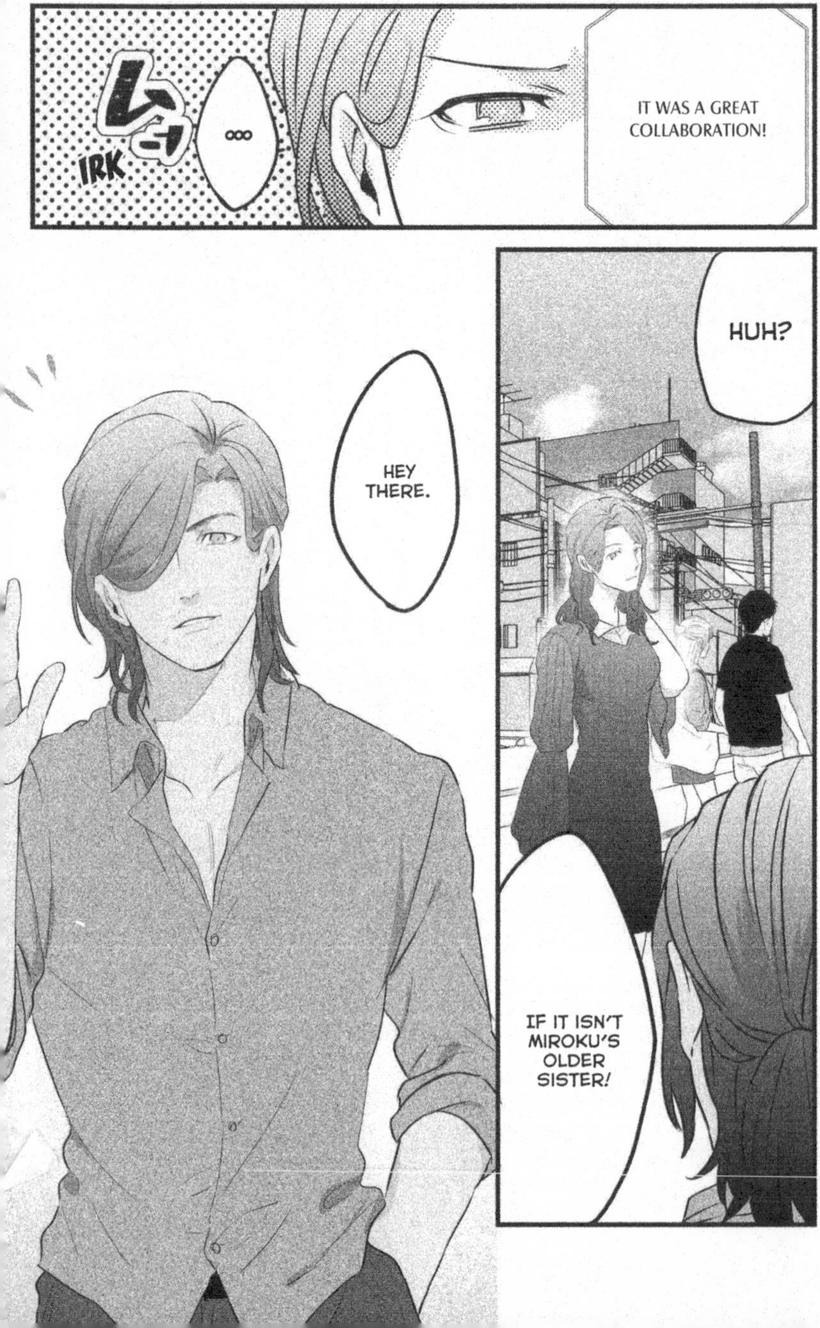
IT WAS A GREAT COLLABORATION!
...
IRK
HUH?
IF IT ISN'T MIROKU'S OLDER SISTER!
HEY THERE.

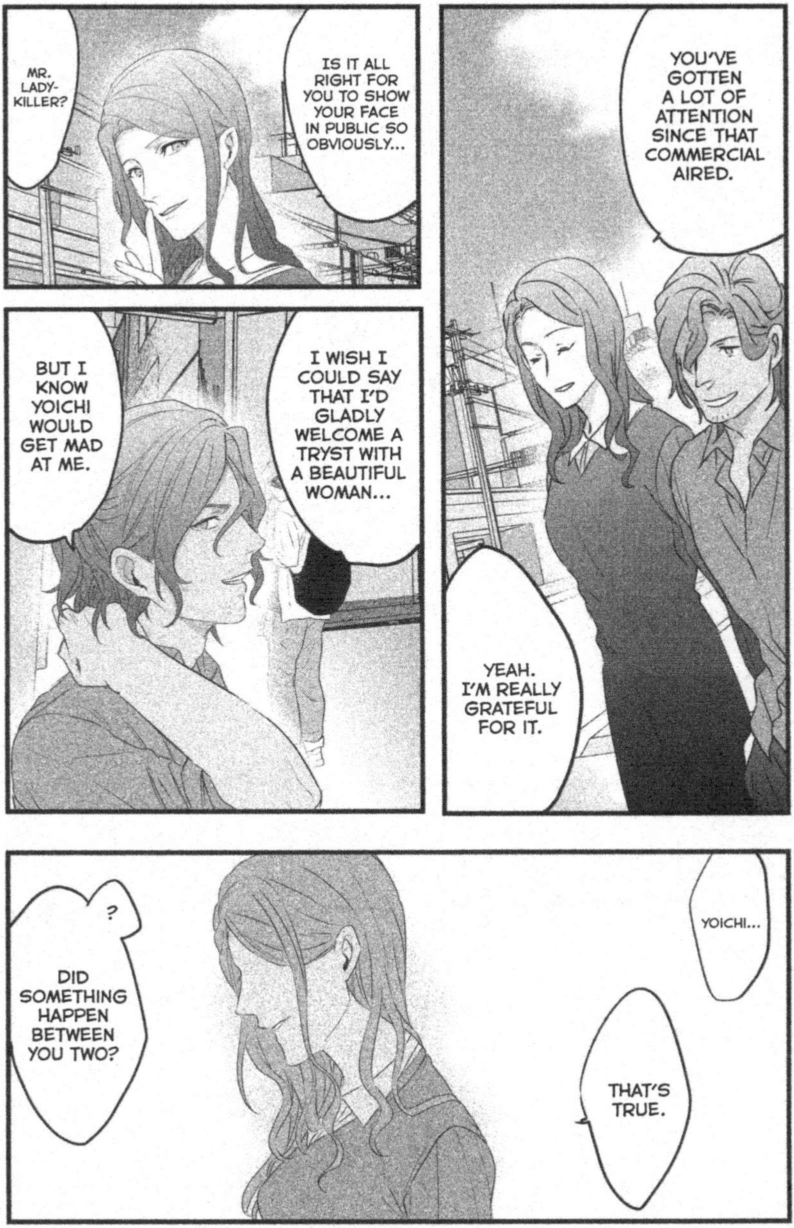
YOU'VE GOTTEN A LOT OF ATTENTION SINCE THAT COMMERCIAL AIRED.
YEAH. I'M REALLY GRATEFUL FOR IT.
IS IT ALL RIGHT FOR YOU TO SHOW YOUR FACE IN PUBLIC SO OBVIOUSLY...
MR. LADY-KILLER?
I WISH I COULD SAY THAT I'D GLADLY WELCOME A TRYST WITH A BEAUTIFUL WOMAN...
BUT I KNOW YOICHI WOULD GET MAD AT ME.
YOICHI...
THAT'S TRUE.
?
DID SOMETHING HAPPEN BETWEEN YOU TWO?

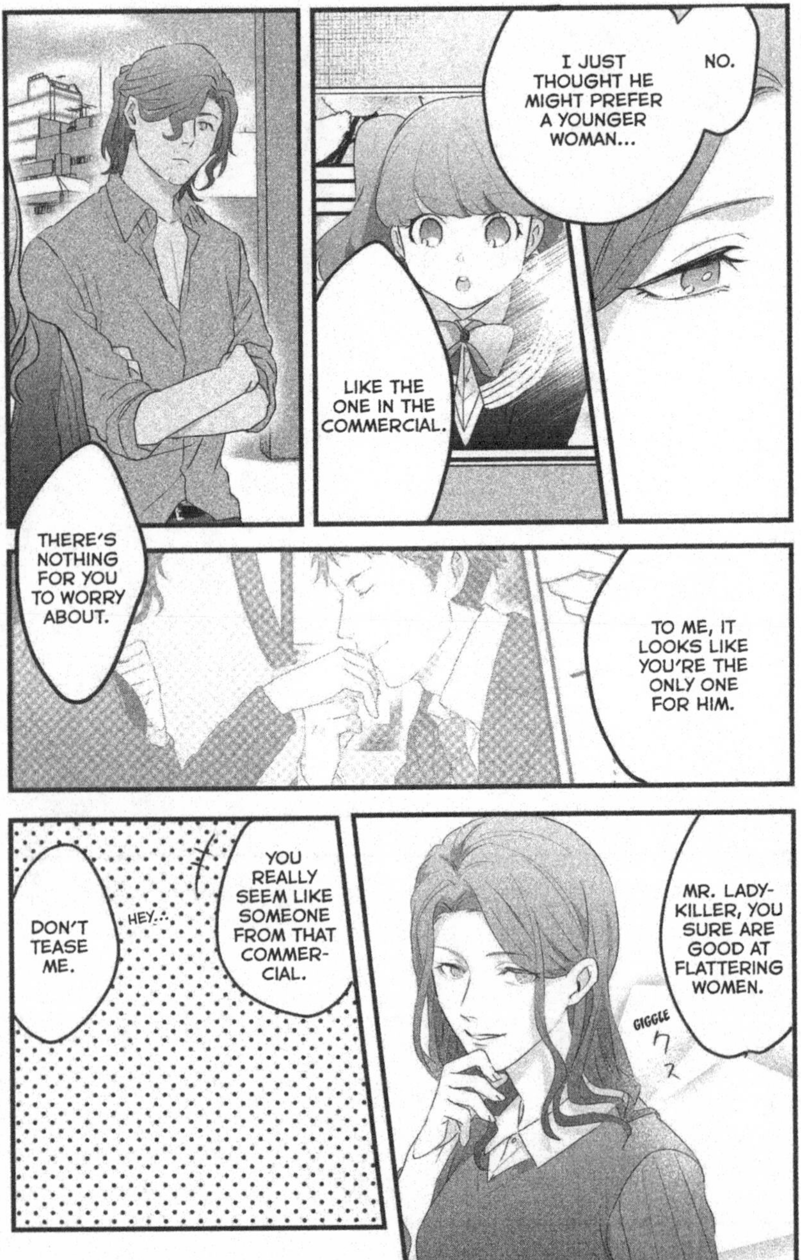
NO.
I JUST THOUGHT HE MIGHT PREFER A YOUNGER WOMAN...
LIKE THE ONE IN THE COMMERCIAL.
THERE'S NOTHING FOR YOU TO WORRY ABOUT.
TO ME, IT LOOKS LIKE YOU'RE THE ONLY ONE FOR HIM.
MR. LADY-KILLER, YOU SURE ARE GOOD AT FLATTERING WOMEN.
GIGGLE
YOU REALLY SEEM LIKE SOMEONE FROM THAT COMMERCIAL.
HEY...
DON'T TEASE ME.

BY THE WAY, IS THE GIRL ACTING WITH MIROKU...?

YEAH.

OUR MANAGER HAS BEEN USELESS FOR THE PAST FEW DAYS BECAUSE OF ALL THIS.

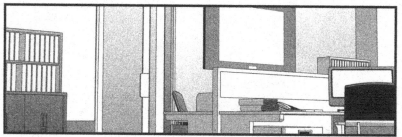

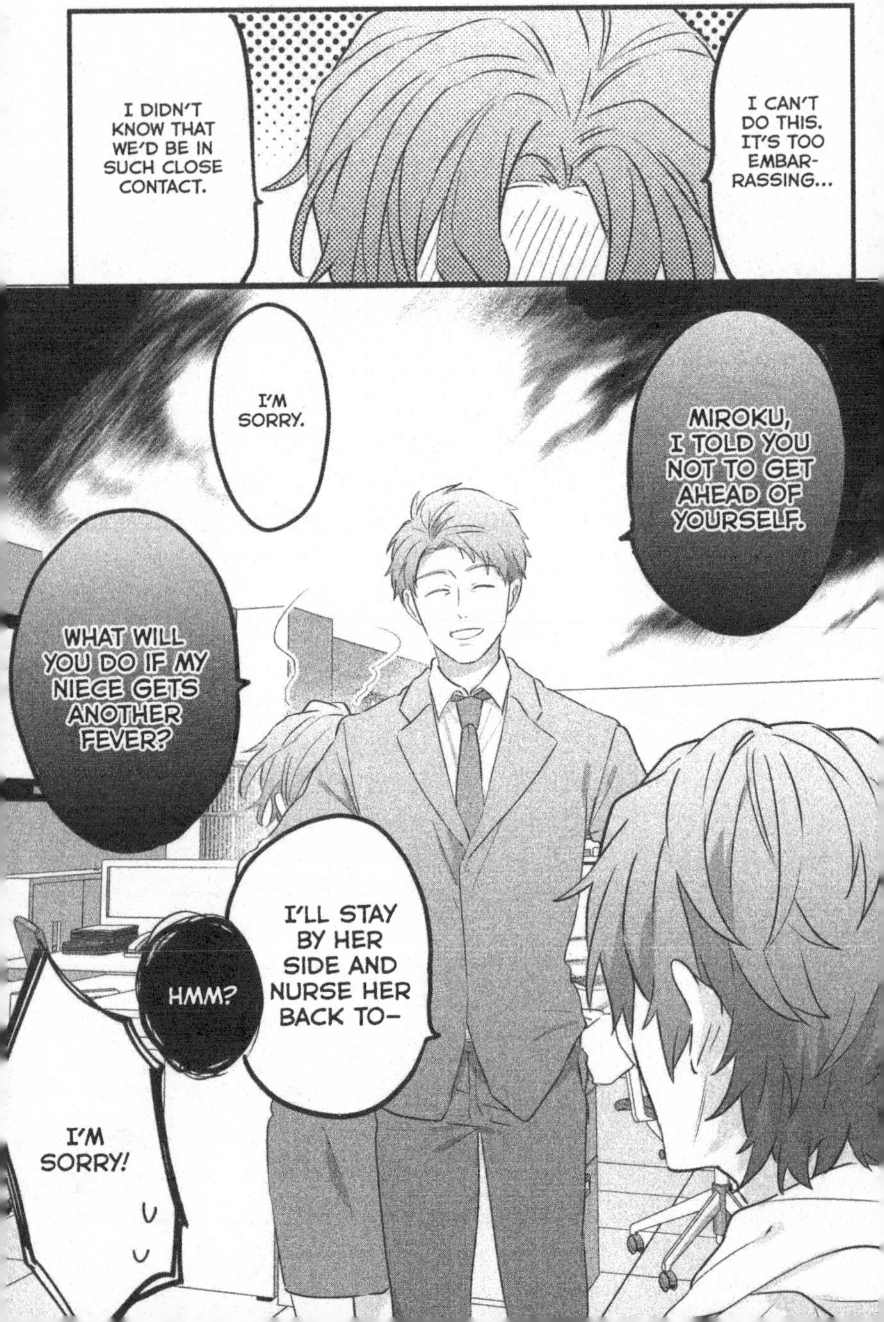
I CAN'T DO THIS. IT'S TOO EMBAR-RASSING...
I DIDN'T KNOW THAT WE'D BE IN SUCH CLOSE CONTACT.
MIROKU, I TOLD YOU NOT TO GET AHEAD OF YOURSELF.
I'M SORRY.
WHAT WILL YOU DO IF MY NIECE GETS ANOTHER FEVER?
I'LL STAY BY HER SIDE AND NURSE HER BACK TO–
HMM?
I'M SORRY!

Chapter 25

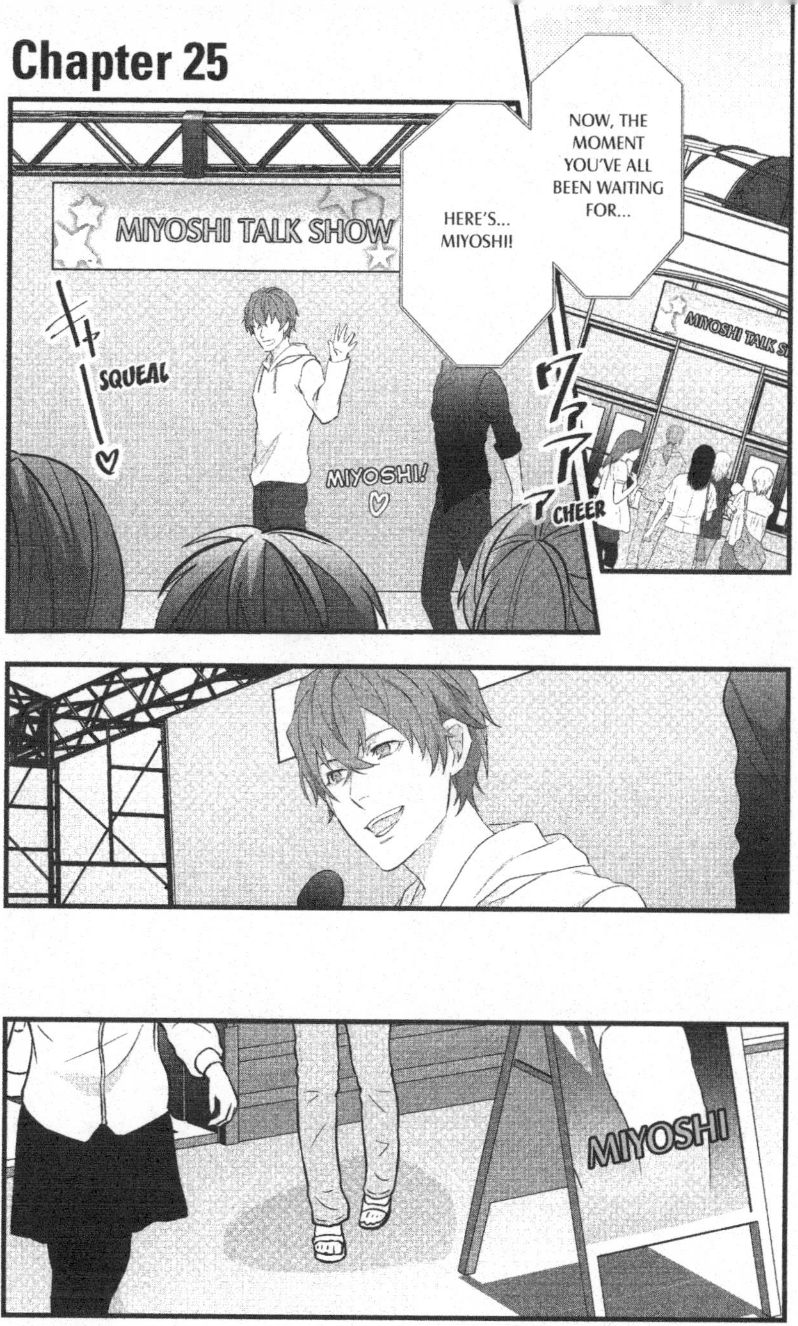

MIYOSHI TALK SHOW
NOW, THE MOMENT YOU'VE ALL BEEN WAITING FOR...
HERE'S... MIYOSHI!
CHEER
SQUEAL
MIYOSHI!
MIYOSHI

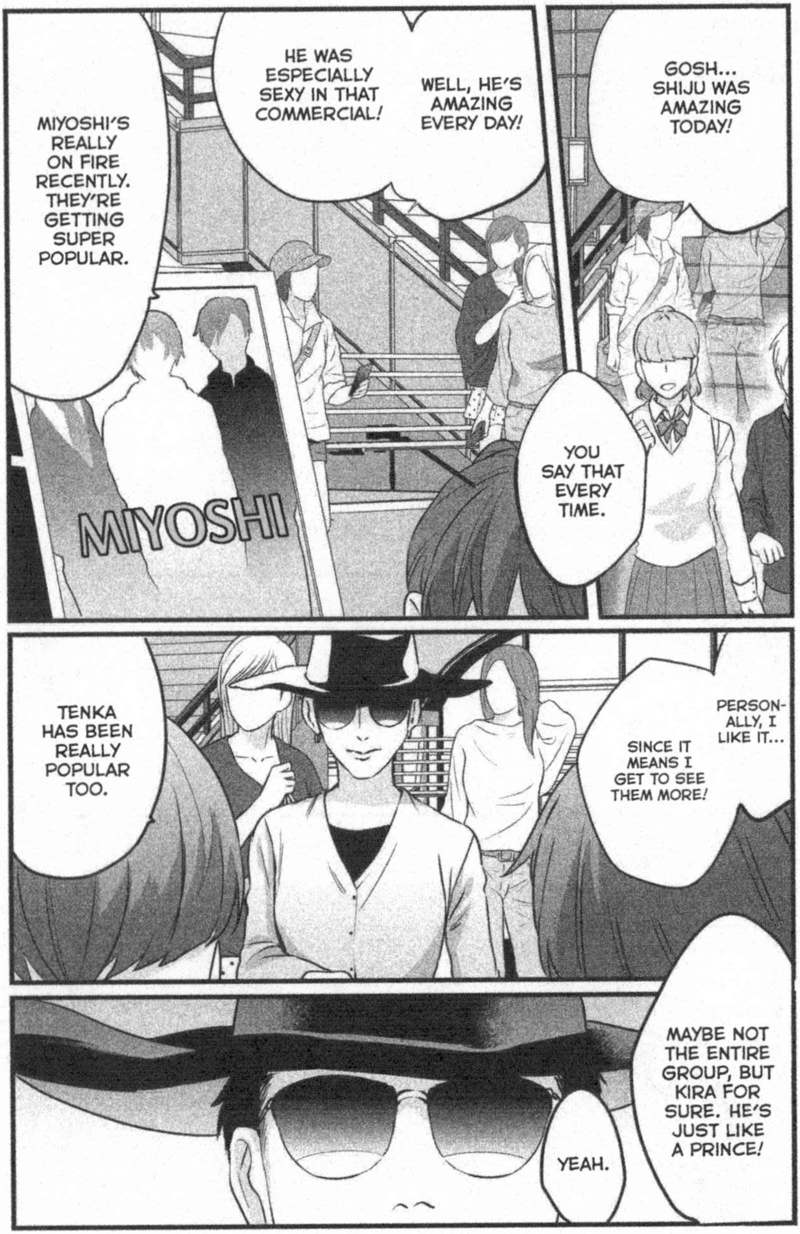
GOSH... SHIJU WAS AMAZING TODAY!
YOU SAY THAT EVERY TIME.
WELL, HE'S AMAZING EVERY DAY!
HE WAS ESPECIALLY SEXY IN THAT COMMERCIAL!
MIYOSHI'S REALLY ON FIRE RECENTLY. THEY'RE GETTING SUPER POPULAR.
MIYOSHI
PERSON-ALLY, I LIKE IT...
SINCE IT MEANS I GET TO SEE THEM MORE!
TENKA HAS BEEN REALLY POPULAR TOO.
MAYBE NOT THE ENTIRE GROUP, BUT KIRA FOR SURE. HE'S JUST LIKE A PRINCE!
YEAH.

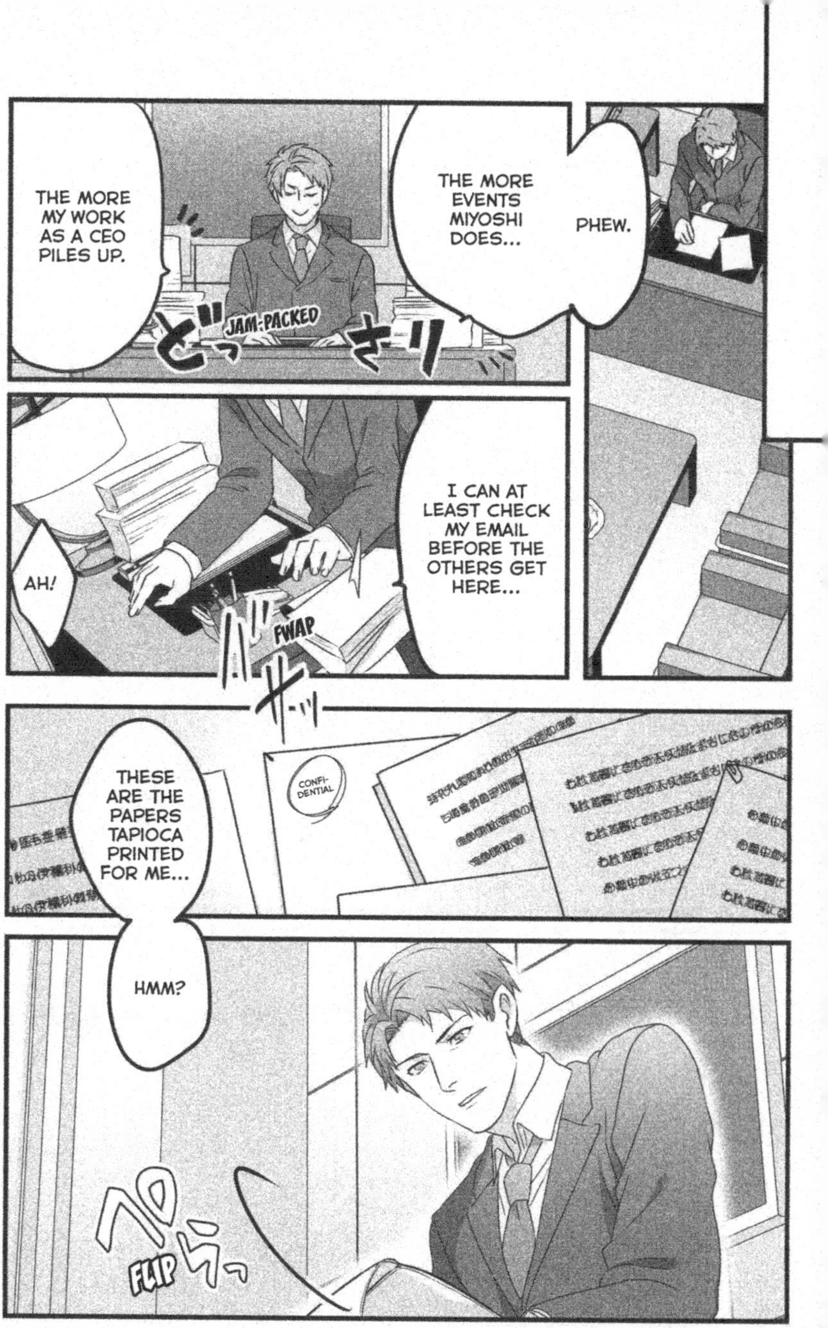
PHEW.
THE MORE EVENTS MIYOSHI DOES...
THE MORE MY WORK AS A CEO PILES UP.
JAM-PACKED
I CAN AT LEAST CHECK MY EMAIL BEFORE THE OTHERS GET HERE...
FWAP
AH!
CONFI-DENTIAL
THESE ARE THE PAPERS TAPIOCA PRINTED FOR ME...
HMM?
FLIP

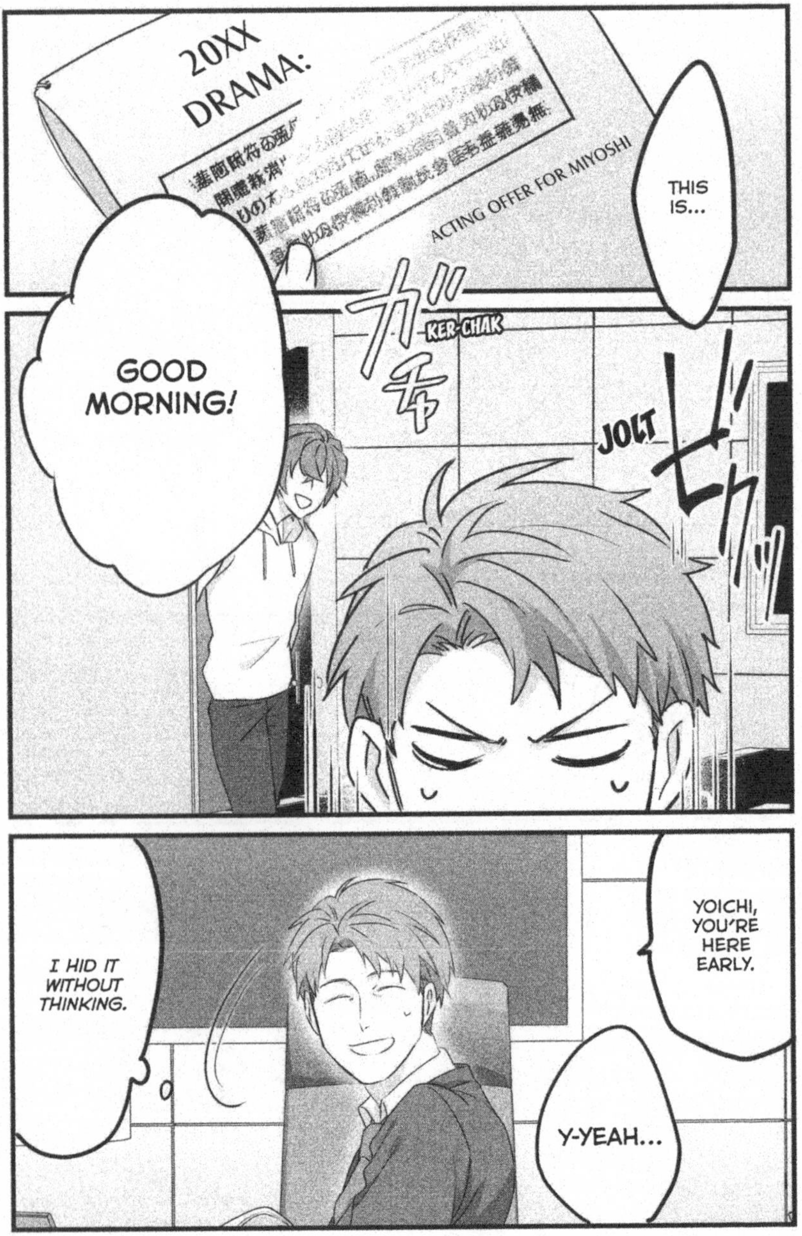

20XX DRAMA:
ACTING OFFER FOR MIYOSHI
THIS IS...
KER-CHAK
JOLT
GOOD MORNING!
YOICHI, YOU'RE HERE EARLY.
Y-YEAH...
I HID IT WITHOUT THINKING.

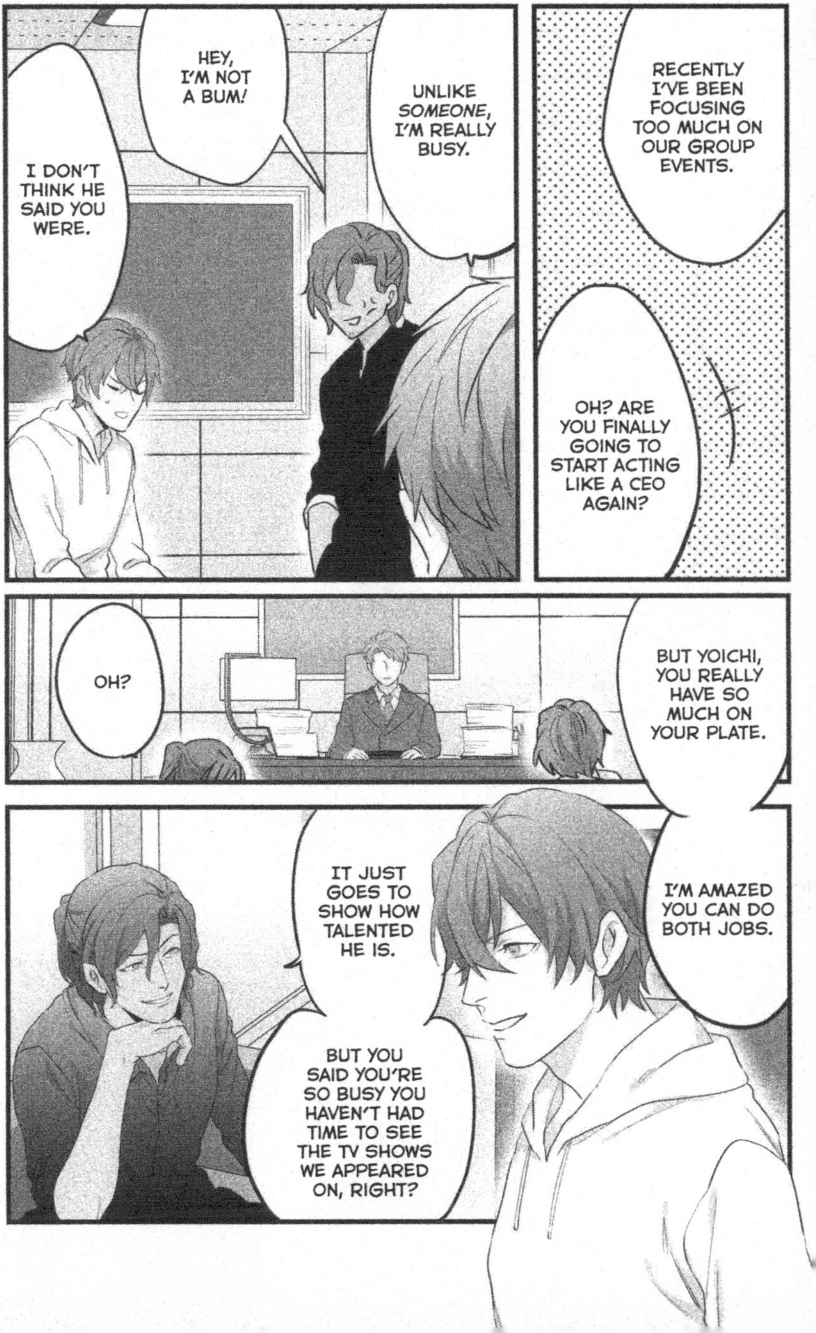
RECENTLY I'VE BEEN FOCUSING TOO MUCH ON OUR GROUP EVENTS.
OH? ARE YOU FINALLY GOING TO START ACTING LIKE A CEO AGAIN?
UNLIKE *SOMEONE*, I'M REALLY BUSY.
HEY, I'M NOT A BUM!
I DON'T THINK HE SAID YOU WERE.
BUT YOICHI, YOU REALLY HAVE SO MUCH ON YOUR PLATE.
OH?
I'M AMAZED YOU CAN DO BOTH JOBS.
IT JUST GOES TO SHOW HOW TALENTED HE IS.
BUT YOU SAID YOU'RE SO BUSY YOU HAVEN'T HAD TIME TO SEE THE TV SHOWS WE APPEARED ON, RIGHT?

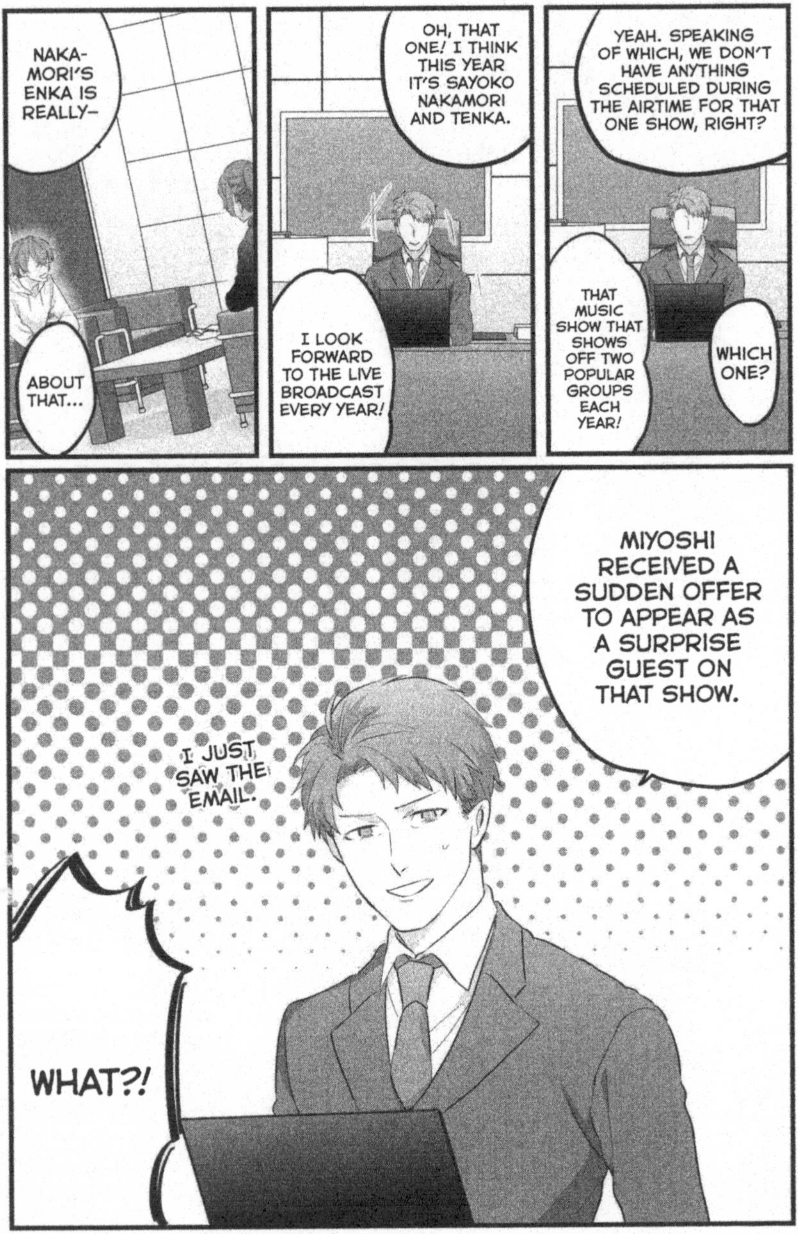
YEAH. SPEAKING OF WHICH, WE DON'T HAVE ANYTHING SCHEDULED DURING THE AIRTIME FOR THAT ONE SHOW, RIGHT?
WHICH ONE?
THAT MUSIC SHOW THAT SHOWS OFF TWO POPULAR GROUPS EACH YEAR!
OH, THAT ONE! I THINK THIS YEAR IT'S SAYOKO NAKAMORI AND TENKA.
I LOOK FORWARD TO THE LIVE BROADCAST EVERY YEAR!
NAKA-MORI'S ENKA IS REALLY–
ABOUT THAT...
MIYOSHI RECEIVED A SUDDEN OFFER TO APPEAR AS A SURPRISE GUEST ON THAT SHOW.
I JUST SAW THE EMAIL.
WHAT?!

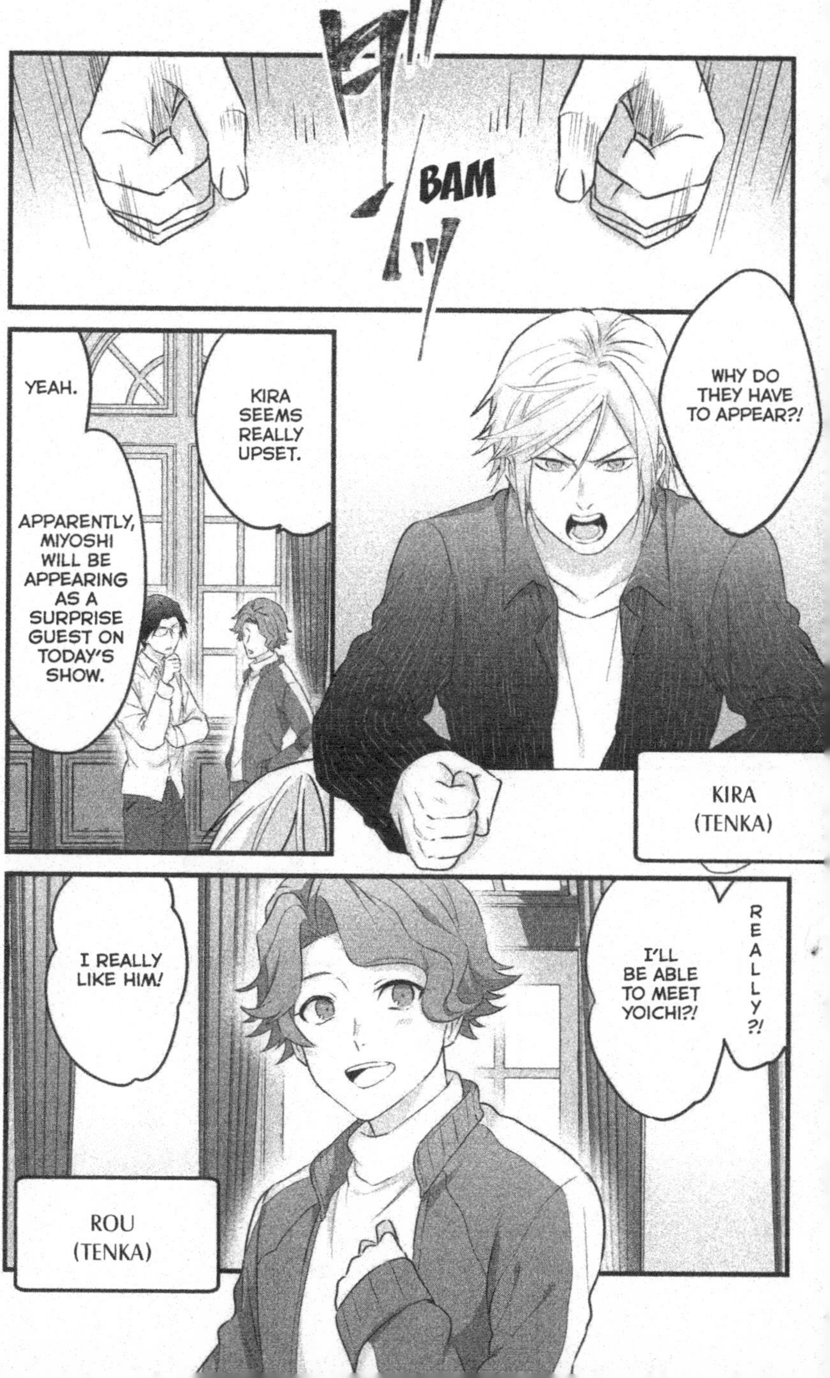
BAM
WHY DO THEY HAVE TO APPEAR?!
KIRA (TENKA)
KIRA SEEMS REALLY UPSET.
YEAH.
APPARENTLY, MIYOSHI WILL BE APPEARING AS A SURPRISE GUEST ON TODAY'S SHOW.
REALLY?!
I'LL BE ABLE TO MEET YOICHI?!
I REALLY LIKE HIM!
ROU (TENKA)

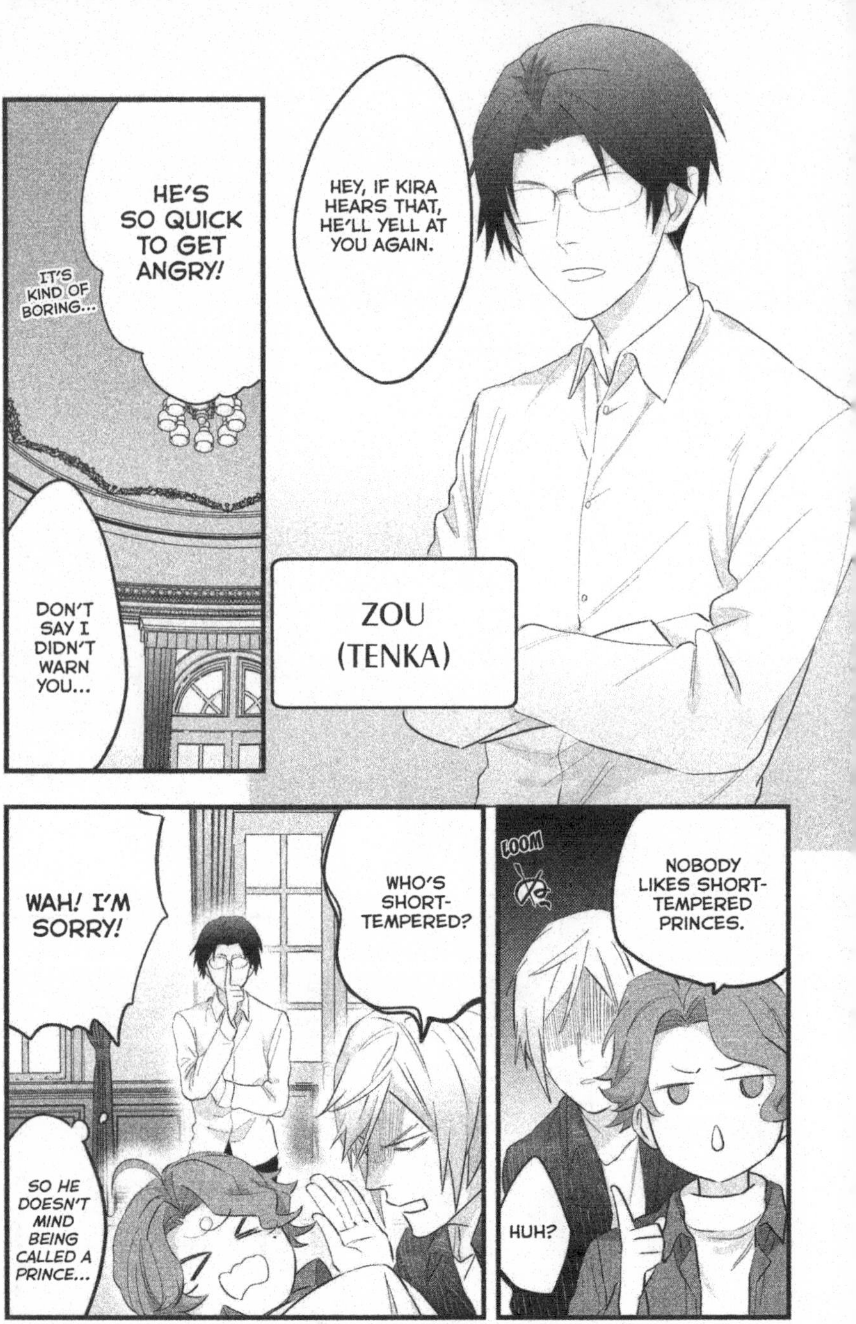
HEY, IF KIRA HEARS THAT, HE'LL YELL AT YOU AGAIN.
ZOU (TENKA)
HE'S SO QUICK TO GET ANGRY!
IT'S KIND OF BORING...
DON'T SAY I DIDN'T WARN YOU...
NOBODY LIKES SHORT-TEMPERED PRINCES.
LOOM
HUH?
WHO'S SHORT-TEMPERED?
WAH! I'M SORRY!
SO HE DOESN'T MIND BEING CALLED A PRINCE...

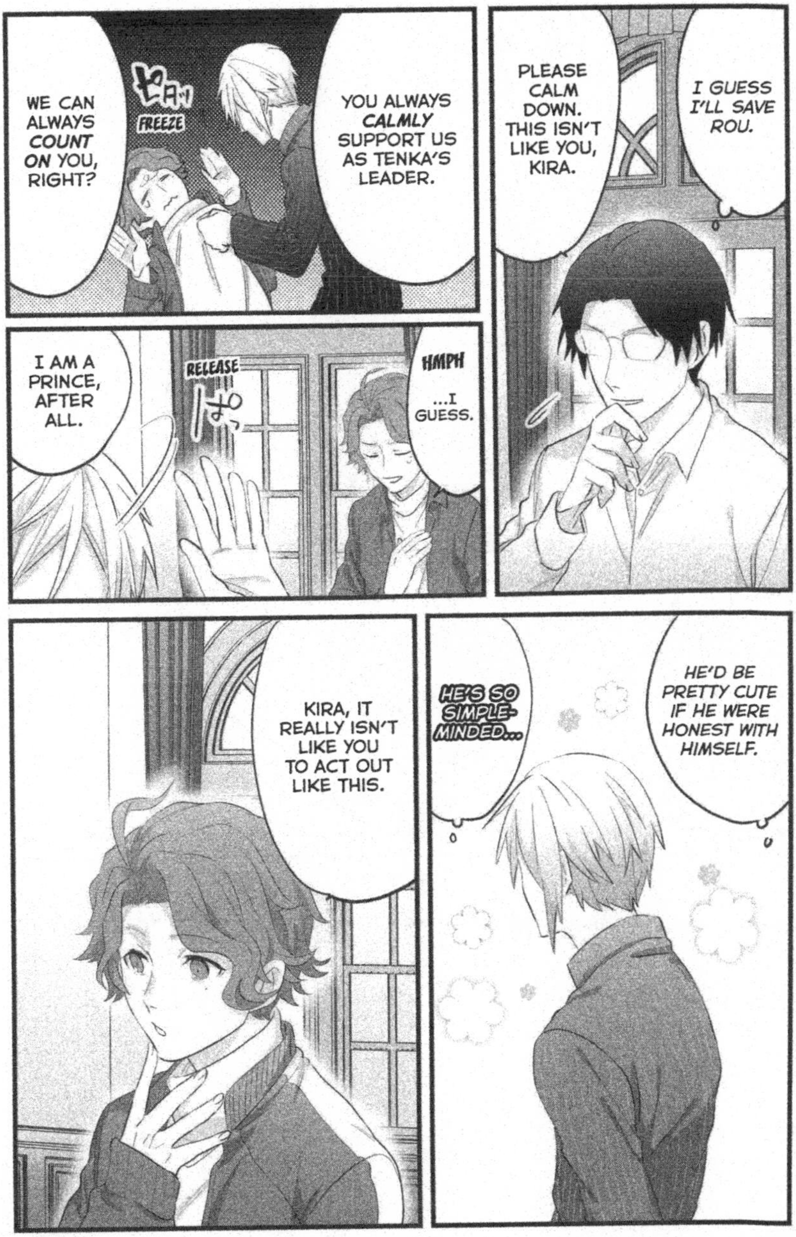
I GUESS I'LL SAVE ROU.
PLEASE CALM DOWN. THIS ISN'T LIKE YOU, KIRA.
YOU ALWAYS CALMLY SUPPORT US AS TENKA'S LEADER.
FREEZE
WE CAN ALWAYS COUNT ON YOU, RIGHT?
HMPH
...I GUESS.
RELEASE
I AM A PRINCE, AFTER ALL.
HE'D BE PRETTY CUTE IF HE WERE HONEST WITH HIMSELF.
HE'S SO SIMPLE-MINDED...
KIRA, IT REALLY ISN'T LIKE YOU TO ACT OUT LIKE THIS.

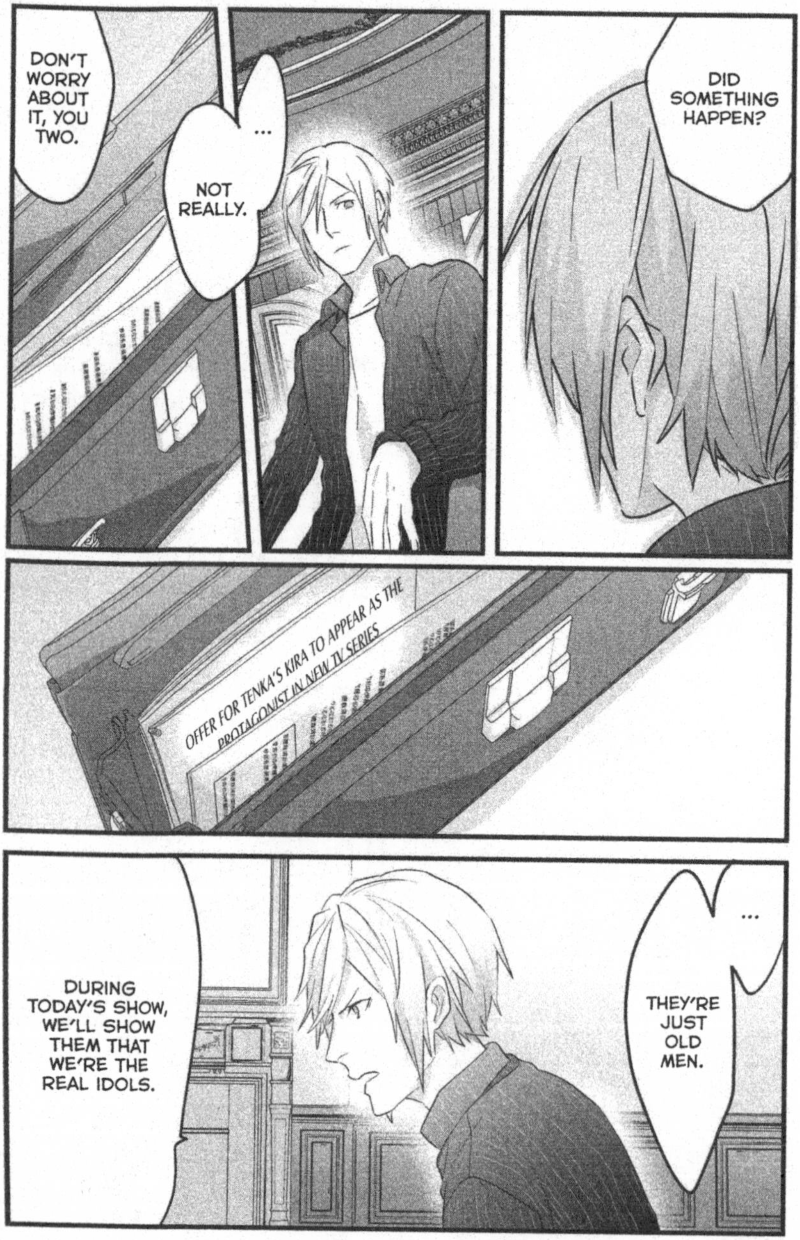
DID SOMETHING HAPPEN?
...
NOT REALLY.
DON'T WORRY ABOUT IT, YOU TWO.
OFFER FOR TENKA'S KIRA TO APPEAR AS THE PROTAGONIST IN NEW TV SERIES
...
THEY'RE JUST OLD MEN.
DURING TODAY'S SHOW, WE'LL SHOW THEM THAT WE'RE THE REAL IDOLS.

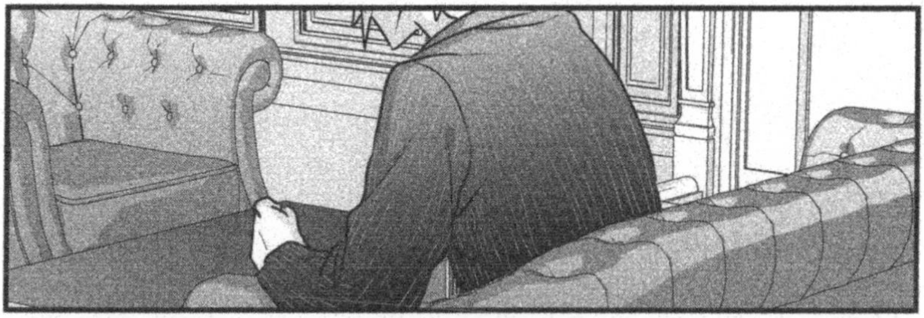

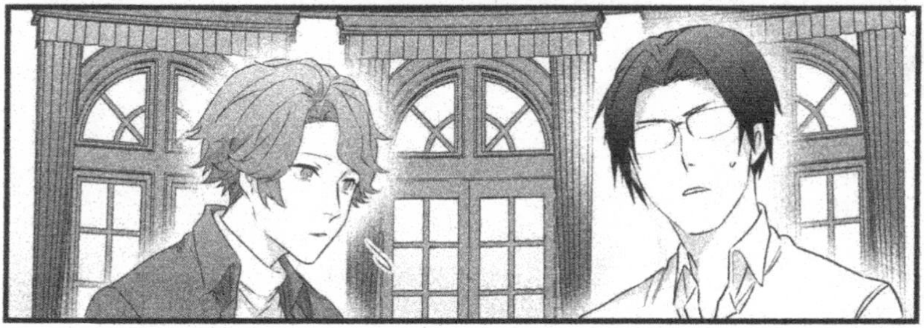

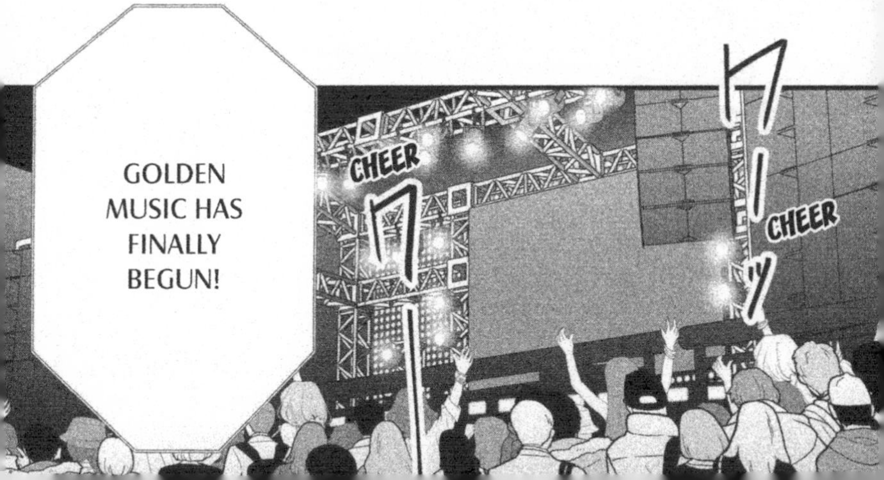
GOLDEN MUSIC HAS FINALLY BEGUN!
CHEER
CHEER

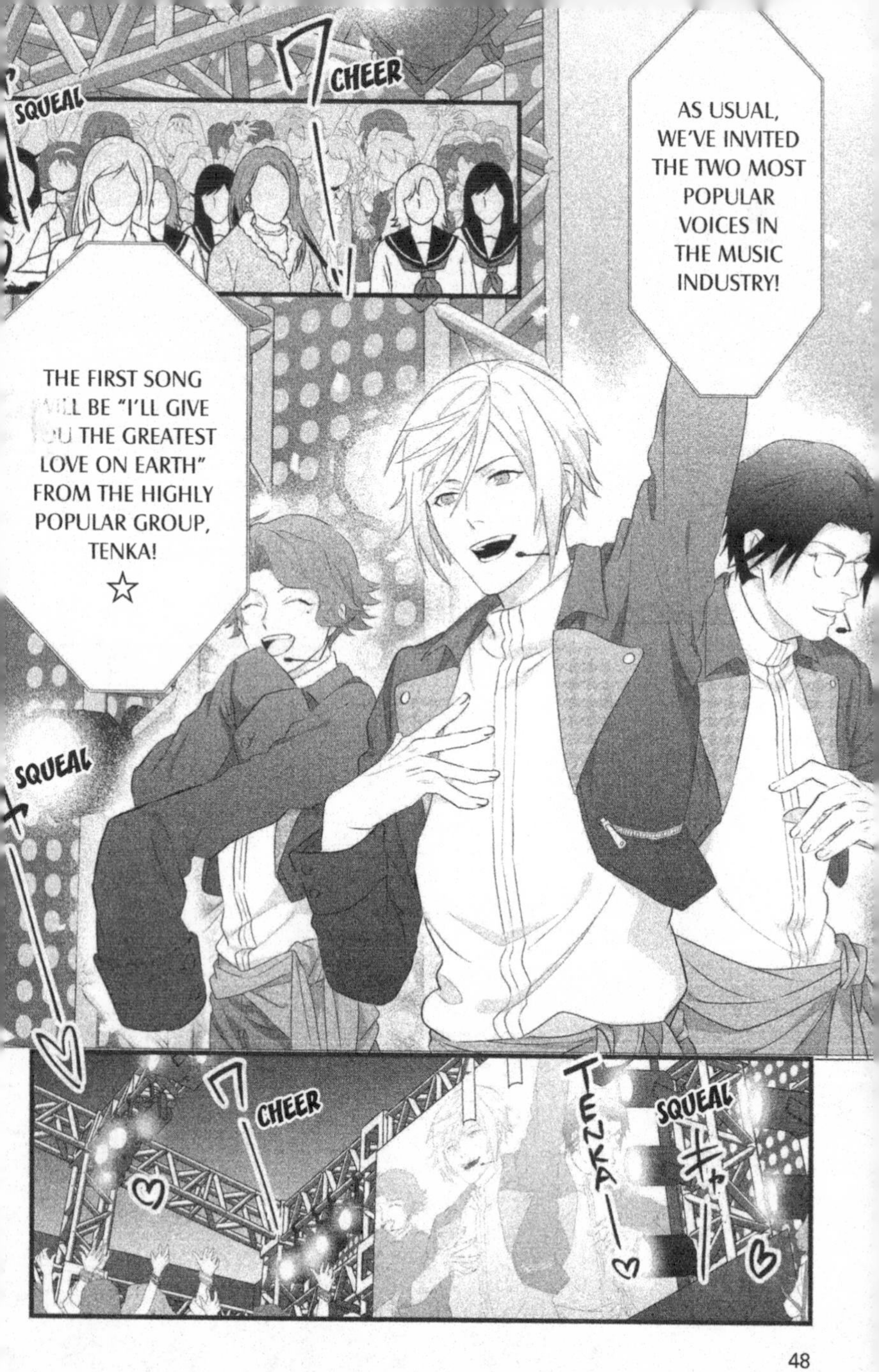
AS USUAL, WE'VE INVITED THE TWO MOST POPULAR VOICES IN THE MUSIC INDUSTRY!
CHEER
SQUEAL
THE FIRST SONG WILL BE "I'LL GIVE YOU THE GREATEST LOVE ON EARTH" FROM THE HIGHLY POPULAR GROUP, TENKA! ☆
SQUEAL
SQUEAL
TENKA—
CHEER

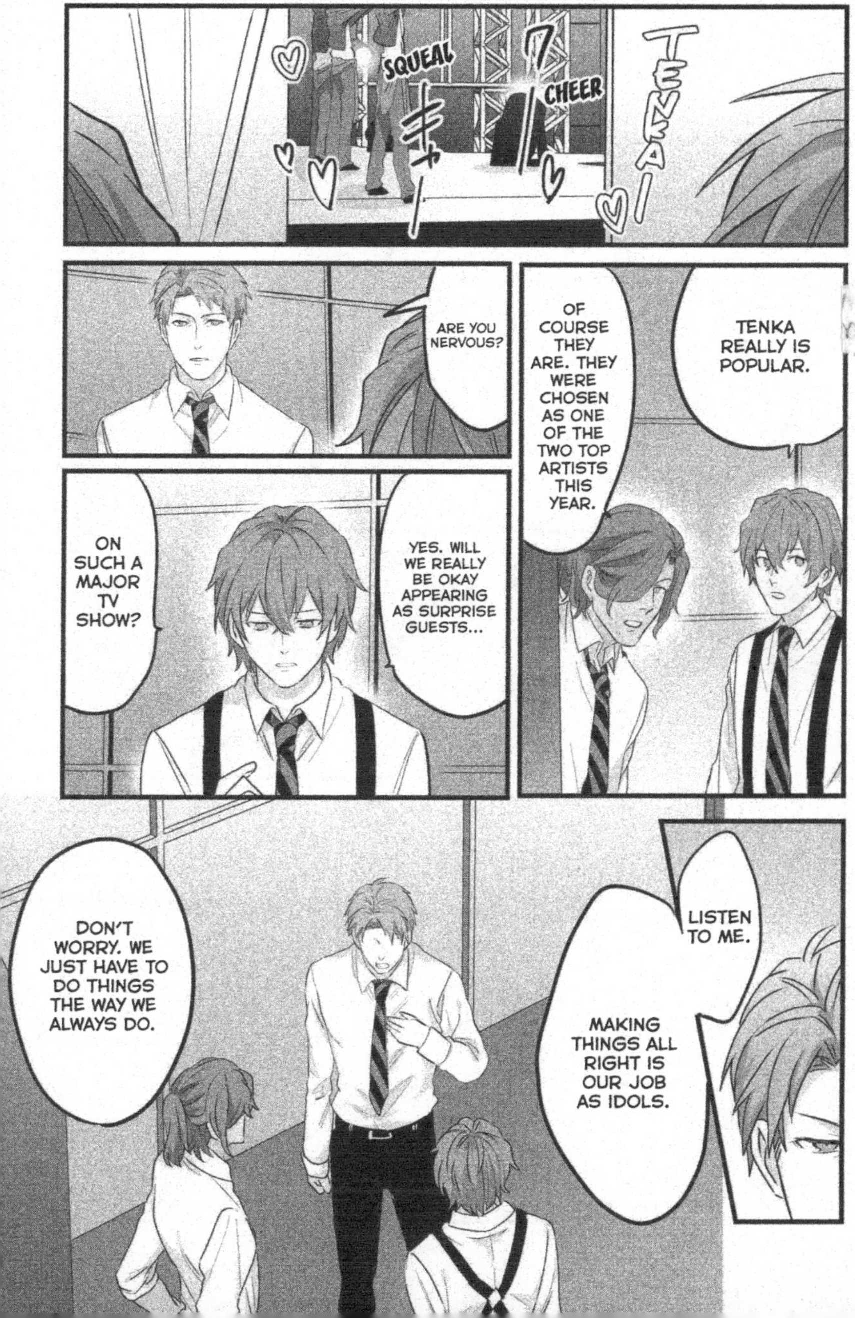
TENKAI
CHEER
SQUEAL
TENKA REALLY IS POPULAR.
OF COURSE THEY ARE. THEY WERE CHOSEN AS ONE OF THE TWO TOP ARTISTS THIS YEAR.
ARE YOU NERVOUS?
YES. WILL WE REALLY BE OKAY APPEARING AS SURPRISE GUESTS...
ON SUCH A MAJOR TV SHOW?
LISTEN TO ME.
MAKING THINGS ALL RIGHT IS OUR JOB AS IDOLS.
DON'T WORRY. WE JUST HAVE TO DO THINGS THE WAY WE ALWAYS DO.

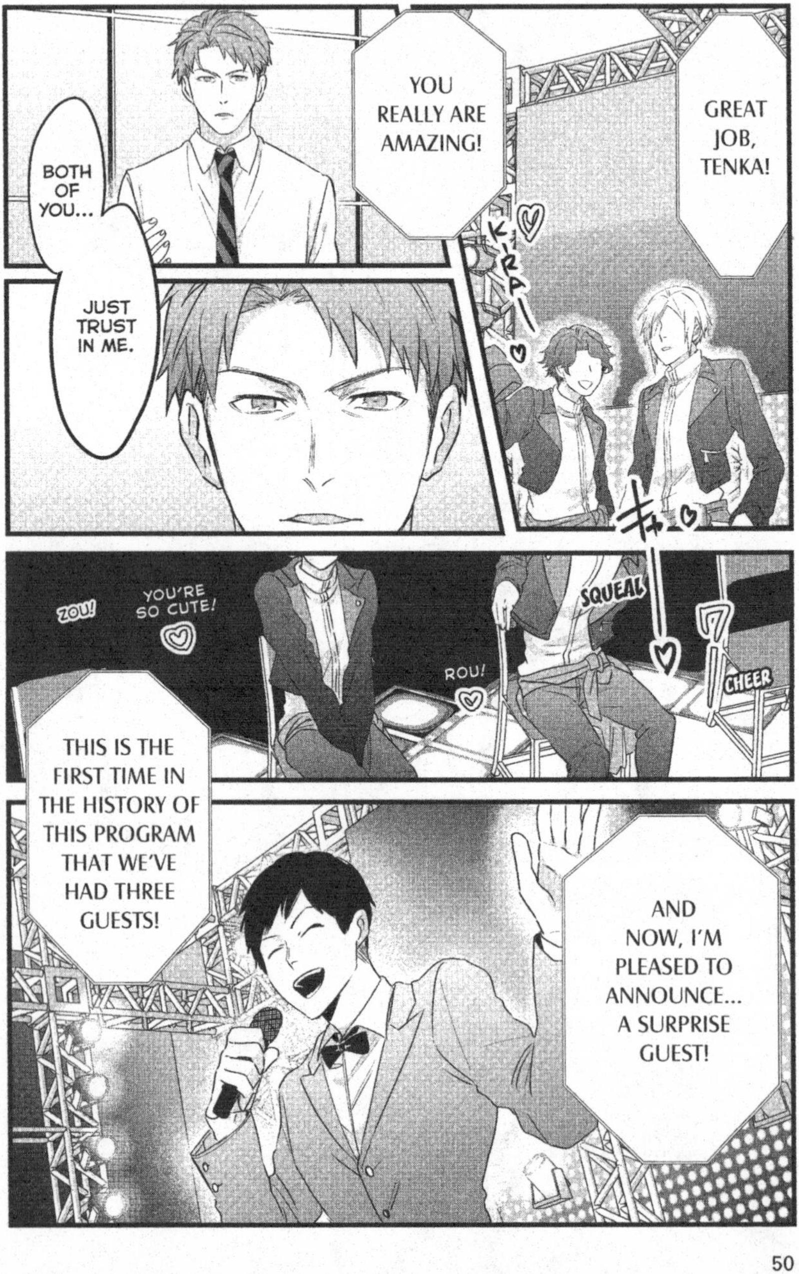
GREAT JOB, TENKA!
YOU REALLY ARE AMAZING!
KIRA
BOTH OF YOU...
JUST TRUST IN ME.
SQUEAL
CHEER
ROU!
YOU'RE SO CUTE!
ZOU!
THIS IS THE FIRST TIME IN THE HISTORY OF THIS PROGRAM THAT WE'VE HAD THREE GUESTS!
AND NOW, I'M PLEASED TO ANNOUNCE... A SURPRISE GUEST!

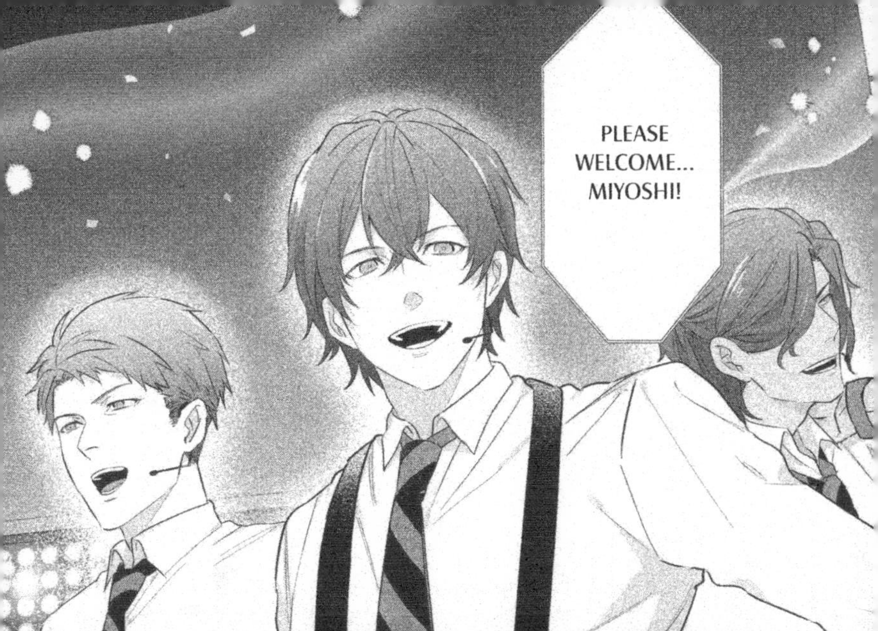
PLEASE WELCOME... MIYOSHI!
CHEER
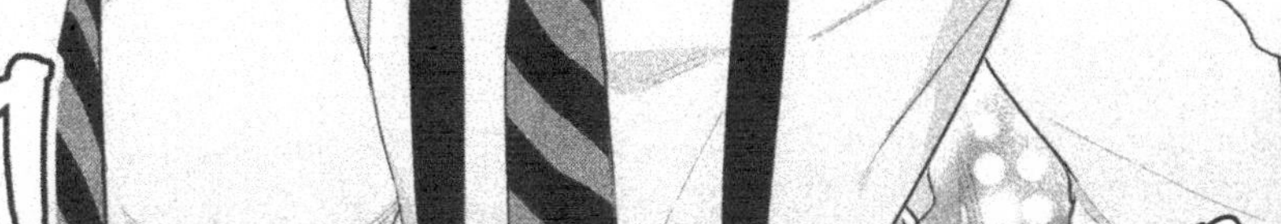

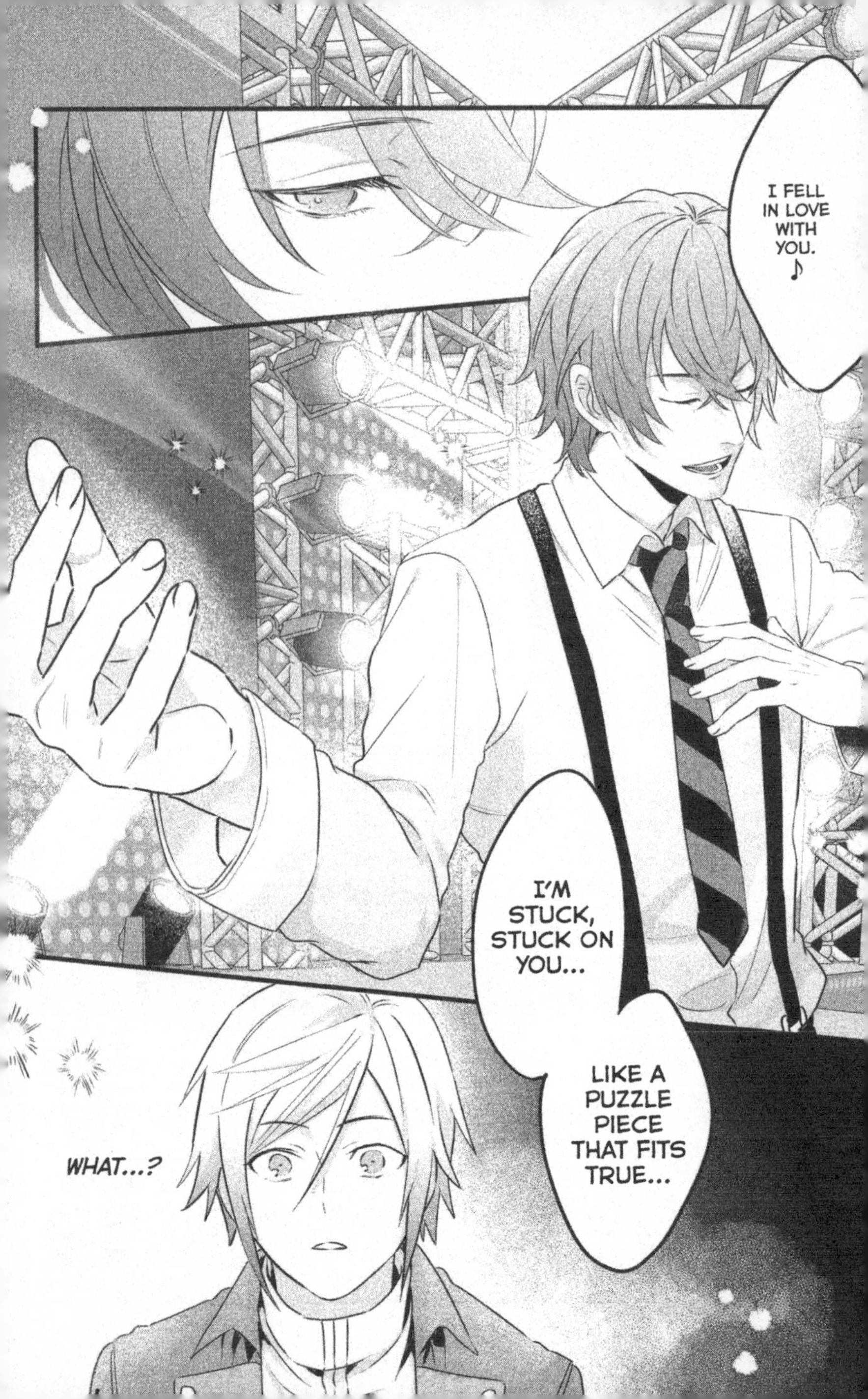
I FELL IN LOVE WITH YOU. ♪
I'M STUCK, STUCK ON YOU...
LIKE A PUZZLE PIECE THAT FITS TRUE...
WHAT...?

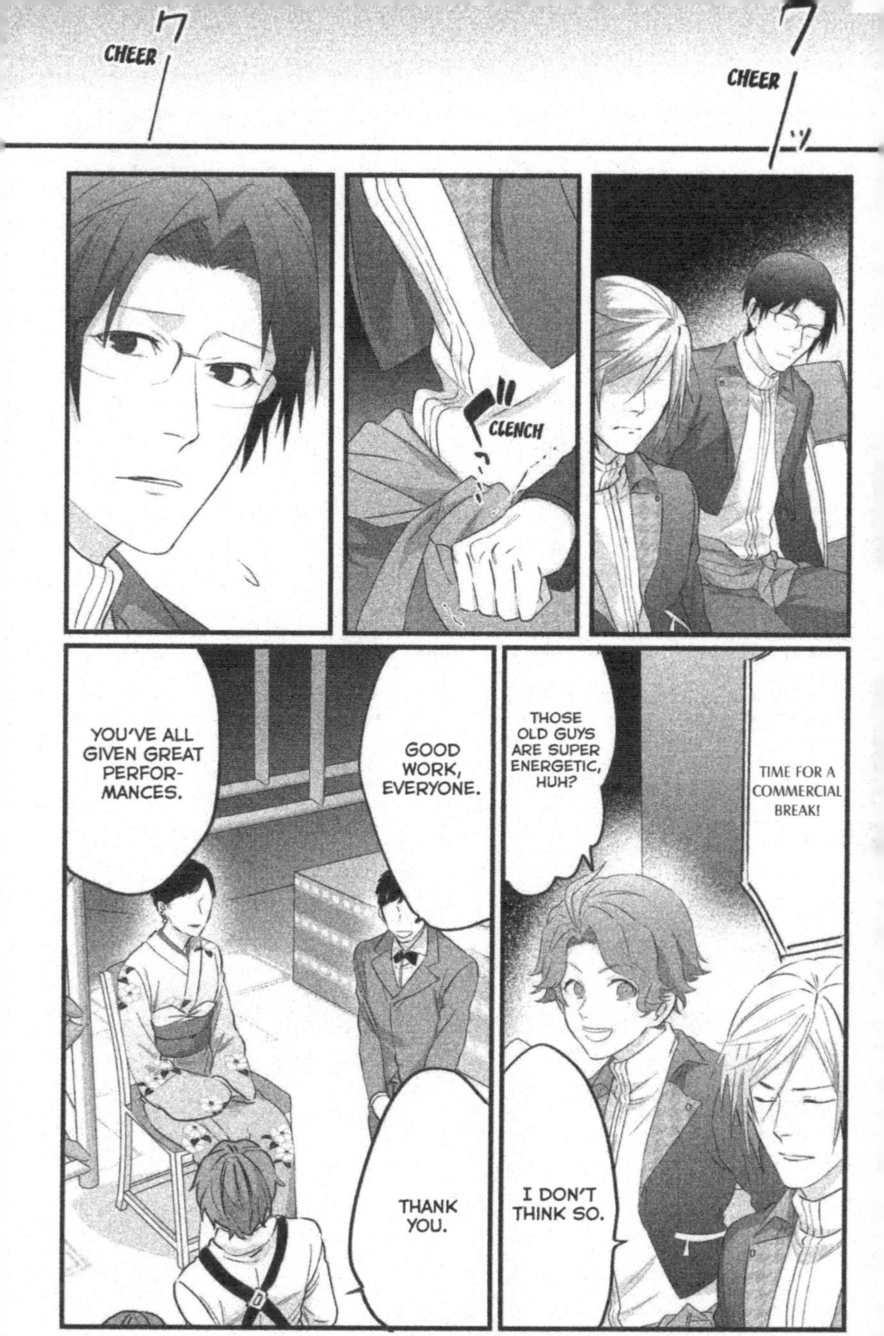
CHEER
CHEER
CLENCH
TIME FOR A COMMERCIAL BREAK!
THOSE OLD GUYS ARE SUPER ENERGETIC, HUH?
I DON'T THINK SO.
GOOD WORK, EVERYONE.
YOU'VE ALL GIVEN GREAT PERFOR-MANCES.
THANK YOU.

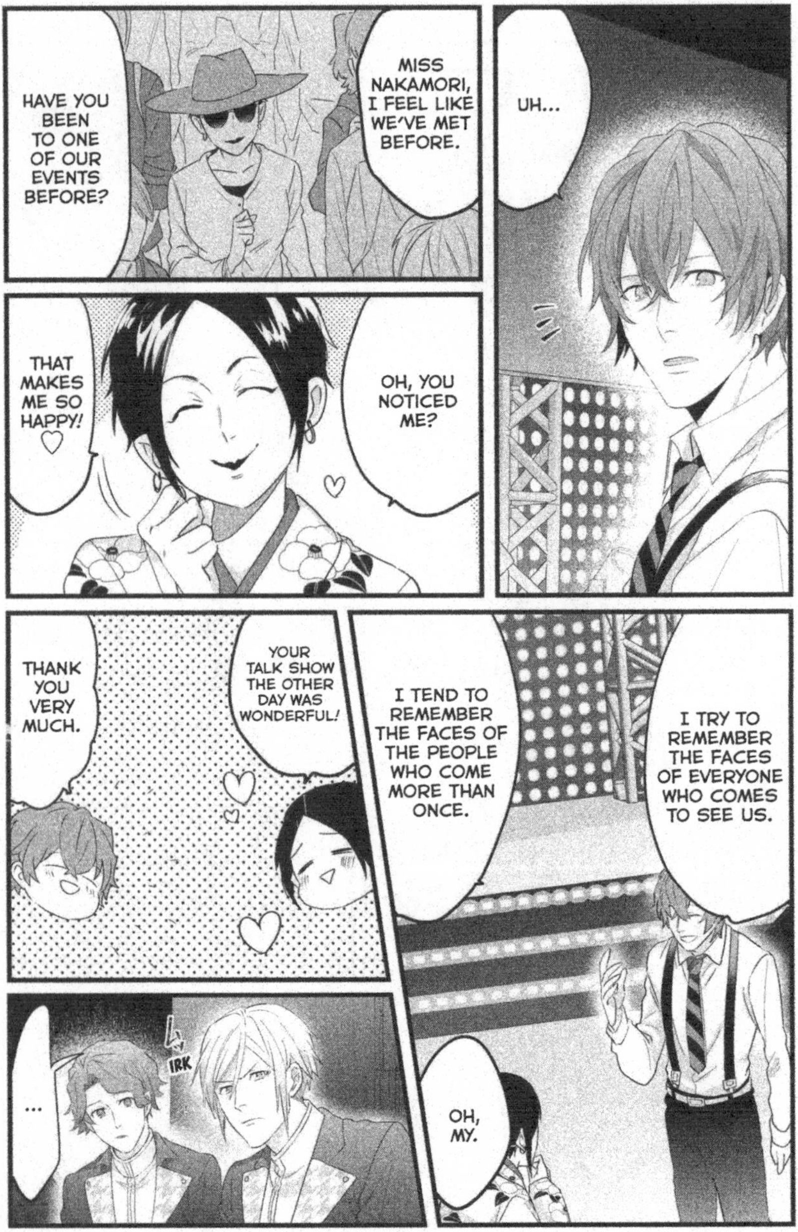
UH...
MISS NAKAMORI, I FEEL LIKE WE'VE MET BEFORE.
HAVE YOU BEEN TO ONE OF OUR EVENTS BEFORE?
OH, YOU NOTICED ME?
THAT MAKES ME SO HAPPY! ♡
I TRY TO REMEMBER THE FACES OF EVERYONE WHO COMES TO SEE US.
I TEND TO REMEMBER THE FACES OF THE PEOPLE WHO COME MORE THAN ONCE.
OH, MY.
YOUR TALK SHOW THE OTHER DAY WAS WONDERFUL!
THANK YOU VERY MUCH.
IRK
...

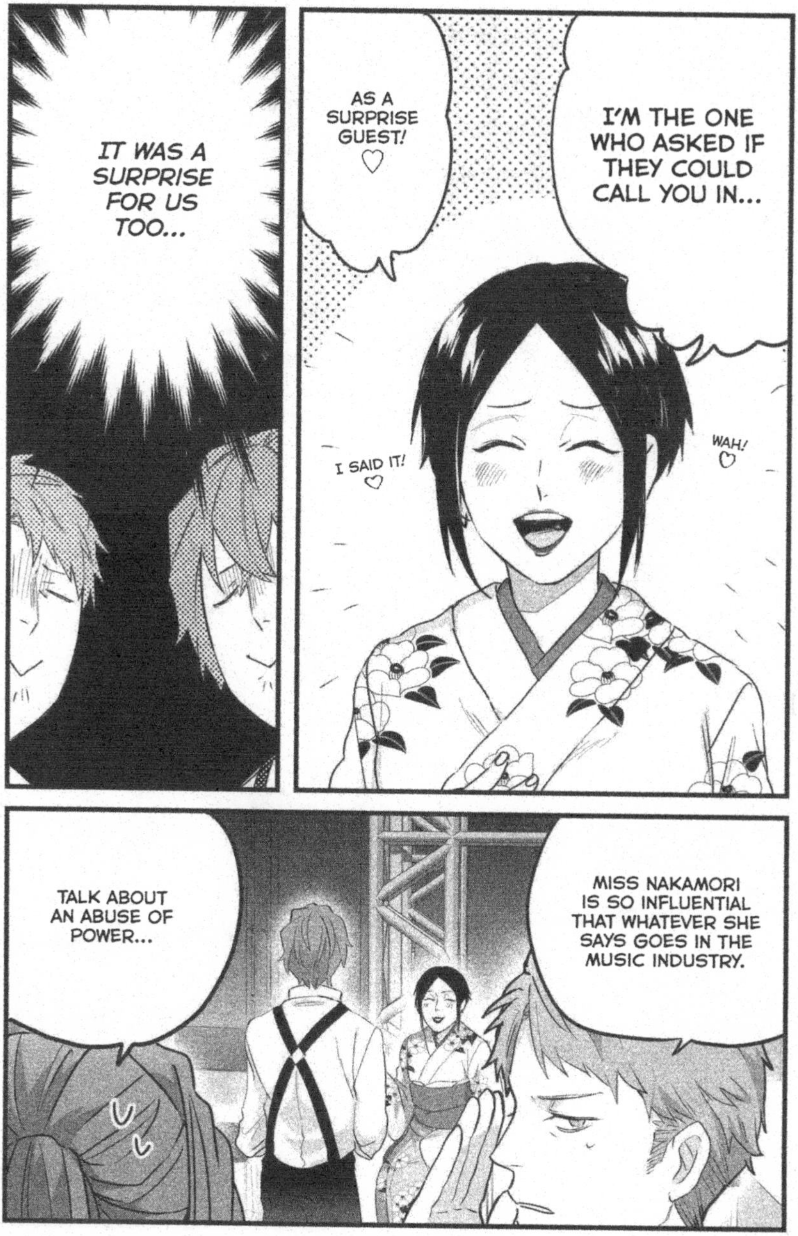
I'M THE ONE WHO ASKED IF THEY COULD CALL YOU IN...
AS A SURPRISE GUEST! ♡
WAH! ♡
I SAID IT! ♡
IT WAS A SURPRISE FOR US TOO...
MISS NAKAMORI IS SO INFLUENTIAL THAT WHATEVER SHE SAYS GOES IN THE MUSIC INDUSTRY.
TALK ABOUT AN ABUSE OF POWER...

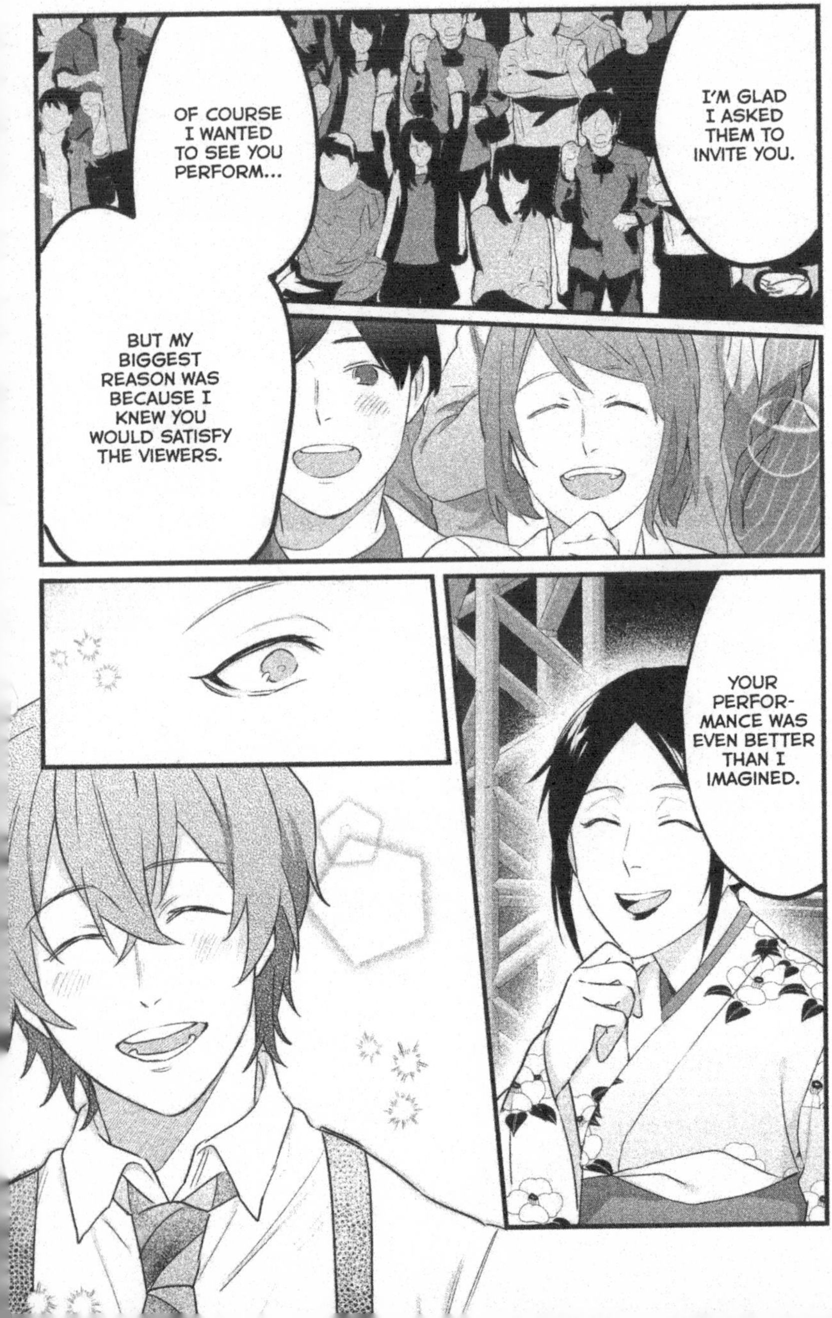
I'M GLAD I ASKED THEM TO INVITE YOU.
OF COURSE I WANTED TO SEE YOU PERFORM...
BUT MY BIGGEST REASON WAS BECAUSE I KNEW YOU WOULD SATISFY THE VIEWERS.
YOUR PERFOR-MANCE WAS EVEN BETTER THAN I IMAGINED.

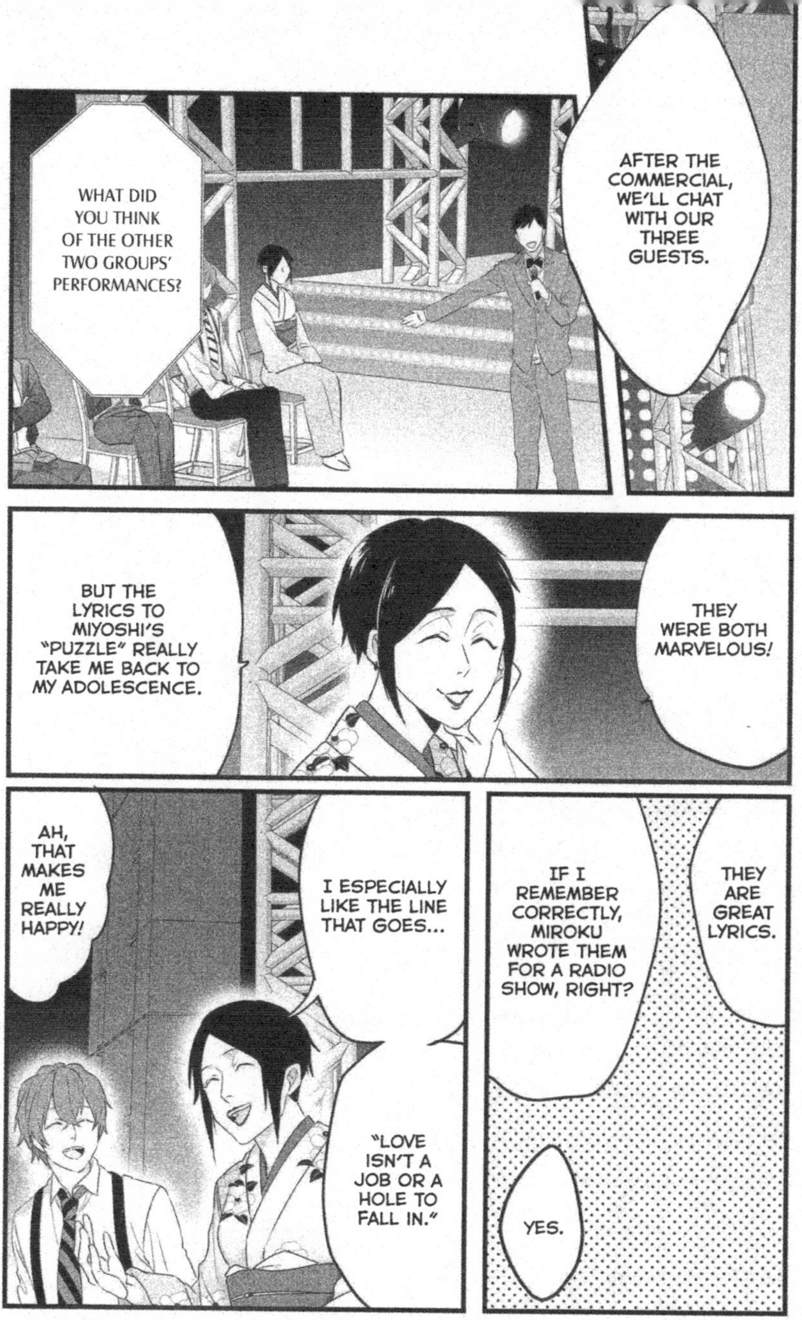
AFTER THE COMMERCIAL, WE'LL CHAT WITH OUR THREE GUESTS.
WHAT DID YOU THINK OF THE OTHER TWO GROUPS' PERFORMANCES?
THEY WERE BOTH MARVELOUS!
BUT THE LYRICS TO MIYOSHI'S "PUZZLE" REALLY TAKE ME BACK TO MY ADOLESCENCE.
THEY ARE GREAT LYRICS.
IF I REMEMBER CORRECTLY, MIROKU WROTE THEM FOR A RADIO SHOW, RIGHT?
YES.
I ESPECIALLY LIKE THE LINE THAT GOES...
"LOVE ISN'T A JOB OR A HOLE TO FALL IN."
AH, THAT MAKES ME REALLY HAPPY!

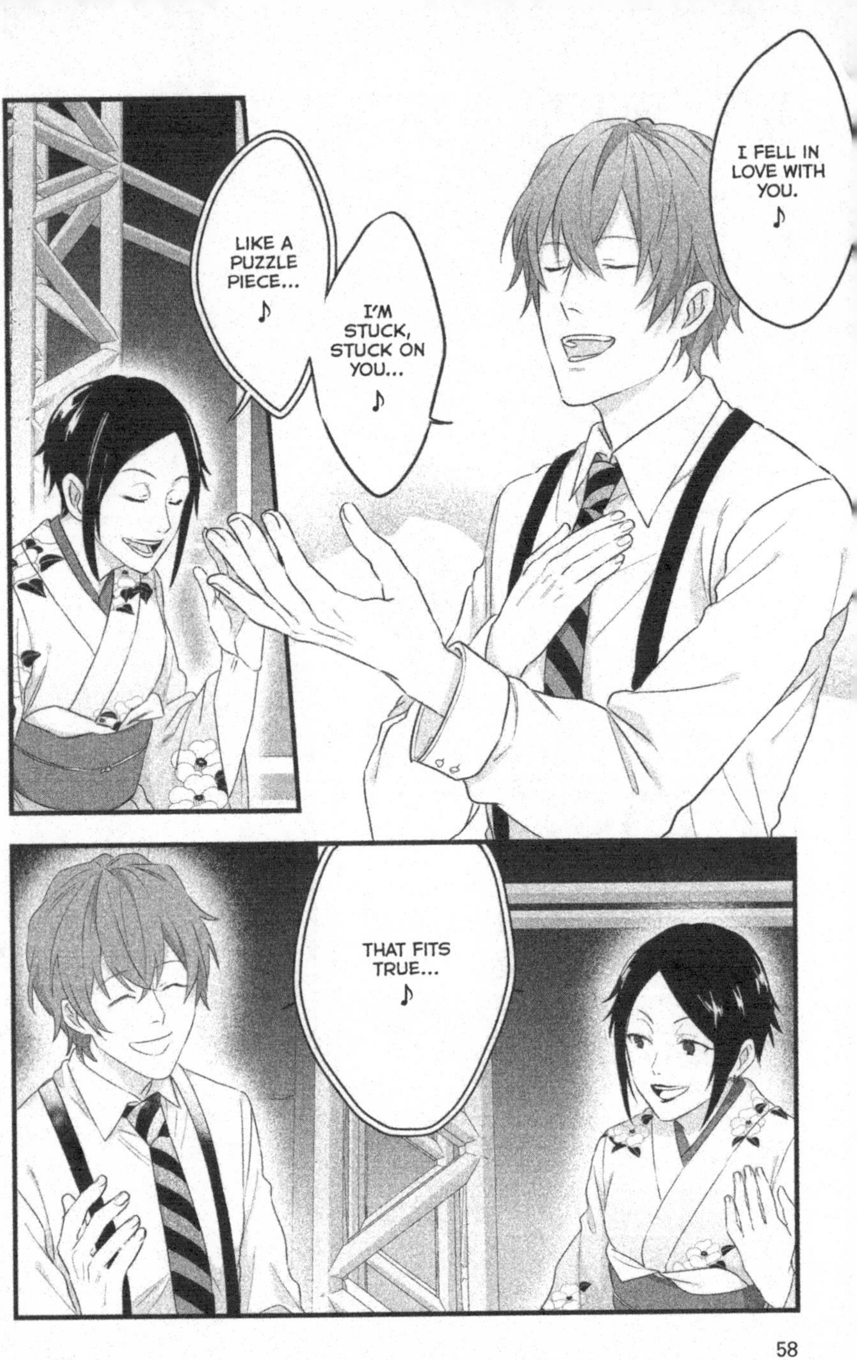
I FELL IN LOVE WITH YOU. ♪
I'M STUCK, STUCK ON YOU... ♪
LIKE A PUZZLE PIECE... ♪
THAT FITS TRUE... ♪

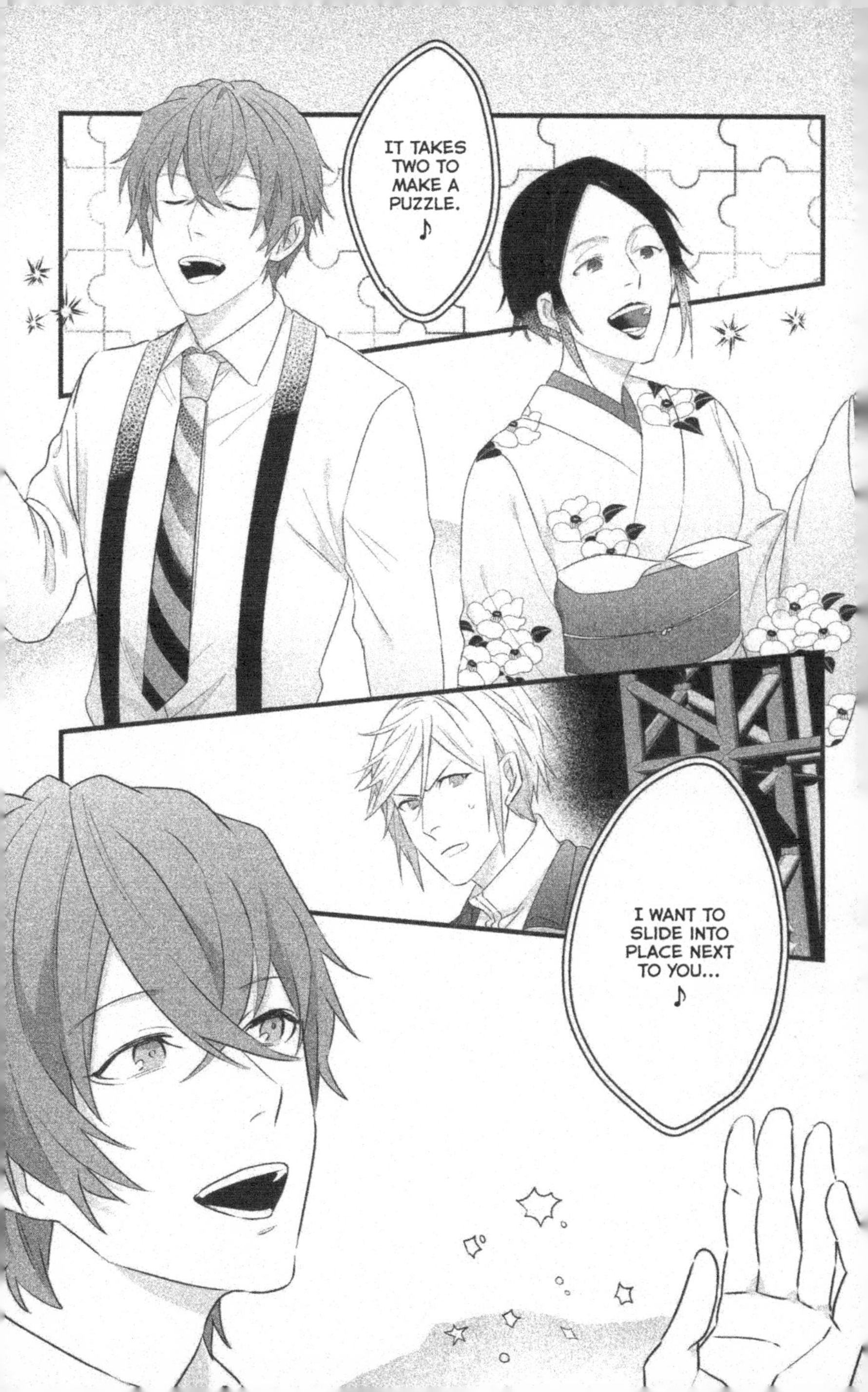
IT TAKES TWO TO MAKE A PUZZLE. ♪
I WANT TO SLIDE INTO PLACE NEXT TO YOU... ♪

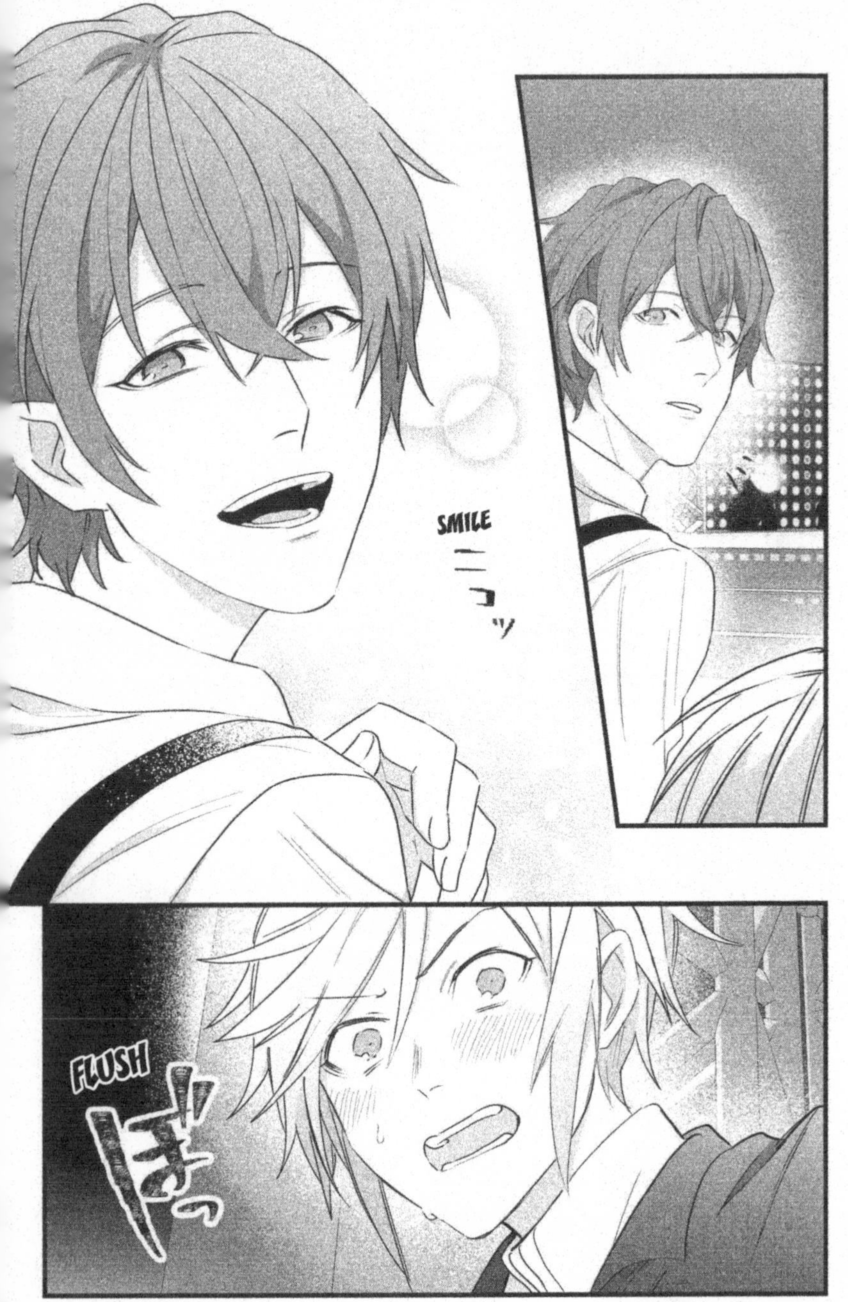
SMILE
ニコッ
FLUSH

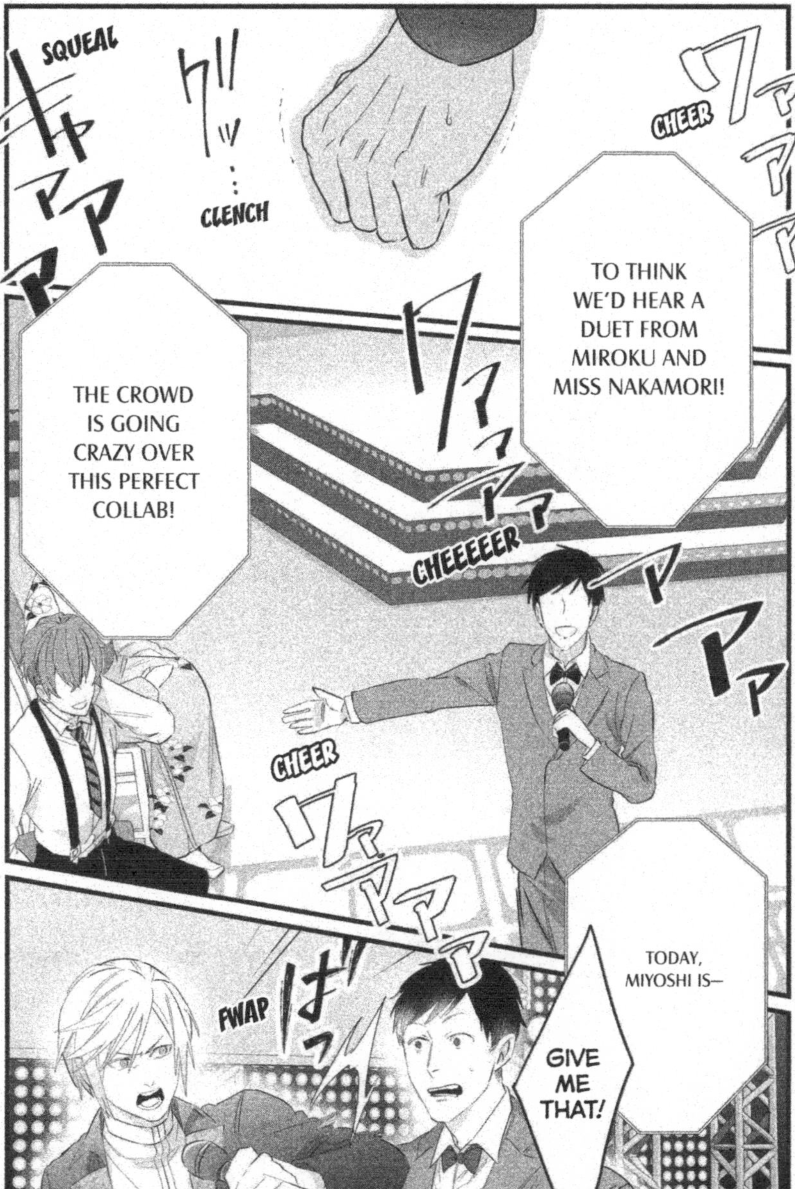
CHEER
CLENCH
SQUEAL
TO THINK WE'D HEAR A DUET FROM MIROKU AND MISS NAKAMORI!
THE CROWD IS GOING CRAZY OVER THIS PERFECT COLLAB!
CHEEEEER
CHEER
TODAY, MIYOSHI IS—
GIVE ME THAT!
FWAP

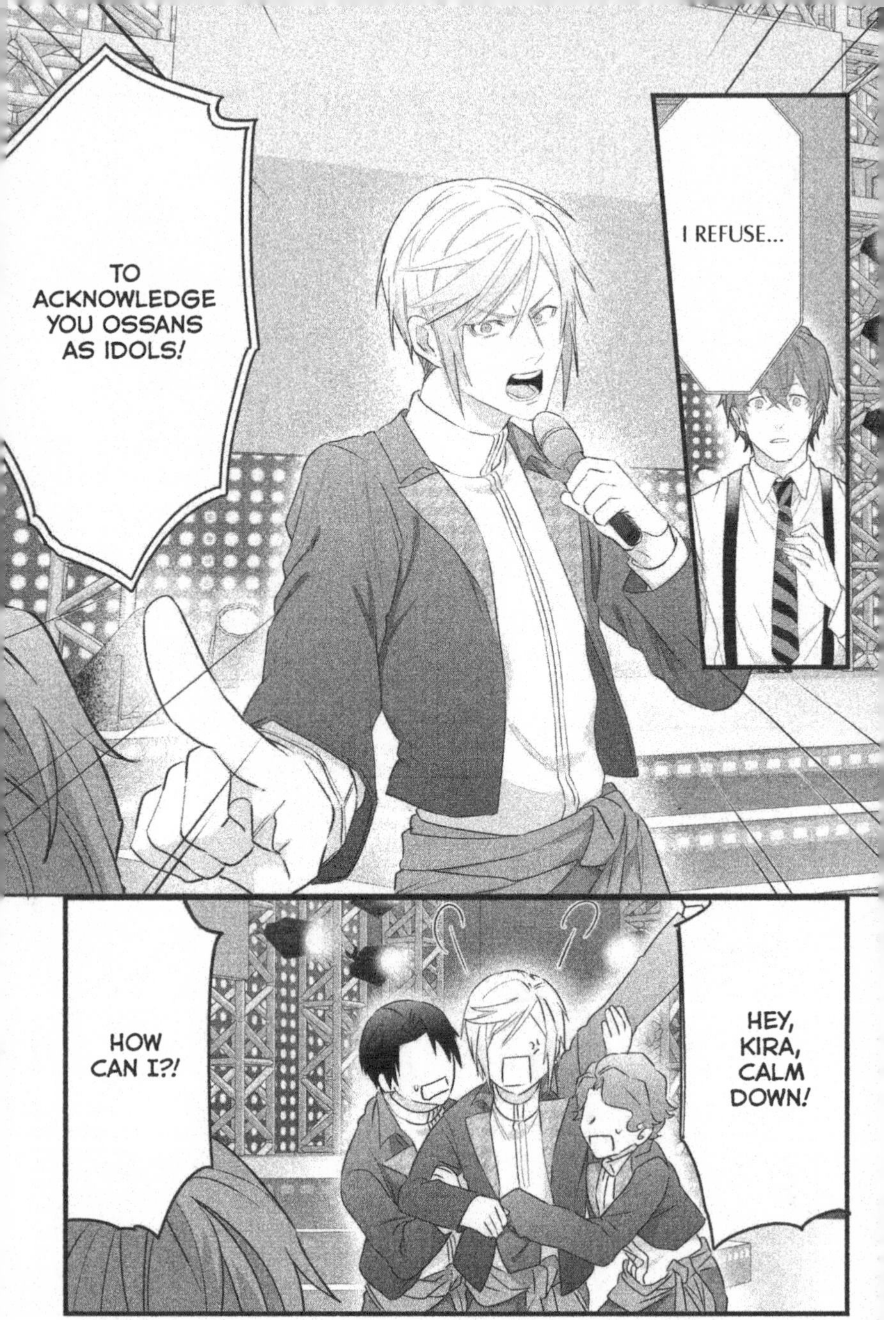
I REFUSE...
TO ACKNOWLEDGE YOU OSSANS AS IDOLS!
HEY, KIRA, CALM DOWN!
HOW CAN I?!

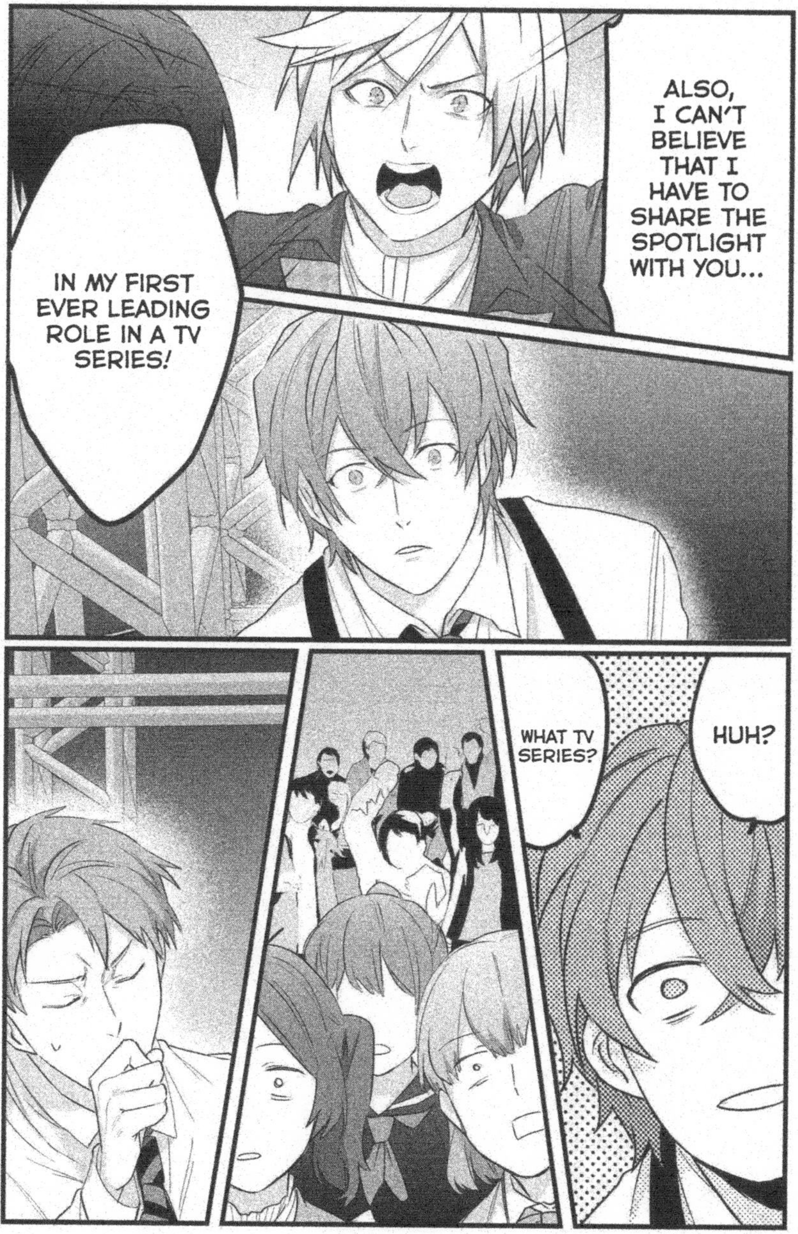
ALSO, I CAN'T BELIEVE THAT I HAVE TO SHARE THE SPOTLIGHT WITH YOU...
IN MY FIRST EVER LEADING ROLE IN A TV SERIES!
HUH?
WHAT TV SERIES?

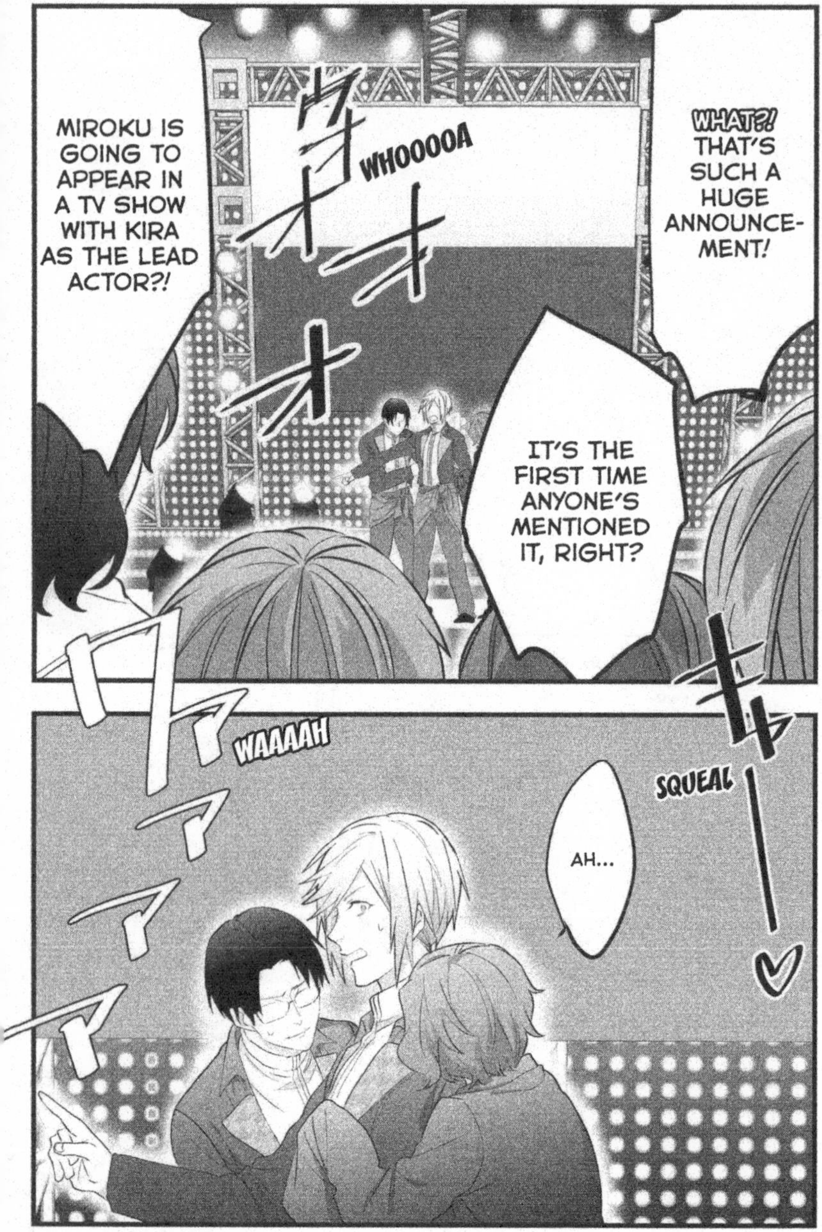
WHAT?! THAT'S SUCH A HUGE ANNOUNCEMENT!
MIROKU IS GOING TO APPEAR IN A TV SHOW WITH KIRA AS THE LEAD ACTOR?!
WHOOOOA
IT'S THE FIRST TIME ANYONE'S MENTIONED IT, RIGHT?
SQUEAL
AH...
WAAAAH

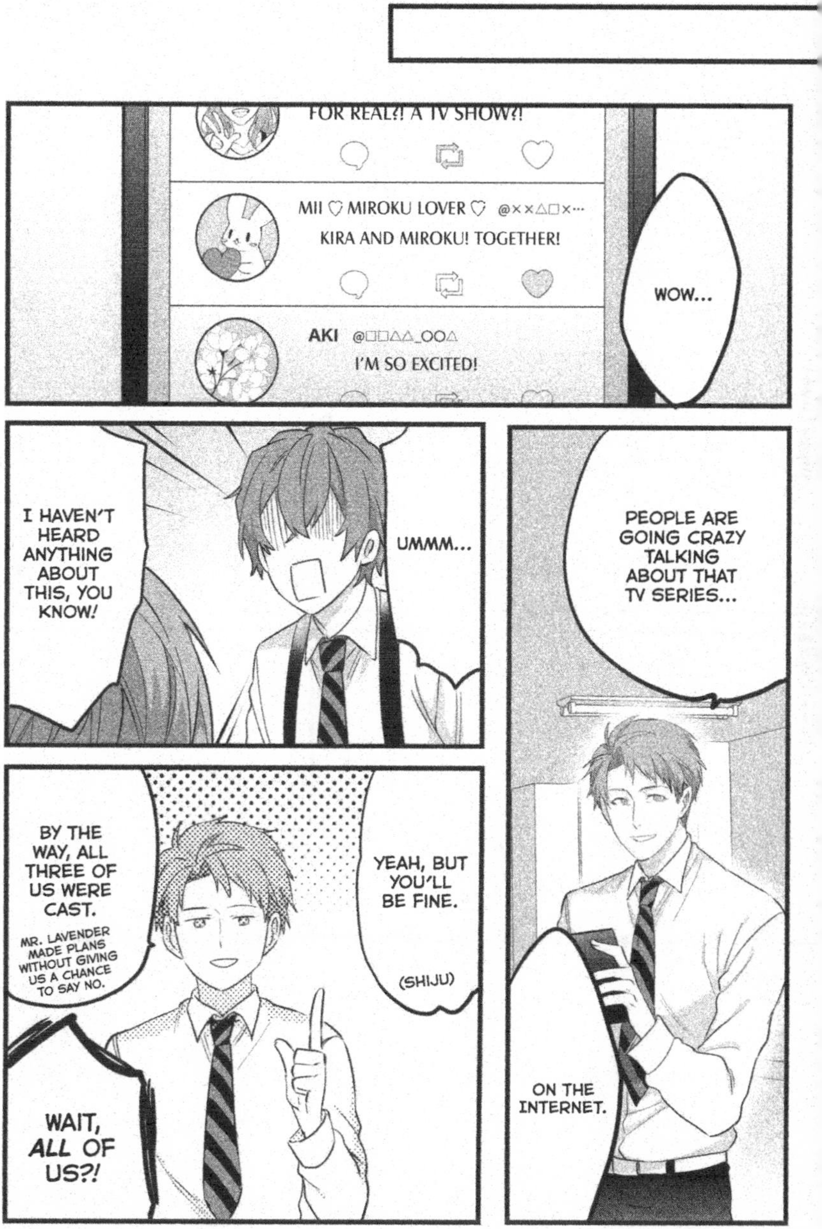
WOW...
FOR REAL?! A TV SHOW?!
MII ♡ MIROKU LOVER ♡ @××△□×···
KIRA AND MIROKU! TOGETHER!
AKI @□□△△_○○△
I'M SO EXCITED!
PEOPLE ARE GOING CRAZY TALKING ABOUT THAT TV SERIES...
ON THE INTERNET.
UMMM...
I HAVEN'T HEARD ANYTHING ABOUT THIS, YOU KNOW!
YEAH, BUT YOU'LL BE FINE.
(SHIJU)
BY THE WAY, ALL THREE OF US WERE CAST.
MR. LAVENDER MADE PLANS WITHOUT GIVING US A CHANCE TO SAY NO.
WAIT, ALL OF US?!

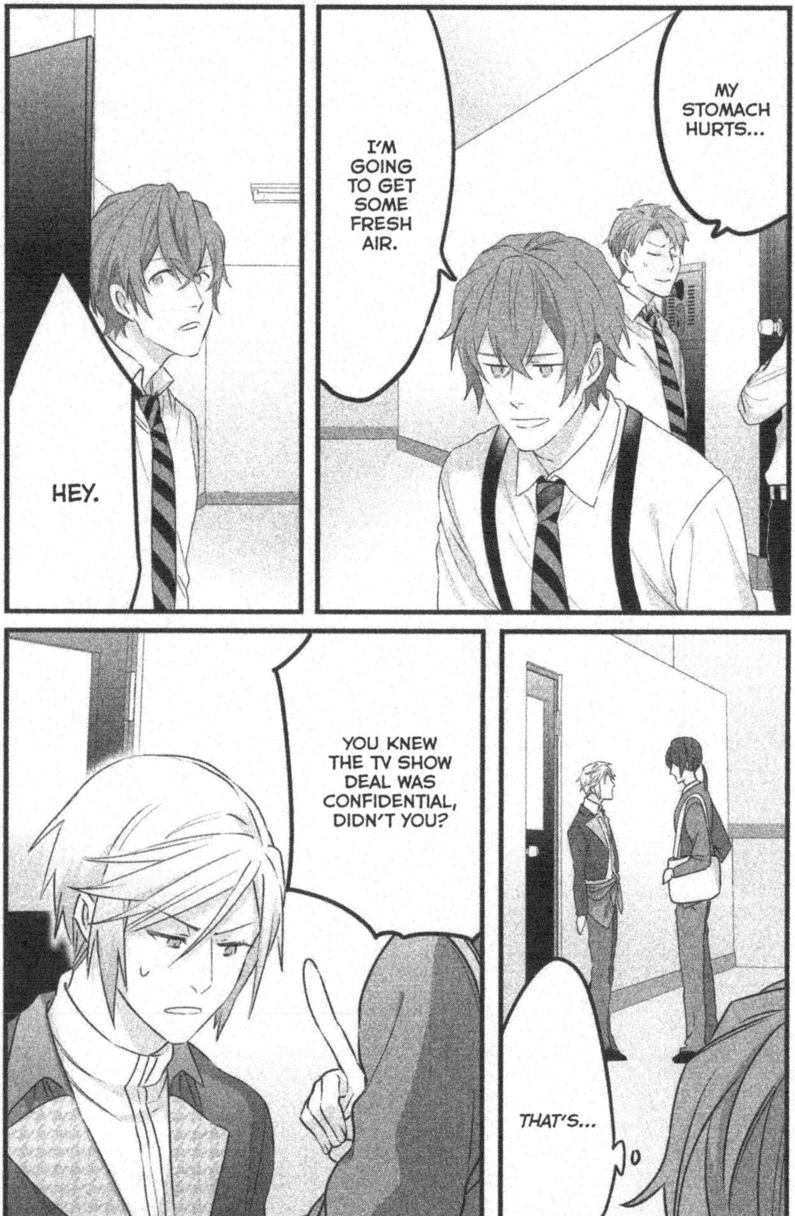
MY STOMACH HURTS...
I'M GOING TO GET SOME FRESH AIR.
HEY.
THAT'S...
YOU KNEW THE TV SHOW DEAL WAS CONFIDENTIAL, DIDN'T YOU?

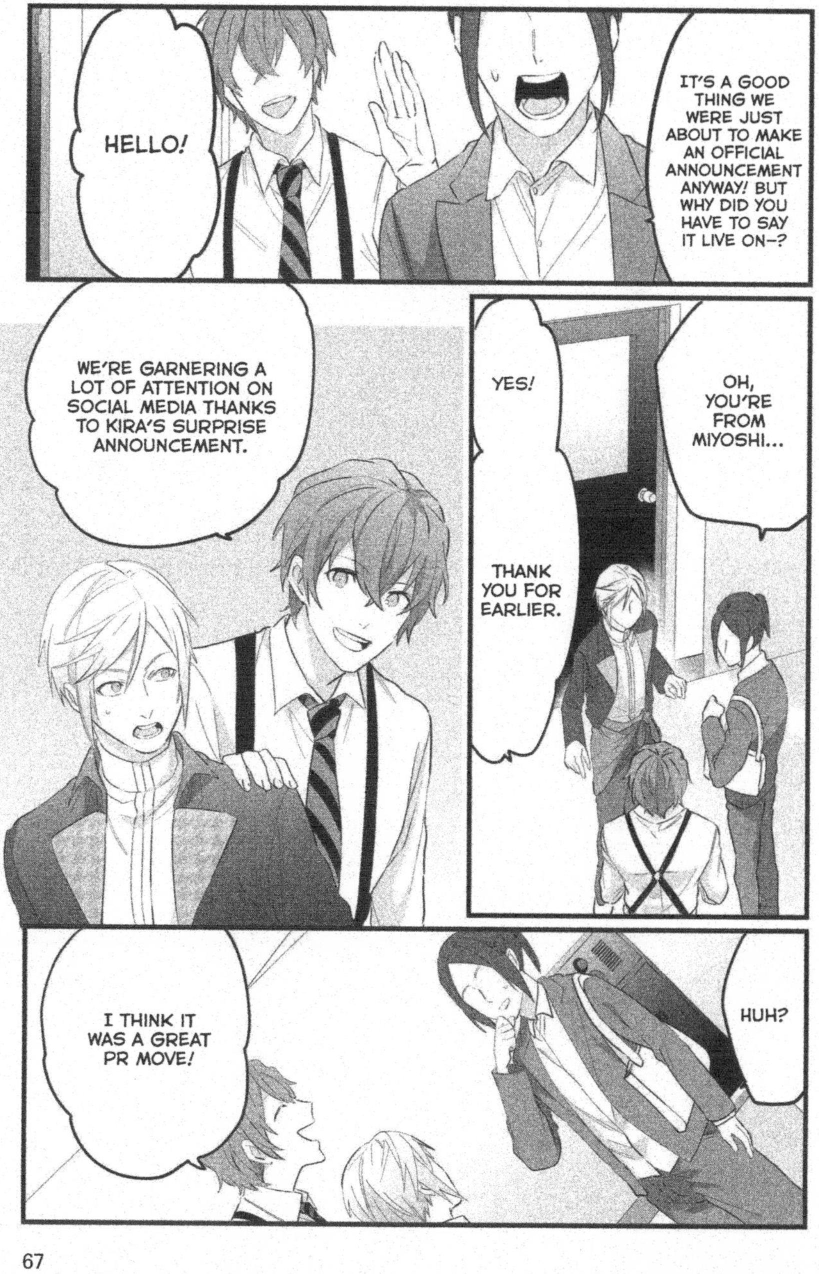
IT'S A GOOD THING WE WERE JUST ABOUT TO MAKE AN OFFICIAL ANNOUNCEMENT ANYWAY! BUT WHY DID YOU HAVE TO SAY IT LIVE ON–?
HELLO!
OH, YOU'RE FROM MIYOSHI...
YES!
THANK YOU FOR EARLIER.
WE'RE GARNERING A LOT OF ATTENTION ON SOCIAL MEDIA THANKS TO KIRA'S SURPRISE ANNOUNCEMENT.
HUH?
I THINK IT WAS A GREAT PR MOVE!

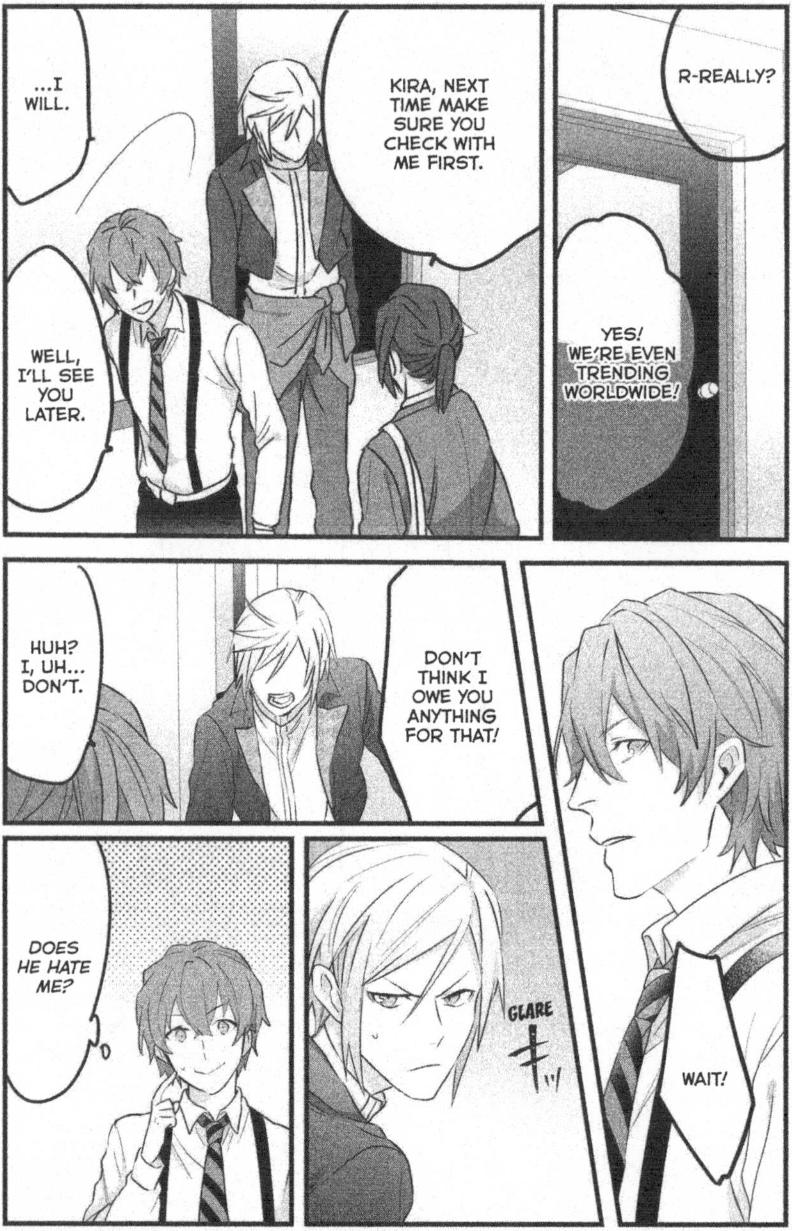
R-REALLY?
YES! WE'RE EVEN TRENDING WORLDWIDE!
KIRA, NEXT TIME MAKE SURE YOU CHECK WITH ME FIRST.
...I WILL.
WELL, I'LL SEE YOU LATER.
WAIT!
DON'T THINK I OWE YOU ANYTHING FOR THAT!
HUH? I, UH... DON'T.
GLARE
DOES HE HATE ME?

Chapter 26

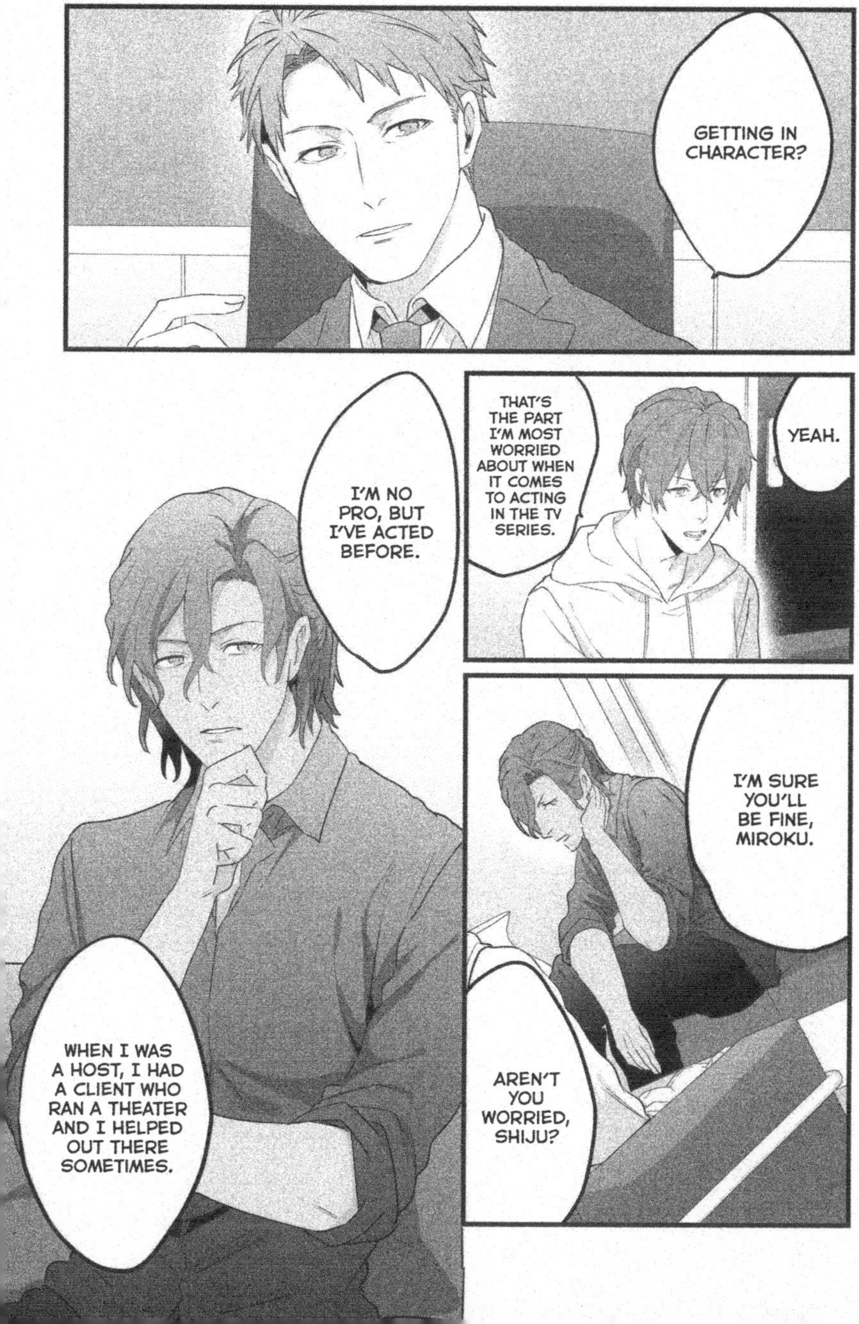

GETTING IN CHARACTER?
YEAH.
THAT'S THE PART I'M MOST WORRIED ABOUT WHEN IT COMES TO ACTING IN THE TV SERIES.
I'M SURE YOU'LL BE FINE, MIROKU.
AREN'T YOU WORRIED, SHIJU?
I'M NO PRO, BUT I'VE ACTED BEFORE.
WHEN I WAS A HOST, I HAD A CLIENT WHO RAN A THEATER AND I HELPED OUT THERE SOMETIMES.

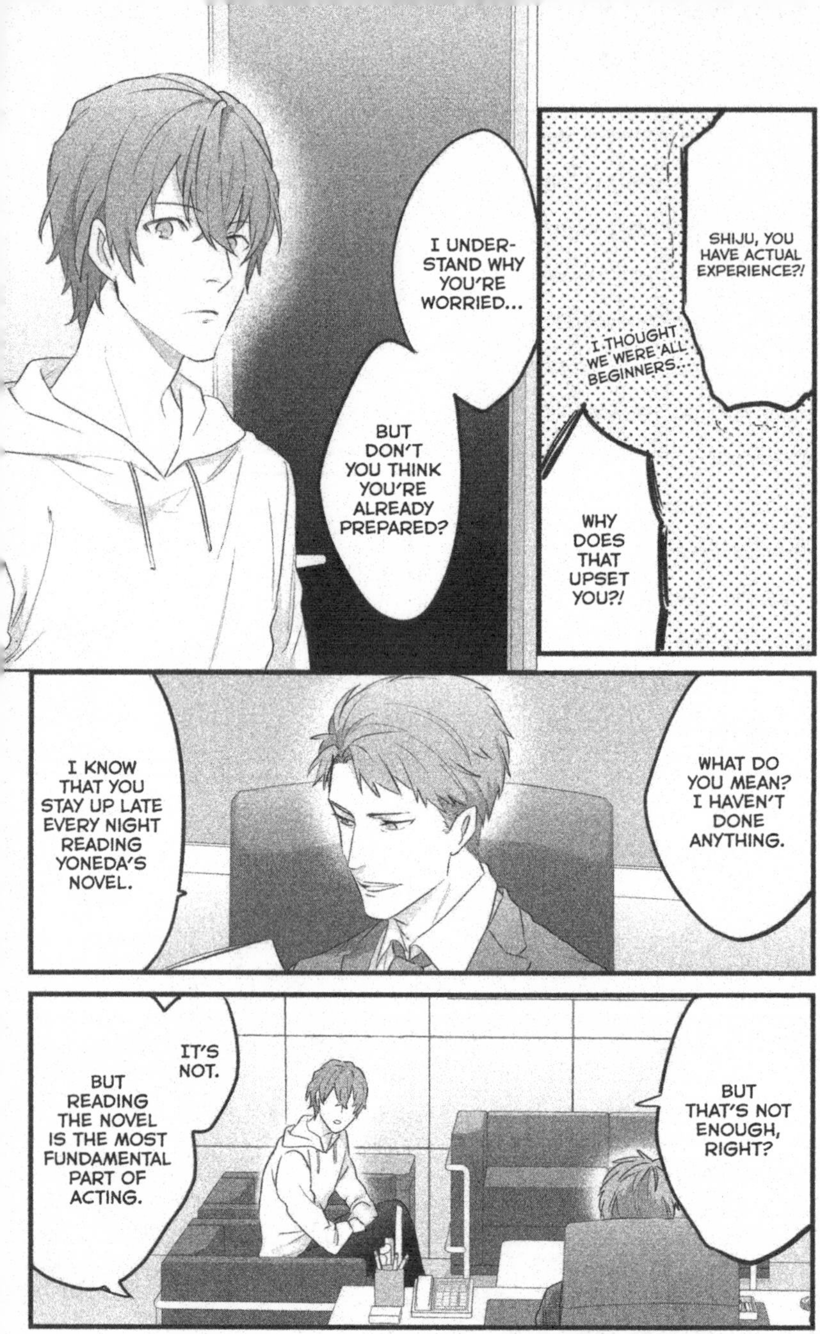
SHIJU, YOU HAVE ACTUAL EXPERIENCE?!
I THOUGHT WE WERE ALL BEGINNERS...
WHY DOES THAT UPSET YOU?!
I UNDERSTAND WHY YOU'RE WORRIED...
BUT DON'T YOU THINK YOU'RE ALREADY PREPARED?
WHAT DO YOU MEAN? I HAVEN'T DONE ANYTHING.
I KNOW THAT YOU STAY UP LATE EVERY NIGHT READING YONEDA'S NOVEL.
BUT THAT'S NOT ENOUGH, RIGHT?
IT'S NOT.
BUT READING THE NOVEL IS THE MOST FUNDAMENTAL PART OF ACTING.

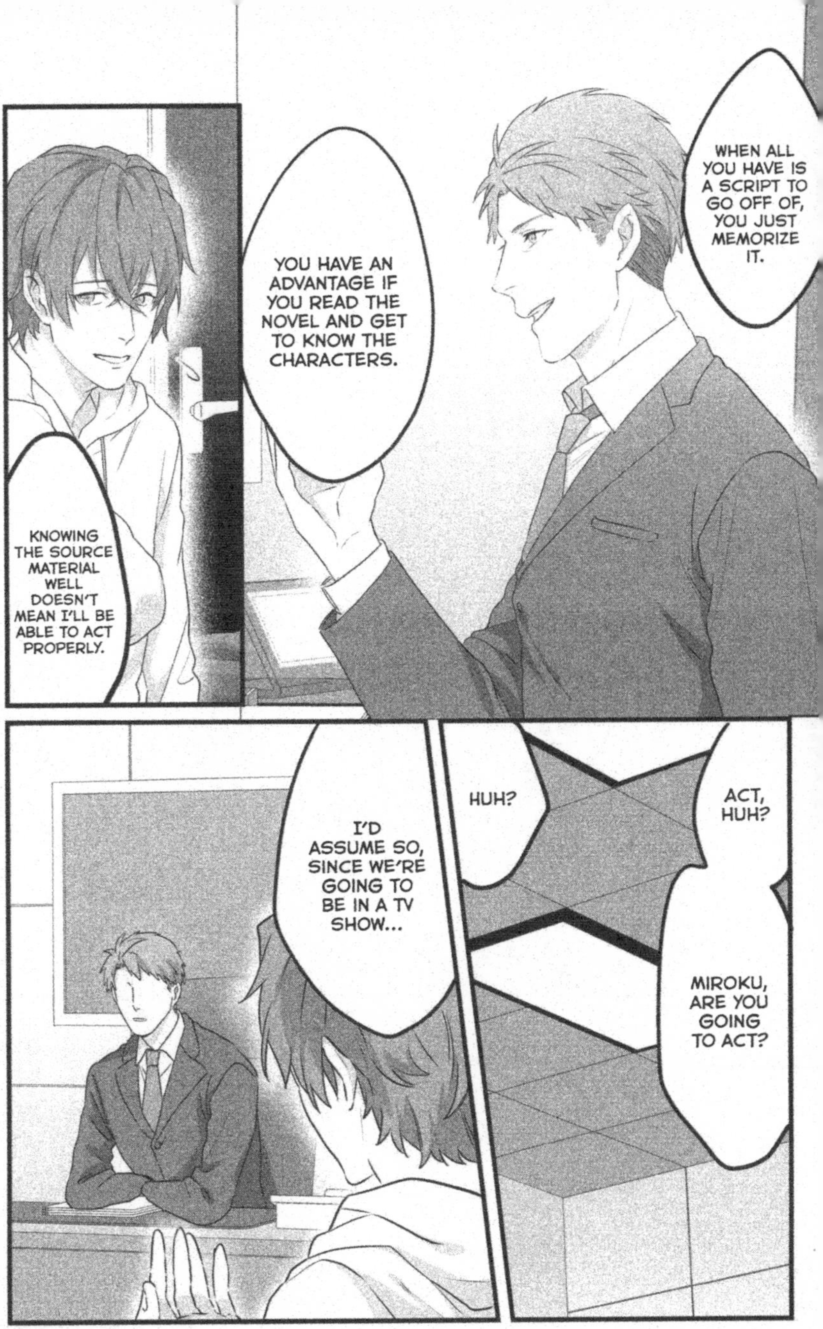
WHEN ALL YOU HAVE IS A SCRIPT TO GO OFF OF, YOU JUST MEMORIZE IT.
YOU HAVE AN ADVANTAGE IF YOU READ THE NOVEL AND GET TO KNOW THE CHARACTERS.
KNOWING THE SOURCE MATERIAL WELL DOESN'T MEAN I'LL BE ABLE TO ACT PROPERLY.
ACT, HUH?
HUH?
MIROKU, ARE YOU GOING TO ACT?
I'D ASSUME SO, SINCE WE'RE GOING TO BE IN A TV SHOW...

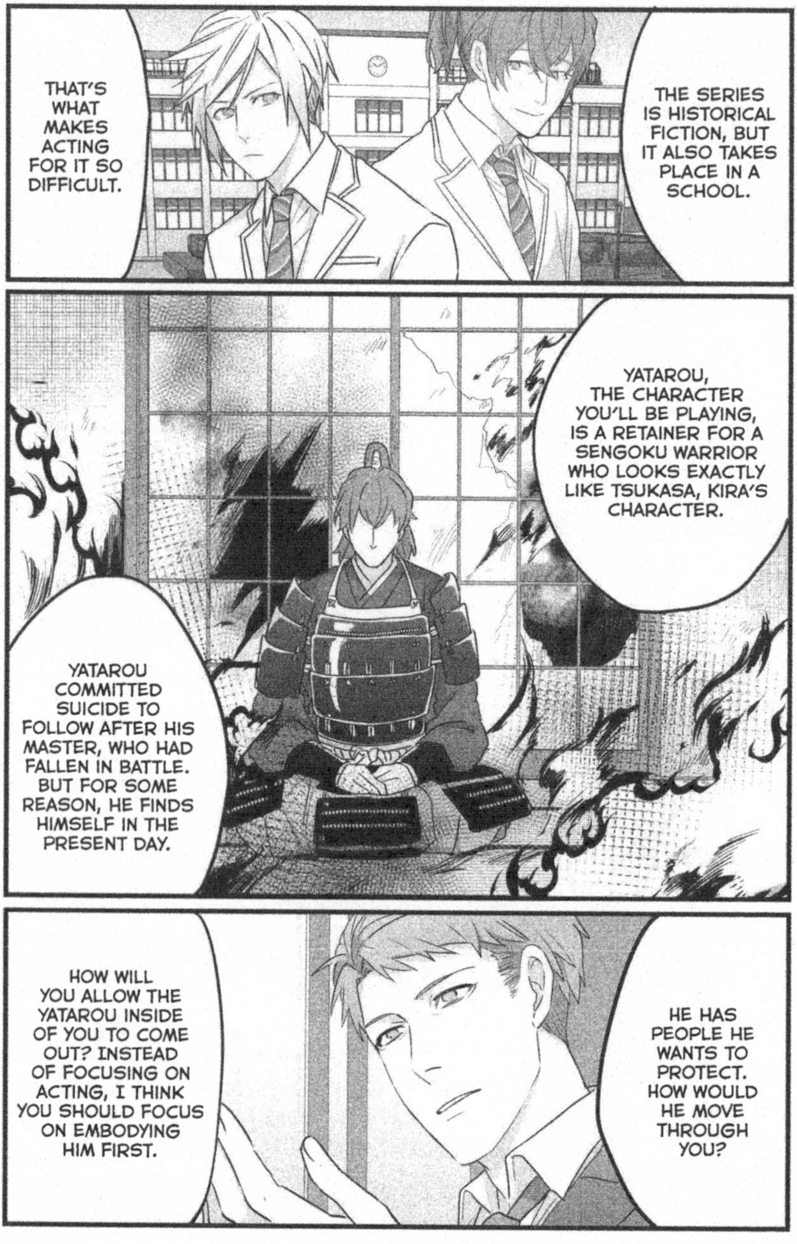
THE SERIES IS HISTORICAL FICTION, BUT IT ALSO TAKES PLACE IN A SCHOOL.
THAT'S WHAT MAKES ACTING FOR IT SO DIFFICULT.
YATAROU, THE CHARACTER YOU'LL BE PLAYING, IS A RETAINER FOR A SENGOKU WARRIOR WHO LOOKS EXACTLY LIKE TSUKASA, KIRA'S CHARACTER.
YATAROU COMMITTED SUICIDE TO FOLLOW AFTER HIS MASTER, WHO HAD FALLEN IN BATTLE. BUT FOR SOME REASON, HE FINDS HIMSELF IN THE PRESENT DAY.
HE HAS PEOPLE HE WANTS TO PROTECT. HOW WOULD HE MOVE THROUGH YOU?
HOW WILL YOU ALLOW THE YATAROU INSIDE OF YOU TO COME OUT? INSTEAD OF FOCUSING ON ACTING, I THINK YOU SHOULD FOCUS ON EMBODYING HIM FIRST.

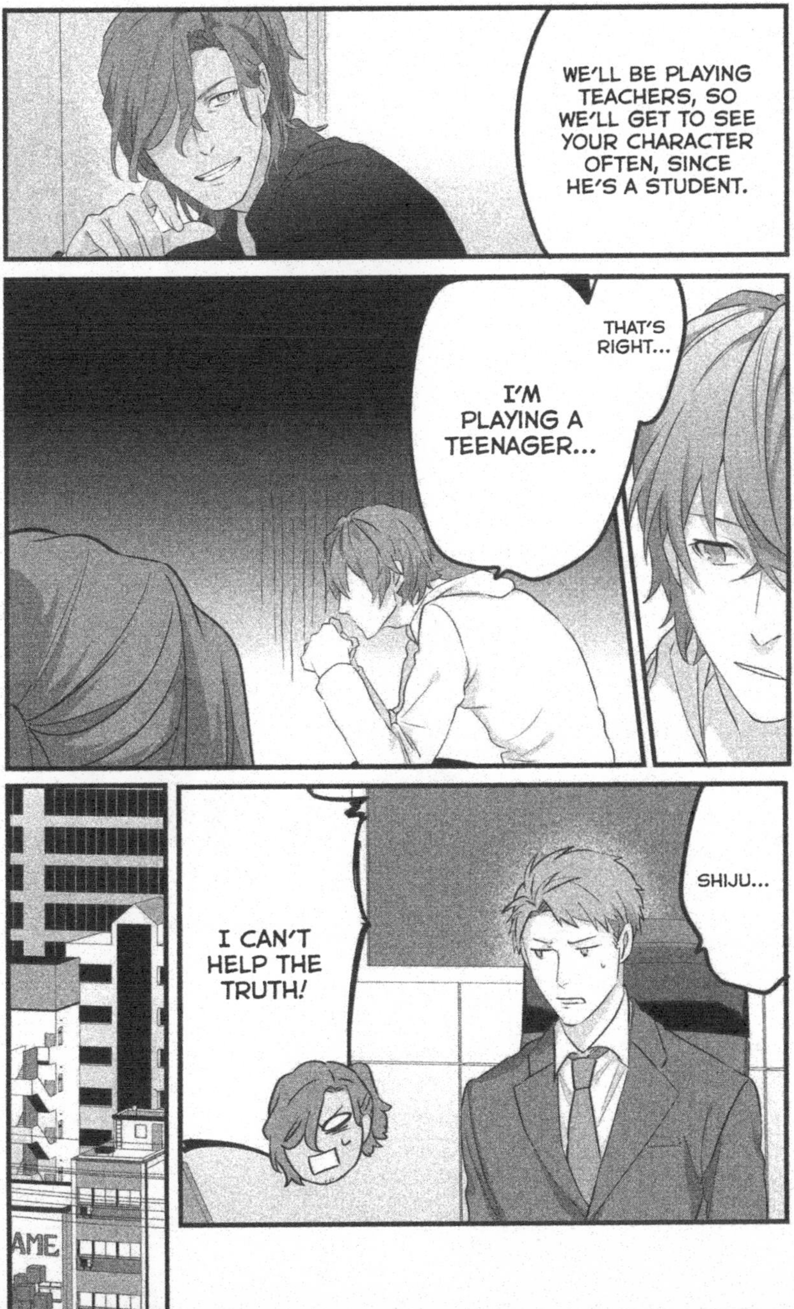
WE'LL BE PLAYING TEACHERS, SO WE'LL GET TO SEE YOUR CHARACTER OFTEN, SINCE HE'S A STUDENT.
THAT'S RIGHT...
I'M PLAYING A TEENAGER...
SHIJU...
I CAN'T HELP THE TRUTH!

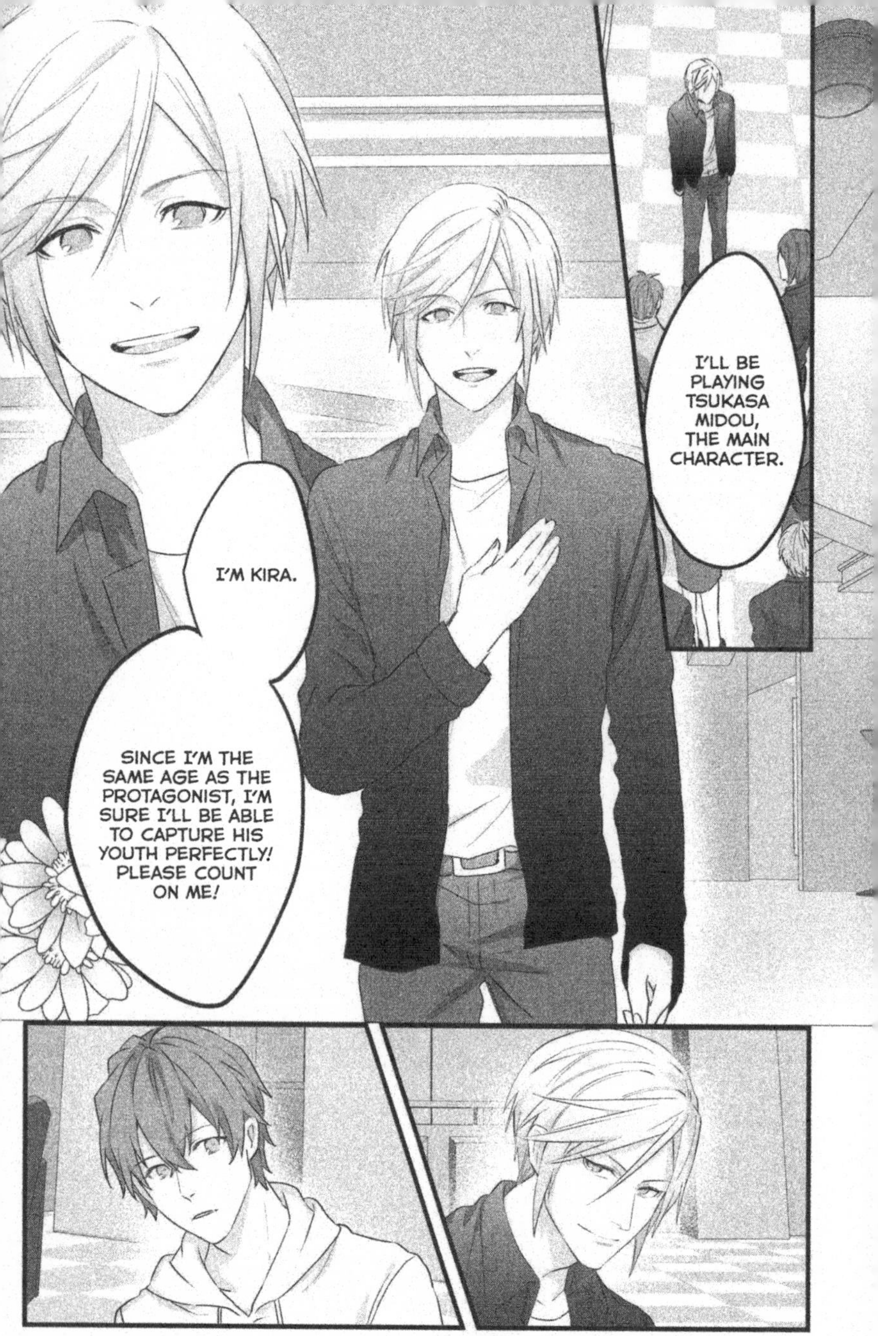
I'LL BE PLAYING TSUKASA MIDOU, THE MAIN CHARACTER.
I'M KIRA.
SINCE I'M THE SAME AGE AS THE PROTAGONIST, I'M SURE I'LL BE ABLE TO CAPTURE HIS YOUTH PERFECTLY! PLEASE COUNT ON ME!

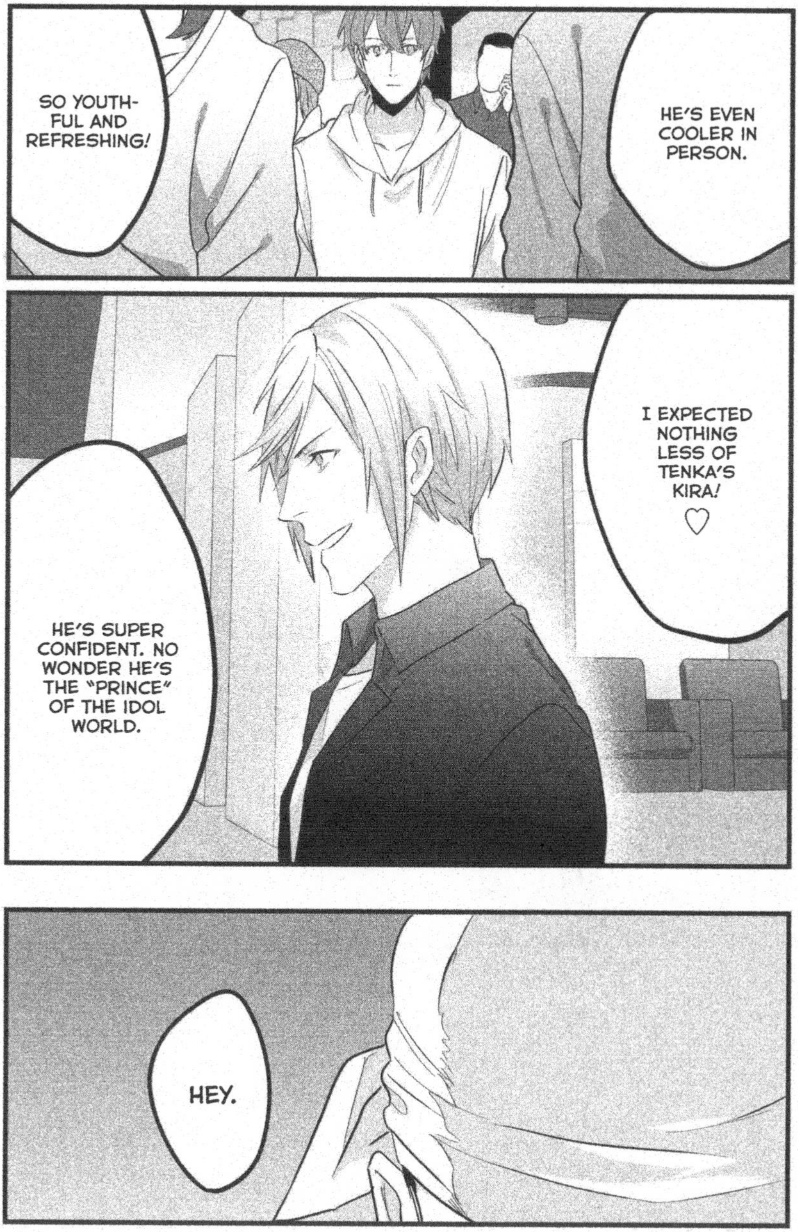
HE'S EVEN COOLER IN PERSON.
SO YOUTH-FUL AND REFRESHING!
I EXPECTED NOTHING LESS OF TENKA'S KIRA! ♡
HE'S SUPER CONFIDENT. NO WONDER HE'S THE "PRINCE" OF THE IDOL WORLD.
HEY.

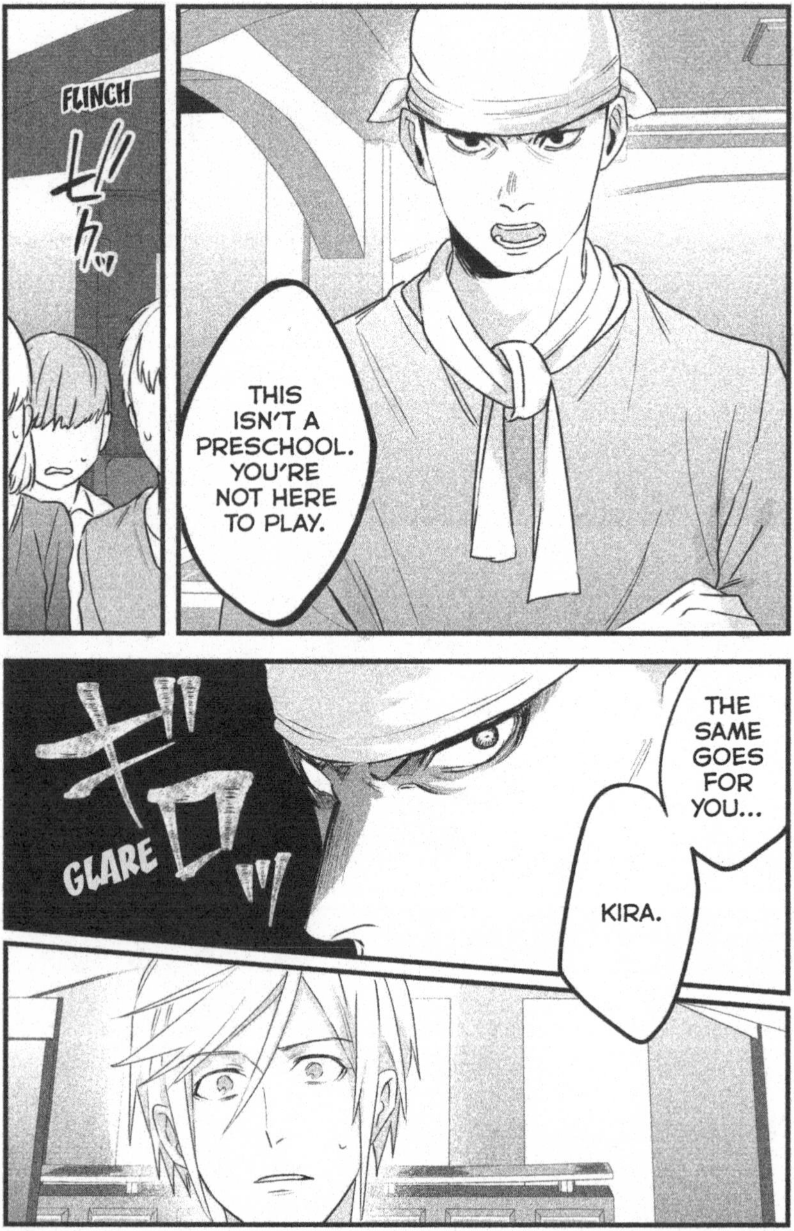
THIS ISN'T A PRESCHOOL. YOU'RE NOT HERE TO PLAY.
FLINCH
ビクッ
THE SAME GOES FOR YOU...
KIRA.
ギロッ
GLARE

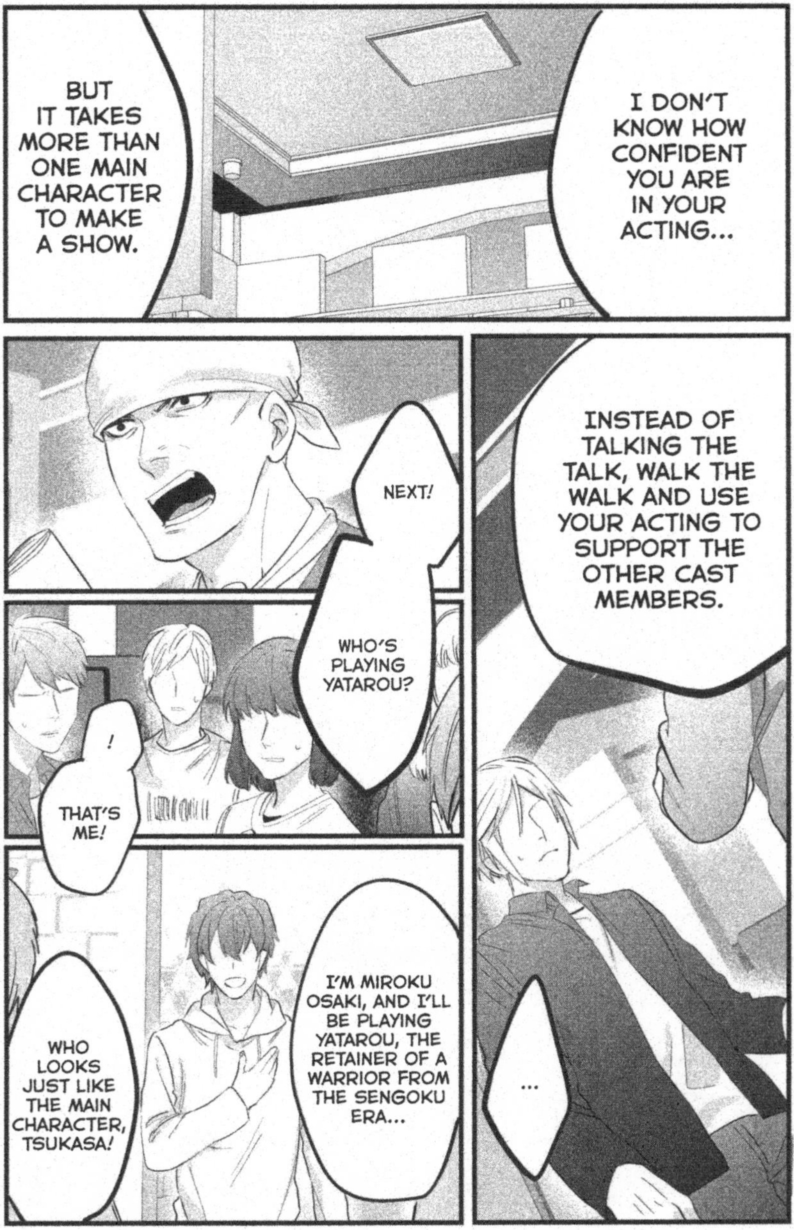
I DON'T KNOW HOW CONFIDENT YOU ARE IN YOUR ACTING...
BUT IT TAKES MORE THAN ONE MAIN CHARACTER TO MAKE A SHOW.
INSTEAD OF TALKING THE TALK, WALK THE WALK AND USE YOUR ACTING TO SUPPORT THE OTHER CAST MEMBERS.
...
NEXT!
WHO'S PLAYING YATAROU?
!
THAT'S ME!
I'M MIROKU OSAKI, AND I'LL BE PLAYING YATAROU, THE RETAINER OF A WARRIOR FROM THE SENGOKU ERA...
WHO LOOKS JUST LIKE THE MAIN CHARACTER, TSUKASA!

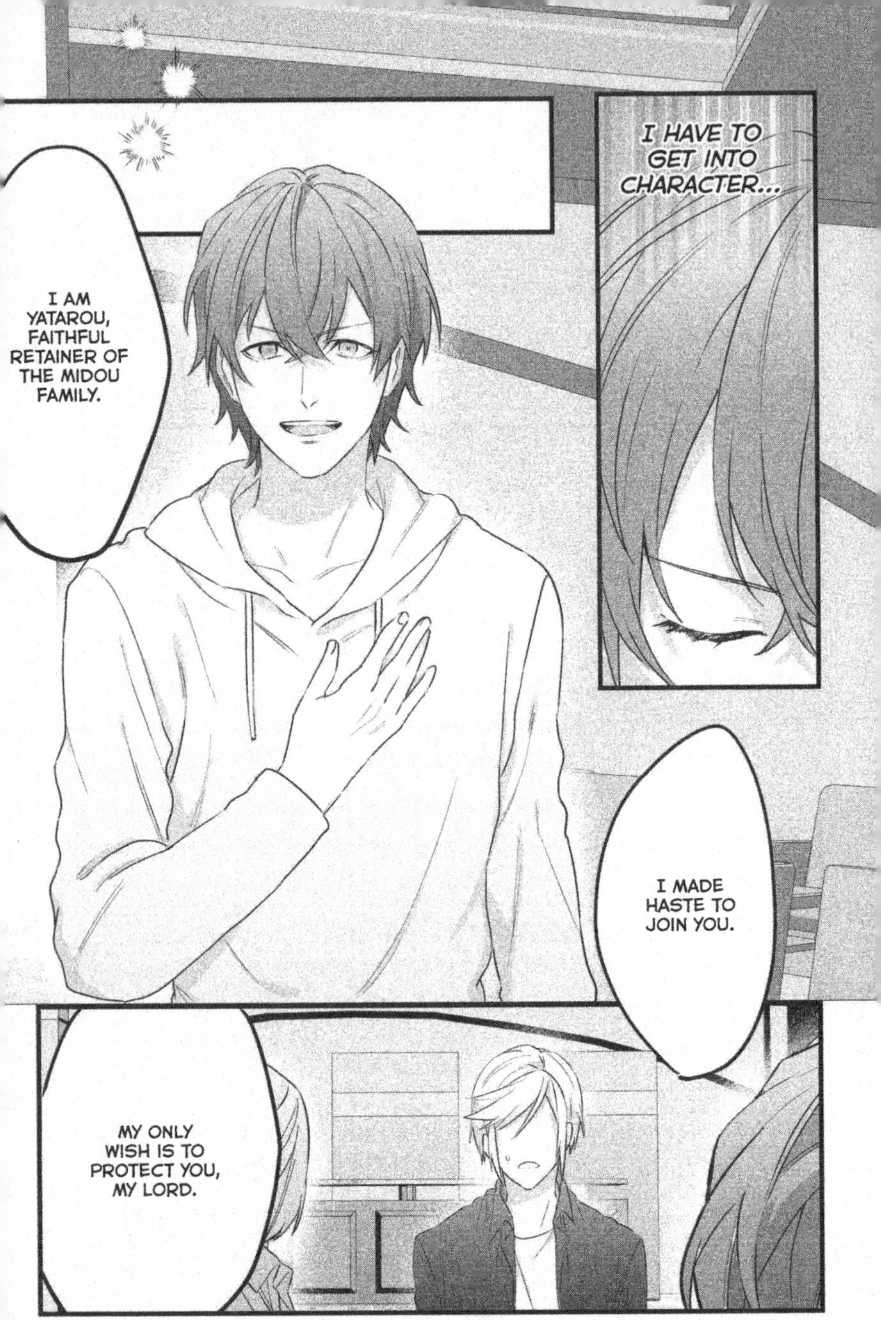
I HAVE TO GET INTO CHARACTER...
I AM YATAROU, FAITHFUL RETAINER OF THE MIDOU FAMILY.
I MADE HASTE TO JOIN YOU.
MY ONLY WISH IS TO PROTECT YOU, MY LORD.

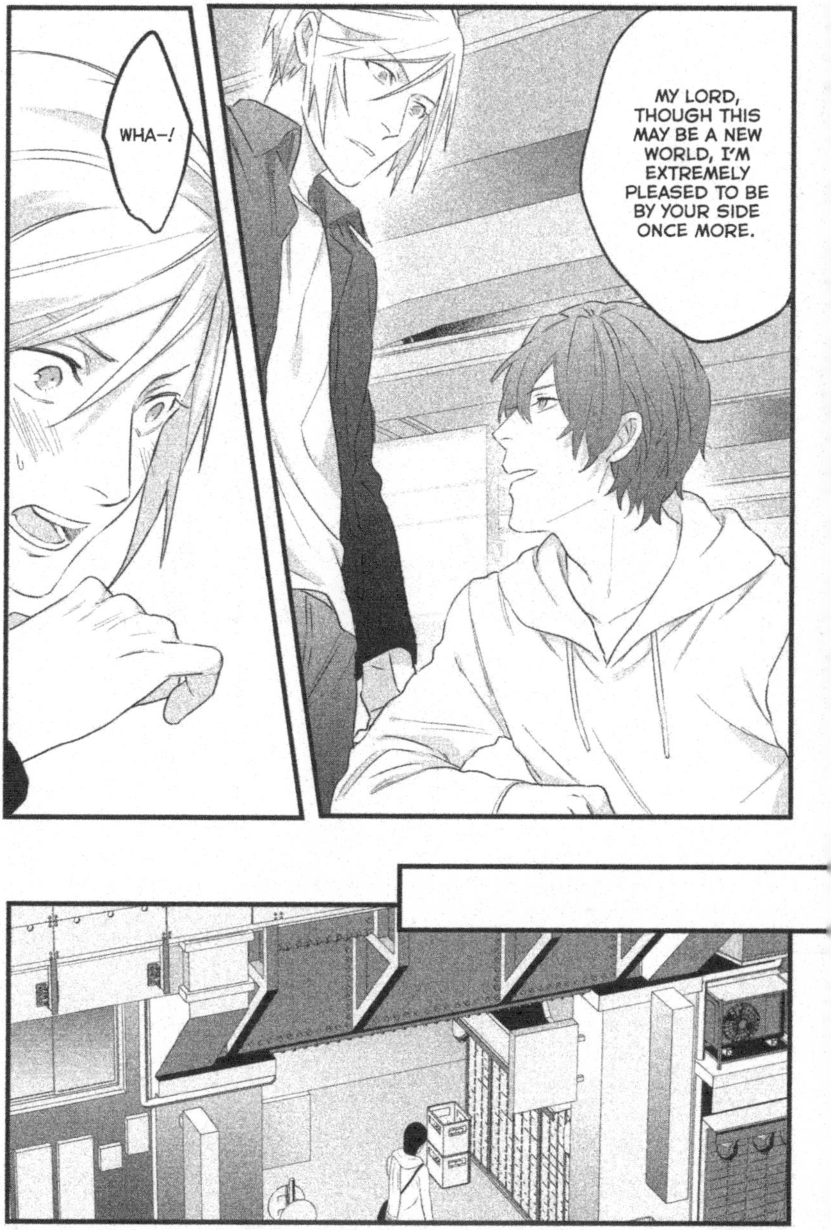
MY LORD, THOUGH THIS MAY BE A NEW WORLD, I'M EXTREMELY PLEASED TO BE BY YOUR SIDE ONCE MORE.
WHA-!

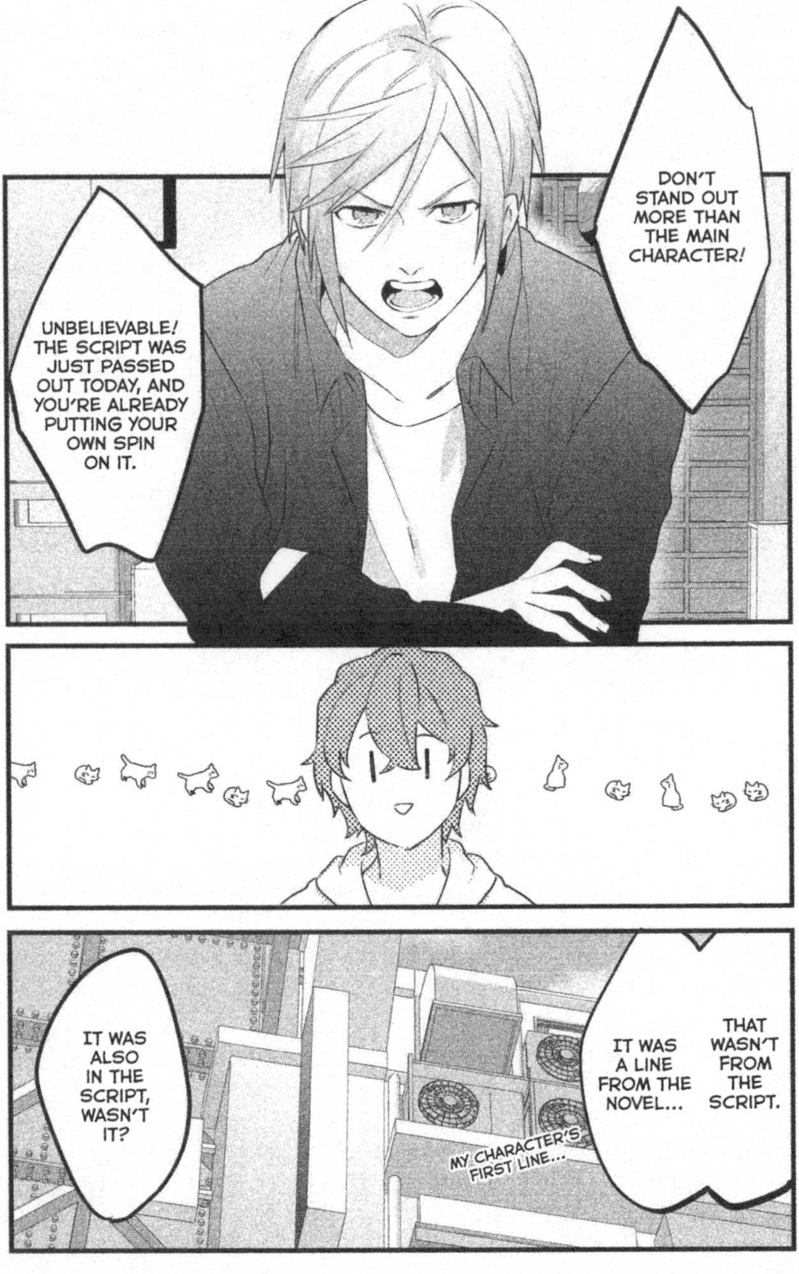
DON'T STAND OUT MORE THAN THE MAIN CHARACTER!
UNBELIEVABLE! THE SCRIPT WAS JUST PASSED OUT TODAY, AND YOU'RE ALREADY PUTTING YOUR OWN SPIN ON IT.
THAT WASN'T FROM THE SCRIPT.
IT WAS A LINE FROM THE NOVEL...
MY CHARACTER'S FIRST LINE...
IT WAS ALSO IN THE SCRIPT, WASN'T IT?

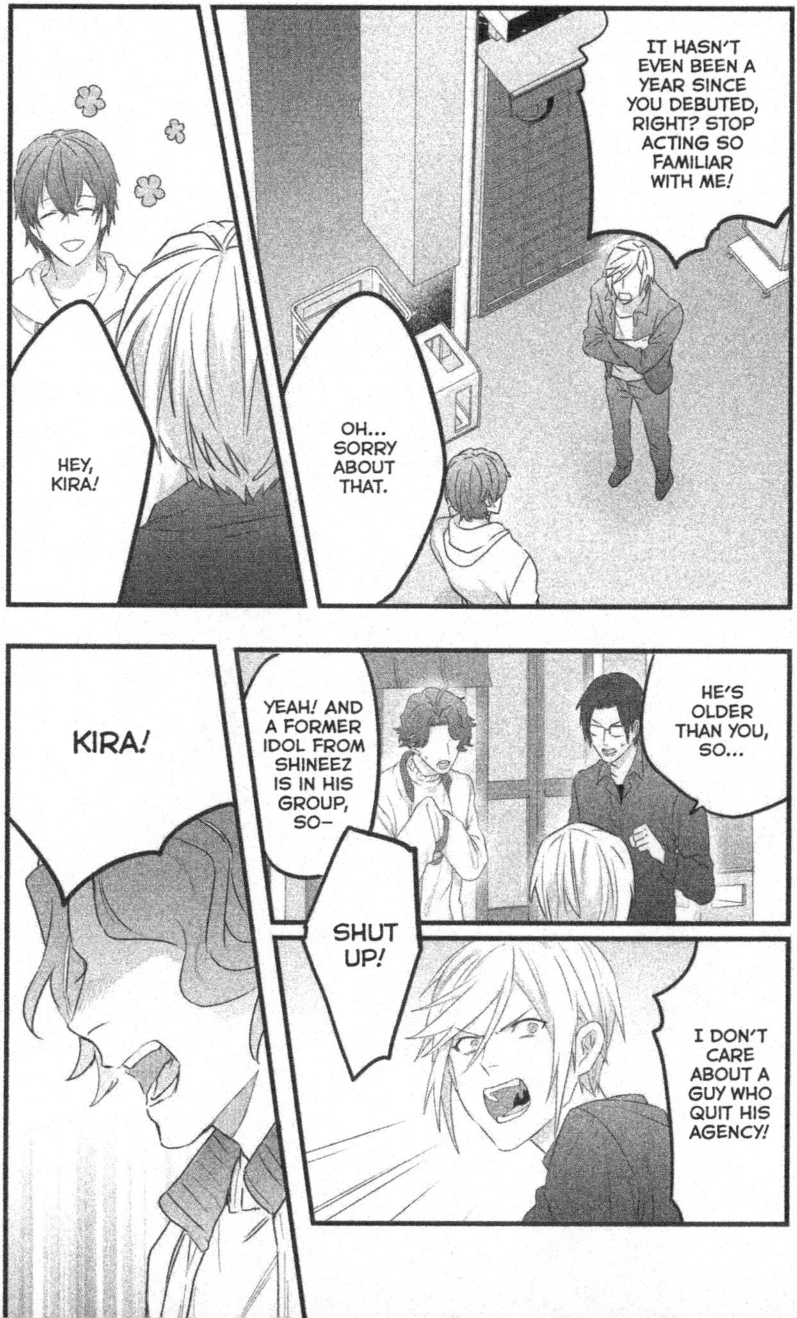
IT HASN'T EVEN BEEN A YEAR SINCE YOU DEBUTED, RIGHT? STOP ACTING SO FAMILIAR WITH ME!
OH... SORRY ABOUT THAT.
HEY, KIRA!
HE'S OLDER THAN YOU, SO...
YEAH! AND A FORMER IDOL FROM SHINEEZ IS IN HIS GROUP, SO–
SHUT UP!
I DON'T CARE ABOUT A GUY WHO QUIT HIS AGENCY!
KIRA!

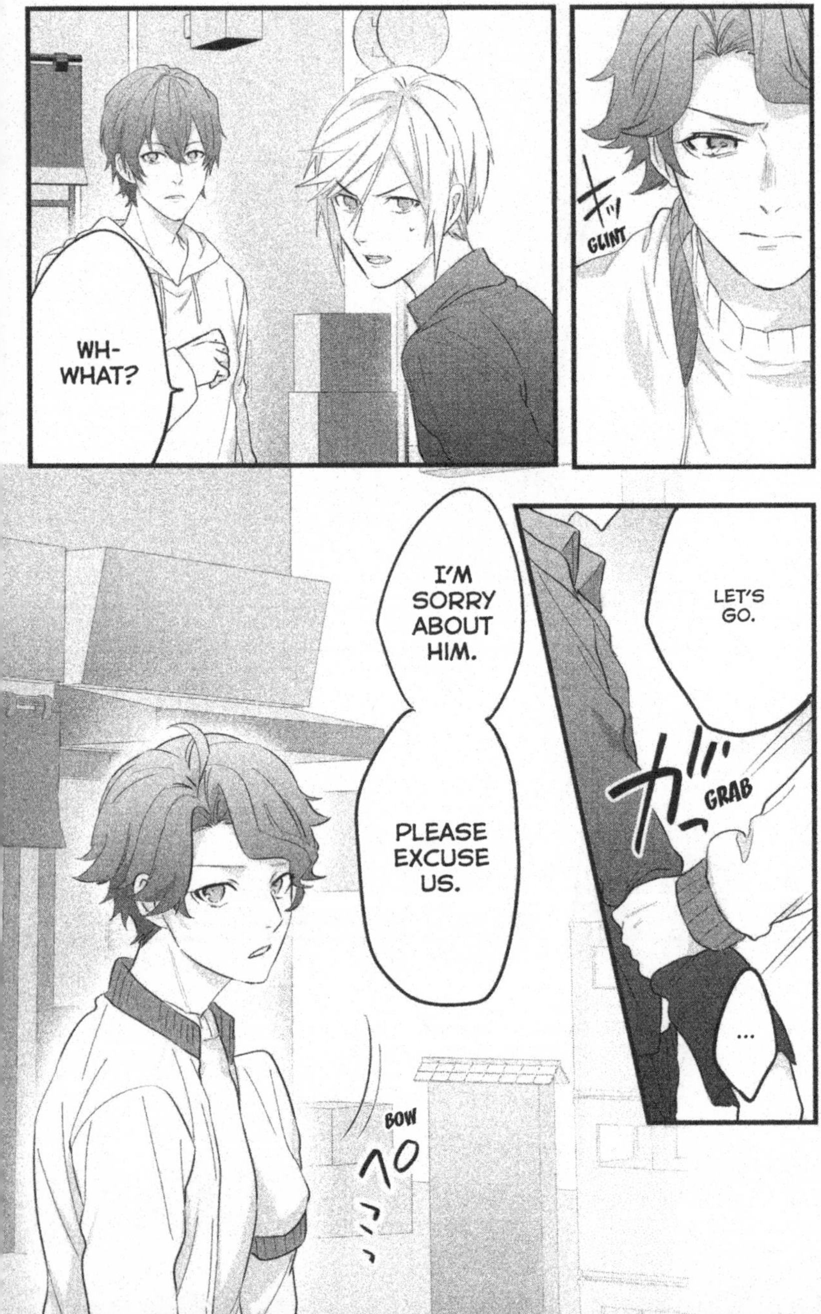
GLINT
WH- WHAT?
LET'S GO.
GRAB
...
I'M SORRY ABOUT HIM.
PLEASE EXCUSE US.
BOW

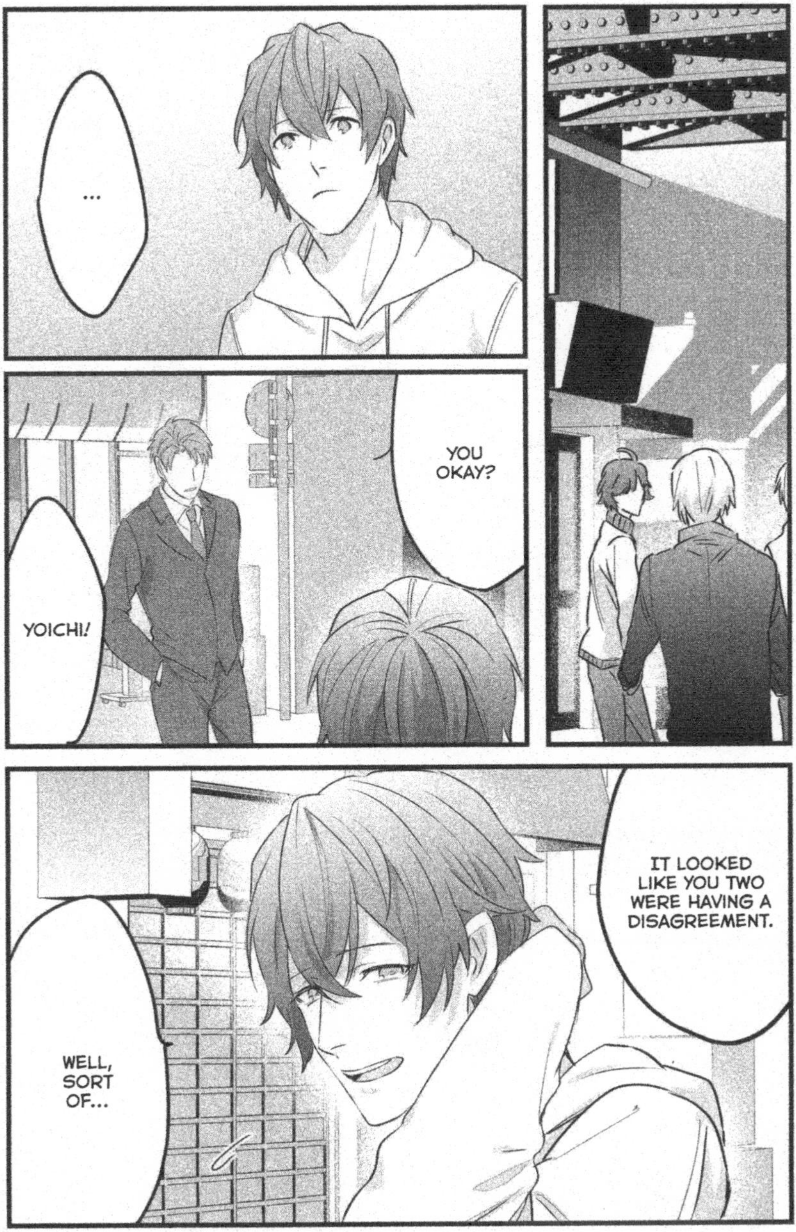
...
YOU OKAY?
YOICHI!
IT LOOKED LIKE YOU TWO WERE HAVING A DISAGREEMENT.
WELL, SORT OF...

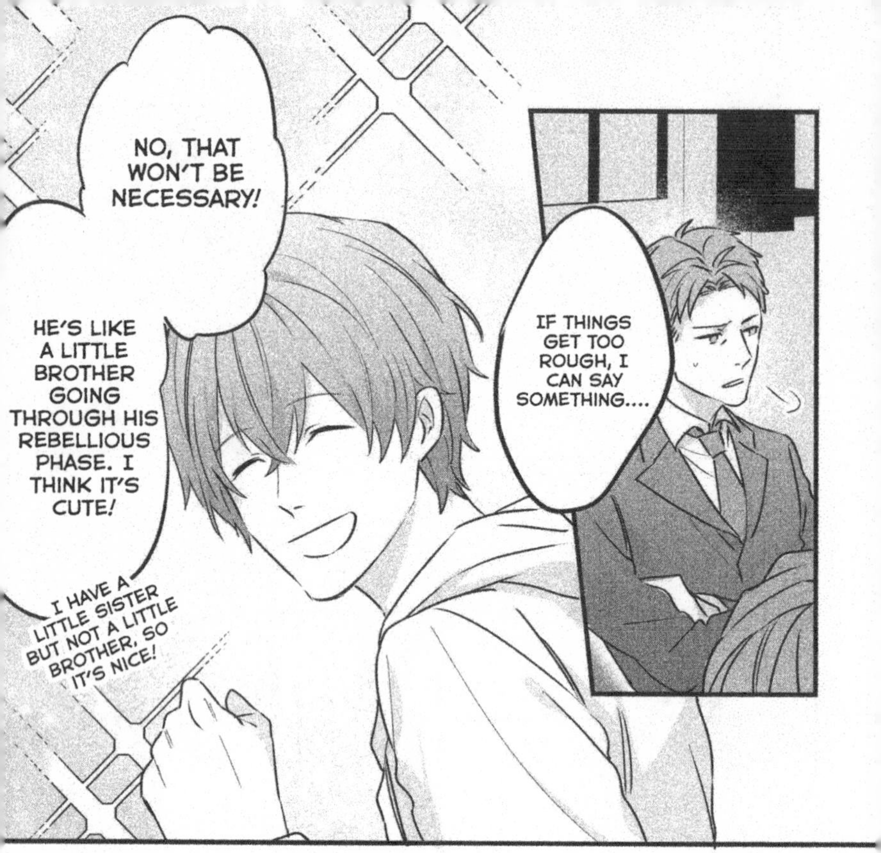
IF THINGS GET TOO ROUGH, I CAN SAY SOMETHING....
NO, THAT WON'T BE NECESSARY!
HE'S LIKE A LITTLE BROTHER GOING THROUGH HIS REBELLIOUS PHASE. I THINK IT'S CUTE!
I HAVE A LITTLE SISTER BUT NOT A LITTLE BROTHER, SO IT'S NICE!
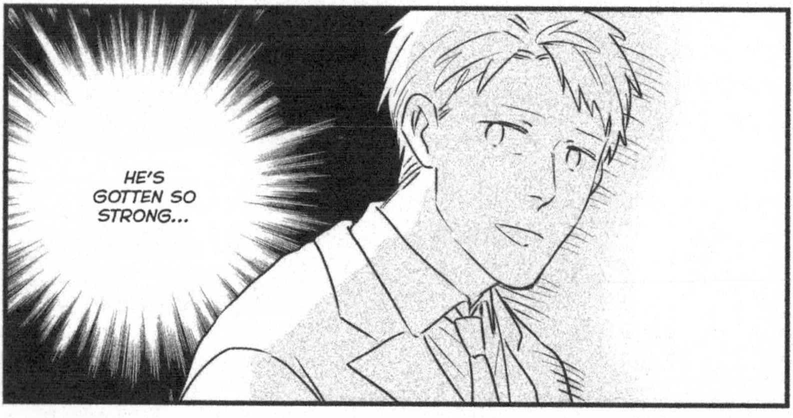
HE'S GOTTEN SO STRONG...

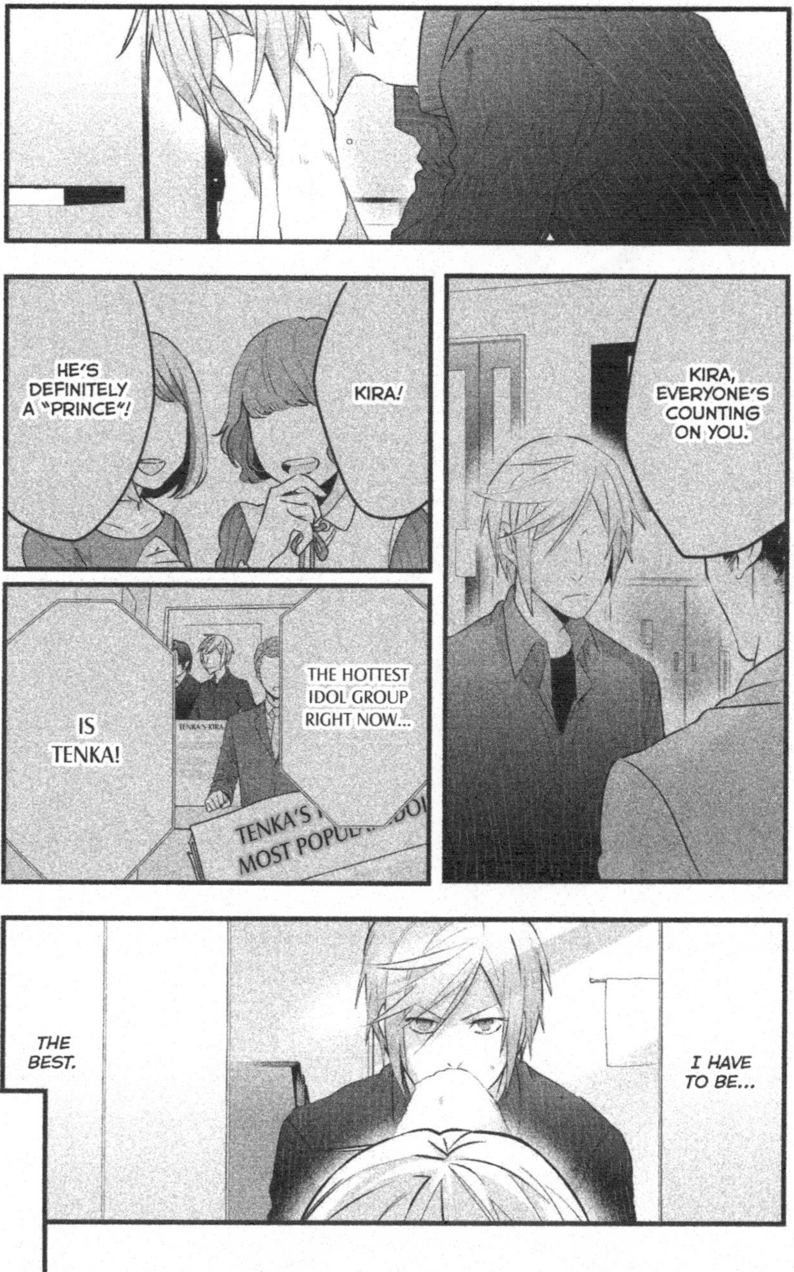
KIRA, EVERYONE'S COUNTING ON YOU.
KIRA!
HE'S DEFINITELY A "PRINCE"!
THE HOTTEST IDOL GROUP RIGHT NOW...
IS TENKA!
I HAVE TO BE...
THE BEST.

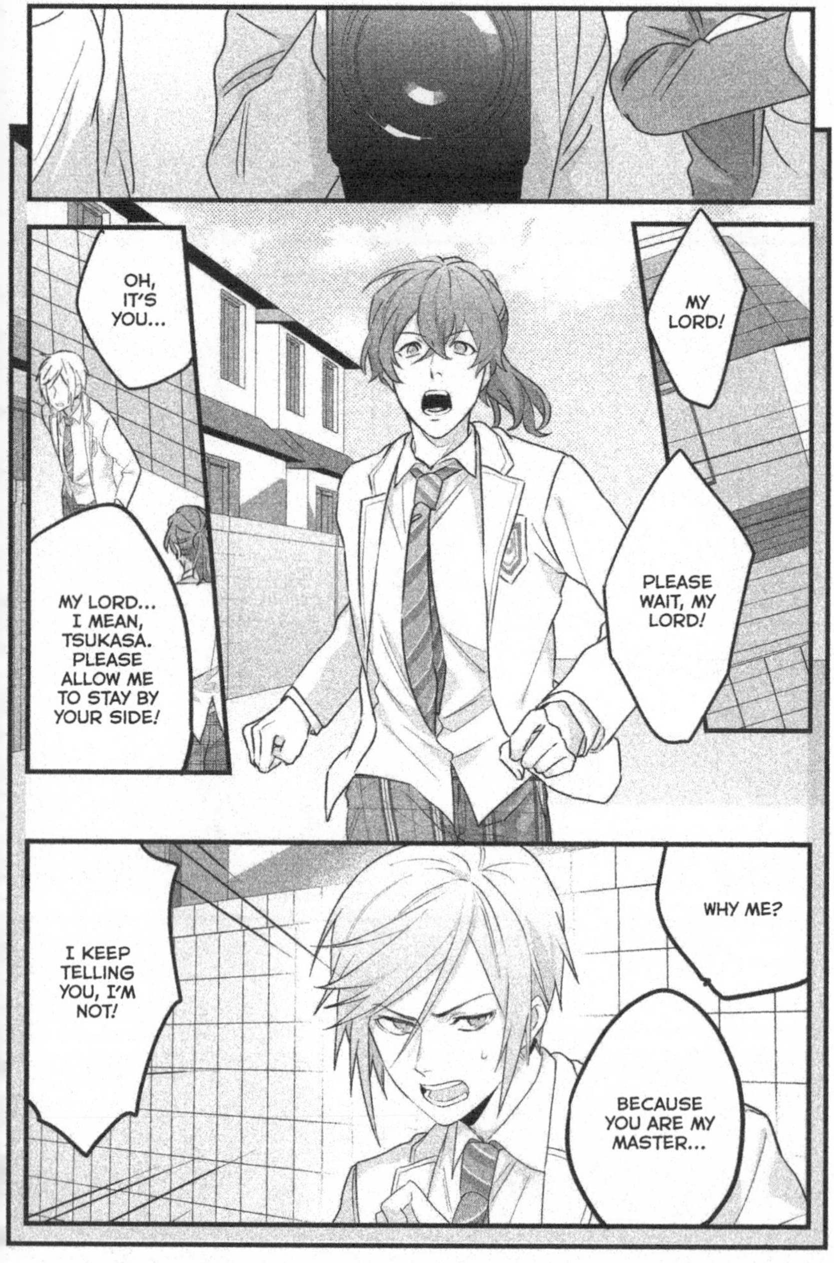
MY LORD!
OH, IT'S YOU...
PLEASE WAIT, MY LORD!
MY LORD... I MEAN, TSUKASA. PLEASE ALLOW ME TO STAY BY YOUR SIDE!
WHY ME?
I KEEP TELLING YOU, I'M NOT!
BECAUSE YOU ARE MY MASTER...

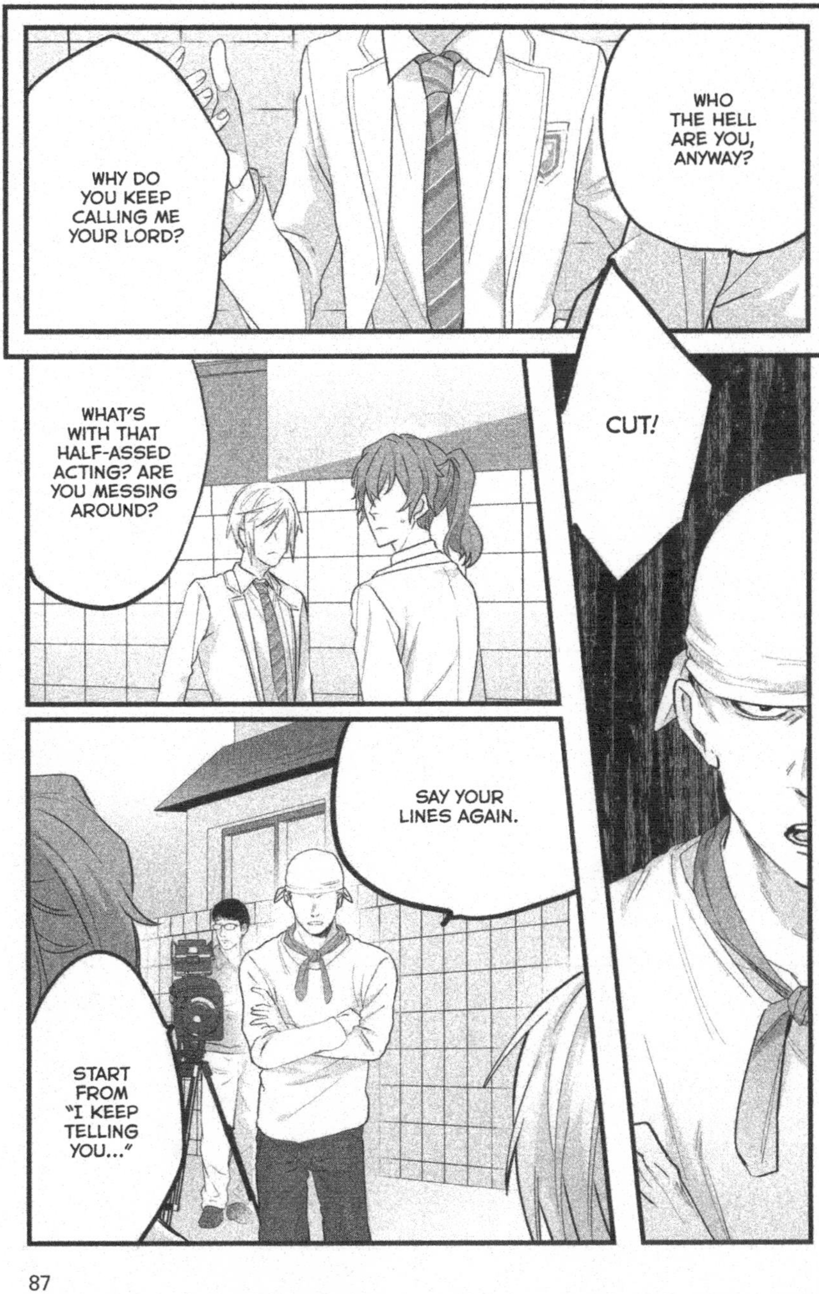
WHO THE HELL ARE YOU, ANYWAY?
WHY DO YOU KEEP CALLING ME YOUR LORD?
CUT!
WHAT'S WITH THAT HALF-ASSED ACTING? ARE YOU MESSING AROUND?
SAY YOUR LINES AGAIN.
START FROM "I KEEP TELLING YOU..."

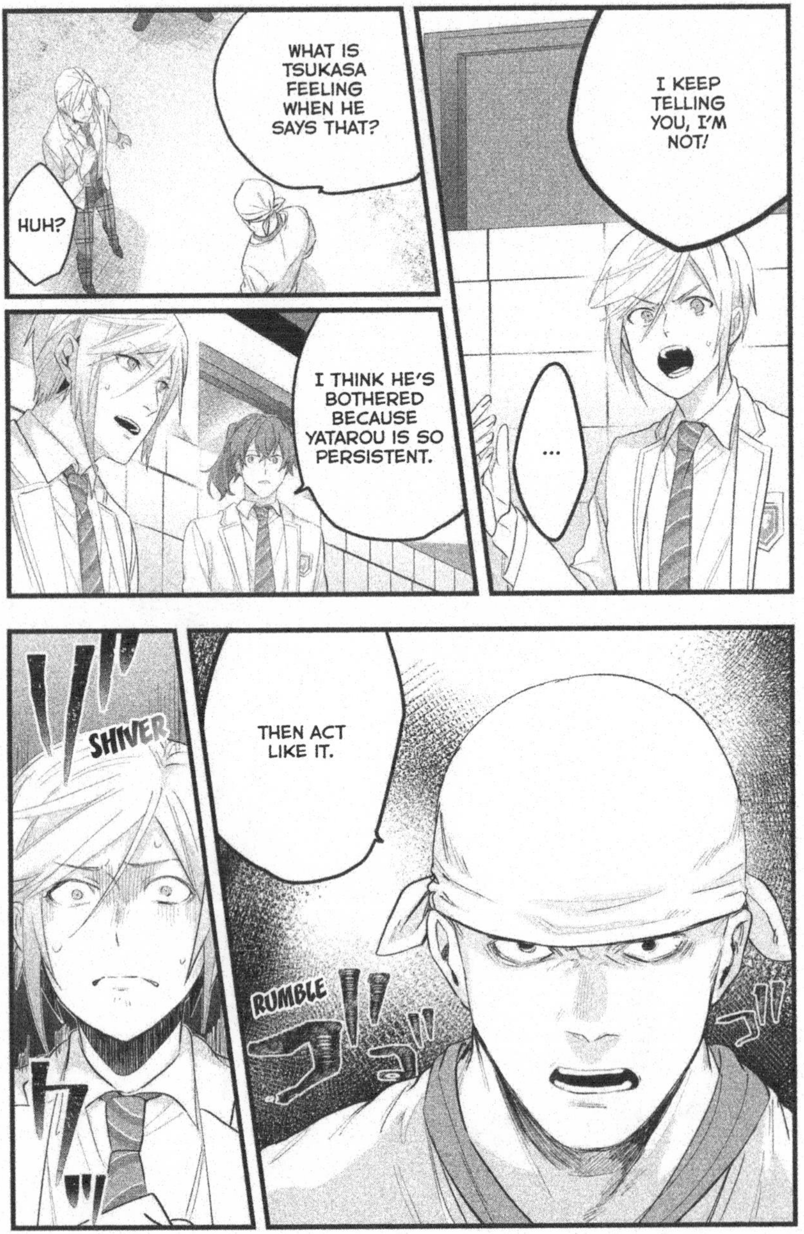
I KEEP TELLING YOU, I'M NOT!
...
WHAT IS TSUKASA FEELING WHEN HE SAYS THAT?
HUH?
I THINK HE'S BOTHERED BECAUSE YATAROU IS SO PERSISTENT.
THEN ACT LIKE IT.
RUMBLE
SHIVER

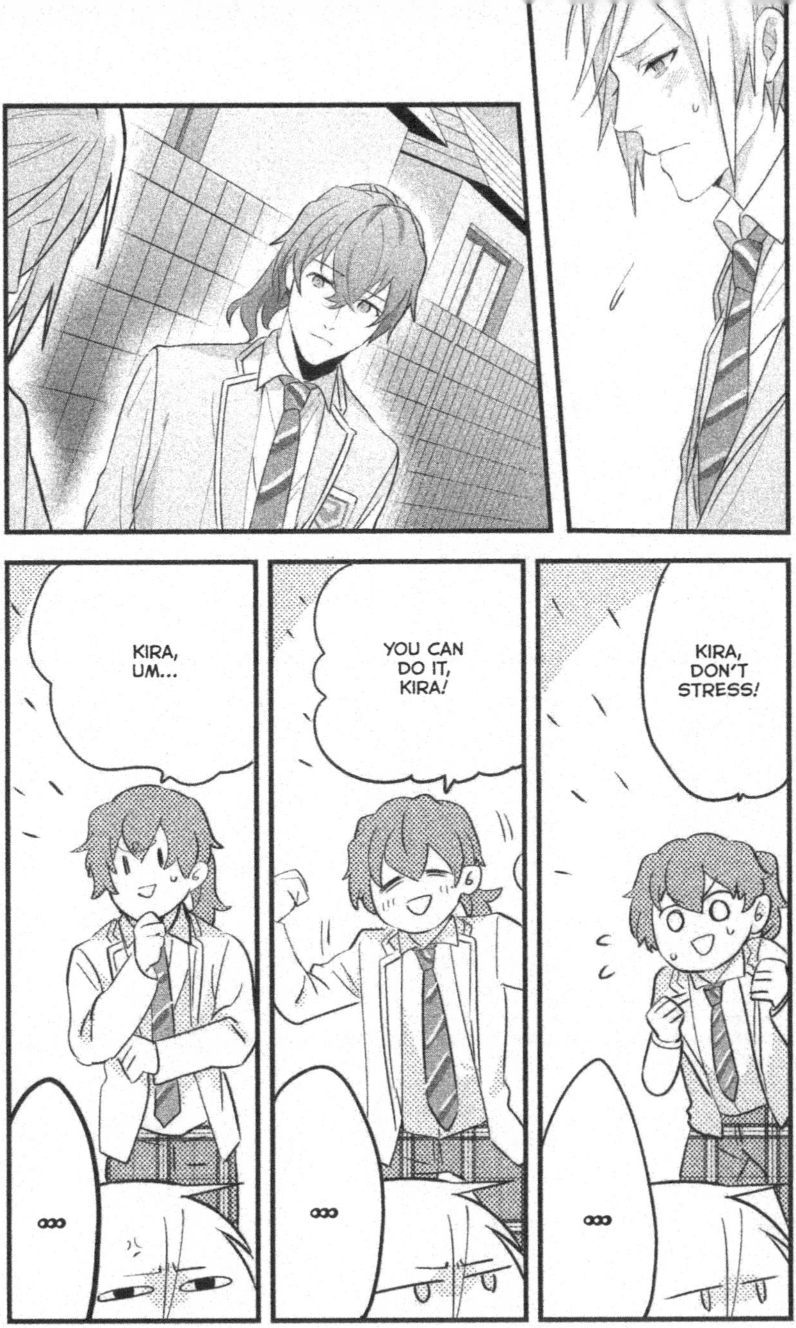
KIRA, DON'T STRESS!
...
YOU CAN DO IT, KIRA!
...
KIRA, UM...
...

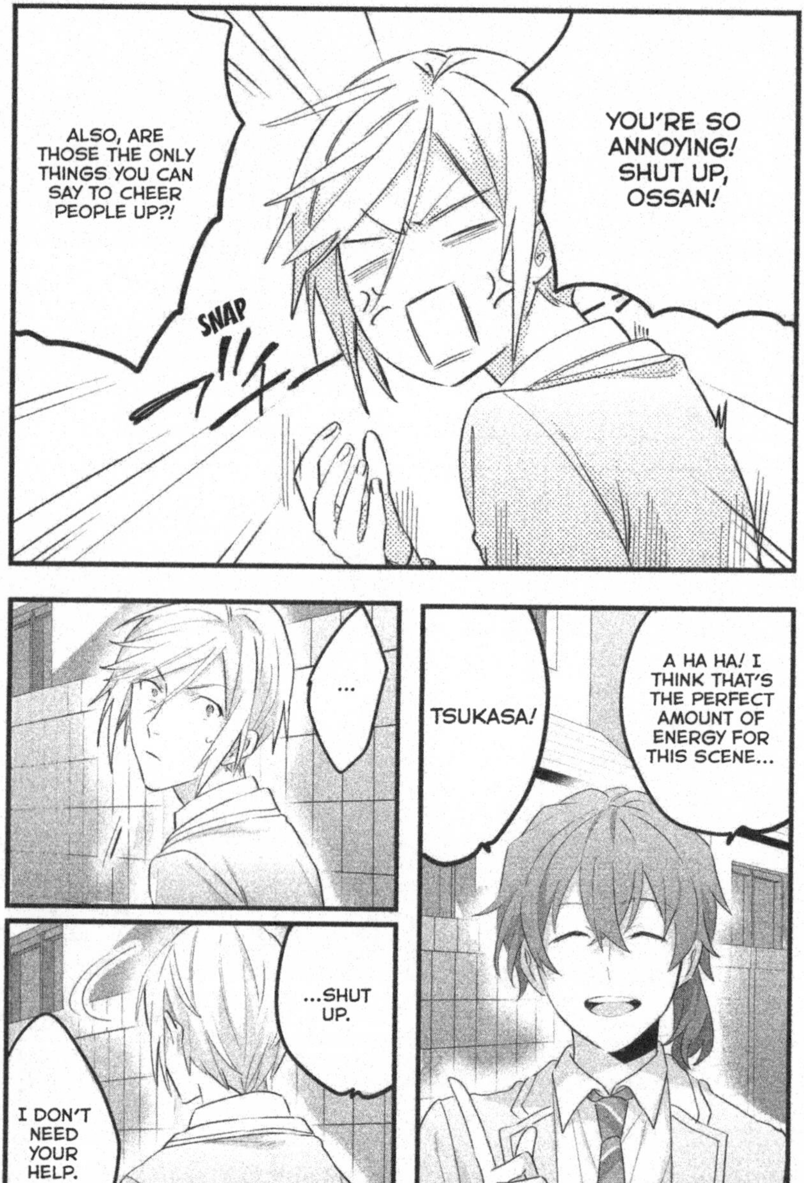
YOU'RE SO ANNOYING! SHUT UP, OSSAN!
ALSO, ARE THOSE THE ONLY THINGS YOU CAN SAY TO CHEER PEOPLE UP?!
SNAP
A HA HA! I THINK THAT'S THE PERFECT AMOUNT OF ENERGY FOR THIS SCENE...
TSUKASA!
...
...SHUT UP.
I DON'T NEED YOUR HELP.

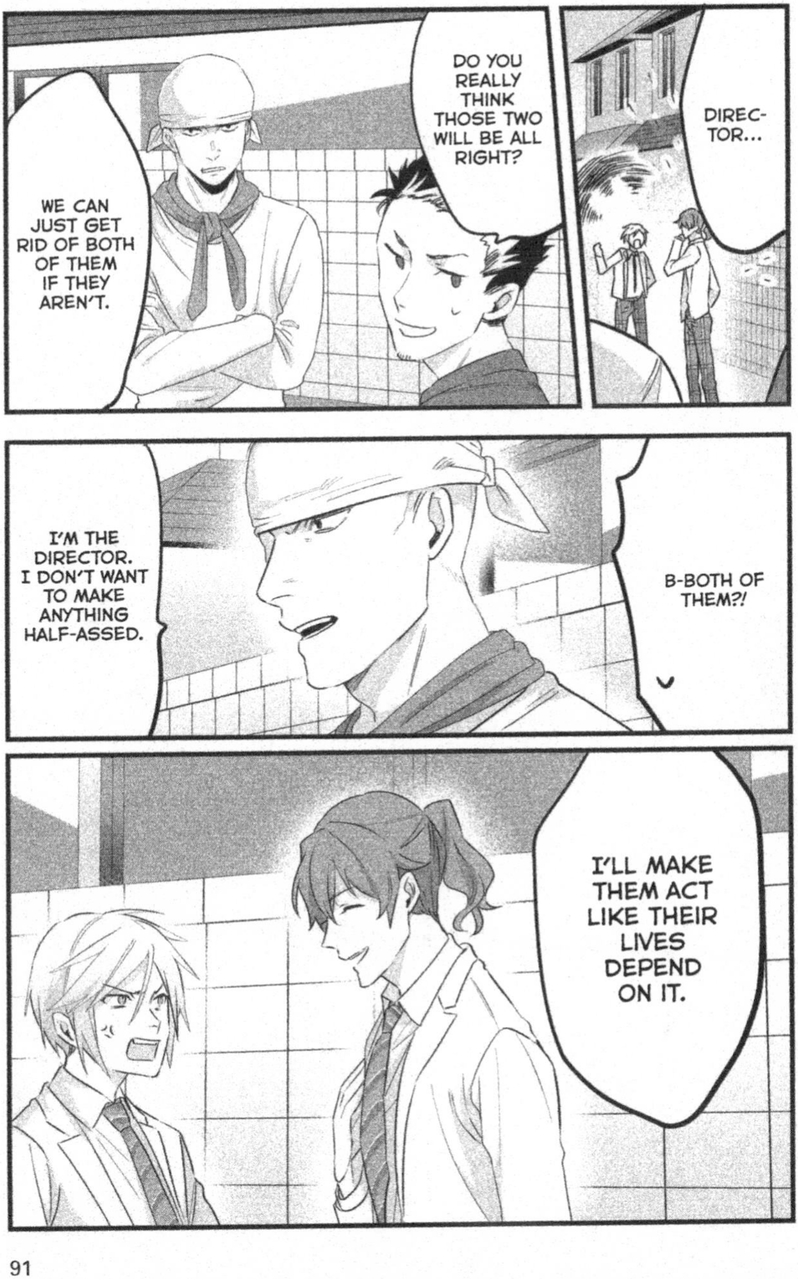
DIREC-TOR...
DO YOU REALLY THINK THOSE TWO WILL BE ALL RIGHT?
WE CAN JUST GET RID OF BOTH OF THEM IF THEY AREN'T.
B-BOTH OF THEM?!
I'M THE DIRECTOR. I DON'T WANT TO MAKE ANYTHING HALF-ASSED.
I'LL MAKE THEM ACT LIKE THEIR LIVES DEPEND ON IT.

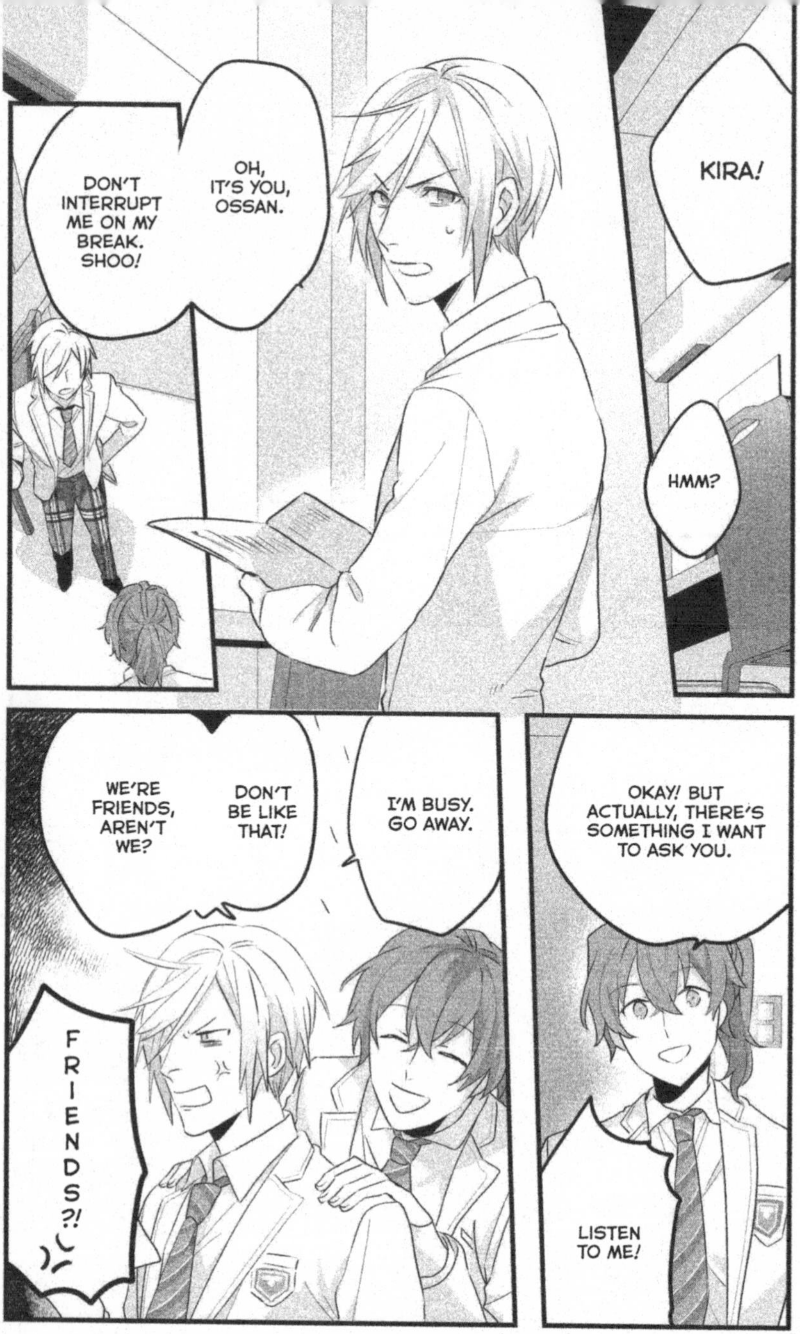
KIRA!
HMM?
OH, IT'S YOU, OSSAN.
DON'T INTERRUPT ME ON MY BREAK. SHOO!
OKAY! BUT ACTUALLY, THERE'S SOMETHING I WANT TO ASK YOU.
LISTEN TO ME!
I'M BUSY. GO AWAY.
DON'T BE LIKE THAT!
WE'RE FRIENDS, AREN'T WE?
FRIENDS?!

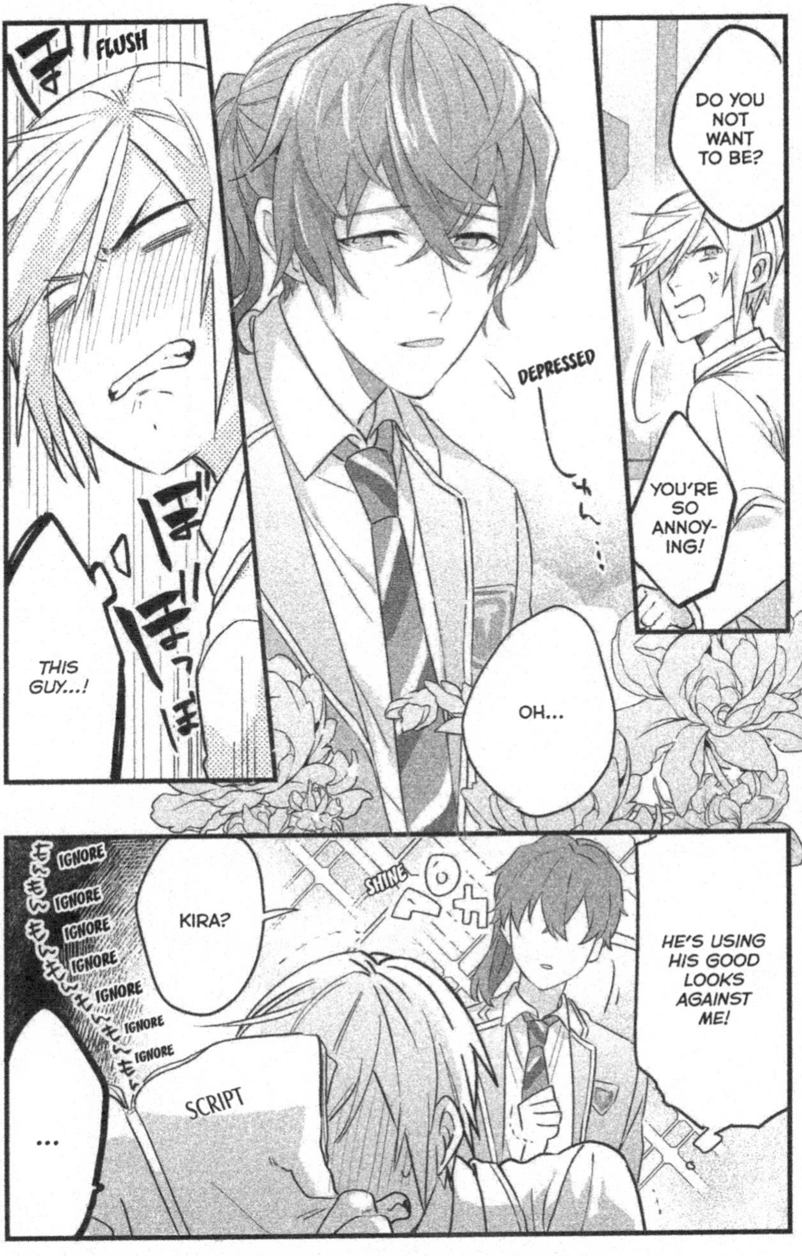
DO YOU NOT WANT TO BE?
YOU'RE SO ANNOYING!
DEPRESSED
OH...
FLUSH
THIS GUY...!
HE'S USING HIS GOOD LOOKS AGAINST ME!
SHINE
KIRA?
IGNORE
IGNORE
IGNORE
IGNORE
IGNORE
IGNORE
IGNORE
SCRIPT
...

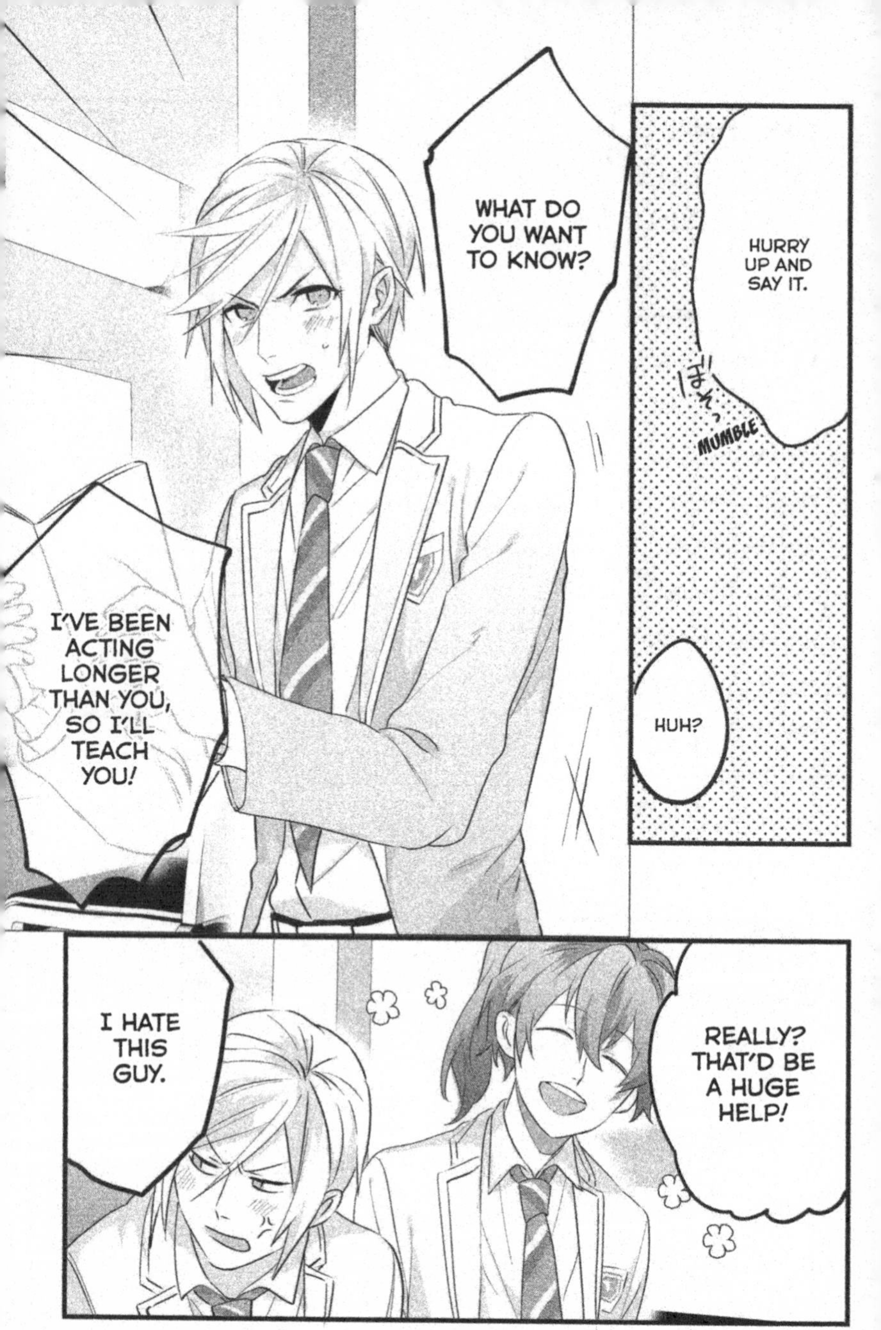
HURRY UP AND SAY IT.
ぼそっ MUMBLE
HUH?
WHAT DO YOU WANT TO KNOW?
I'VE BEEN ACTING LONGER THAN YOU, SO I'LL TEACH YOU!
REALLY? THAT'D BE A HUGE HELP!
I HATE THIS GUY.

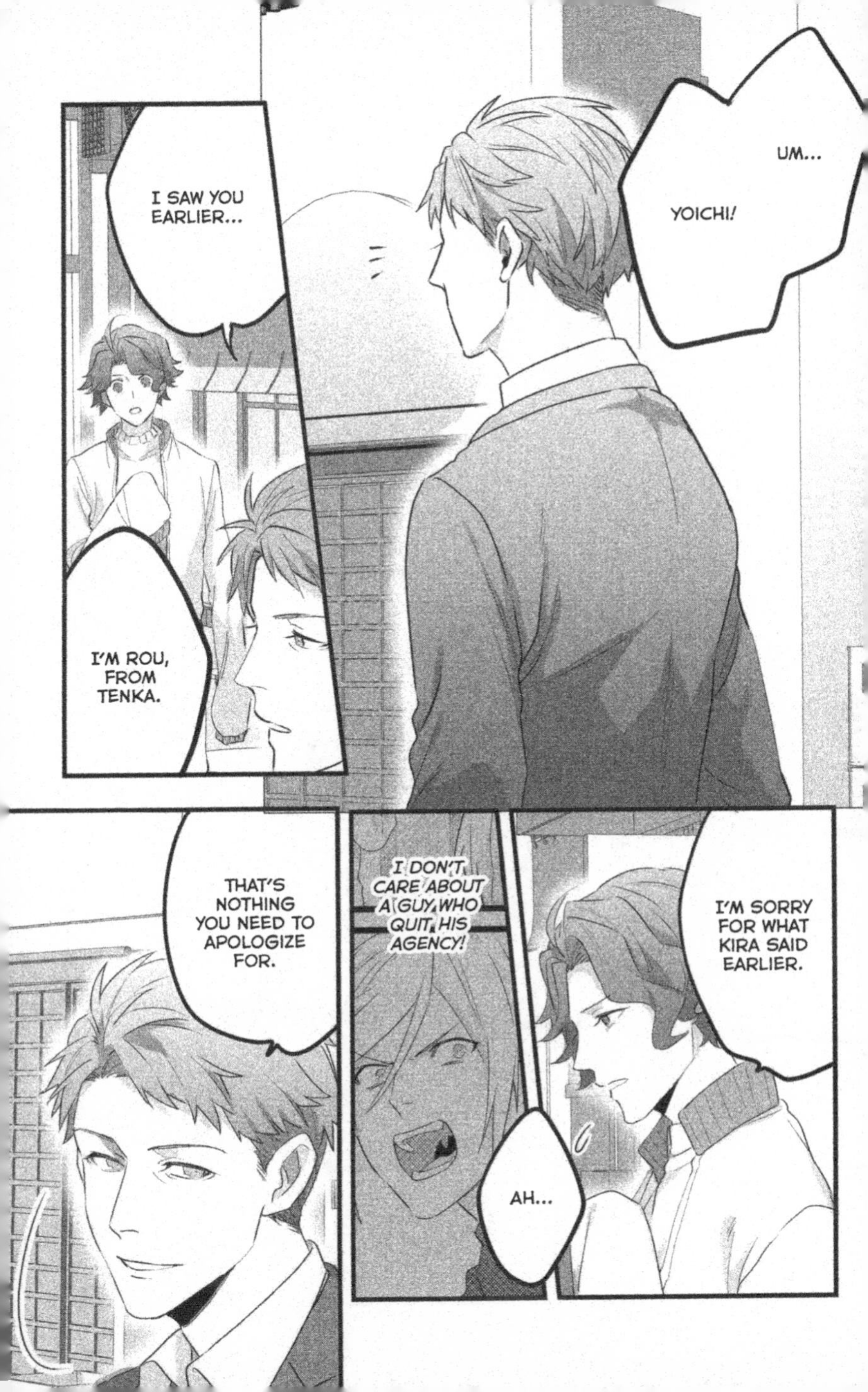
UM...
YOICHI!
I SAW YOU EARLIER...
I'M ROU, FROM TENKA.
I'M SORRY FOR WHAT KIRA SAID EARLIER.
AH...
I DON'T CARE ABOUT A GUY WHO QUIT HIS AGENCY!
THAT'S NOTHING YOU NEED TO APOLOGIZE FOR.

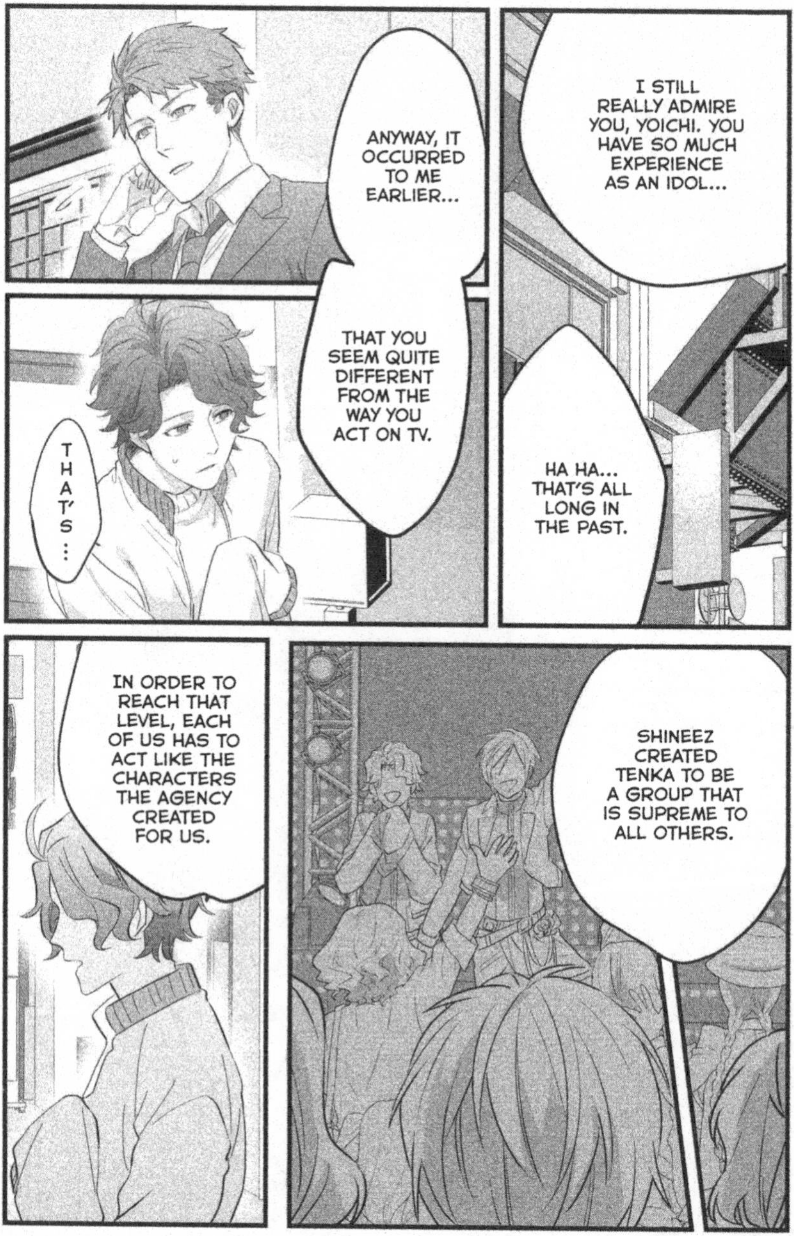
I STILL REALLY ADMIRE YOU, YOICHI. YOU HAVE SO MUCH EXPERIENCE AS AN IDOL...
HA HA... THAT'S ALL LONG IN THE PAST.
ANYWAY, IT OCCURRED TO ME EARLIER...
THAT YOU SEEM QUITE DIFFERENT FROM THE WAY YOU ACT ON TV.
THAT'S...
SHINEEZ CREATED TENKA TO BE A GROUP THAT IS SUPREME TO ALL OTHERS.
IN ORDER TO REACH THAT LEVEL, EACH OF US HAS TO ACT LIKE THE CHARACTERS THE AGENCY CREATED FOR US.

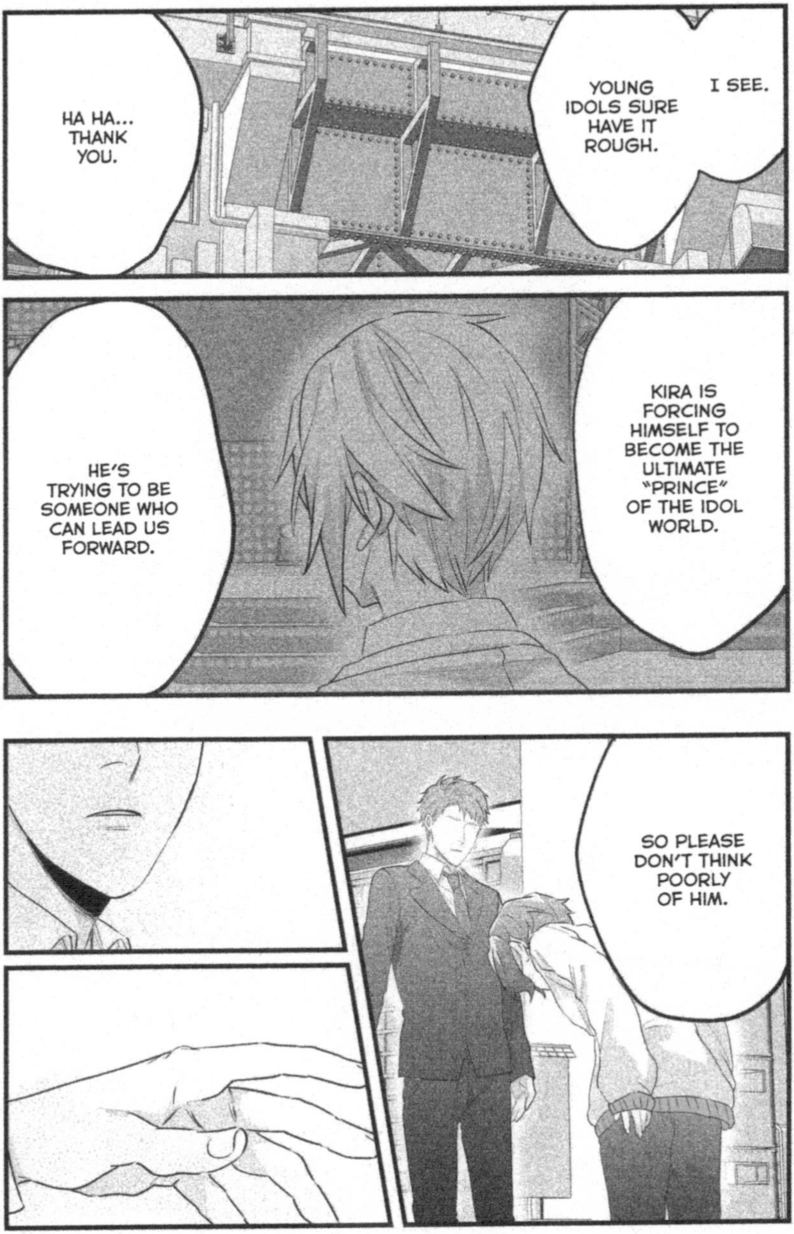
I SEE.
YOUNG IDOLS SURE HAVE IT ROUGH.
HA HA... THANK YOU.
KIRA IS FORCING HIMSELF TO BECOME THE ULTIMATE "PRINCE" OF THE IDOL WORLD.
HE'S TRYING TO BE SOMEONE WHO CAN LEAD US FORWARD.
SO PLEASE DON'T THINK POORLY OF HIM.

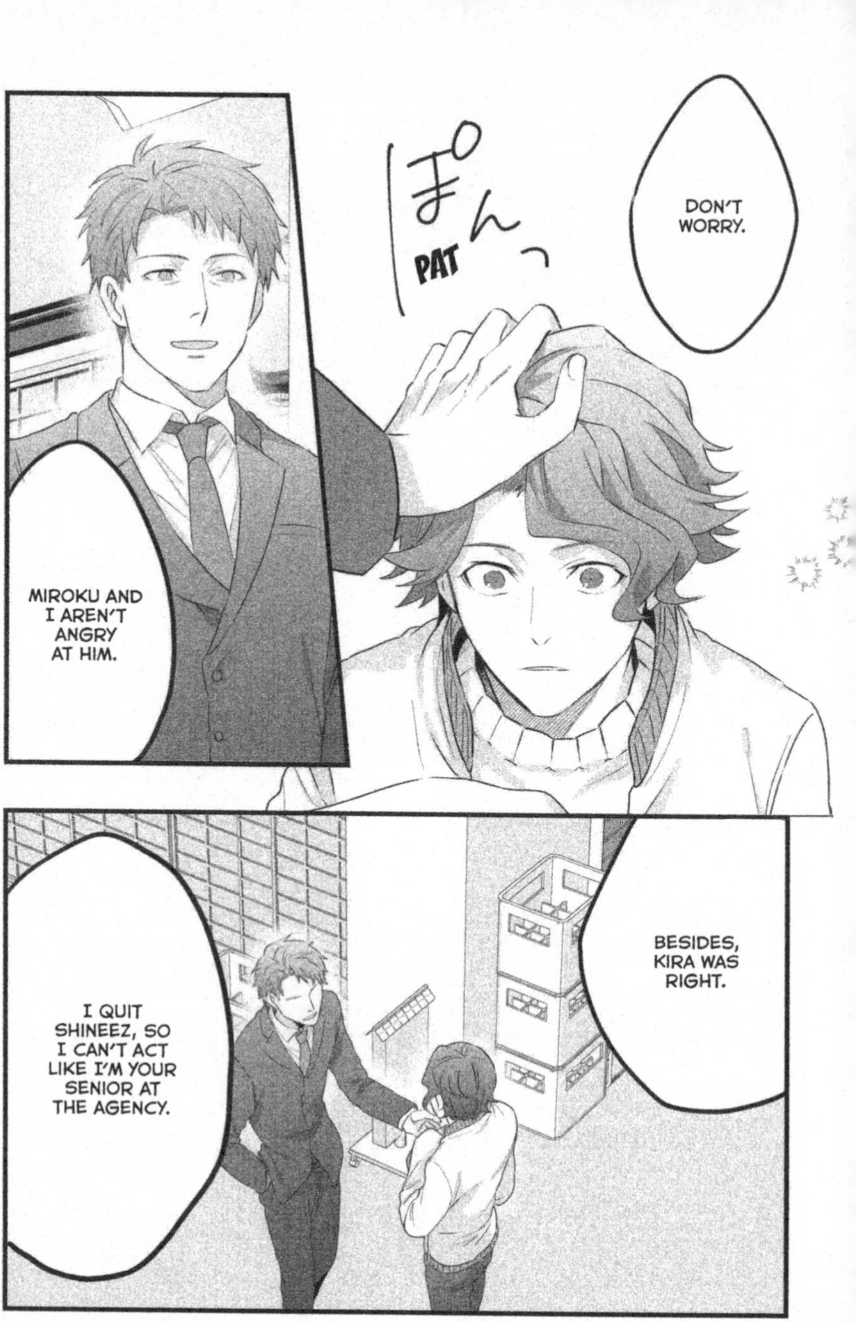
DON'T WORRY.
ぽんっ
PAT
MIROKU AND I AREN'T ANGRY AT HIM.
BESIDES, KIRA WAS RIGHT.
I QUIT SHINEEZ, SO I CAN'T ACT LIKE I'M YOUR SENIOR AT THE AGENCY.

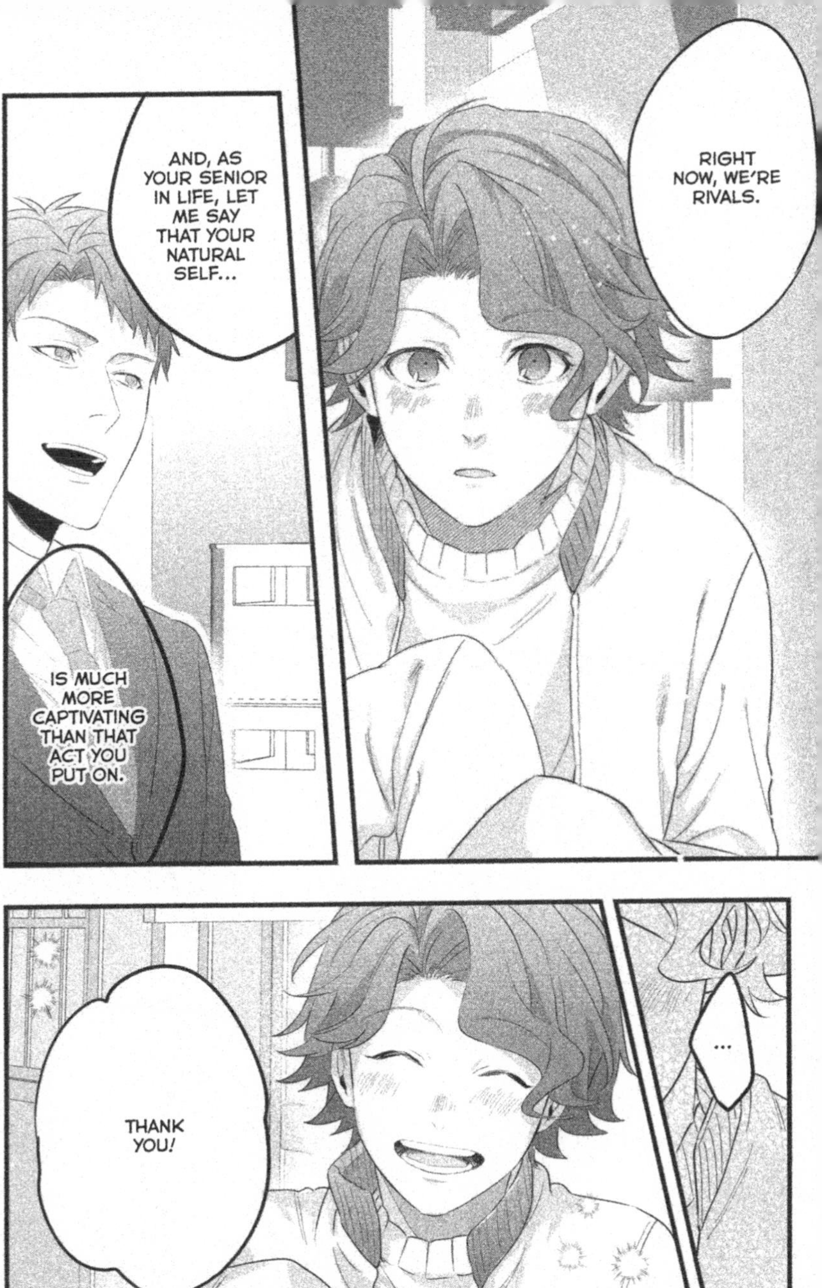
RIGHT NOW, WE'RE RIVALS.
AND, AS YOUR SENIOR IN LIFE, LET ME SAY THAT YOUR NATURAL SELF...
IS MUCH MORE CAPTIVATING THAN THAT ACT YOU PUT ON.
...
THANK YOU!

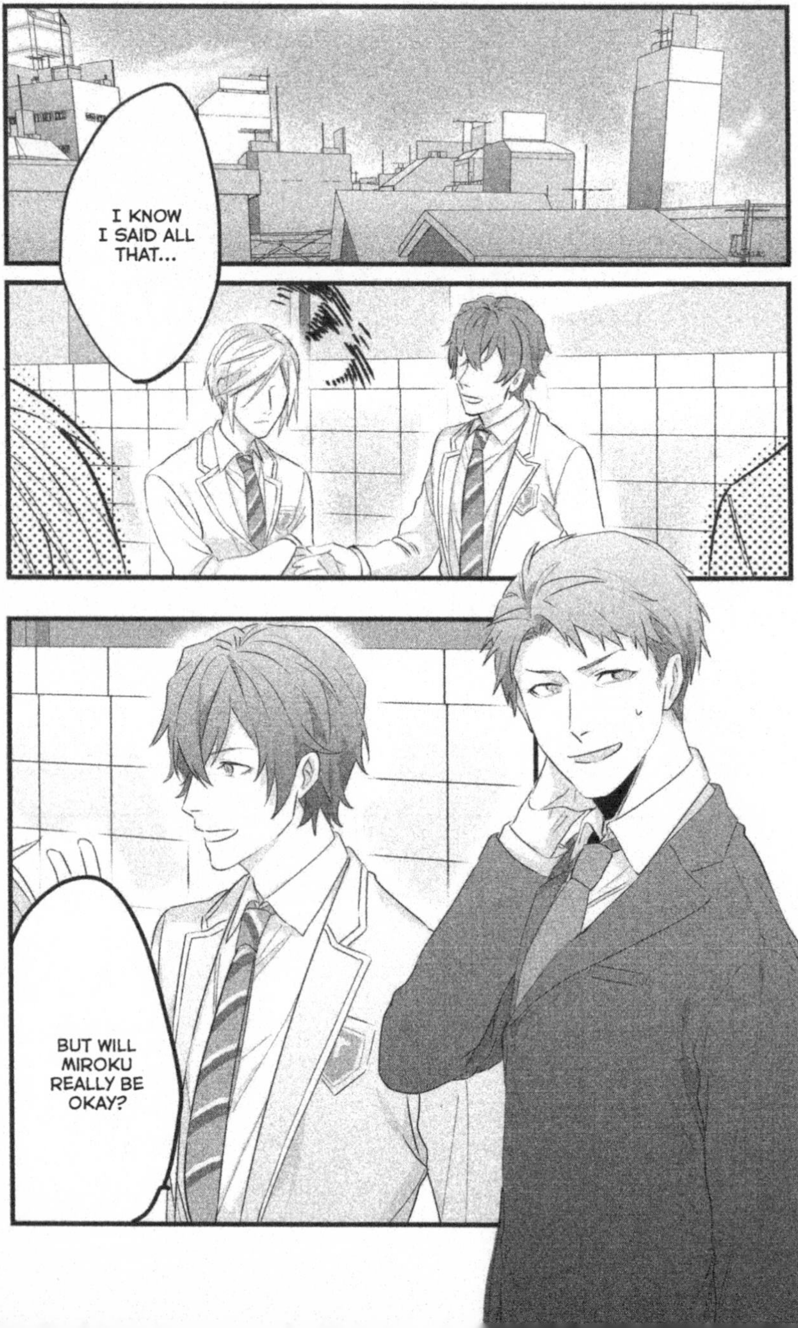
I KNOW I SAID ALL THAT...
BUT WILL MIROKU REALLY BE OKAY?

Chapter 27

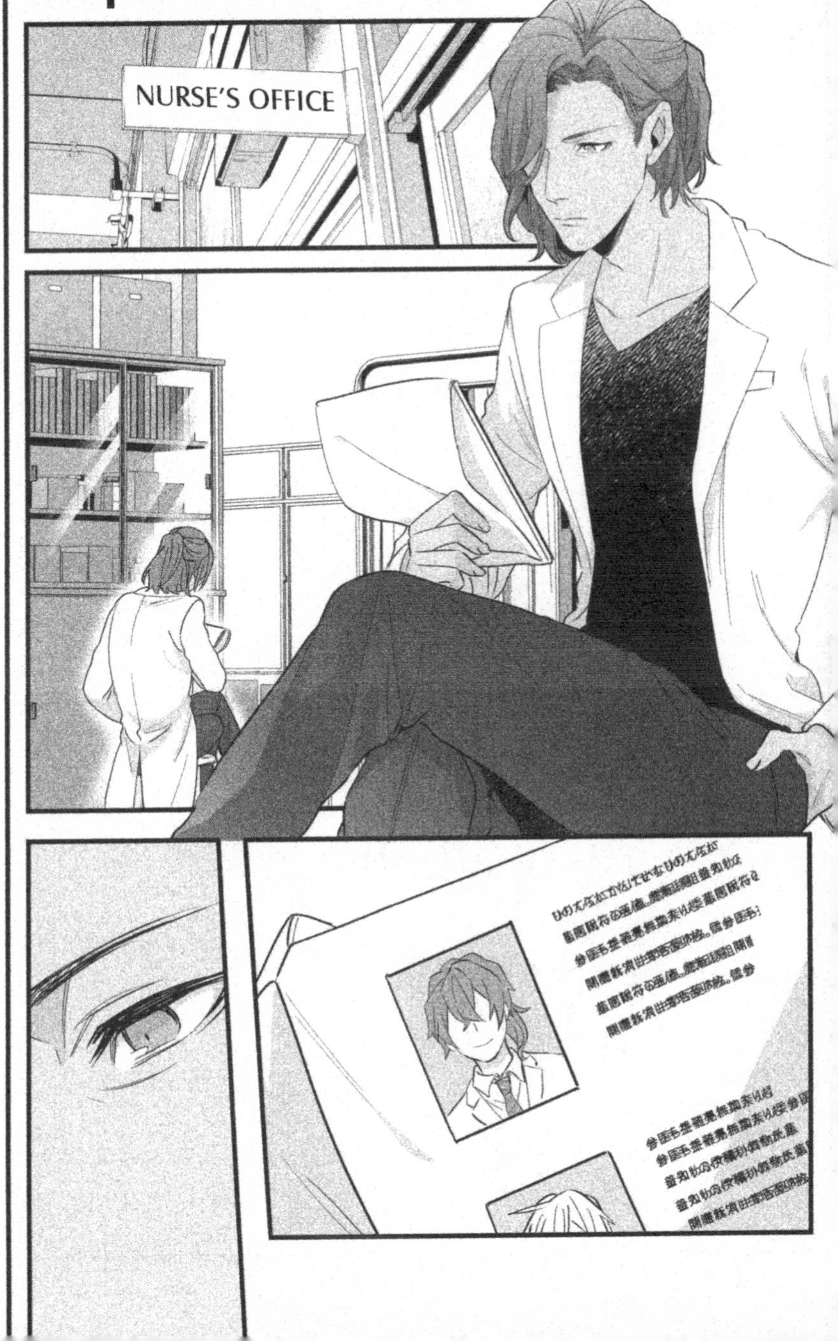
NURSE'S OFFICE

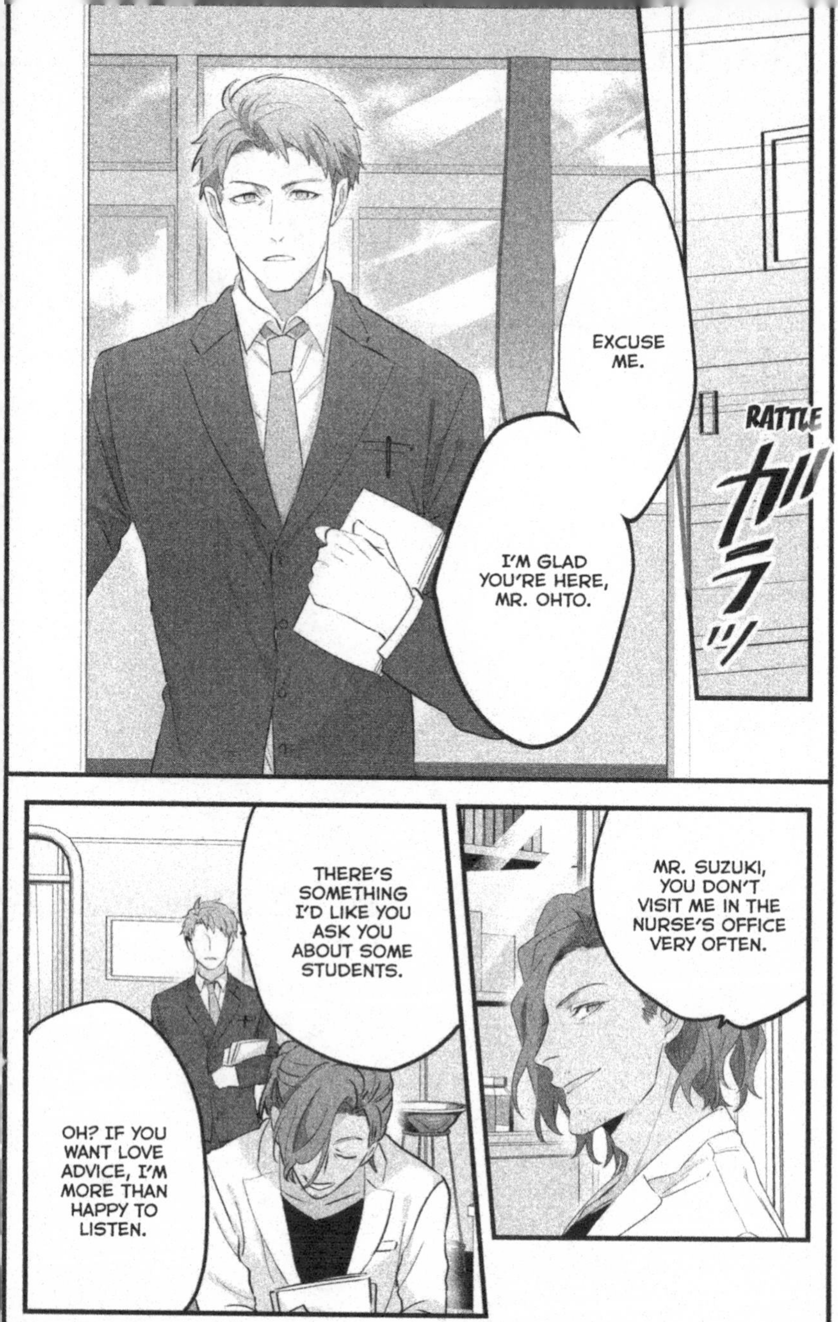
EXCUSE ME.
RATTLE
ガラッ
I'M GLAD YOU'RE HERE, MR. OHTO.
MR. SUZUKI, YOU DON'T VISIT ME IN THE NURSE'S OFFICE VERY OFTEN.
THERE'S SOMETHING I'D LIKE YOU ASK YOU ABOUT SOME STUDENTS.
OH? IF YOU WANT LOVE ADVICE, I'M MORE THAN HAPPY TO LISTEN.

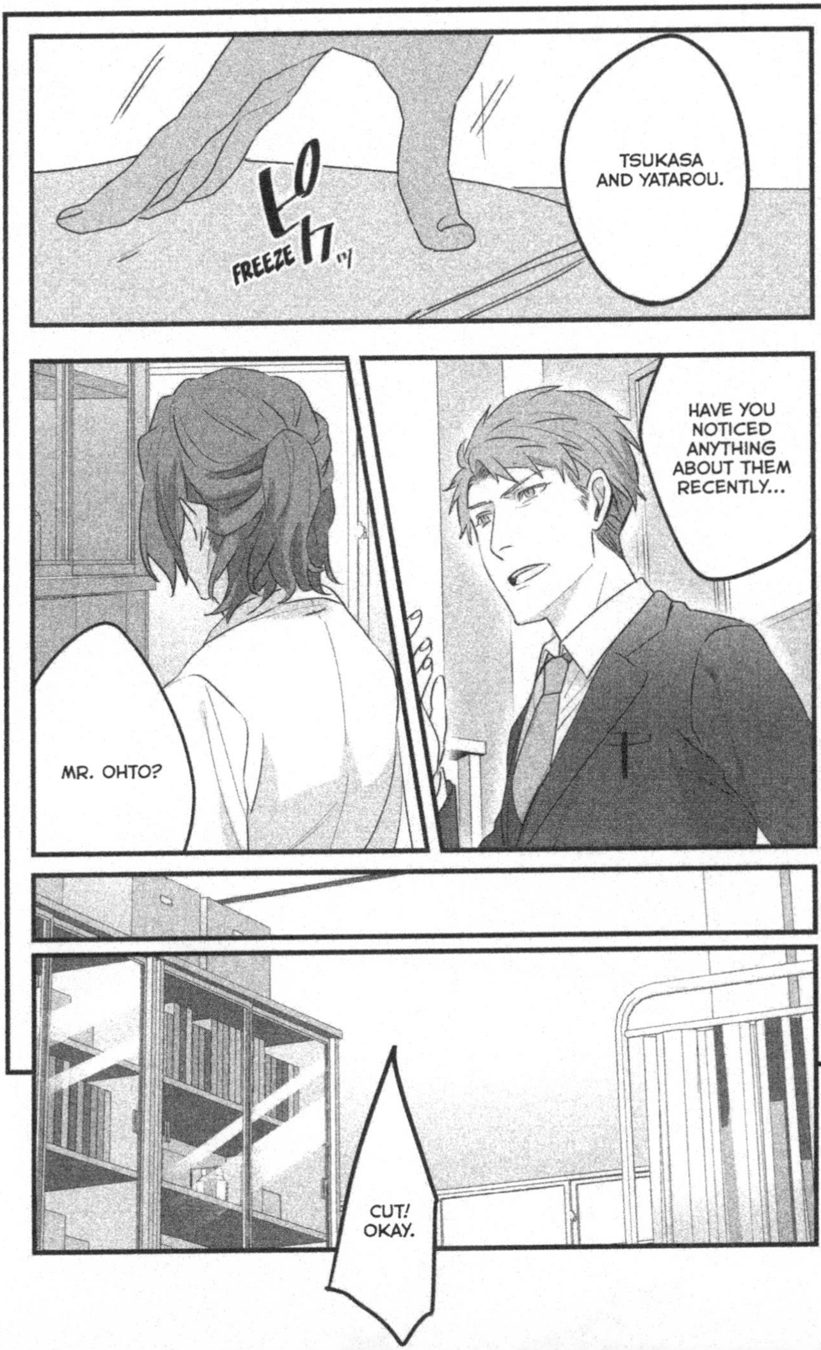
TSUKASA AND YATAROU.
FREEZE
HAVE YOU NOTICED ANYTHING ABOUT THEM RECENTLY...
MR. OHTO?
CUT! OKAY.

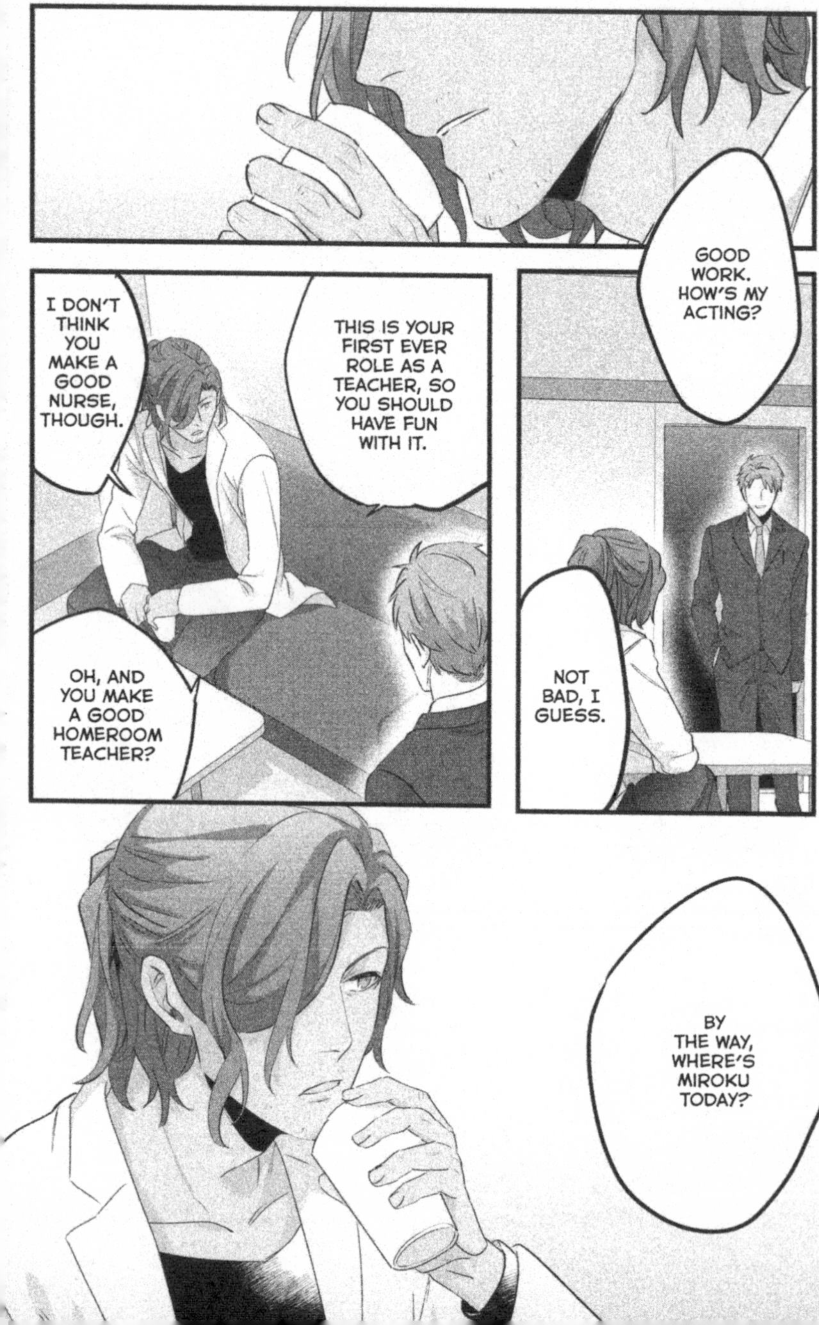
GOOD WORK. HOW'S MY ACTING?
NOT BAD, I GUESS.
THIS IS YOUR FIRST EVER ROLE AS A TEACHER, SO YOU SHOULD HAVE FUN WITH IT.
I DON'T THINK YOU MAKE A GOOD NURSE, THOUGH.
OH, AND YOU MAKE A GOOD HOMEROOM TEACHER?
BY THE WAY, WHERE'S MIROKU TODAY?

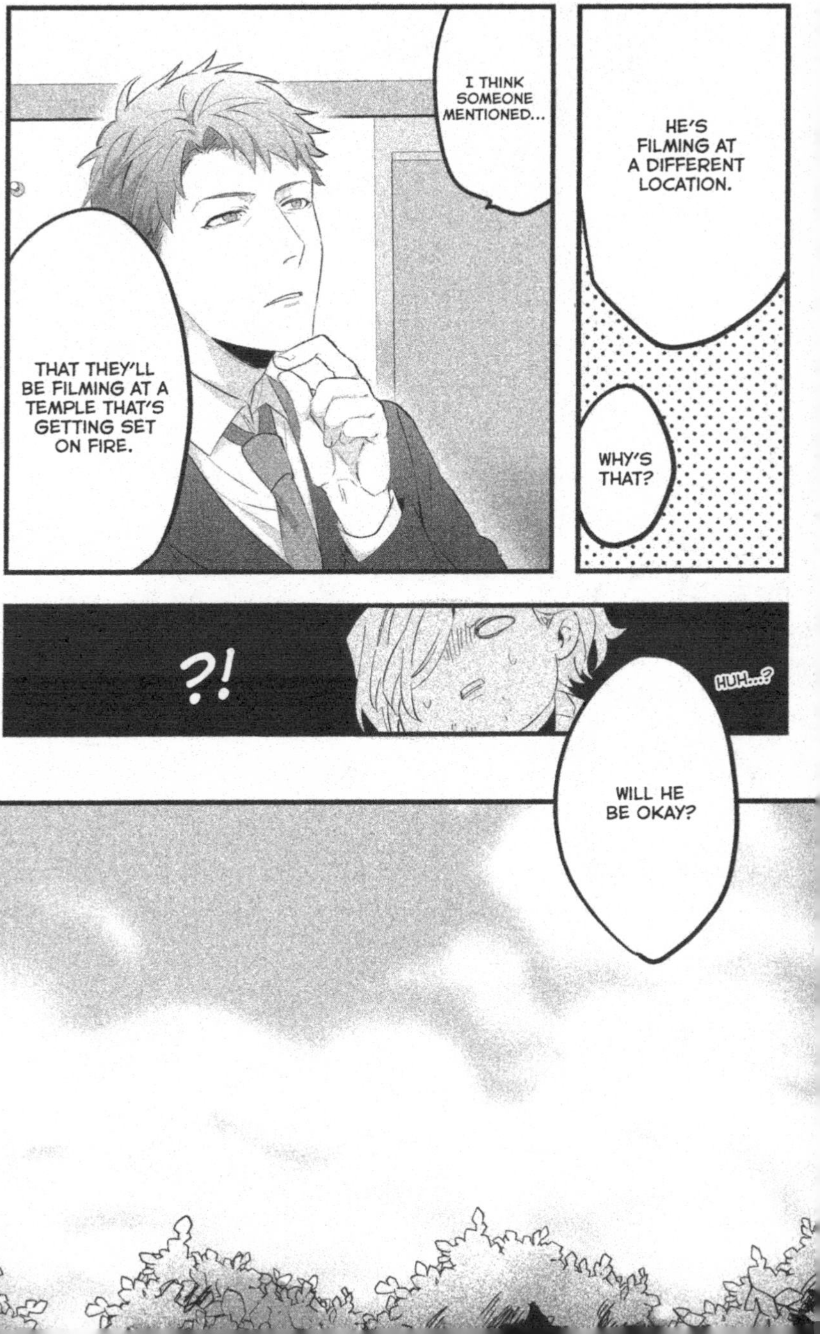
HE'S FILMING AT A DIFFERENT LOCATION.
WHY'S THAT?
I THINK SOMEONE MENTIONED...
THAT THEY'LL BE FILMING AT A TEMPLE THAT'S GETTING SET ON FIRE.
HUH...?
?!
WILL HE BE OKAY?

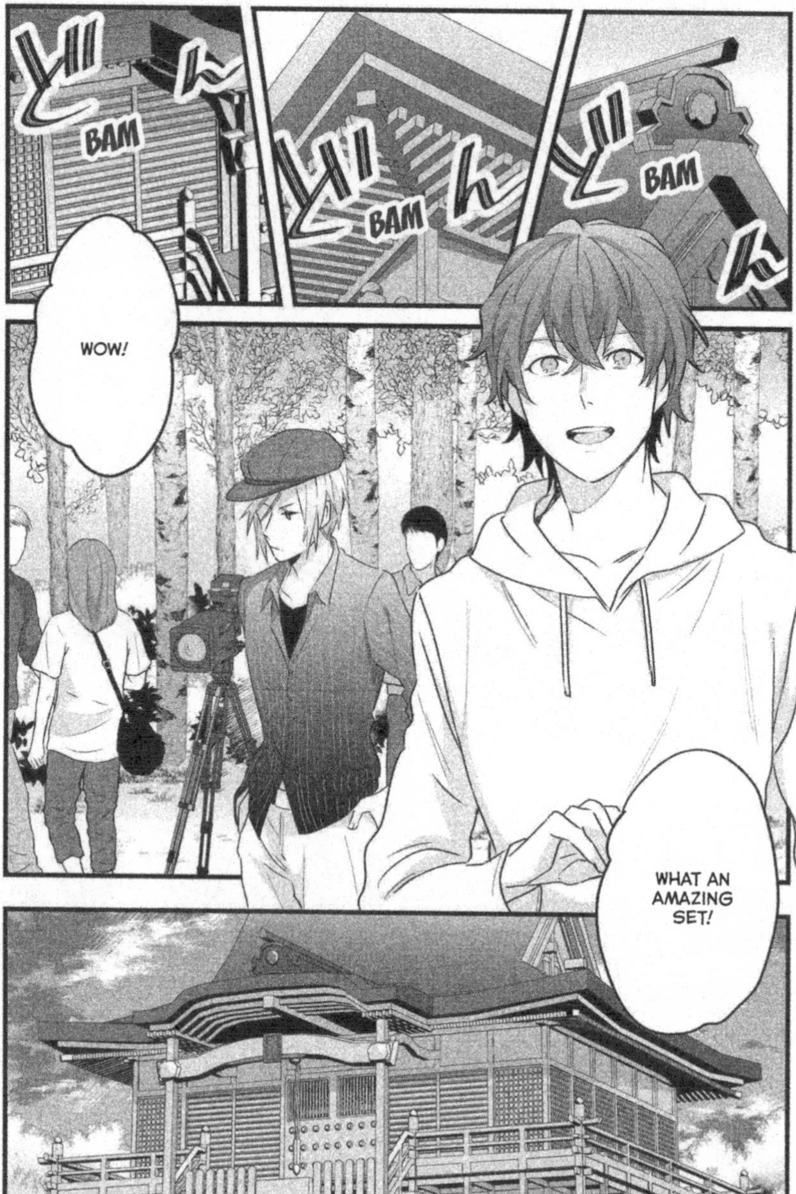
どーん
BAM
どーん
BAM
どーん
BAM
WOW!
WHAT AN AMAZING SET!

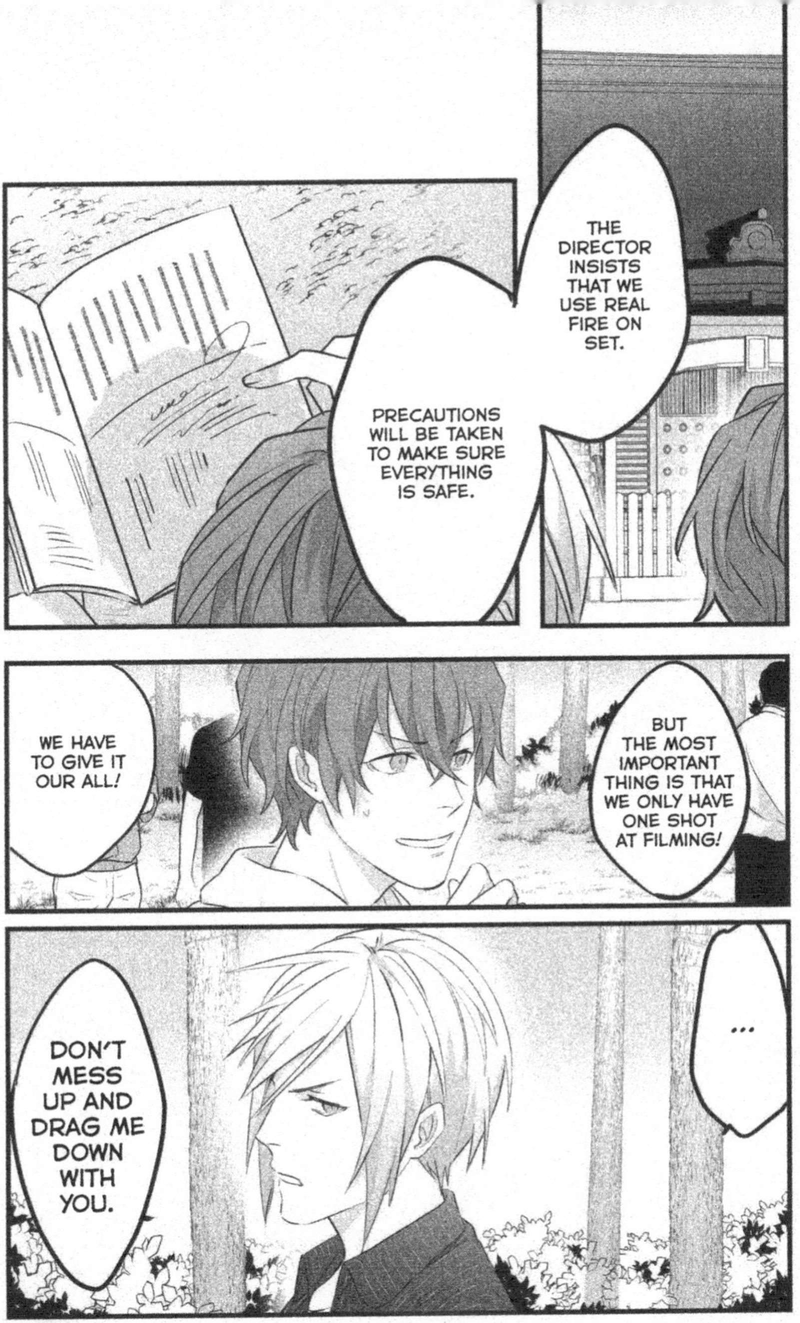
THE DIRECTOR INSISTS THAT WE USE REAL FIRE ON SET.
PRECAUTIONS WILL BE TAKEN TO MAKE SURE EVERYTHING IS SAFE.
BUT THE MOST IMPORTANT THING IS THAT WE ONLY HAVE ONE SHOT AT FILMING!
WE HAVE TO GIVE IT OUR ALL!
...
DON'T MESS UP AND DRAG ME DOWN WITH YOU.

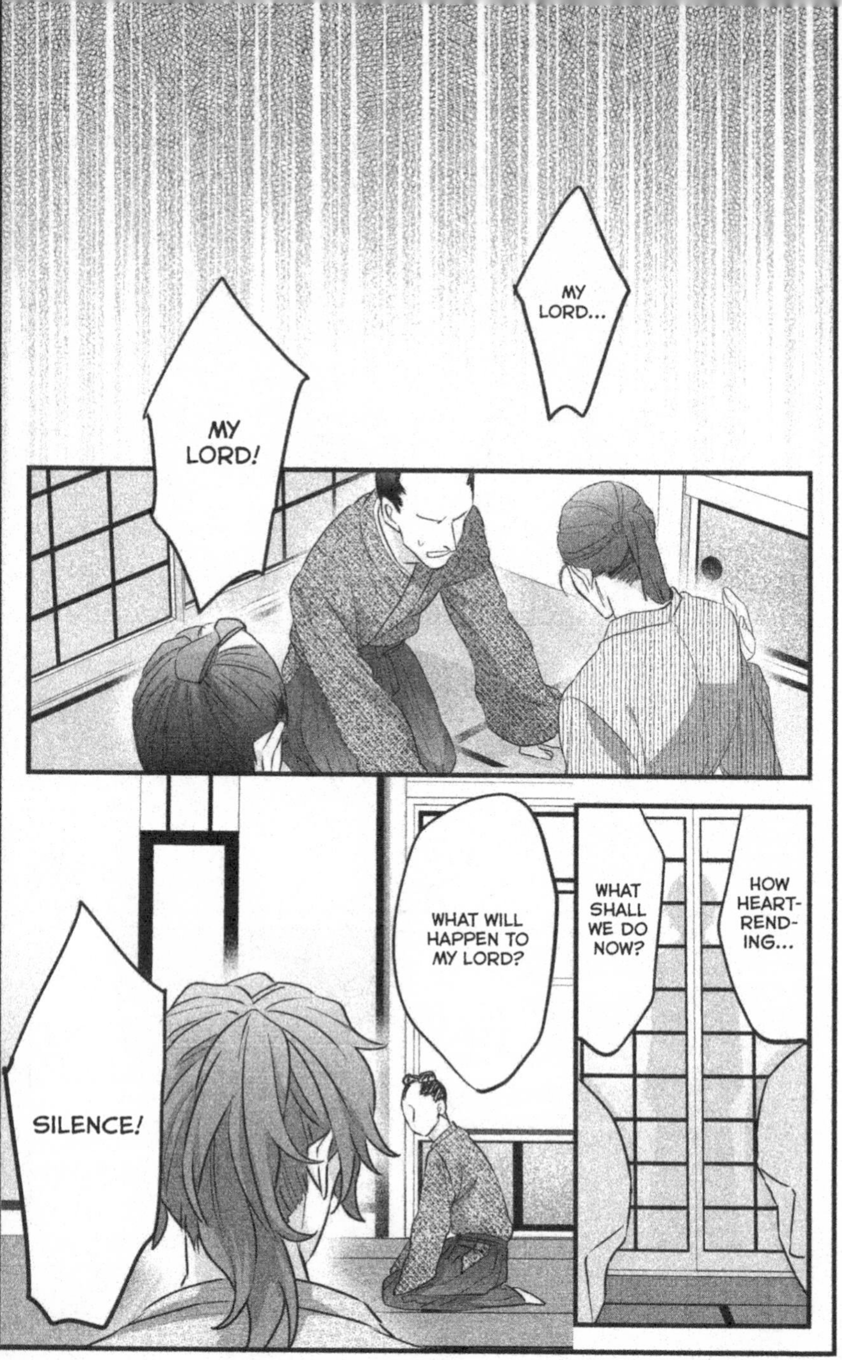

MY LORD...
MY LORD!
HOW HEART-RENDING...
WHAT SHALL WE DO NOW?
WHAT WILL HAPPEN TO MY LORD?
SILENCE!

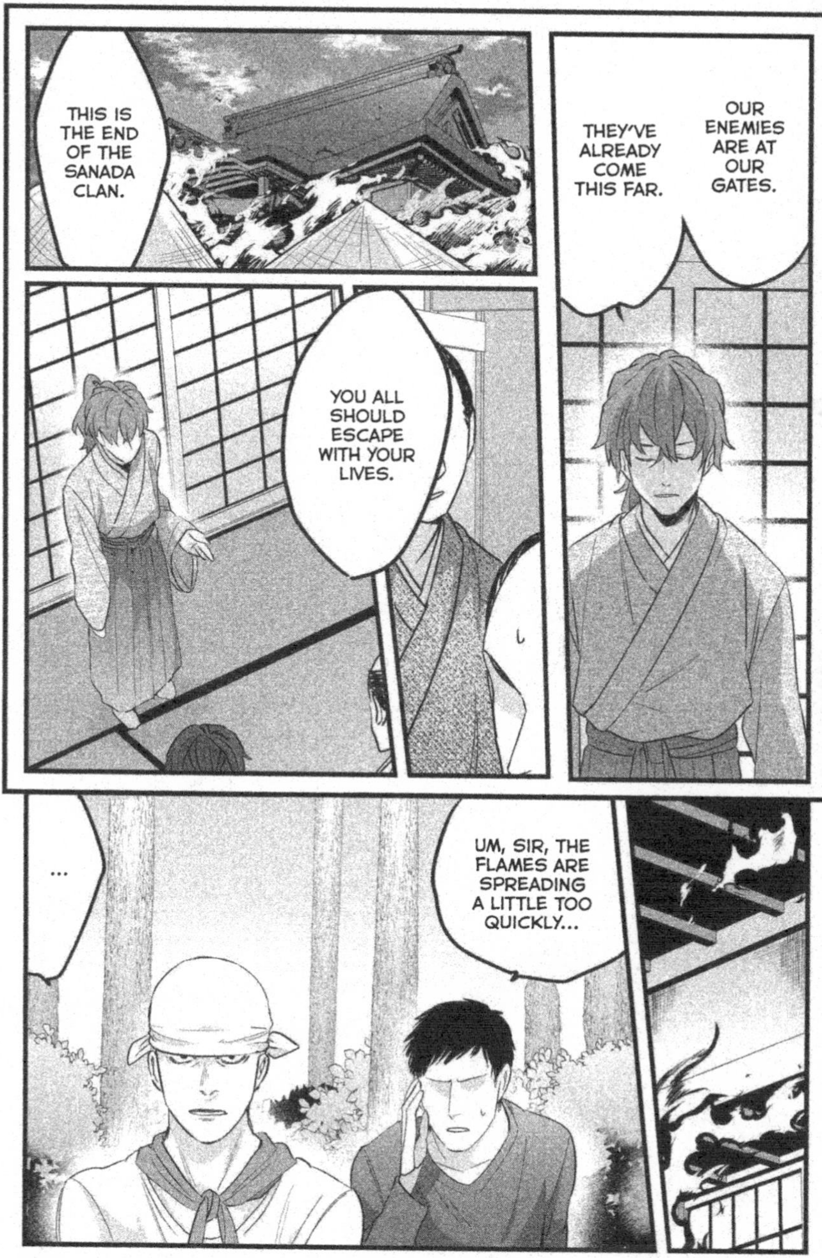
OUR ENEMIES ARE AT OUR GATES.
THEY'VE ALREADY COME THIS FAR.
THIS IS THE END OF THE SANADA CLAN.
YOU ALL SHOULD ESCAPE WITH YOUR LIVES.
UM, SIR, THE FLAMES ARE SPREADING A LITTLE TOO QUICKLY...
...

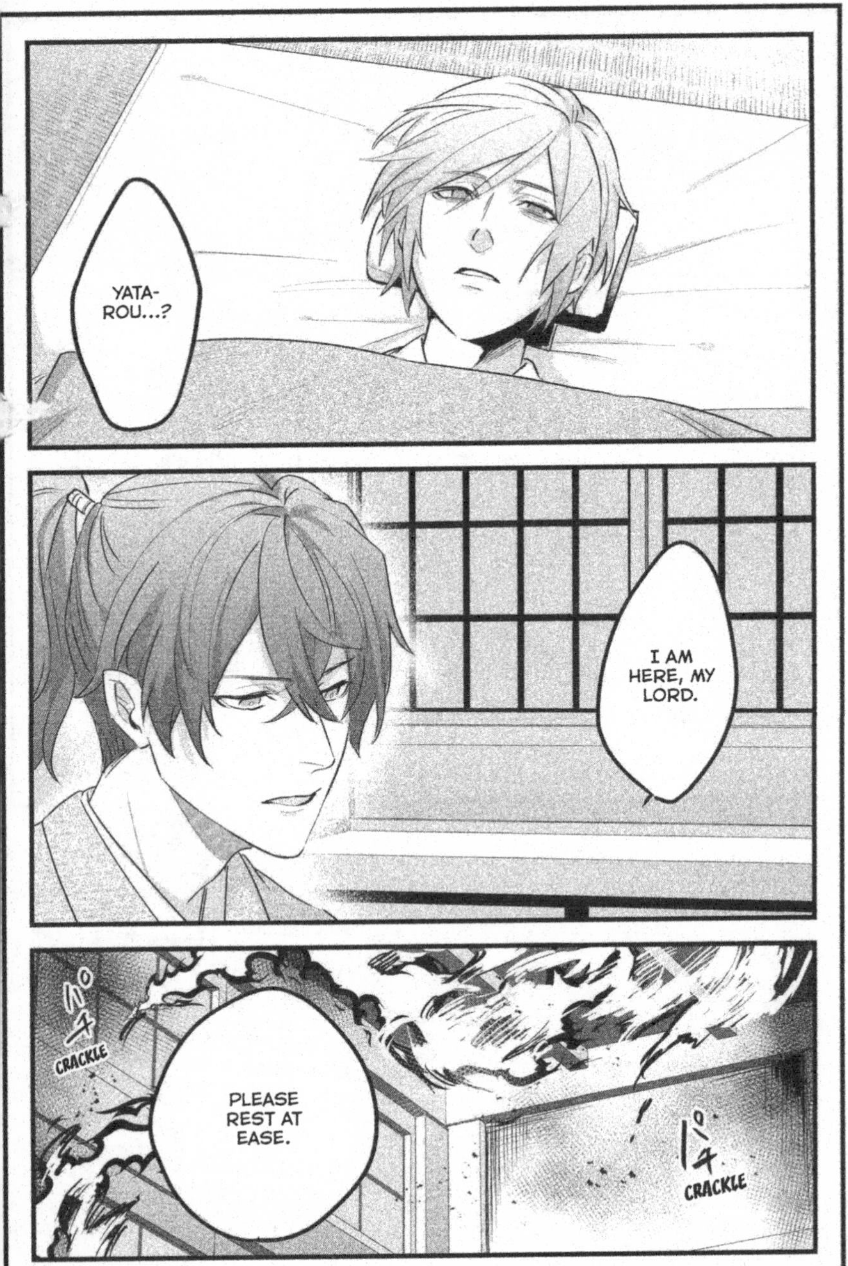
YATA-ROU...?
I AM HERE, MY LORD.
パチ
CRACKLE
PLEASE REST AT EASE.
パチ
CRACKLE

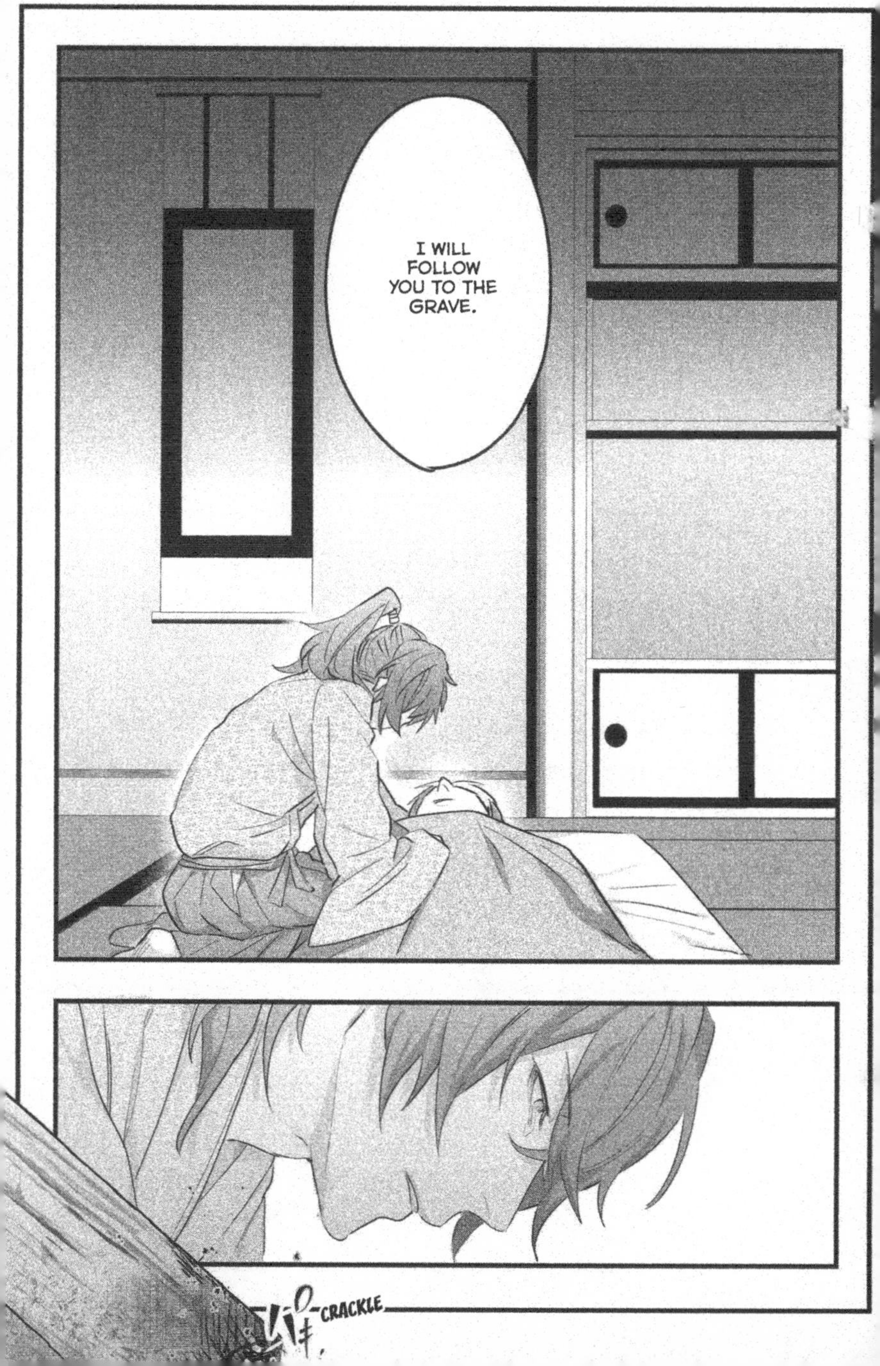
I WILL FOLLOW YOU TO THE GRAVE.
CRACKLE

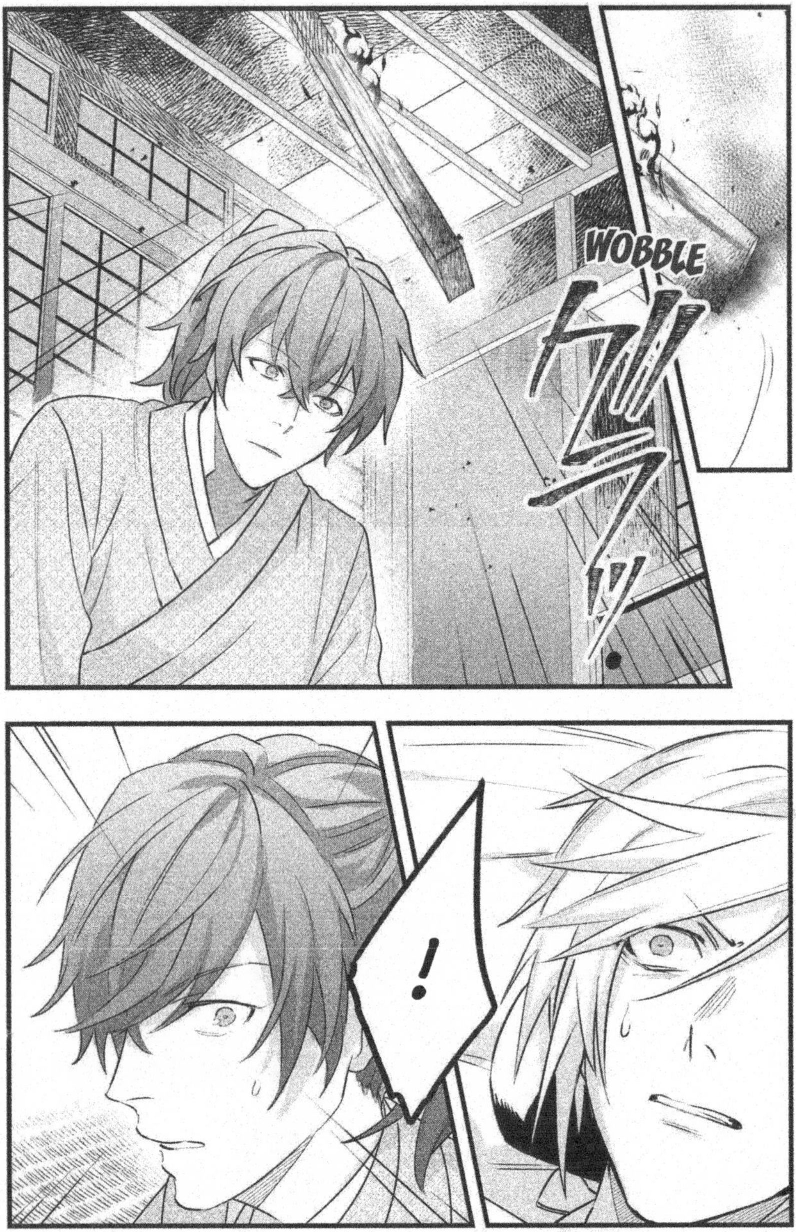
WOBBLE
グラッ
!

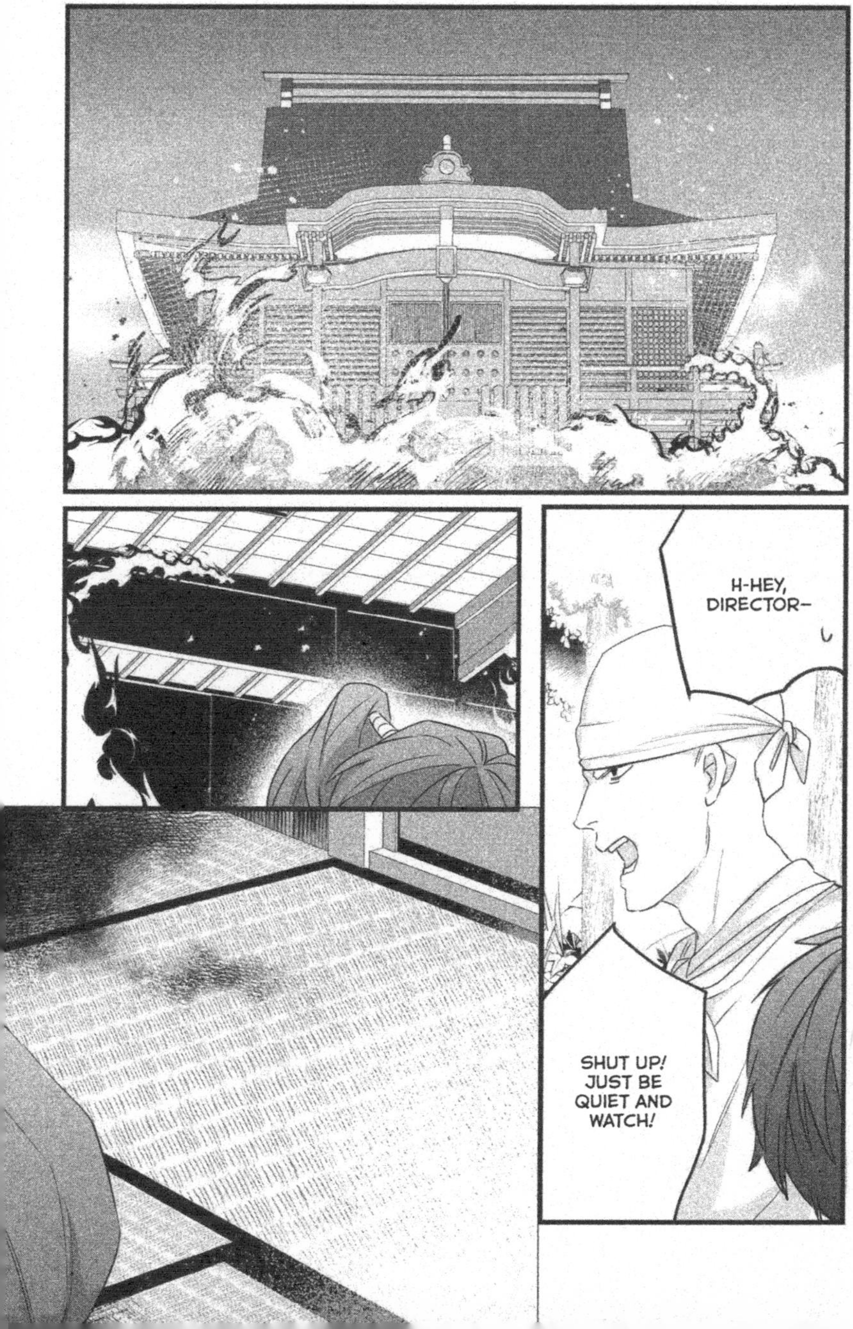
H-HEY, DIRECTOR-
SHUT UP! JUST BE QUIET AND WATCH!

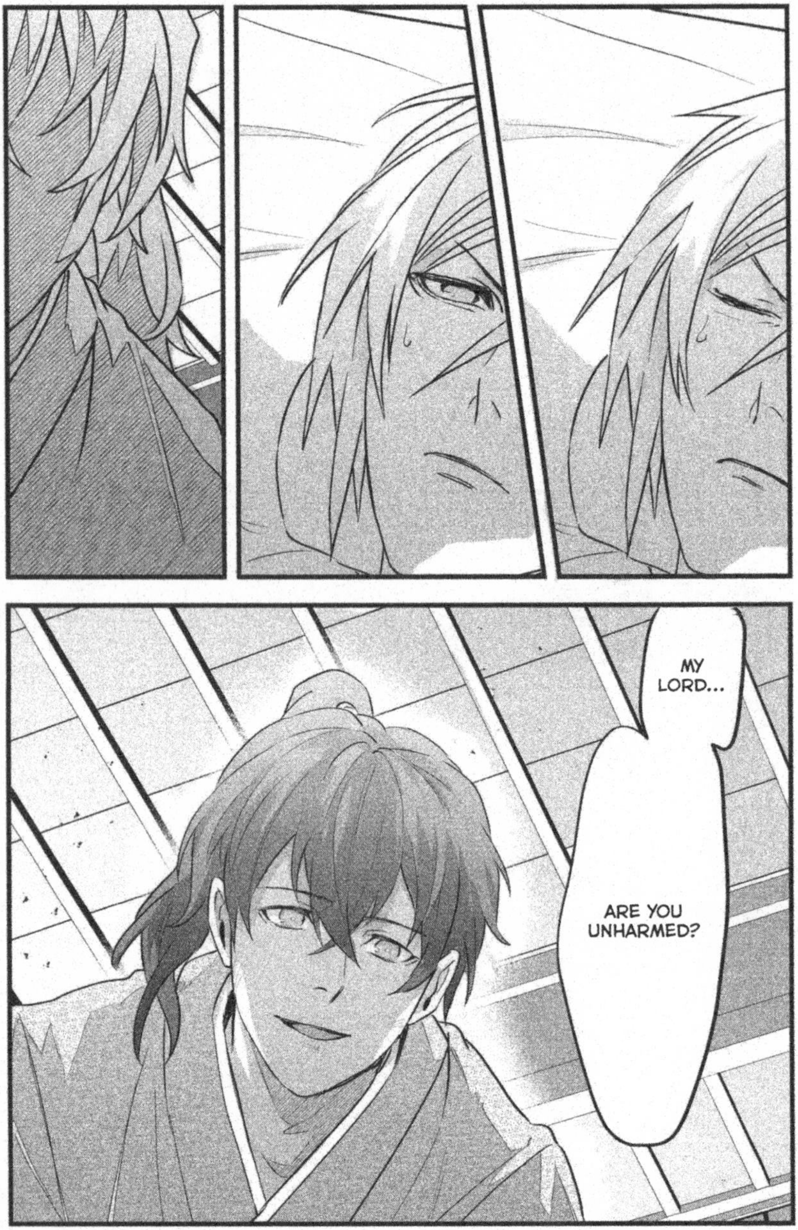
MY LORD...
ARE YOU UNHARMED?

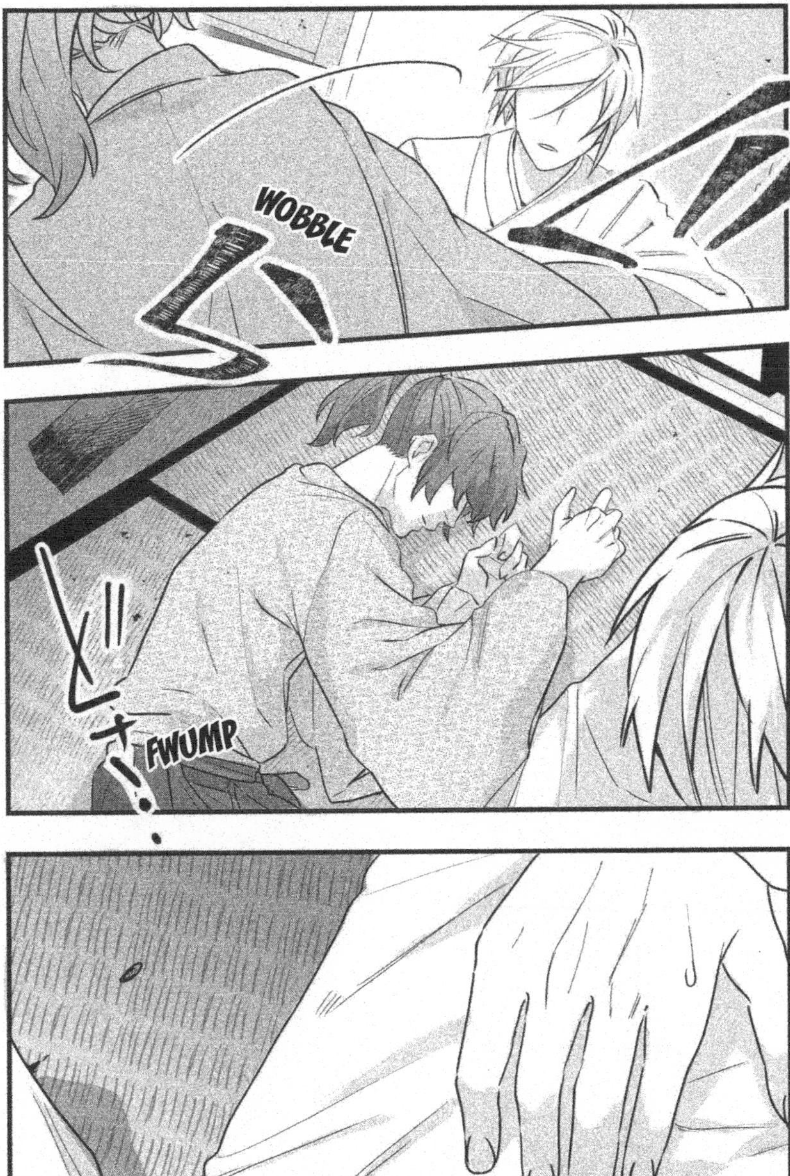
WOBBLE
FWUMP

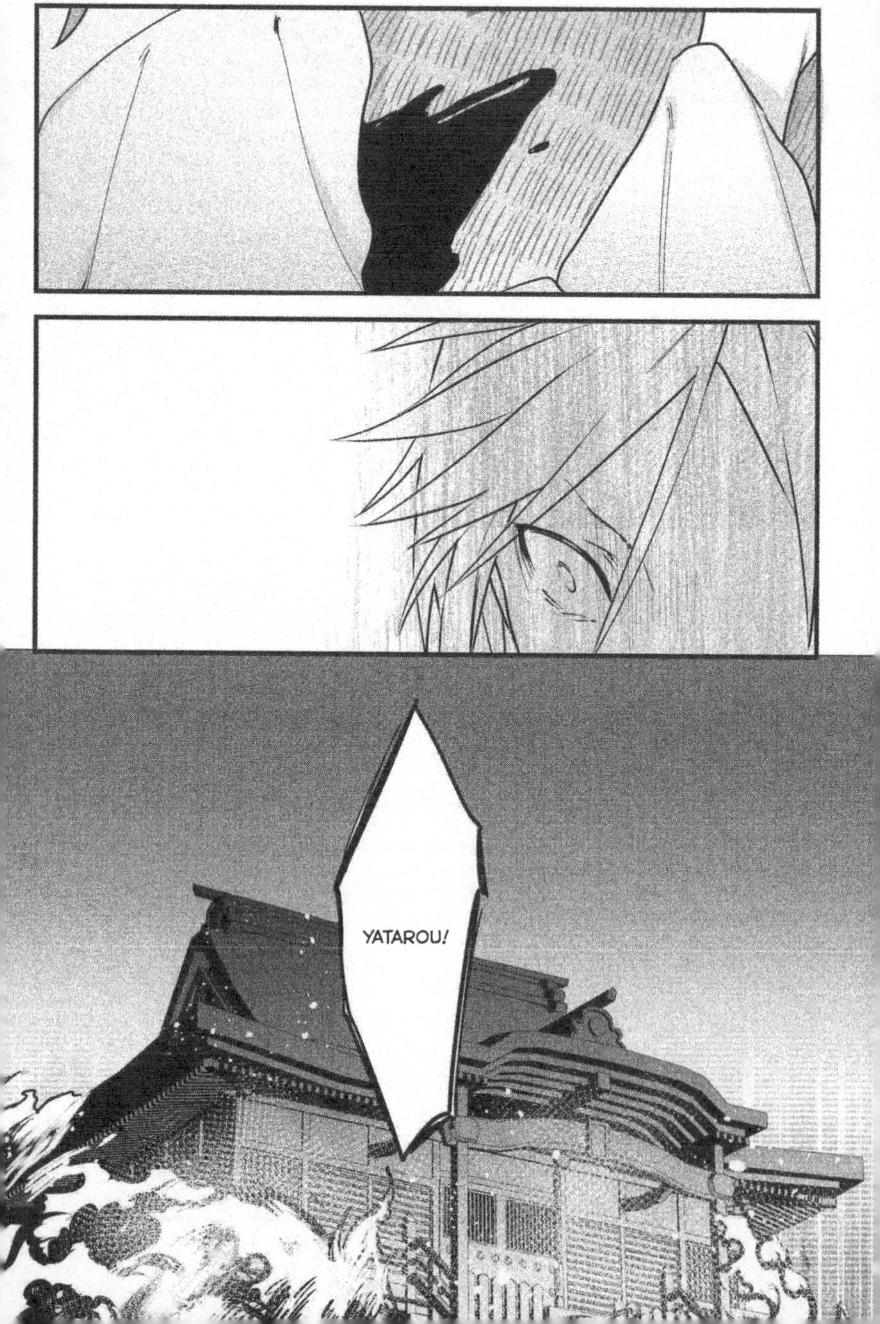
YATAROU!

Chapter 28

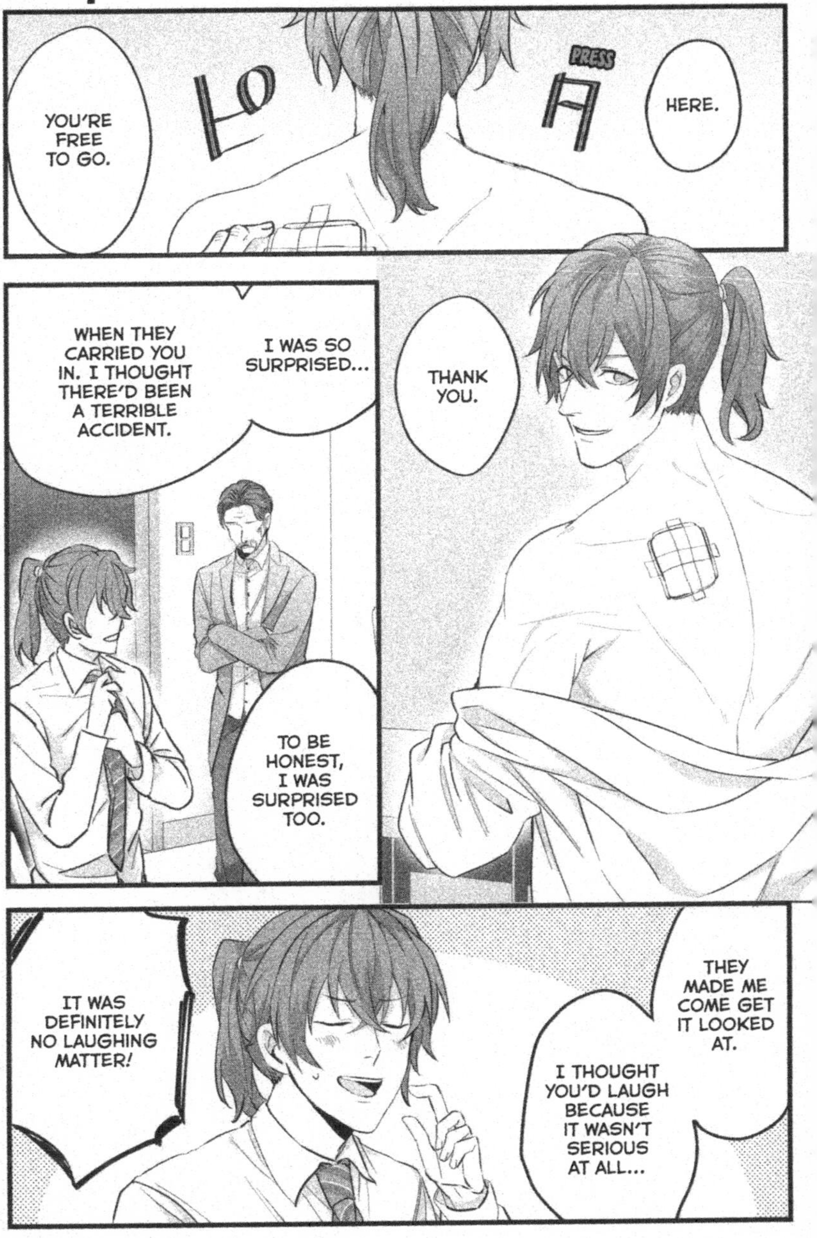
PRESS
HERE.
YOU'RE FREE TO GO.
THANK YOU.
I WAS SO SURPRISED...
WHEN THEY CARRIED YOU IN. I THOUGHT THERE'D BEEN A TERRIBLE ACCIDENT.
TO BE HONEST, I WAS SURPRISED TOO.
THEY MADE ME COME GET IT LOOKED AT.
I THOUGHT YOU'D LAUGH BECAUSE IT WASN'T SERIOUS AT ALL...
IT WAS DEFINITELY NO LAUGHING MATTER!

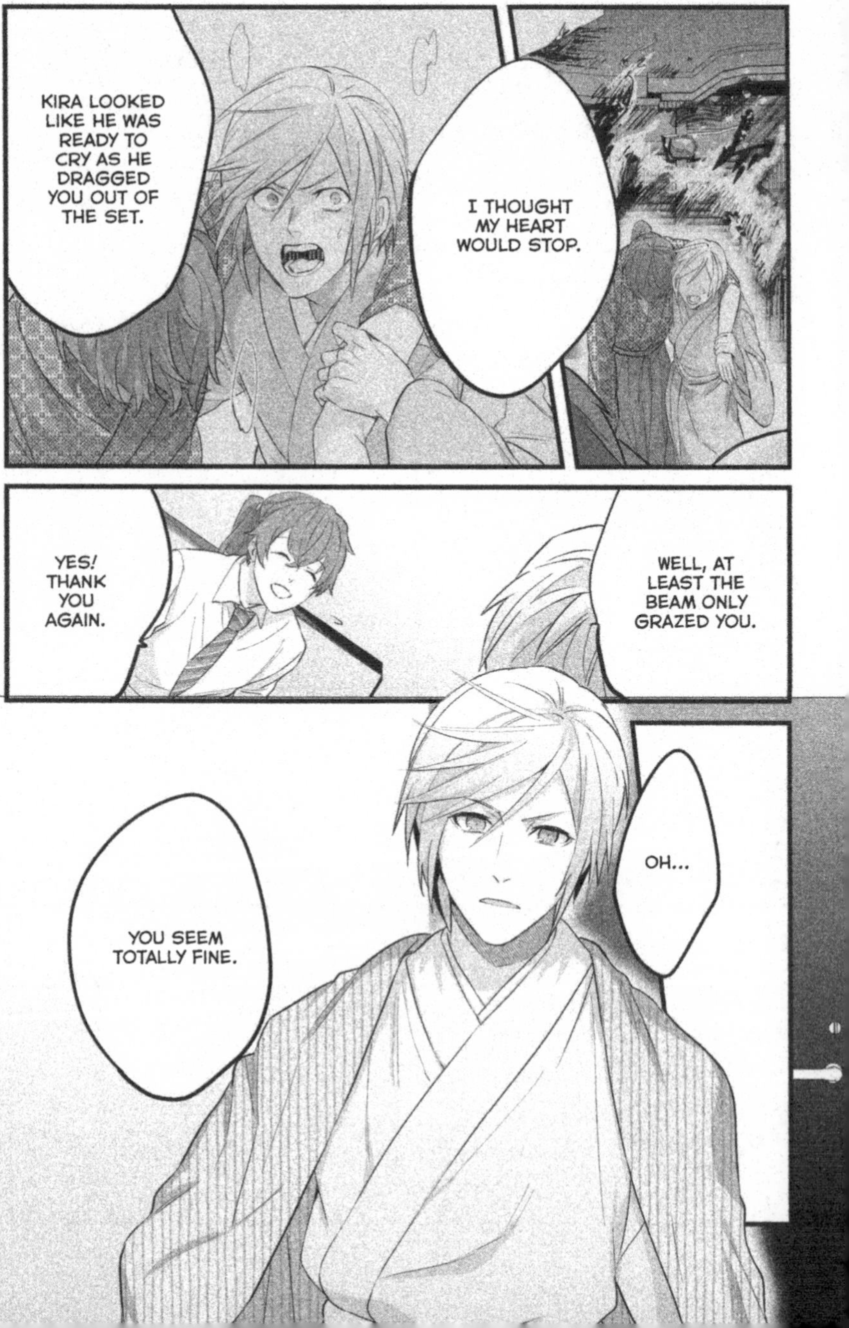
I THOUGHT MY HEART WOULD STOP.
KIRA LOOKED LIKE HE WAS READY TO CRY AS HE DRAGGED YOU OUT OF THE SET.
WELL, AT LEAST THE BEAM ONLY GRAZED YOU.
YES! THANK YOU AGAIN.
OH...
YOU SEEM TOTALLY FINE.

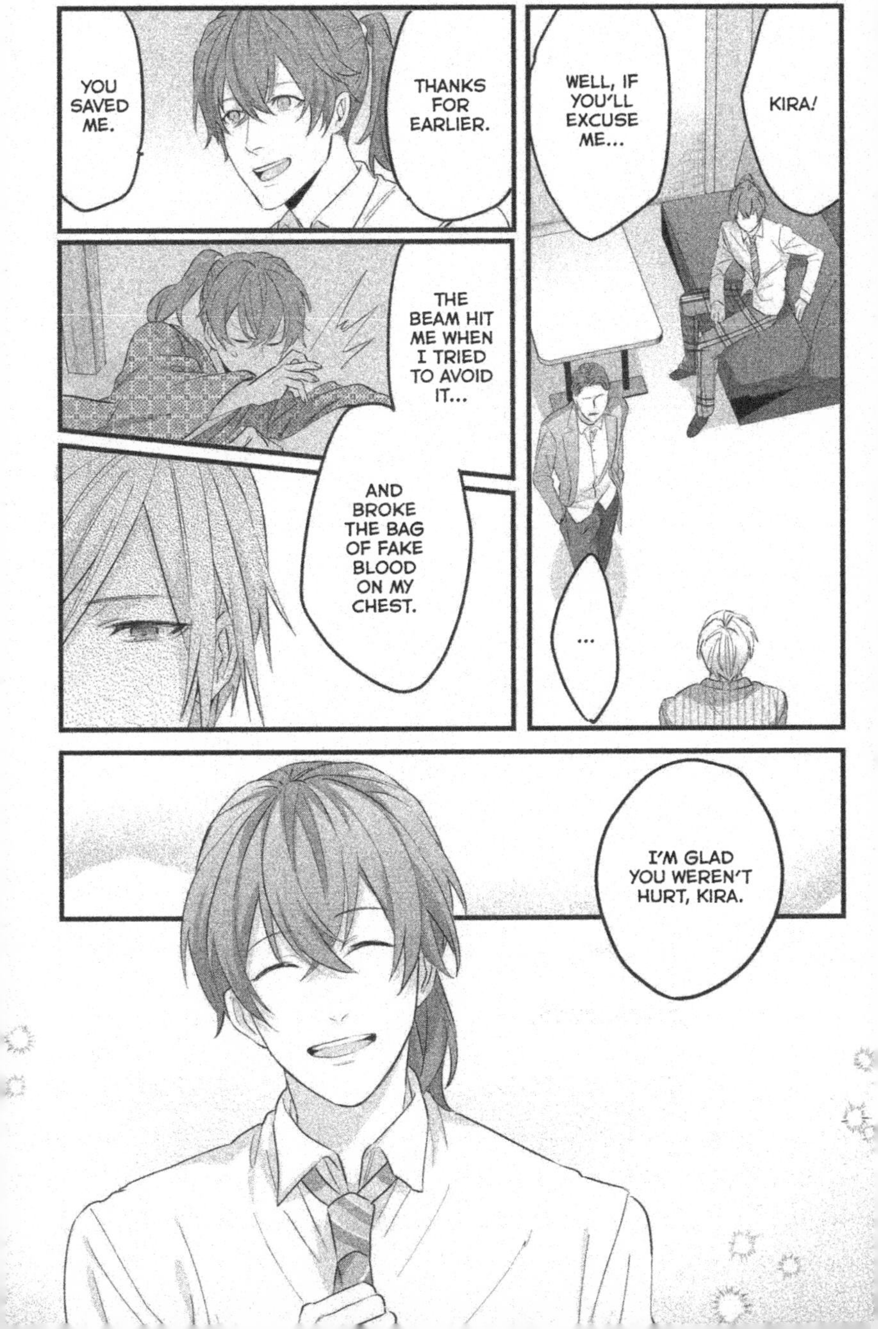
KIRA!
WELL, IF YOU'LL EXCUSE ME...
...
THANKS FOR EARLIER.
YOU SAVED ME.
THE BEAM HIT ME WHEN I TRIED TO AVOID IT...
AND BROKE THE BAG OF FAKE BLOOD ON MY CHEST.
I'M GLAD YOU WEREN'T HURT, KIRA.

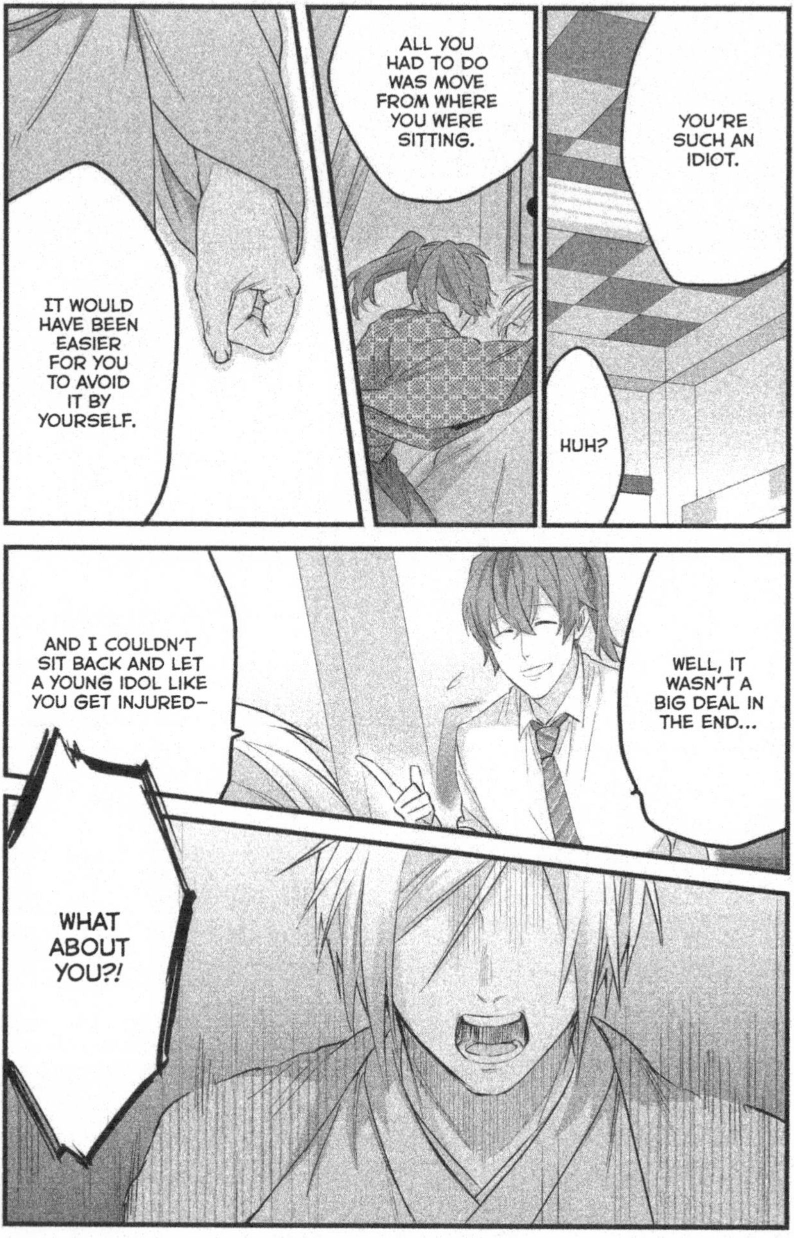
YOU'RE SUCH AN IDIOT.
HUH?
ALL YOU HAD TO DO WAS MOVE FROM WHERE YOU WERE SITTING.
IT WOULD HAVE BEEN EASIER FOR YOU TO AVOID IT BY YOURSELF.
WELL, IT WASN'T A BIG DEAL IN THE END...
AND I COULDN'T SIT BACK AND LET A YOUNG IDOL LIKE YOU GET INJURED–
WHAT ABOUT YOU?!

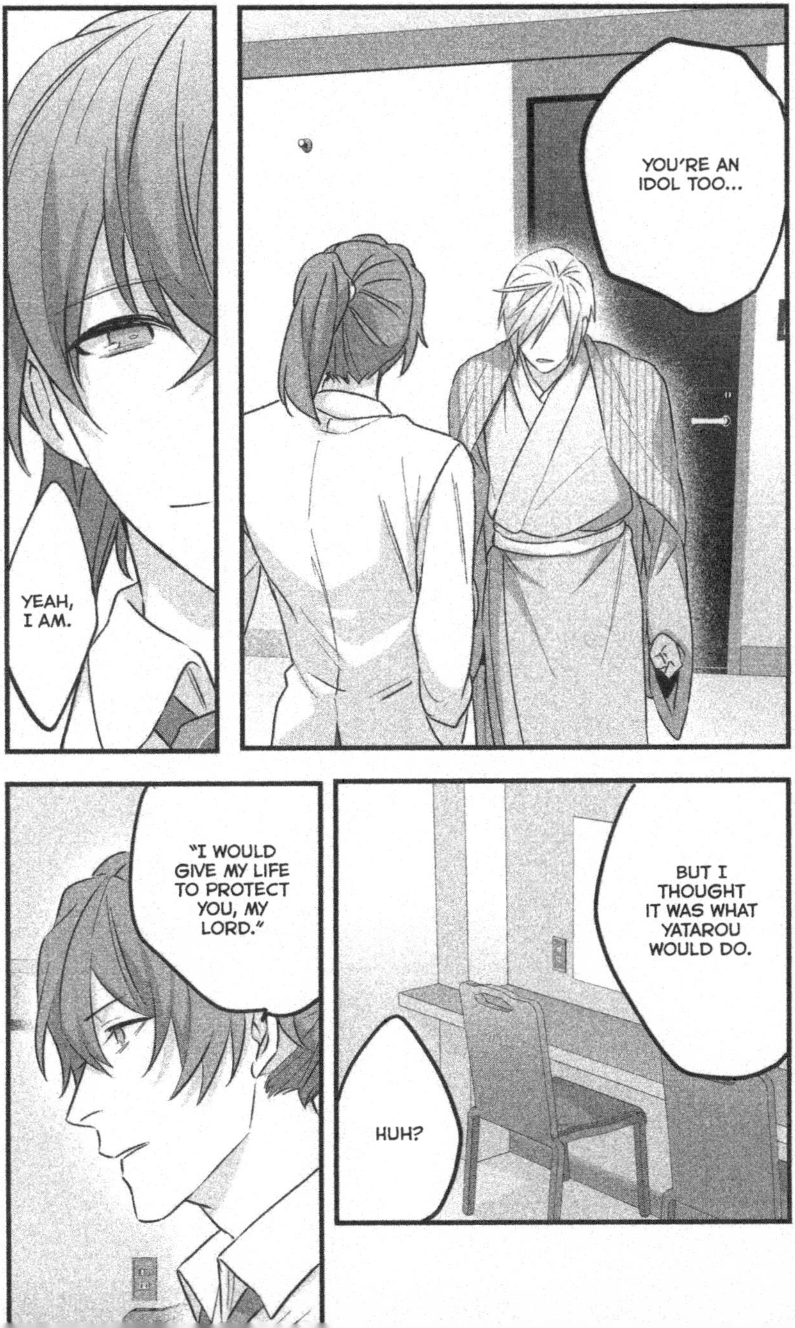
YOU'RE AN IDOL TOO...
YEAH, I AM.
BUT I THOUGHT IT WAS WHAT YATAROU WOULD DO.
HUH?
"I WOULD GIVE MY LIFE TO PROTECT YOU, MY LORD."

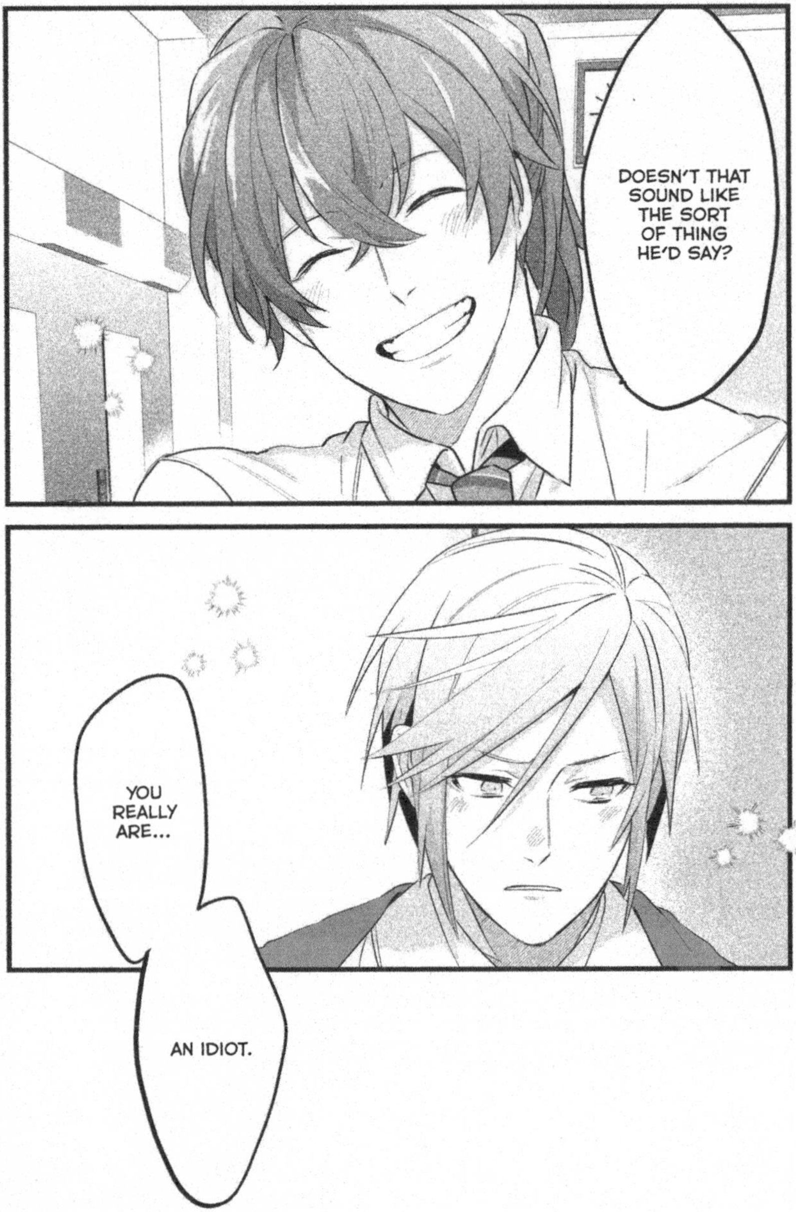
DOESN'T THAT SOUND LIKE THE SORT OF THING HE'D SAY?
YOU REALLY ARE...
AN IDIOT.

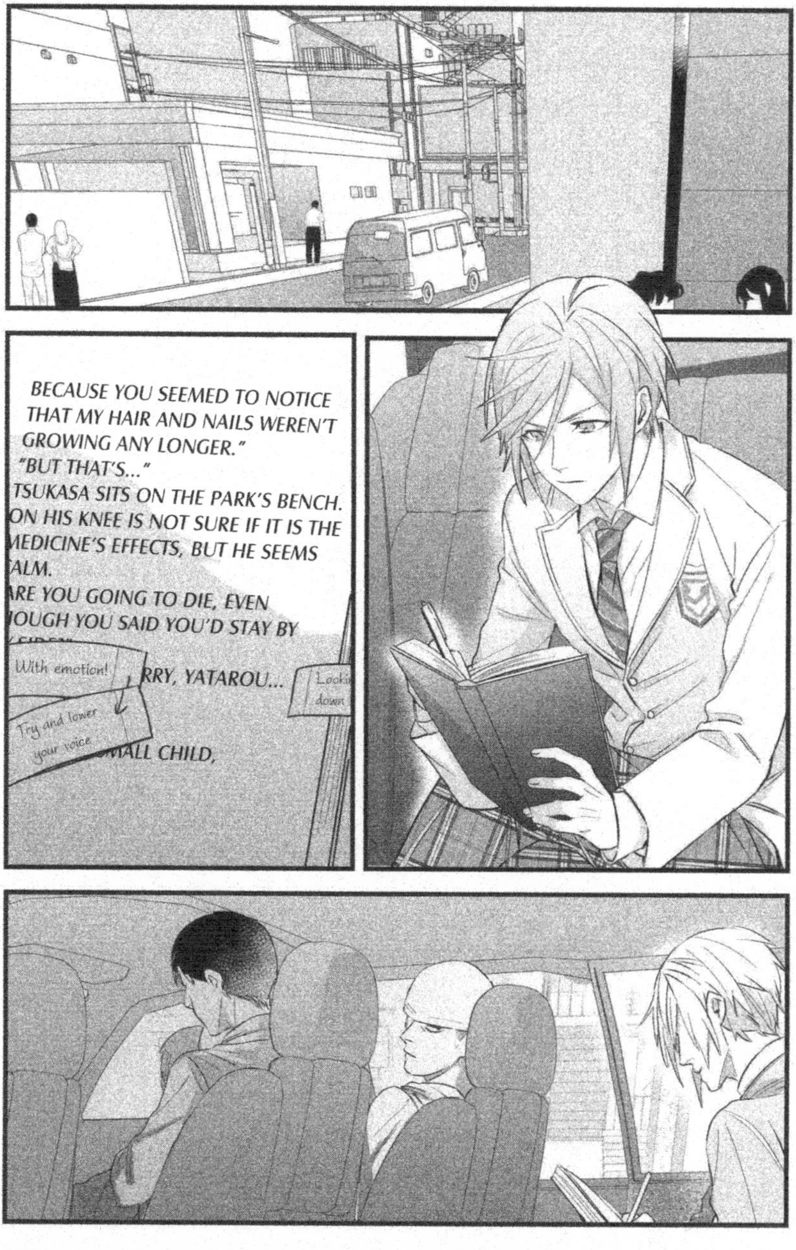
BECAUSE YOU SEEMED TO NOTICE
THAT MY HAIR AND NAILS WEREN'T
GROWING ANY LONGER."
"BUT THAT'S..."
TSUKASA SITS ON THE PARK'S BENCH.
ON HIS KNEE IS NOT SURE IF IT IS THE
MEDICINE'S EFFECTS, BUT HE SEEMS
ALM.
ARE YOU GOING TO DIE, EVEN
OUGH YOU SAID YOU'D STAY BY
With emotion!
RRY, YATAROU...
Try and lower your voice
MALL CHILD,
Looki down

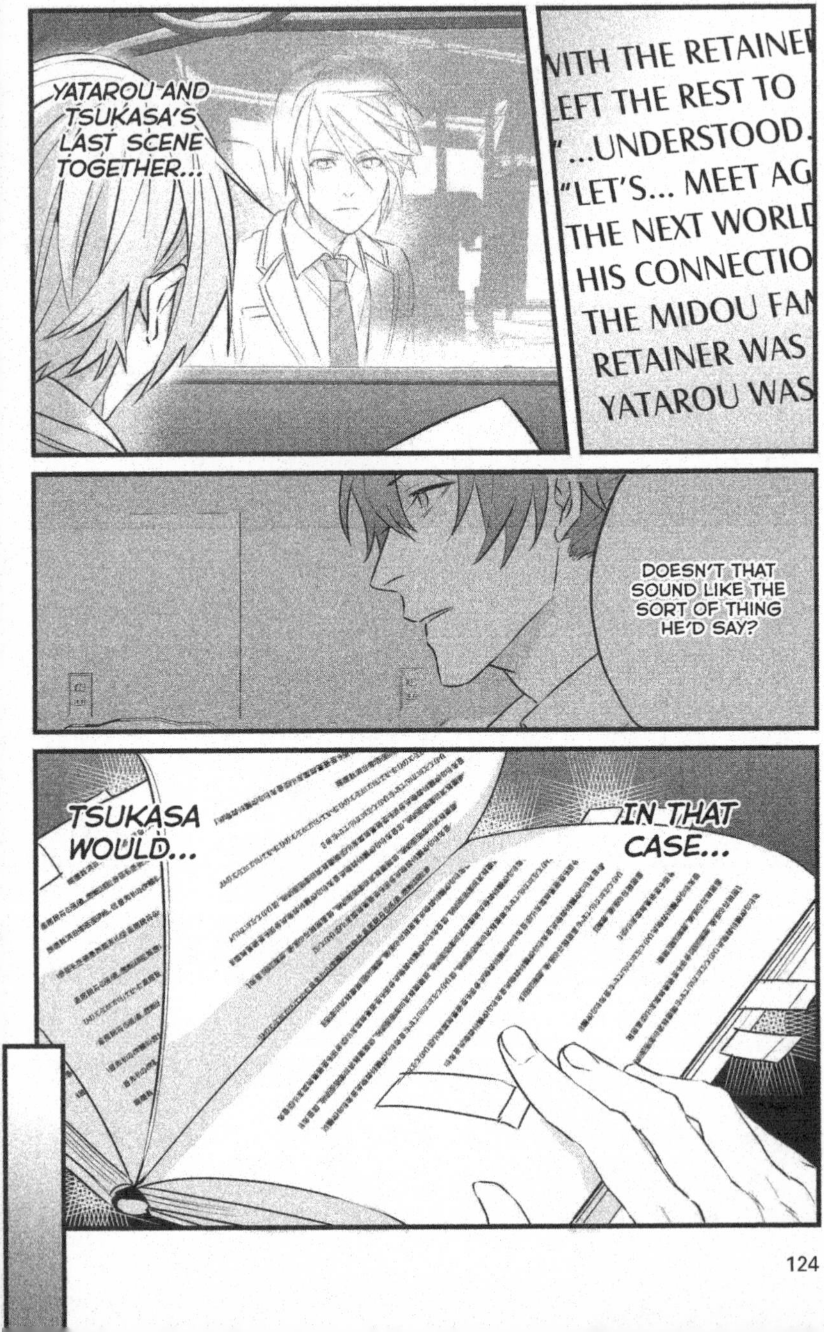
ITH THE RETAINE
EFT THE REST TO
"...UNDERSTOOD.
"LET'S... MEET AG
THE NEXT WORL
HIS CONNECTIO
THE MIDOU FA
RETAINER WAS
YATAROU WAS
YATAROU AND TSUKASA'S LAST SCENE TOGETHER...
DOESN'T THAT SOUND LIKE THE SORT OF THING HE'D SAY?
IN THAT CASE...
TSUKASA WOULD...

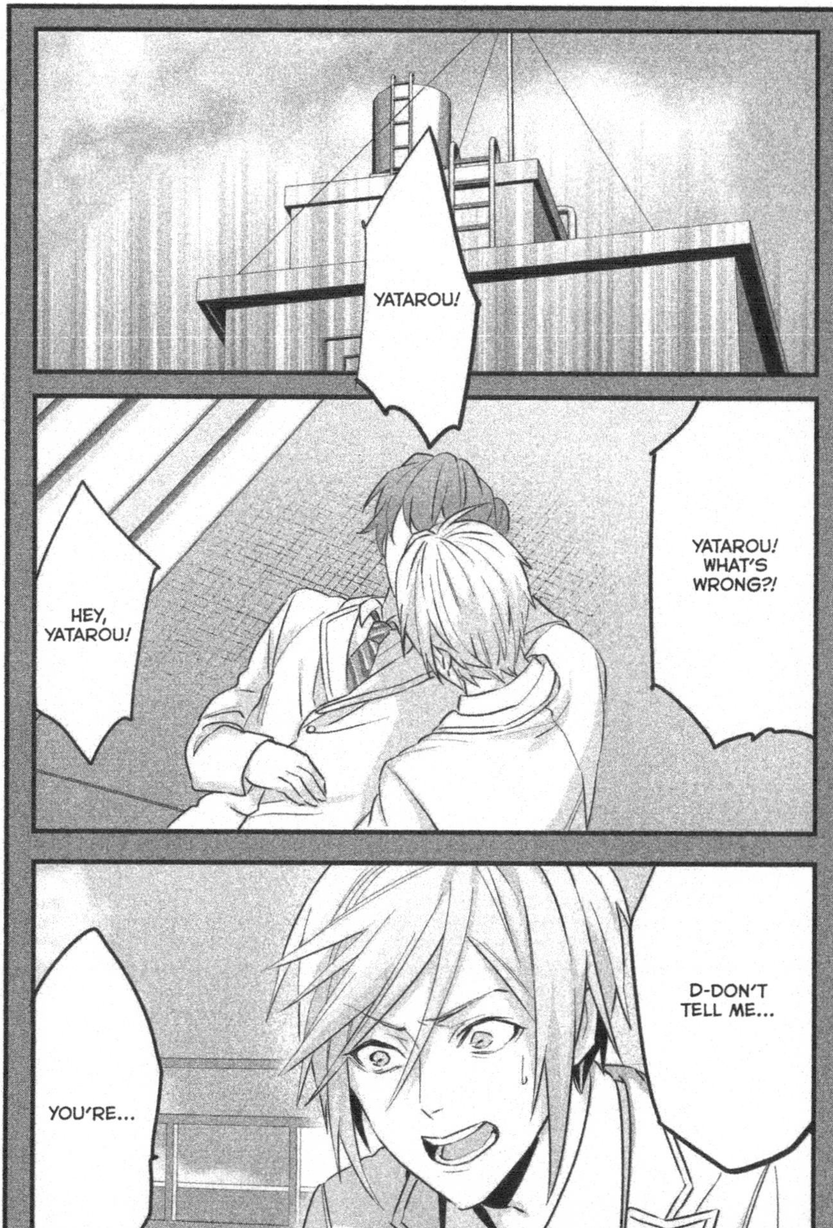
YATAROU!
YATAROU! WHAT'S WRONG?!
HEY, YATAROU!
D-DON'T TELL ME...
YOU'RE...

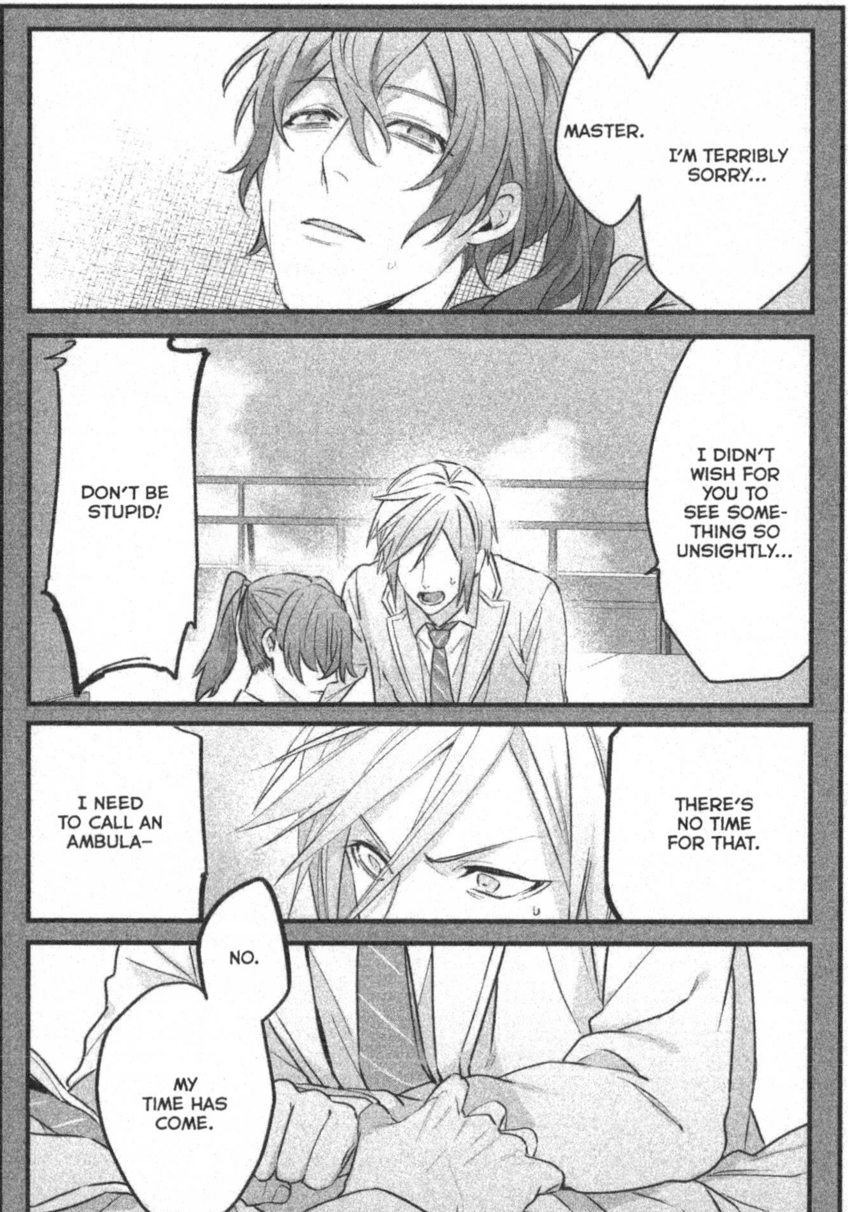
MASTER.
I'M TERRIBLY SORRY...
I DIDN'T WISH FOR YOU TO SEE SOMETHING SO UNSIGHTLY...
DON'T BE STUPID!
THERE'S NO TIME FOR THAT.
I NEED TO CALL AN AMBULA–
NO.
MY TIME HAS COME.

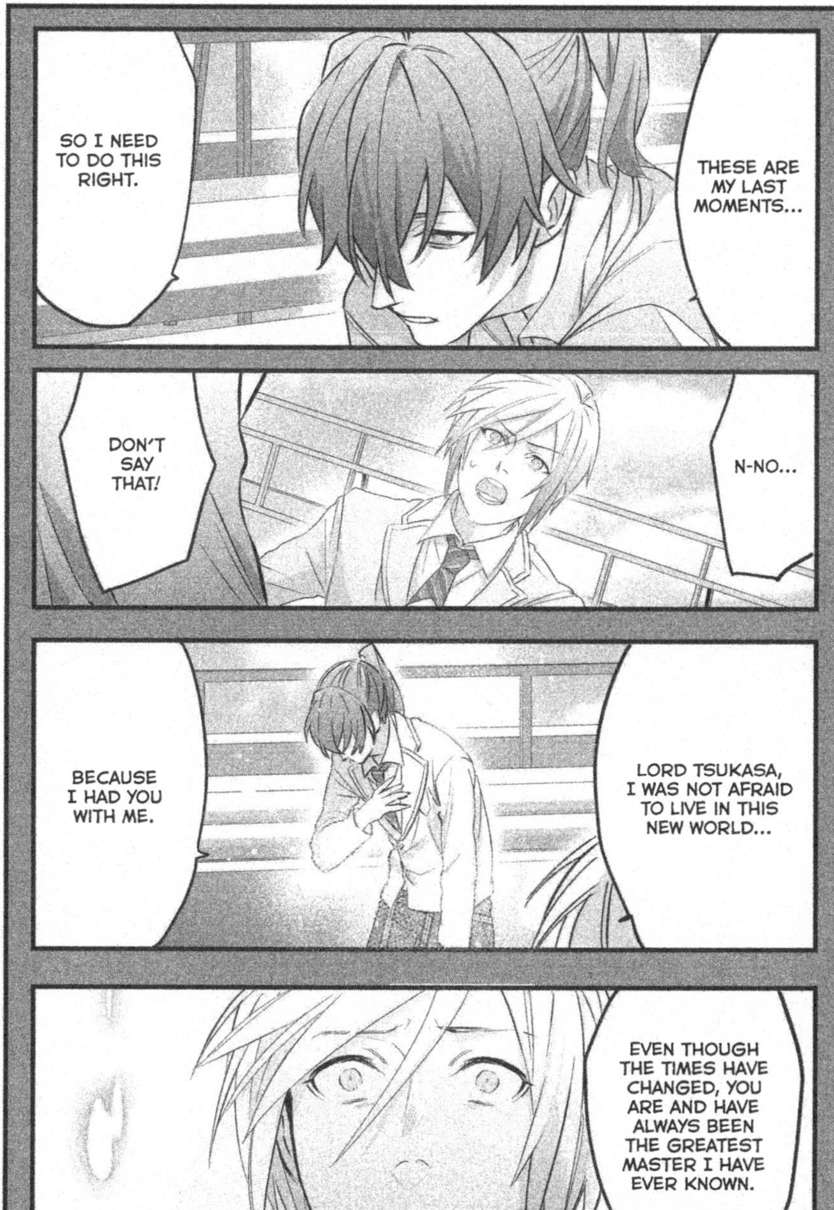
THESE ARE MY LAST MOMENTS...
SO I NEED TO DO THIS RIGHT.
N-NO...
DON'T SAY THAT!
LORD TSUKASA, I WAS NOT AFRAID TO LIVE IN THIS NEW WORLD...
BECAUSE I HAD YOU WITH ME.
EVEN THOUGH THE TIMES HAVE CHANGED, YOU ARE AND HAVE ALWAYS BEEN THE GREATEST MASTER I HAVE EVER KNOWN.

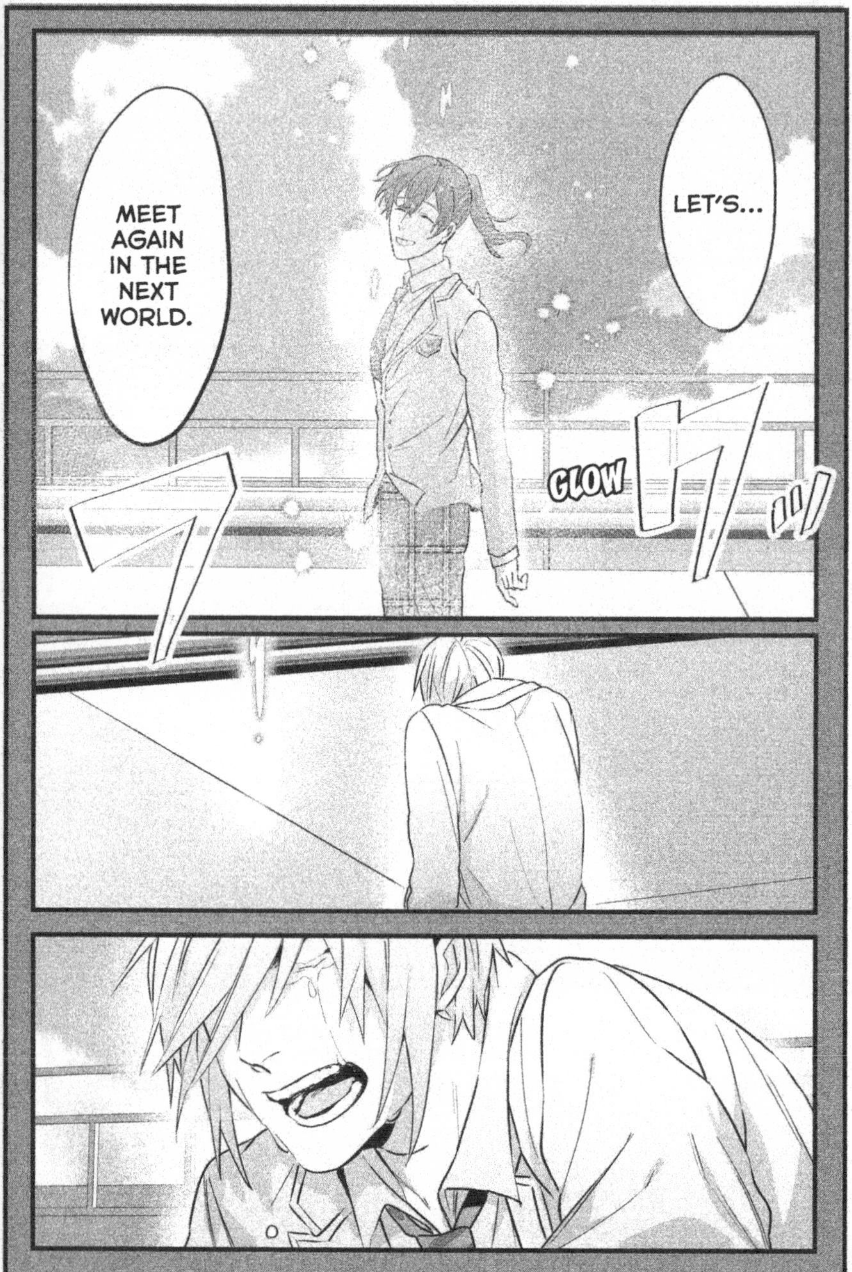
LET'S...
MEET AGAIN IN THE NEXT WORLD.
GLOW

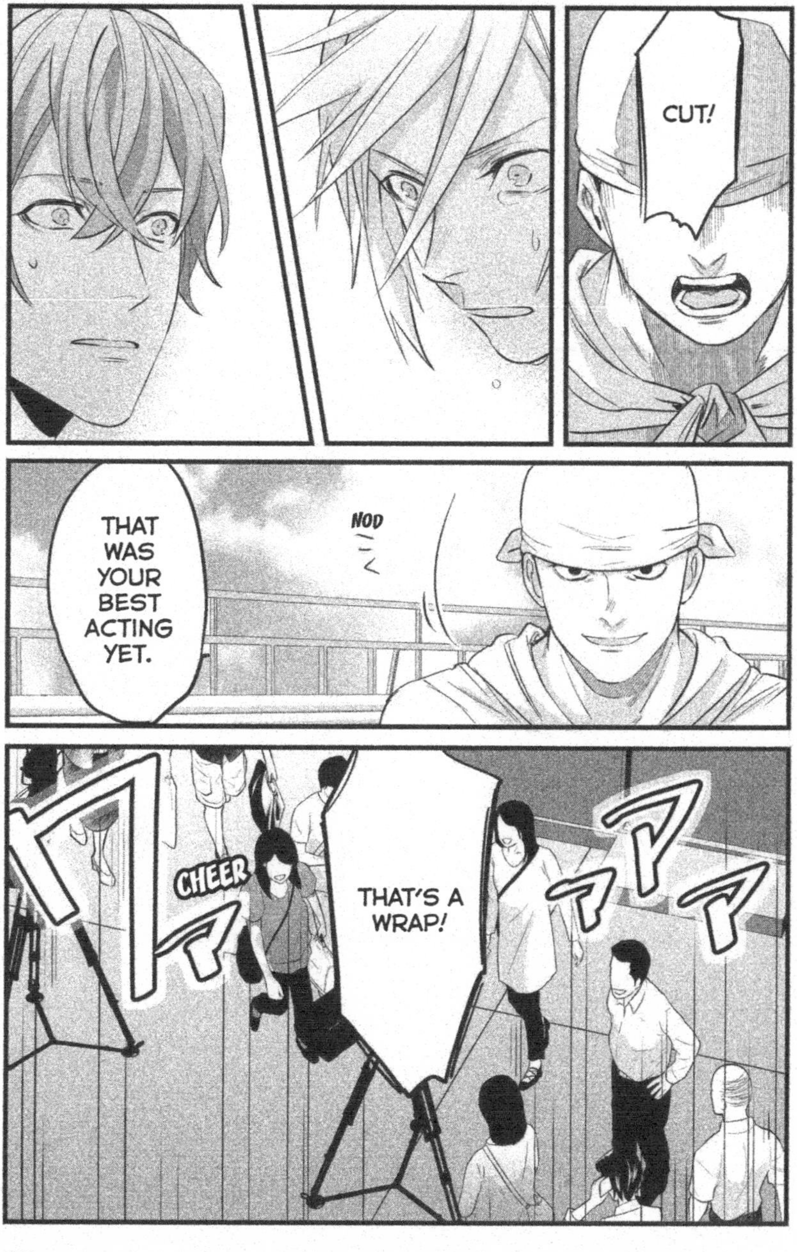
CUT!
NOD
THAT WAS YOUR BEST ACTING YET.
THAT'S A WRAP!
CHEER

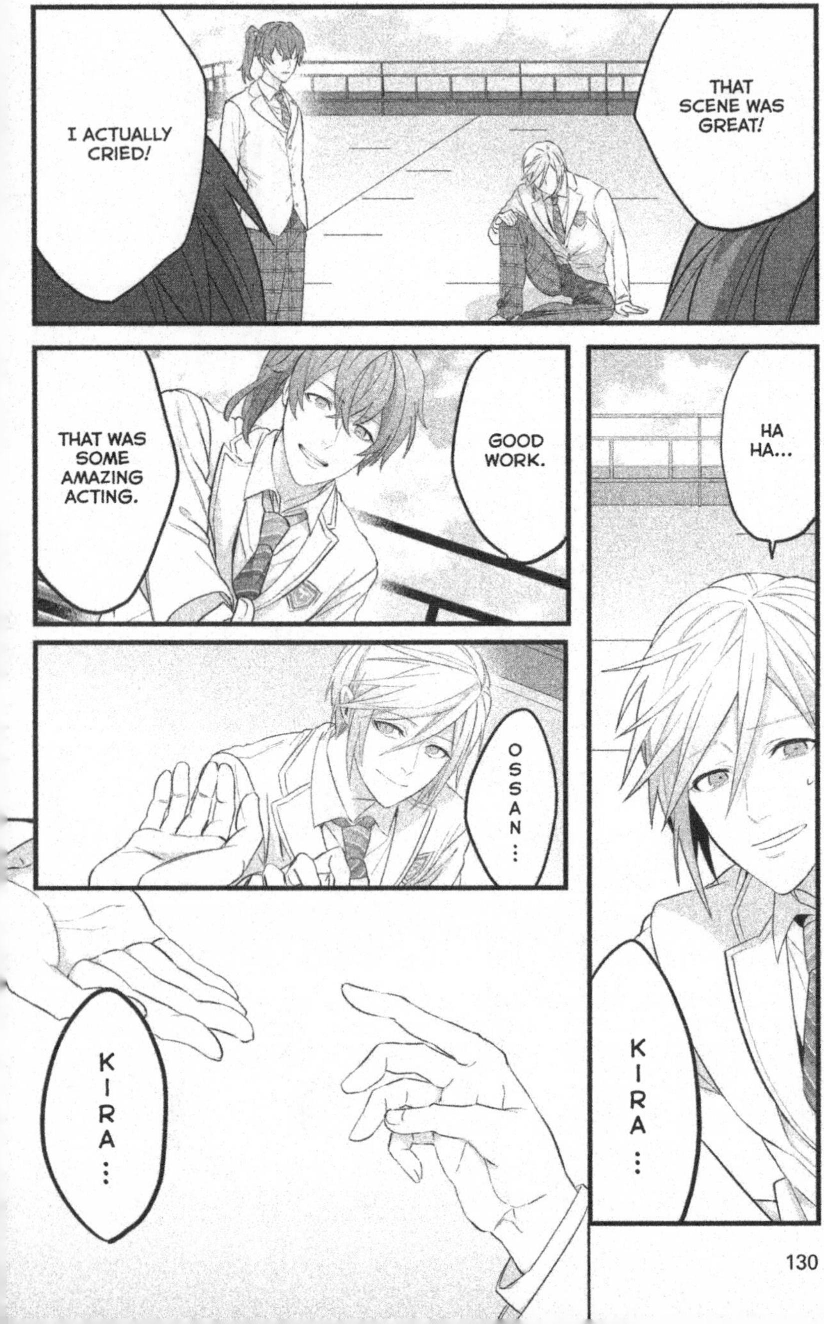
THAT SCENE WAS GREAT!
I ACTUALLY CRIED!
HA HA...
KIRA...
GOOD WORK.
THAT WAS SOME AMAZING ACTING.
OSSAN...
KIRA...

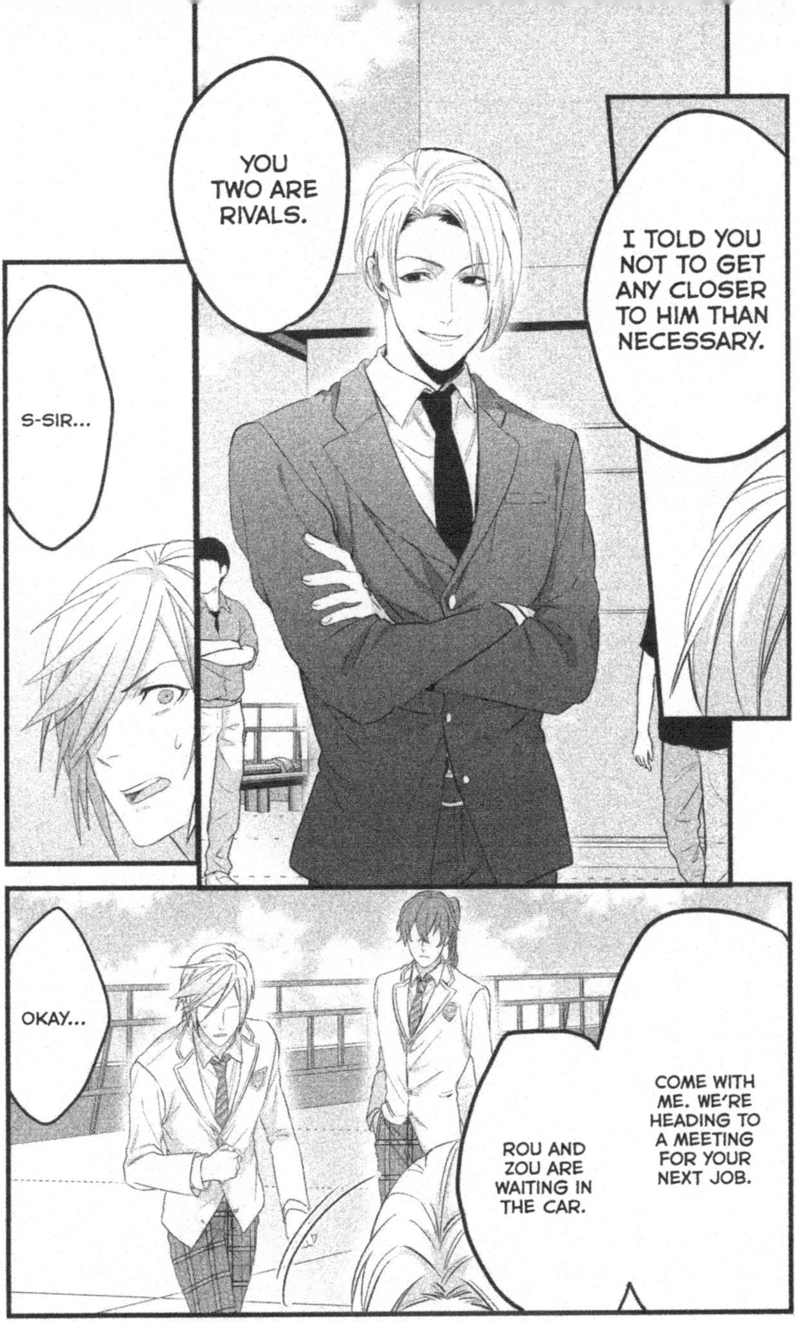
I TOLD YOU NOT TO GET ANY CLOSER TO HIM THAN NECESSARY.
YOU TWO ARE RIVALS.
S-SIR...
COME WITH ME. WE'RE HEADING TO A MEETING FOR YOUR NEXT JOB.
ROU AND ZOU ARE WAITING IN THE CAR.
OKAY...

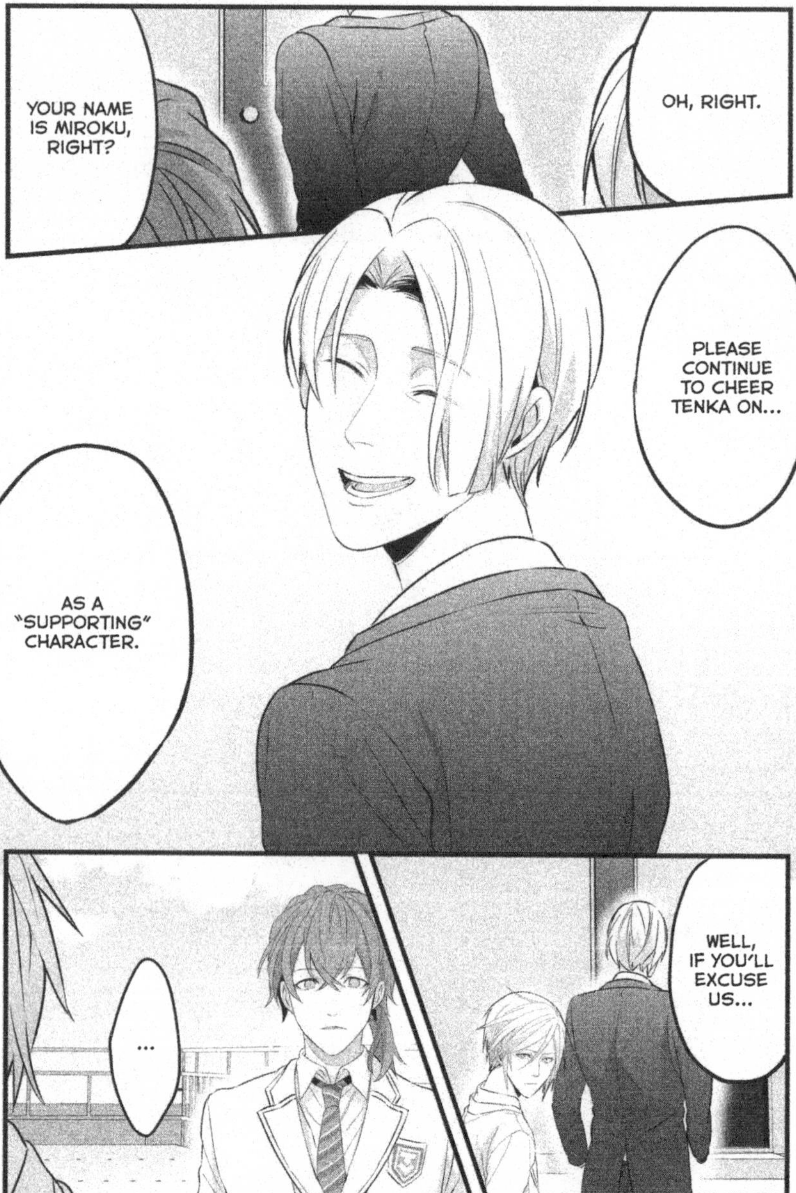
OH, RIGHT.
YOUR NAME IS MIROKU, RIGHT?
PLEASE CONTINUE TO CHEER TENKA ON...
AS A "SUPPORTING" CHARACTER.
WELL, IF YOU'LL EXCUSE US...
...

Chapter 29

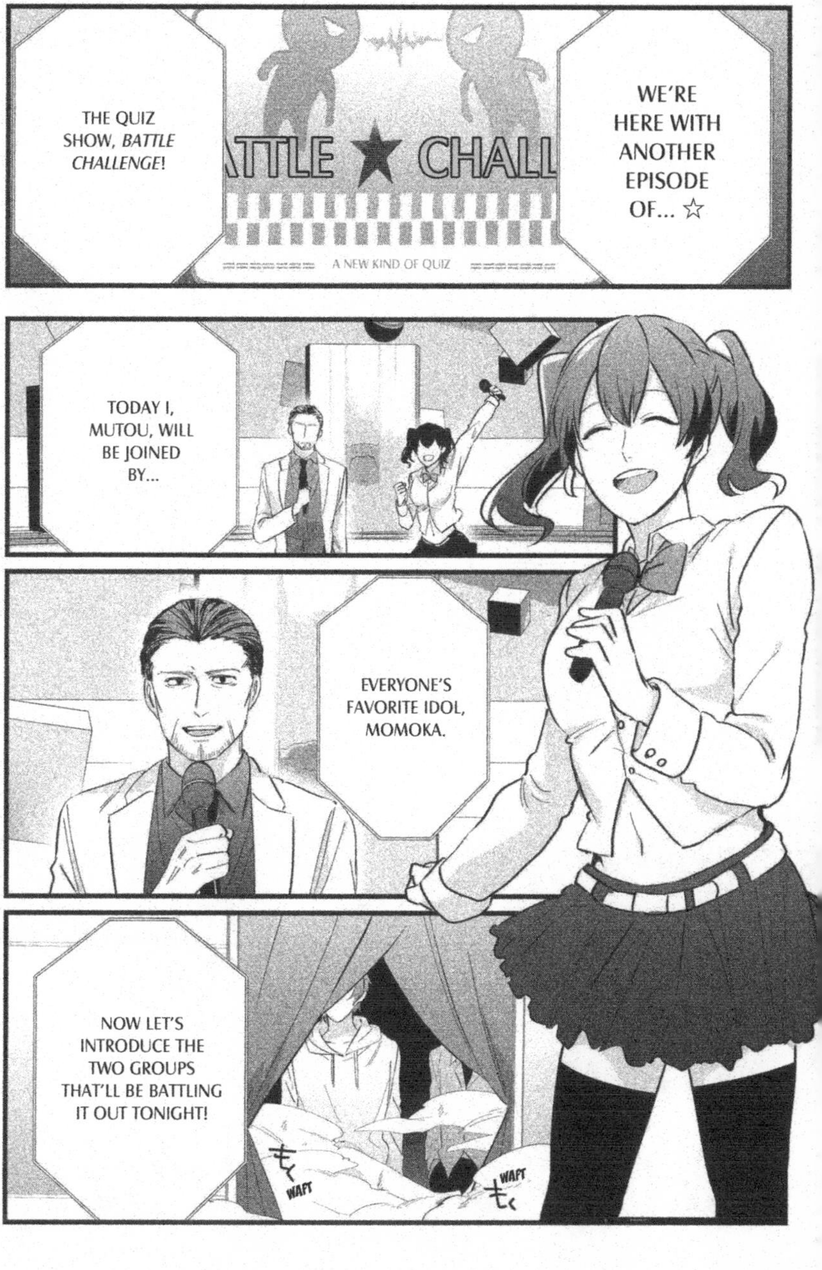
WE'RE HERE WITH ANOTHER EPISODE OF... ☆
THE QUIZ SHOW, *BATTLE CHALLENGE*!
A NEW KIND OF QUIZ
TODAY I, MUTOU, WILL BE JOINED BY...
EVERYONE'S FAVORITE IDOL, MOMOKA.
NOW LET'S INTRODUCE THE TWO GROUPS THAT'LL BE BATTLING IT OUT TONIGHT!
WAPT
WAPT

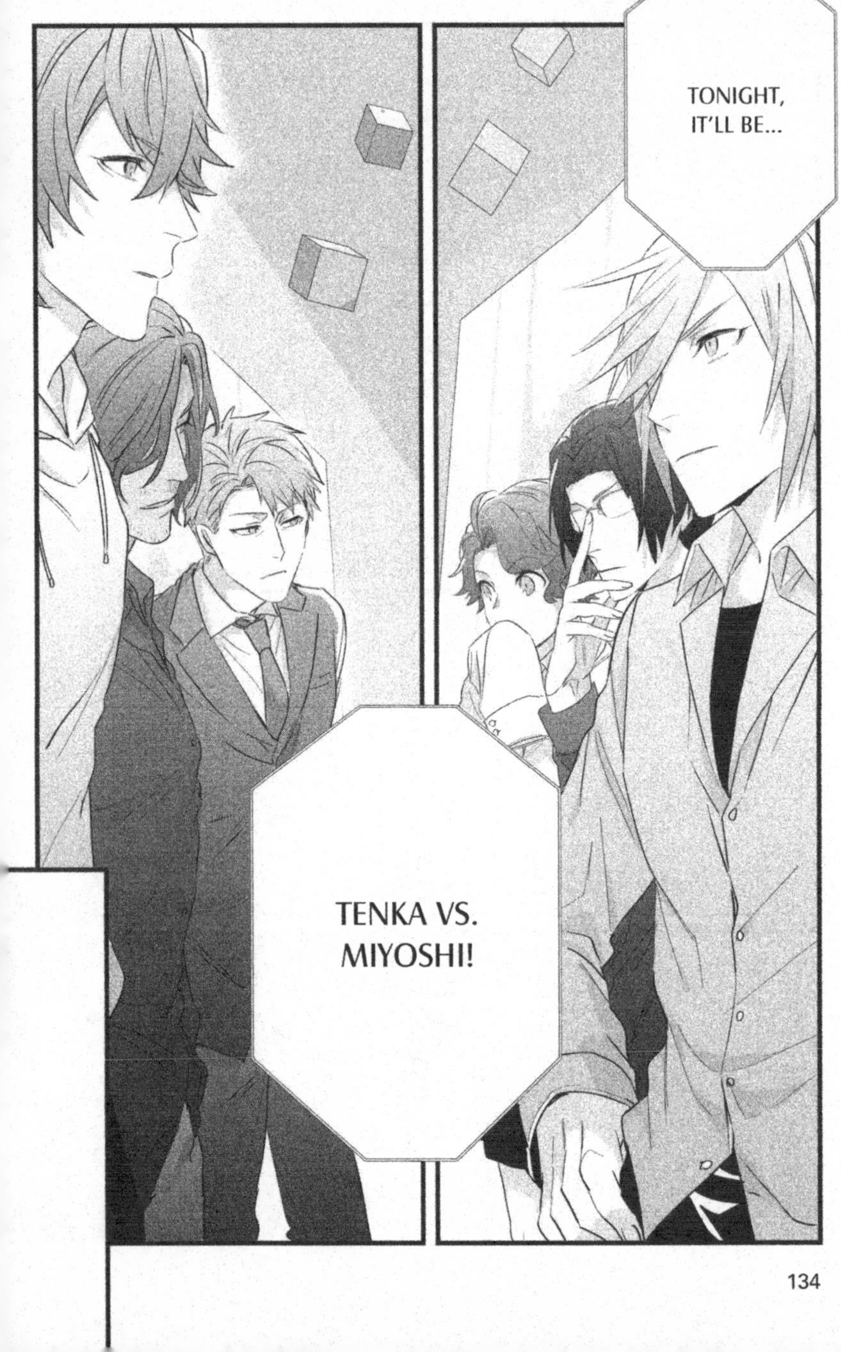
TONIGHT, IT'LL BE...
TENKA VS. MIYOSHI!

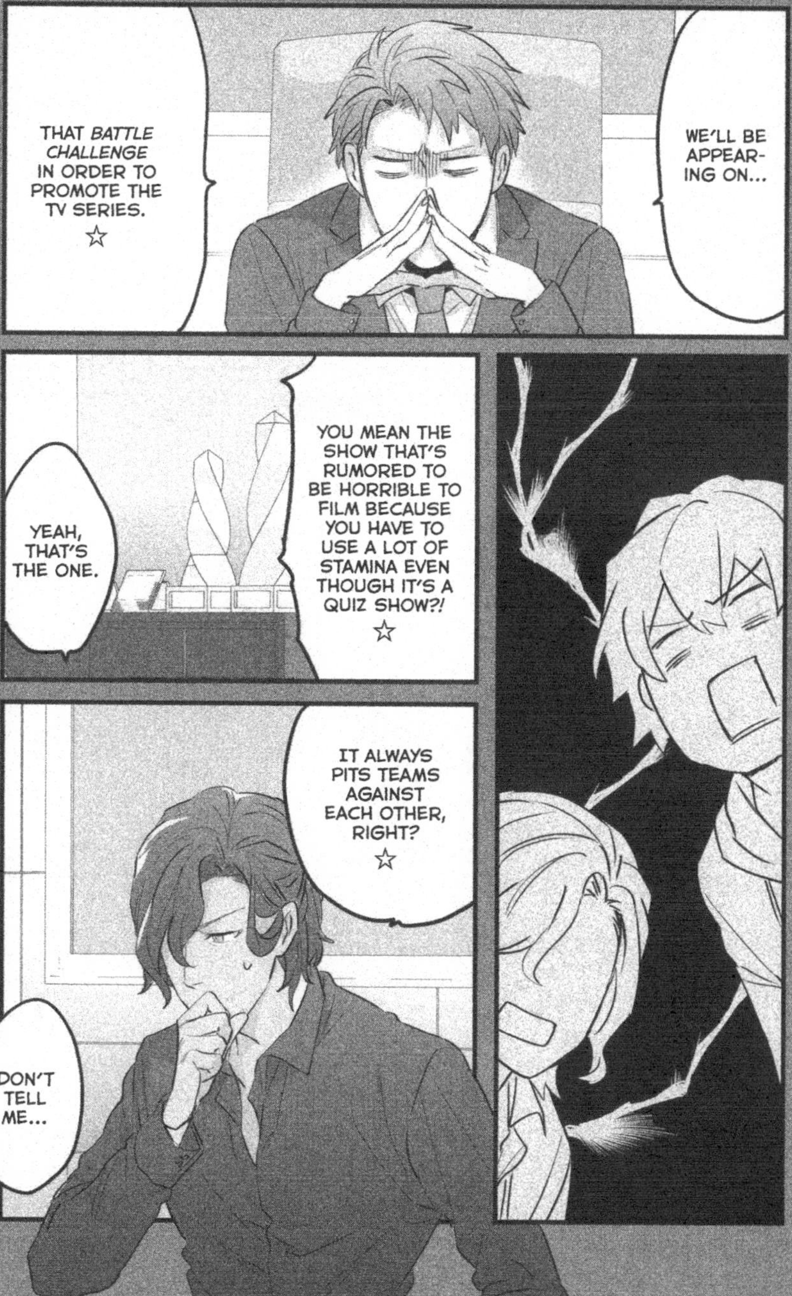
WE'LL BE APPEARING ON...
THAT *BATTLE CHALLENGE* IN ORDER TO PROMOTE THE TV SERIES. ☆
YOU MEAN THE SHOW THAT'S RUMORED TO BE HORRIBLE TO FILM BECAUSE YOU HAVE TO USE A LOT OF STAMINA EVEN THOUGH IT'S A QUIZ SHOW?! ☆
YEAH, THAT'S THE ONE.
IT ALWAYS PITS TEAMS AGAINST EACH OTHER, RIGHT? ☆
DON'T TELL ME...

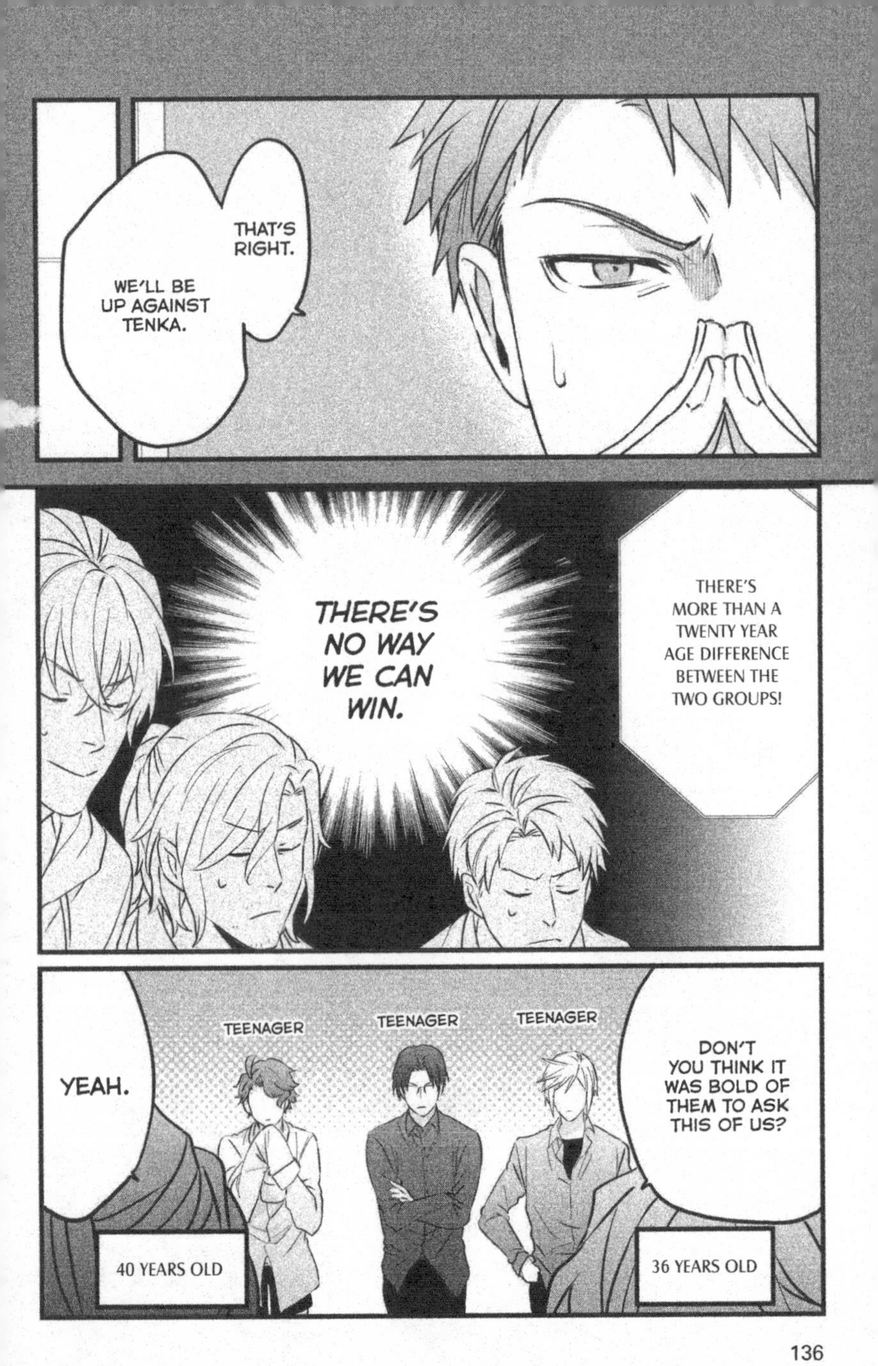
THAT'S RIGHT.
WE'LL BE UP AGAINST TENKA.
THERE'S MORE THAN A TWENTY YEAR AGE DIFFERENCE BETWEEN THE TWO GROUPS!
THERE'S NO WAY WE CAN WIN.
DON'T YOU THINK IT WAS BOLD OF THEM TO ASK THIS OF US?
TEENAGER
TEENAGER
TEENAGER
36 YEARS OLD
YEAH.
40 YEARS OLD

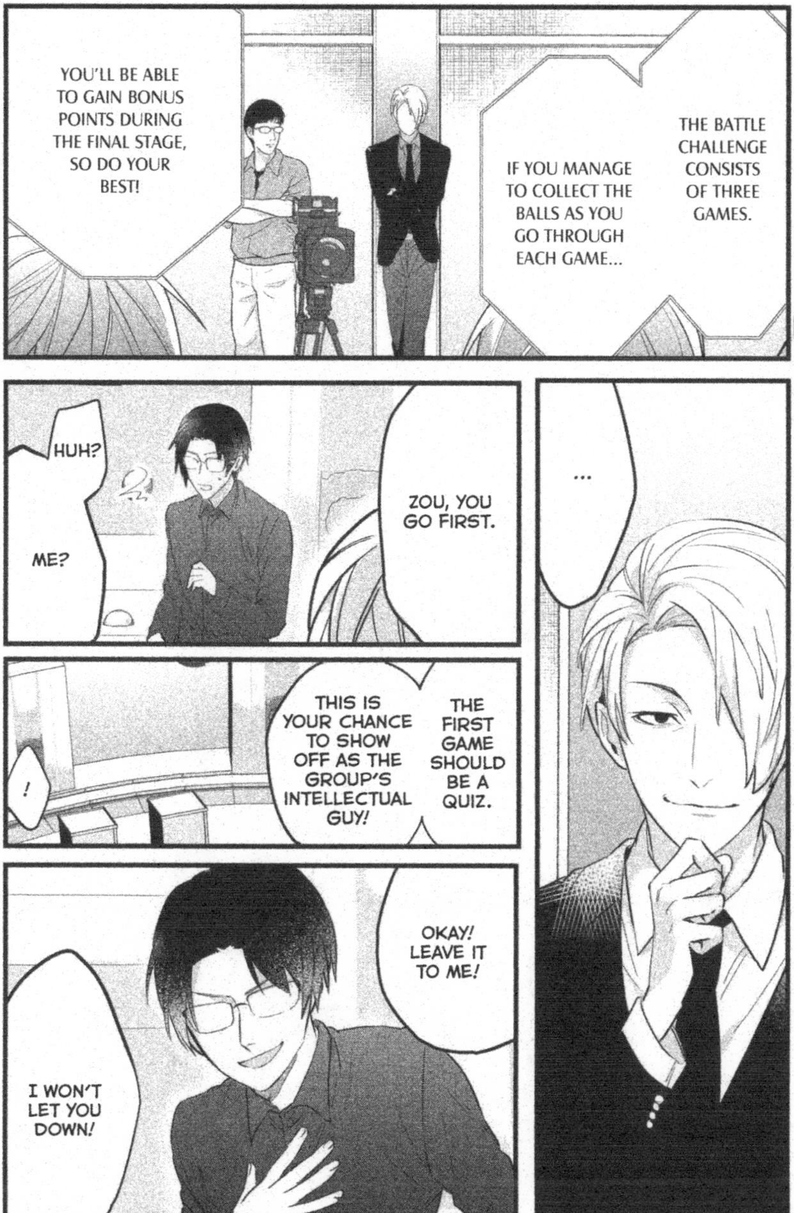
THE BATTLE CHALLENGE CONSISTS OF THREE GAMES.
IF YOU MANAGE TO COLLECT THE BALLS AS YOU GO THROUGH EACH GAME...
YOU'LL BE ABLE TO GAIN BONUS POINTS DURING THE FINAL STAGE, SO DO YOUR BEST!
...
ZOU, YOU GO FIRST.
HUH?
ME?
THE FIRST GAME SHOULD BE A QUIZ.
THIS IS YOUR CHANCE TO SHOW OFF AS THE GROUP'S INTELLECTUAL GUY!
!
OKAY! LEAVE IT TO ME!
I WON'T LET YOU DOWN!

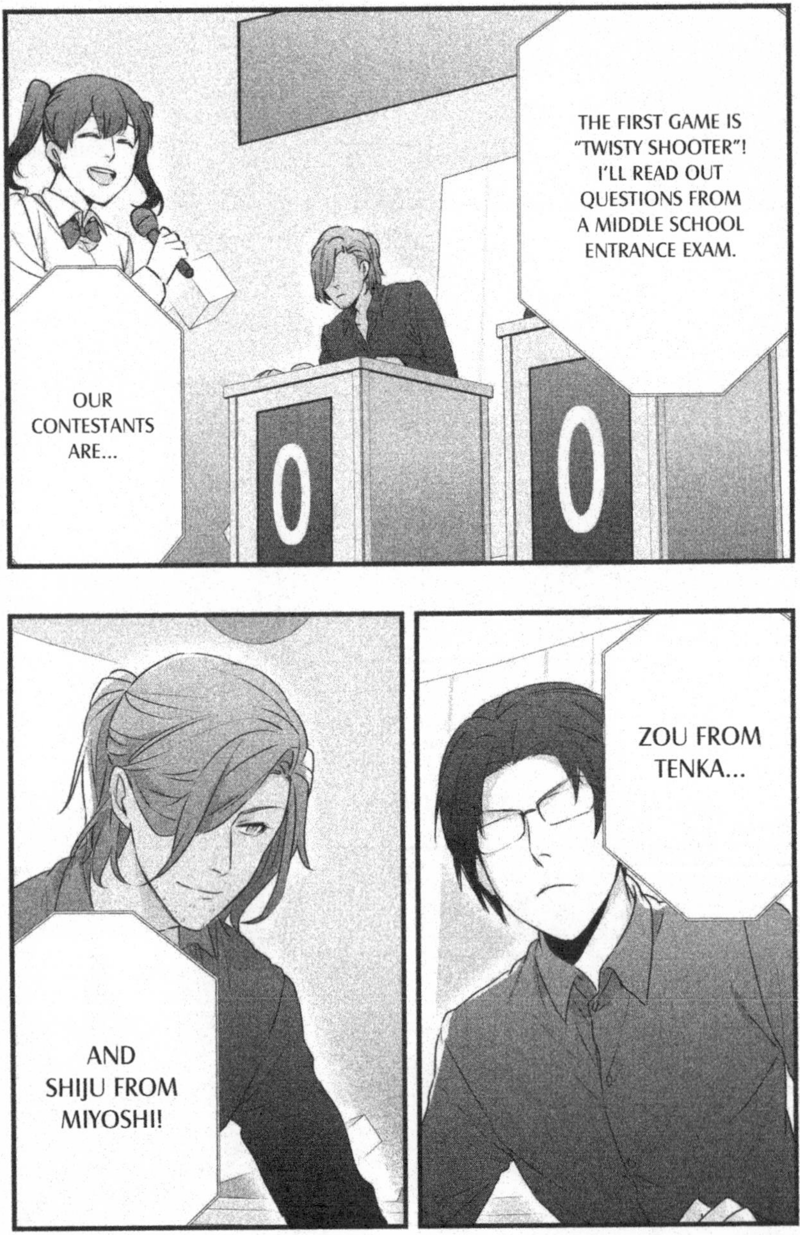
THE FIRST GAME IS "TWISTY SHOOTER"! I'LL READ OUT QUESTIONS FROM A MIDDLE SCHOOL ENTRANCE EXAM.
OUR CONTESTANTS ARE...
ZOU FROM TENKA...
AND SHIJU FROM MIYOSHI!

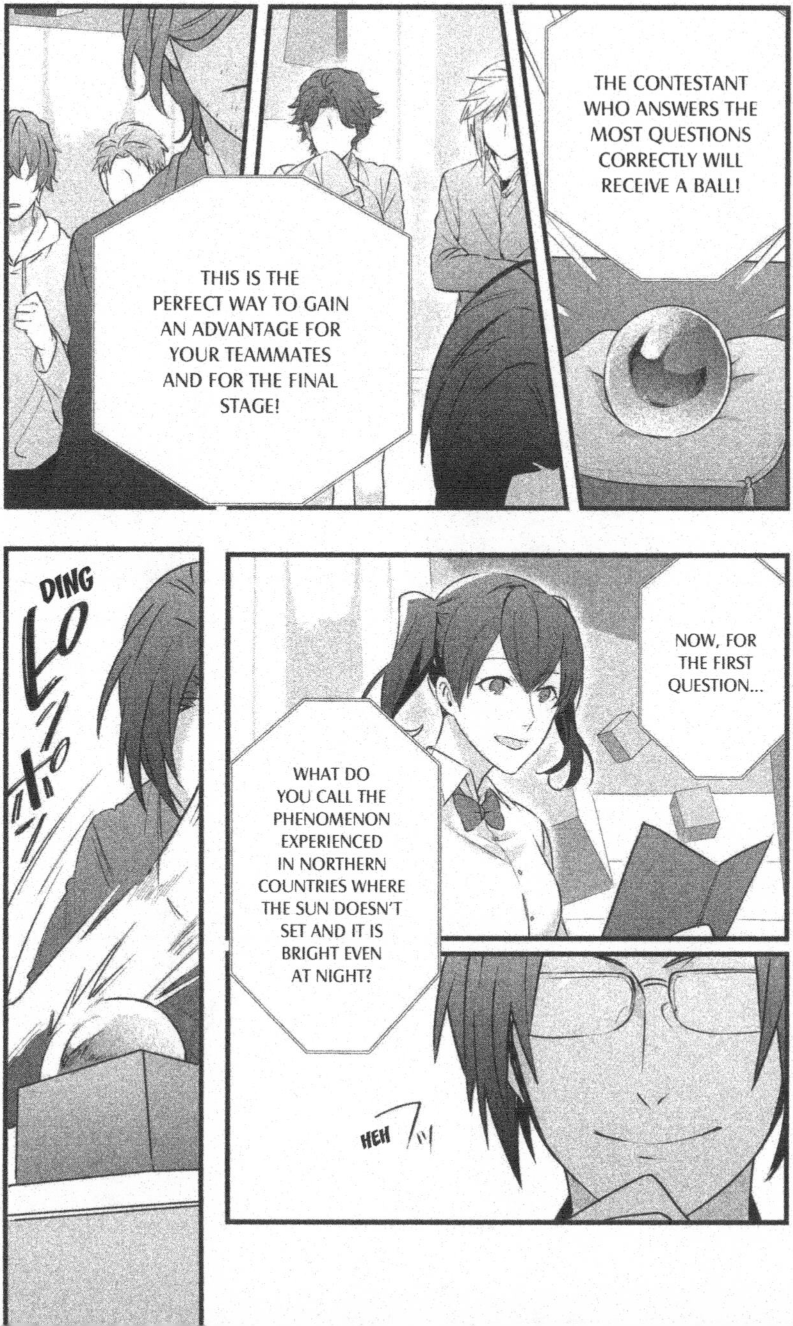
THE CONTESTANT WHO ANSWERS THE MOST QUESTIONS CORRECTLY WILL RECEIVE A BALL!
THIS IS THE PERFECT WAY TO GAIN AN ADVANTAGE FOR YOUR TEAMMATES AND FOR THE FINAL STAGE!
NOW, FOR THE FIRST QUESTION...
WHAT DO YOU CALL THE PHENOMENON EXPERIENCED IN NORTHERN COUNTRIES WHERE THE SUN DOESN'T SET AND IT IS BRIGHT EVEN AT NIGHT?
HEH
DING

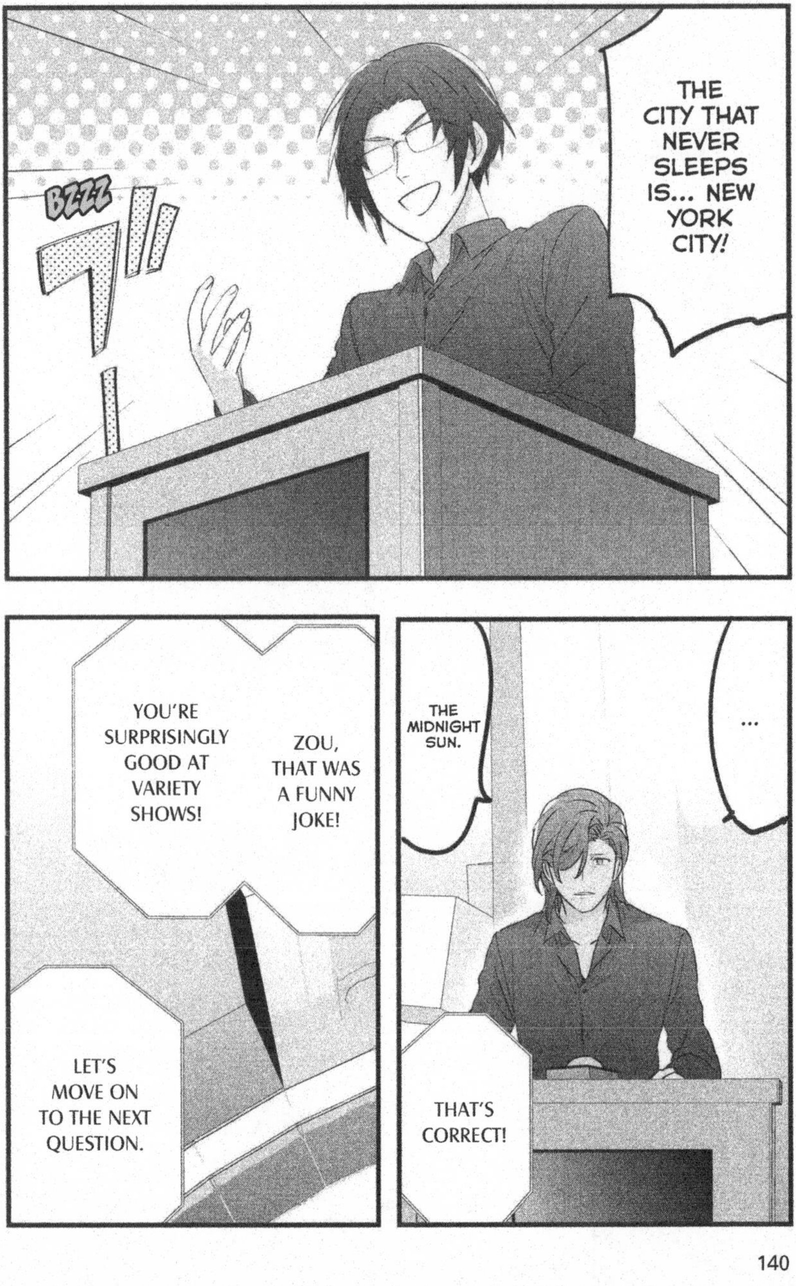
THE CITY THAT NEVER SLEEPS IS... NEW YORK CITY!
BZZZ
...
THE MIDNIGHT SUN.
THAT'S CORRECT!
ZOU, THAT WAS A FUNNY JOKE!
YOU'RE SURPRISINGLY GOOD AT VARIETY SHOWS!
LET'S MOVE ON TO THE NEXT QUESTION.

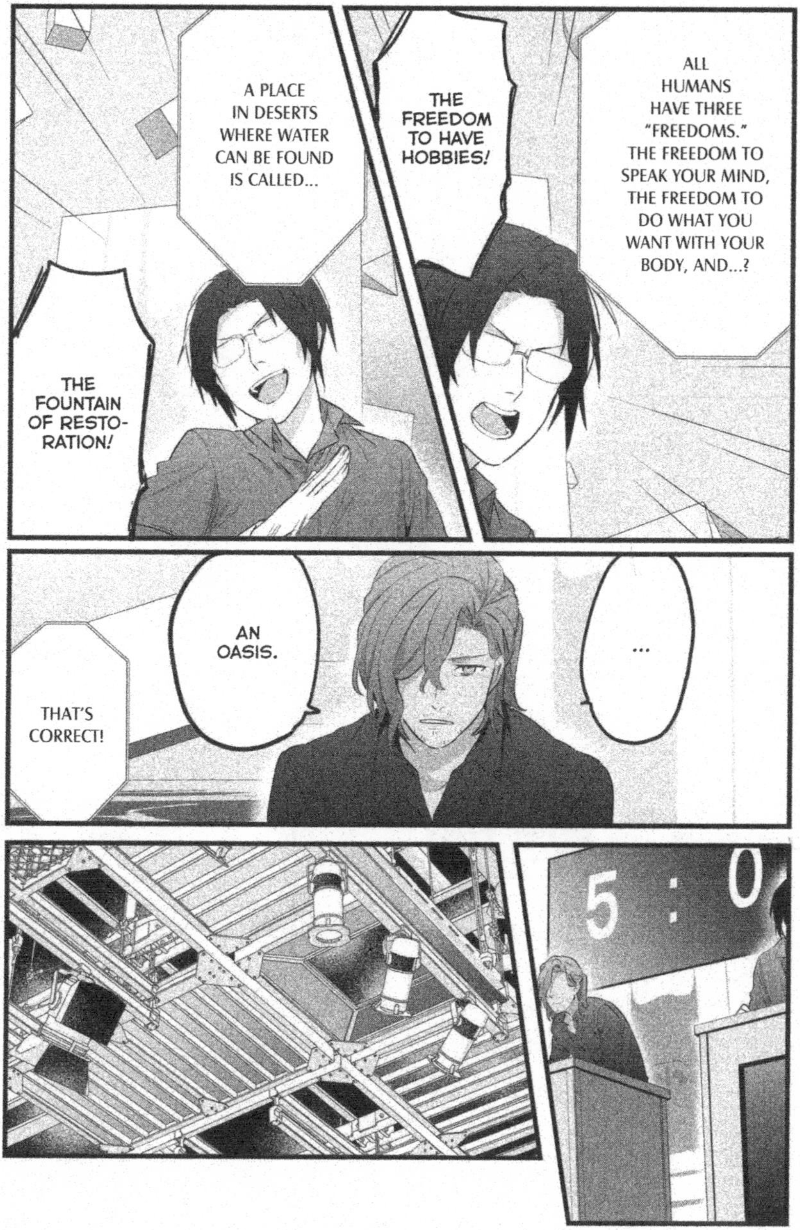
ALL HUMANS HAVE THREE "FREEDOMS." THE FREEDOM TO SPEAK YOUR MIND, THE FREEDOM TO DO WHAT YOU WANT WITH YOUR BODY, AND...?
THE FREEDOM TO HAVE HOBBIES!
A PLACE IN DESERTS WHERE WATER CAN BE FOUND IS CALLED...
THE FOUNTAIN OF RESTO-RATION!
...
AN OASIS.
THAT'S CORRECT!
5 : 0

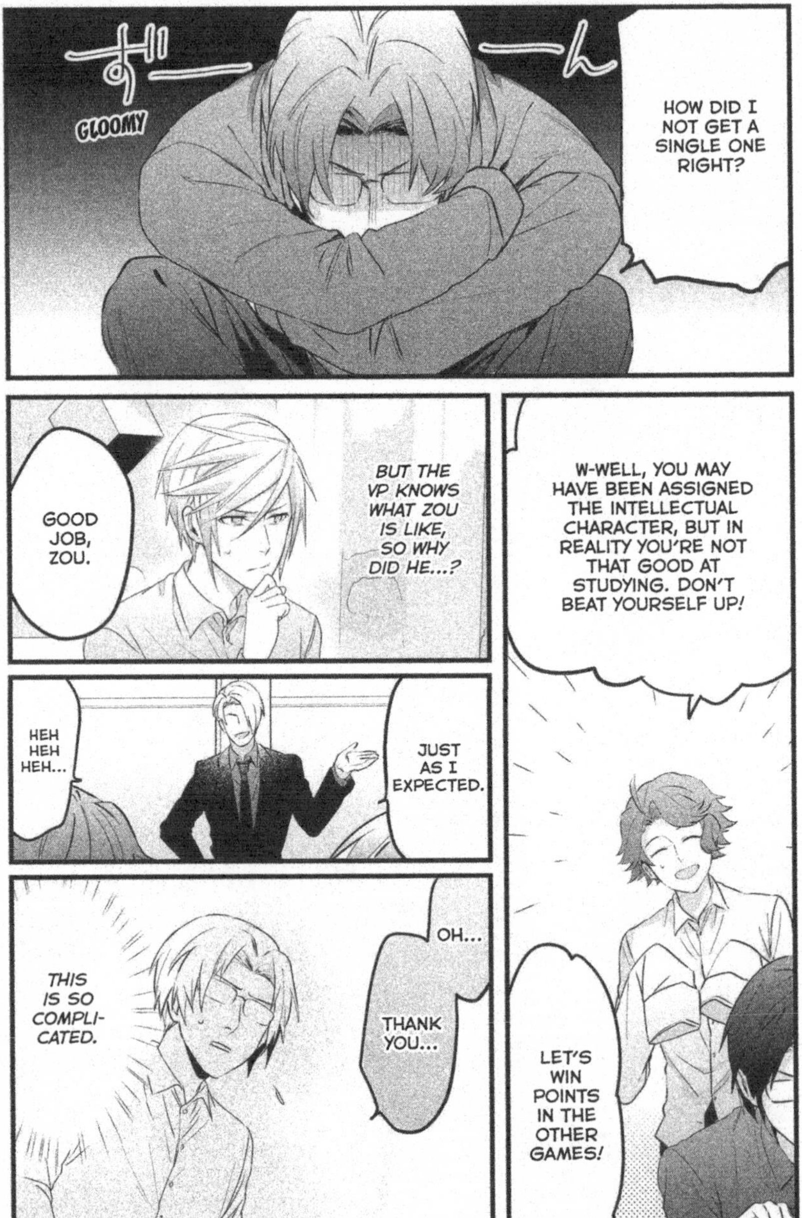
ずーーん
GLOOMY
HOW DID I NOT GET A SINGLE ONE RIGHT?
W-WELL, YOU MAY HAVE BEEN ASSIGNED THE INTELLECTUAL CHARACTER, BUT IN REALITY YOU'RE NOT THAT GOOD AT STUDYING. DON'T BEAT YOURSELF UP!
LET'S WIN POINTS IN THE OTHER GAMES!
BUT THE VP KNOWS WHAT ZOU IS LIKE, SO WHY DID HE...?
GOOD JOB, ZOU.
JUST AS I EXPECTED.
HEH HEH HEH...
OH...
THANK YOU...
THIS IS SO COMPLI-CATED.

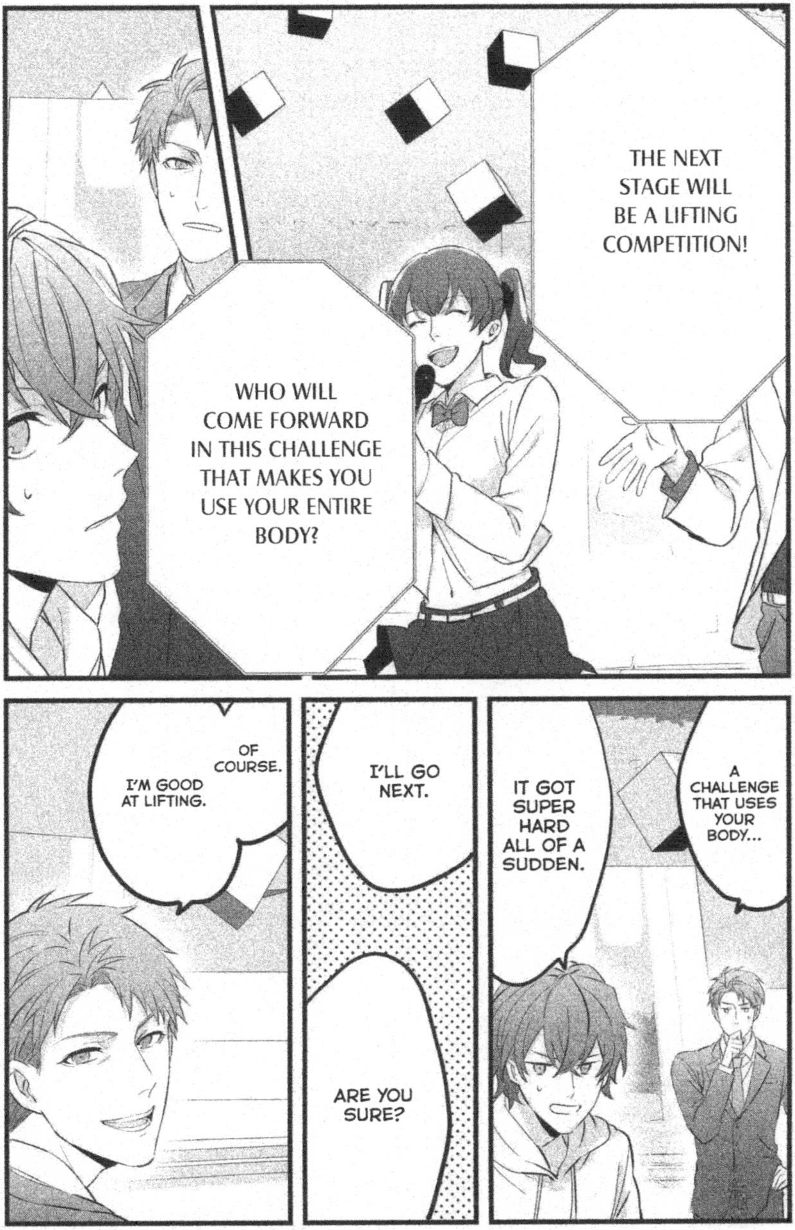
THE NEXT STAGE WILL BE A LIFTING COMPETITION!
WHO WILL COME FORWARD IN THIS CHALLENGE THAT MAKES YOU USE YOUR ENTIRE BODY?
A CHALLENGE THAT USES YOUR BODY...
IT GOT SUPER HARD ALL OF A SUDDEN.
I'LL GO NEXT.
ARE YOU SURE?
OF COURSE.
I'M GOOD AT LIFTING.

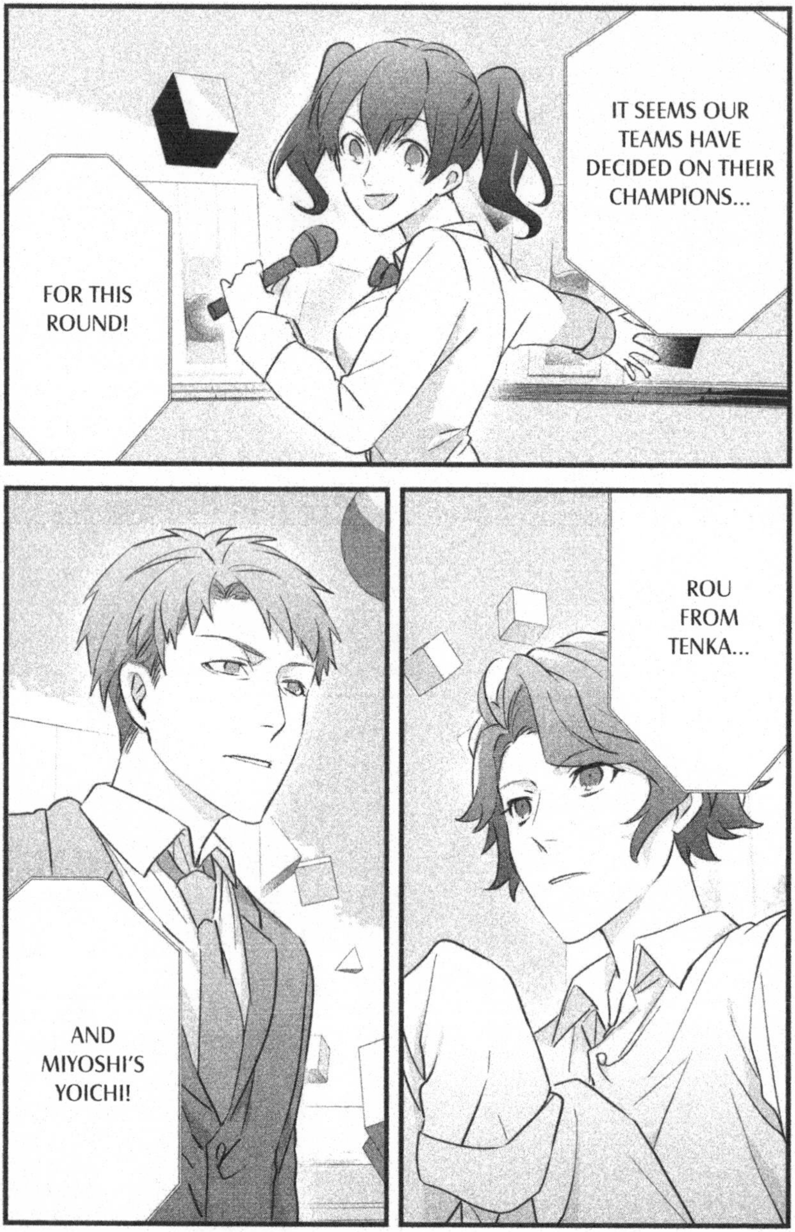
IT SEEMS OUR TEAMS HAVE DECIDED ON THEIR CHAMPIONS...
FOR THIS ROUND!
ROU FROM TENKA...
AND MIYOSHI'S YOICHI!

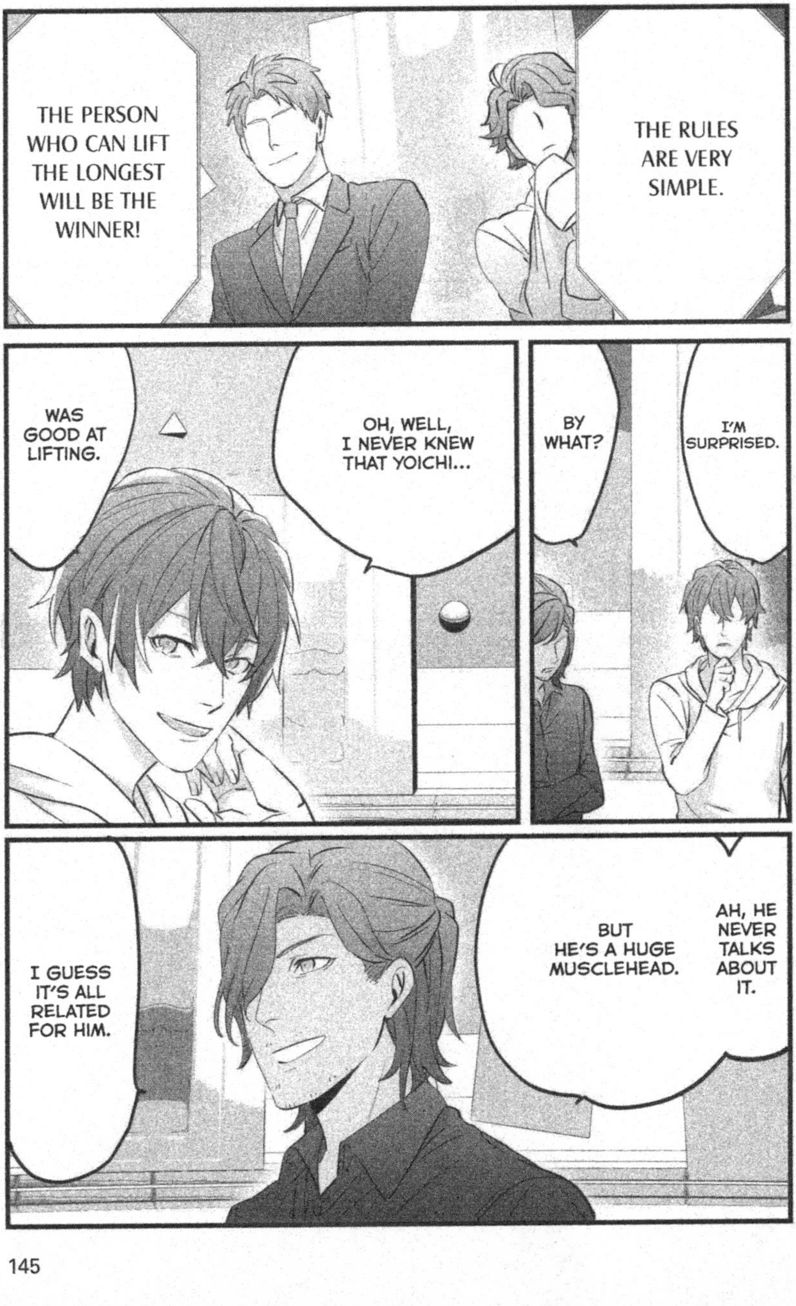
THE RULES ARE VERY SIMPLE.
THE PERSON WHO CAN LIFT THE LONGEST WILL BE THE WINNER!
I'M SURPRISED.
BY WHAT?
OH, WELL, I NEVER KNEW THAT YOICHI...
WAS GOOD AT LIFTING.
AH, HE NEVER TALKS ABOUT IT.
BUT HE'S A HUGE MUSCLEHEAD.
I GUESS IT'S ALL RELATED FOR HIM.

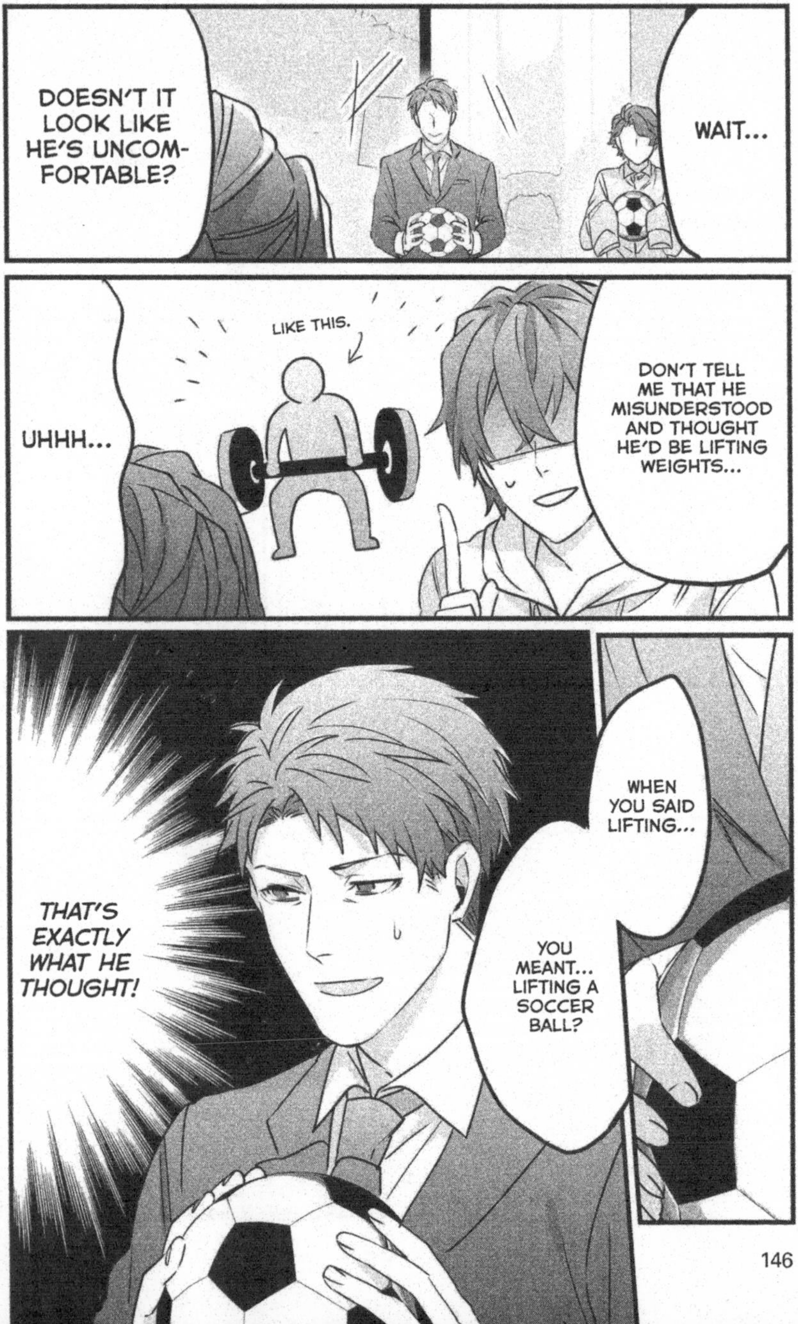
WAIT...
DOESN'T IT LOOK LIKE HE'S UNCOM-FORTABLE?
DON'T TELL ME THAT HE MISUNDERSTOOD AND THOUGHT HE'D BE LIFTING WEIGHTS...
LIKE THIS.
UHHH...
WHEN YOU SAID LIFTING...
YOU MEANT... LIFTING A SOCCER BALL?
THAT'S EXACTLY WHAT HE THOUGHT!

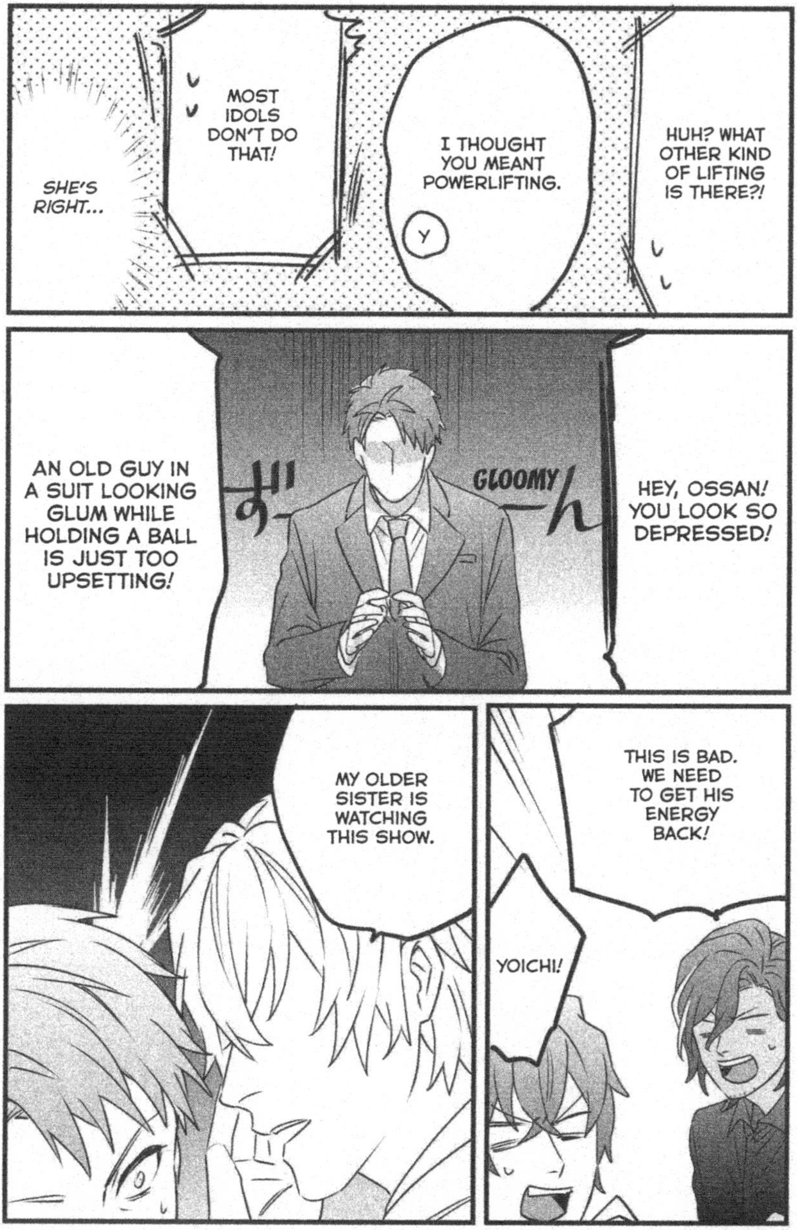

HUH? WHAT OTHER KIND OF LIFTING IS THERE?!
I THOUGHT YOU MEANT POWERLIFTING.
MOST IDOLS DON'T DO THAT!
SHE'S RIGHT...
HEY, OSSAN! YOU LOOK SO DEPRESSED!
GLOOMY
ずーん
AN OLD GUY IN A SUIT LOOKING GLUM WHILE HOLDING A BALL IS JUST TOO UPSETTING!
THIS IS BAD. WE NEED TO GET HIS ENERGY BACK!
YOICHI!
MY OLDER SISTER IS WATCHING THIS SHOW.

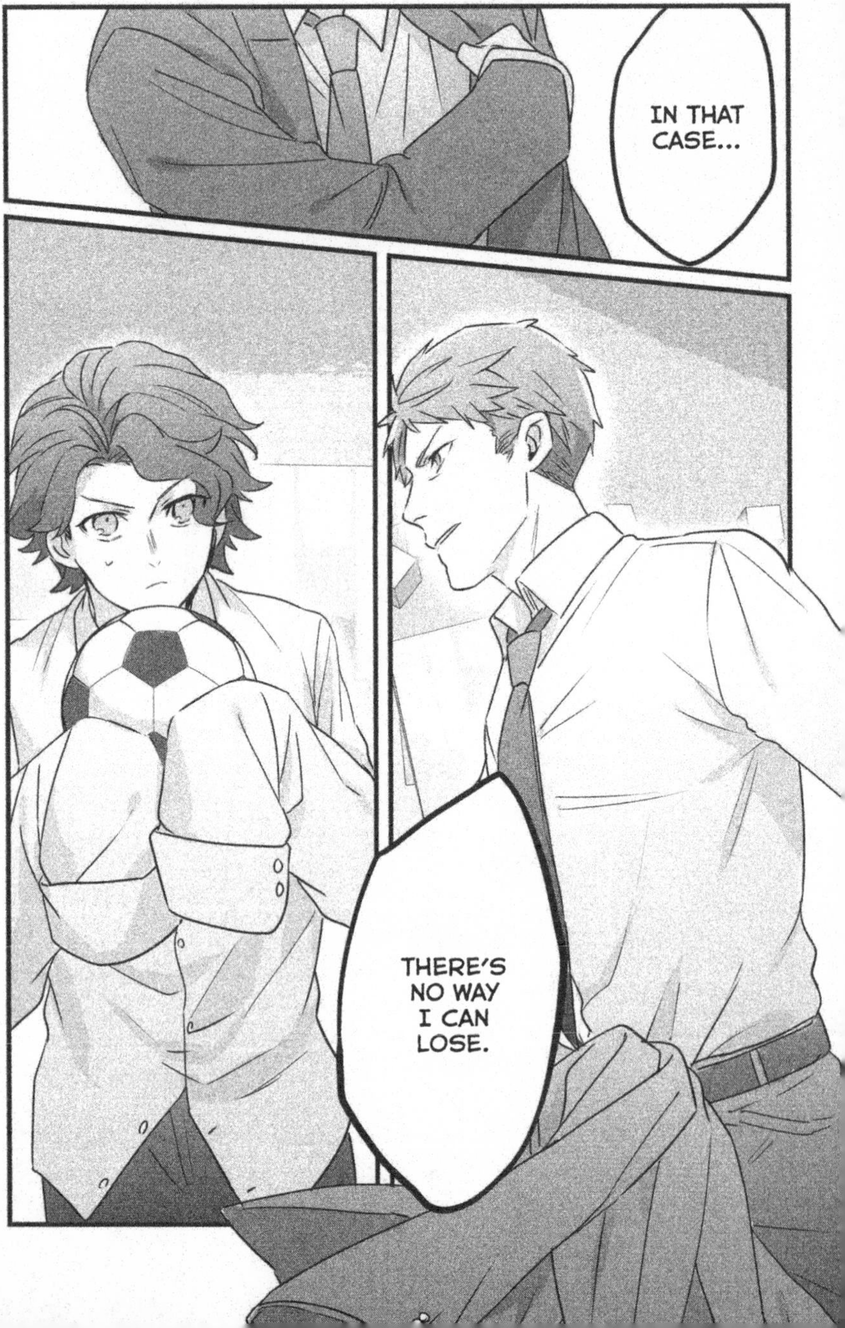
IN THAT CASE...
THERE'S NO WAY I CAN LOSE.

Chapter 30

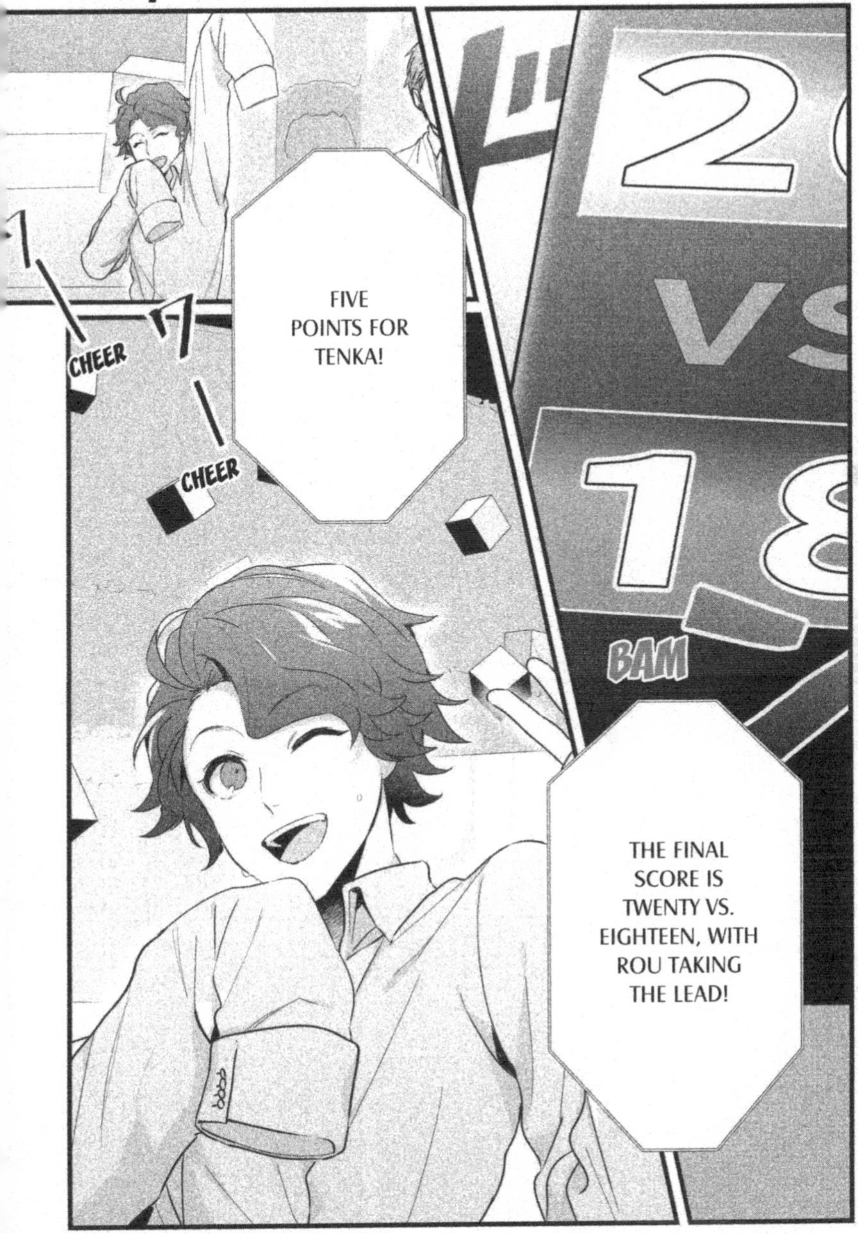
CHEER
CHEER
FIVE POINTS FOR TENKA!
BAM
THE FINAL SCORE IS TWENTY VS. EIGHTEEN, WITH ROU TAKING THE LEAD!

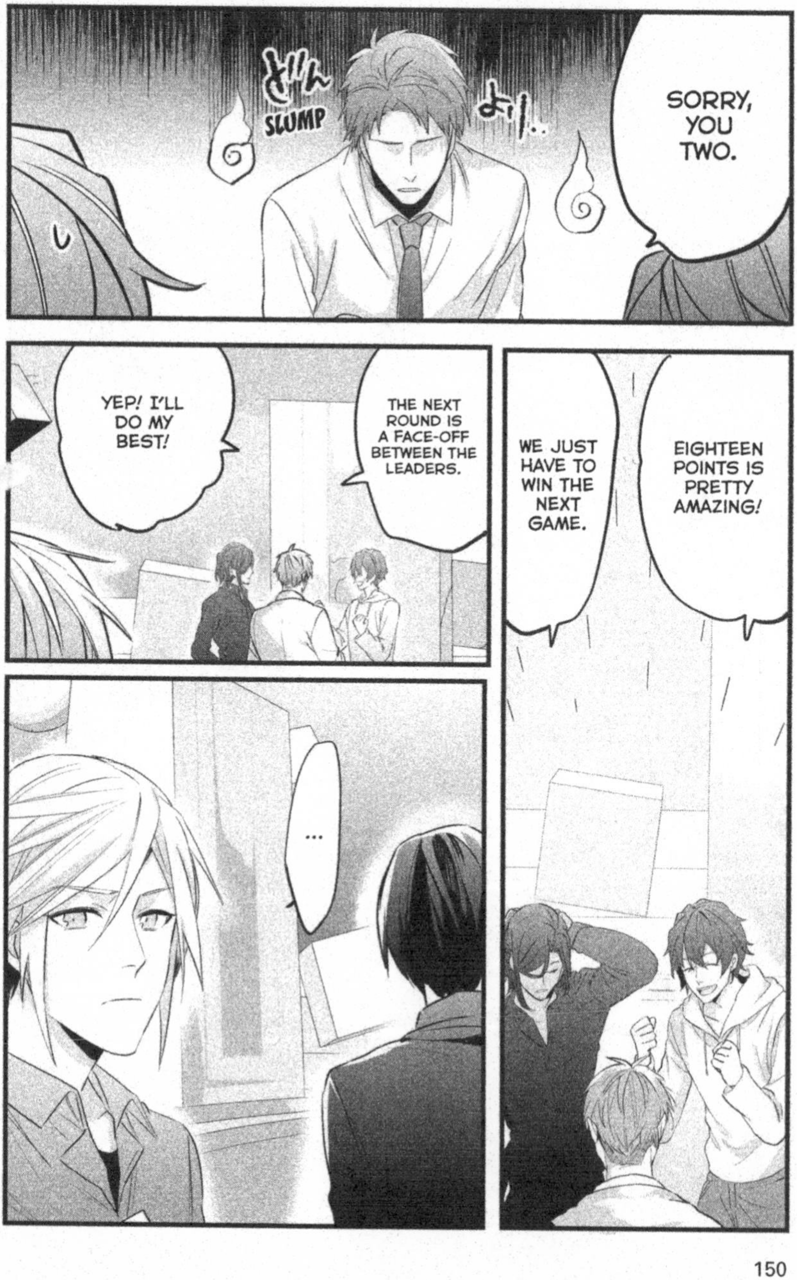
SLUMP
SORRY, YOU TWO.
EIGHTEEN POINTS IS PRETTY AMAZING!
WE JUST HAVE TO WIN THE NEXT GAME.
THE NEXT ROUND IS A FACE-OFF BETWEEN THE LEADERS.
YEP! I'LL DO MY BEST!
...

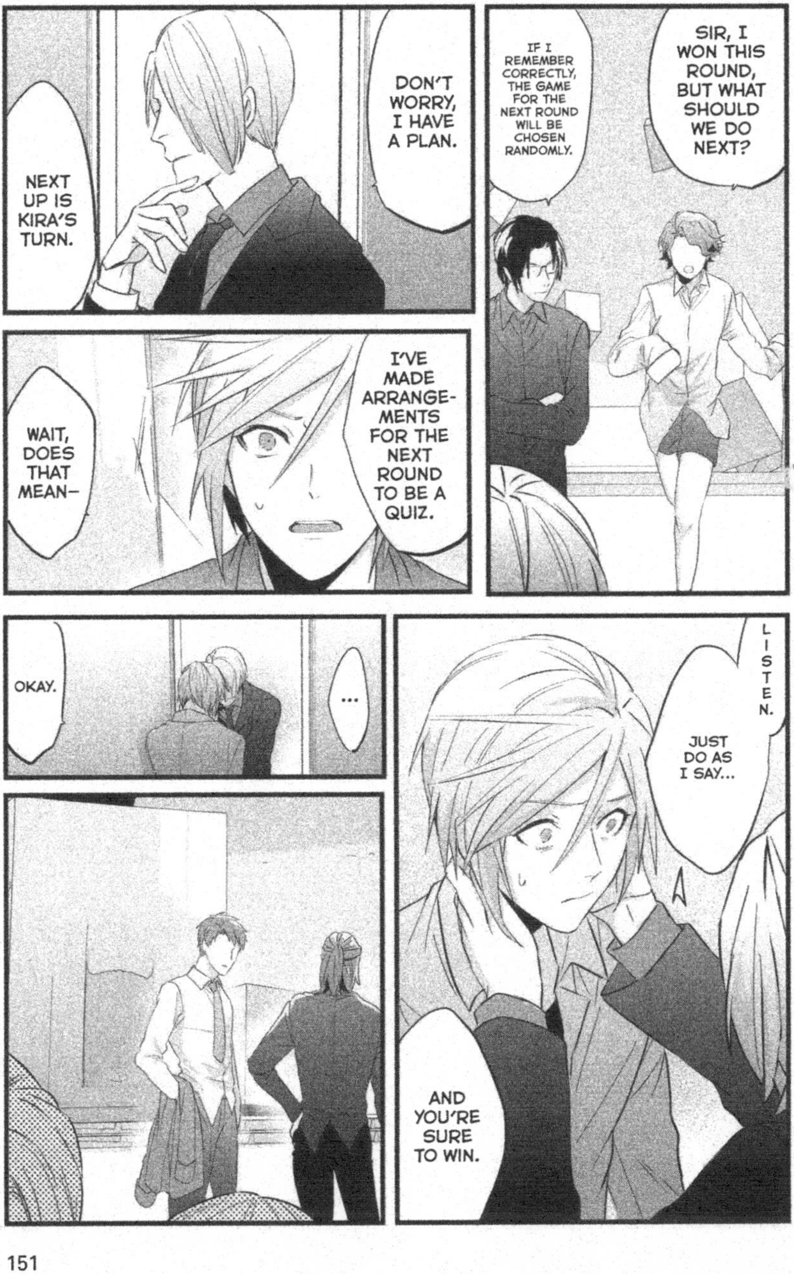
SIR, I WON THIS ROUND, BUT WHAT SHOULD WE DO NEXT?
IF I REMEMBER CORRECTLY, THE GAME FOR THE NEXT ROUND WILL BE CHOSEN RANDOMLY.
DON'T WORRY, I HAVE A PLAN.
NEXT UP IS KIRA'S TURN.
I'VE MADE ARRANGE-MENTS FOR THE NEXT ROUND TO BE A QUIZ.
WAIT, DOES THAT MEAN—
LISTEN.
JUST DO AS I SAY...
AND YOU'RE SURE TO WIN.
...
OKAY.

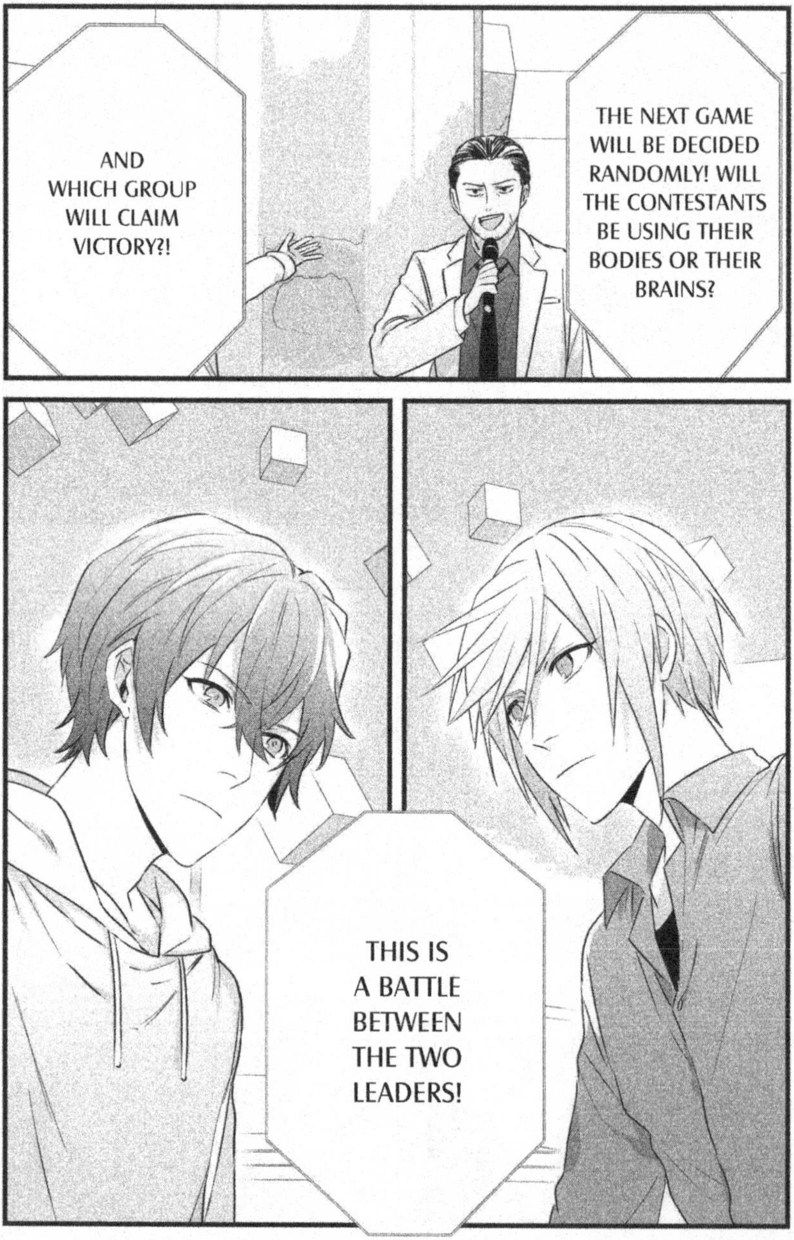
THE NEXT GAME WILL BE DECIDED RANDOMLY! WILL THE CONTESTANTS BE USING THEIR BODIES OR THEIR BRAINS?
AND WHICH GROUP WILL CLAIM VICTORY?!
THIS IS A BATTLE BETWEEN THE TWO LEADERS!

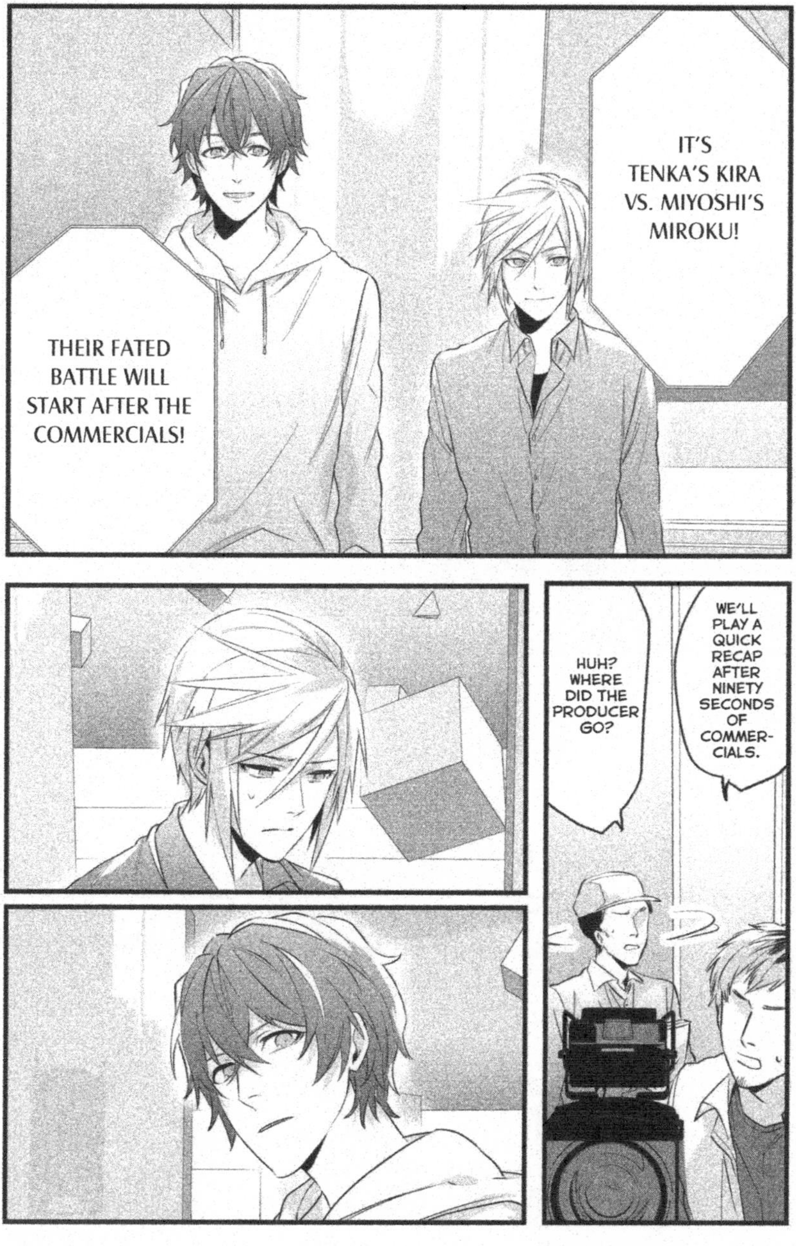
IT'S TENKA'S KIRA VS. MIYOSHI'S MIROKU!
THEIR FATED BATTLE WILL START AFTER THE COMMERCIALS!
WE'LL PLAY A QUICK RECAP AFTER NINETY SECONDS OF COMMER-CIALS.
HUH? WHERE DID THE PRODUCER GO?

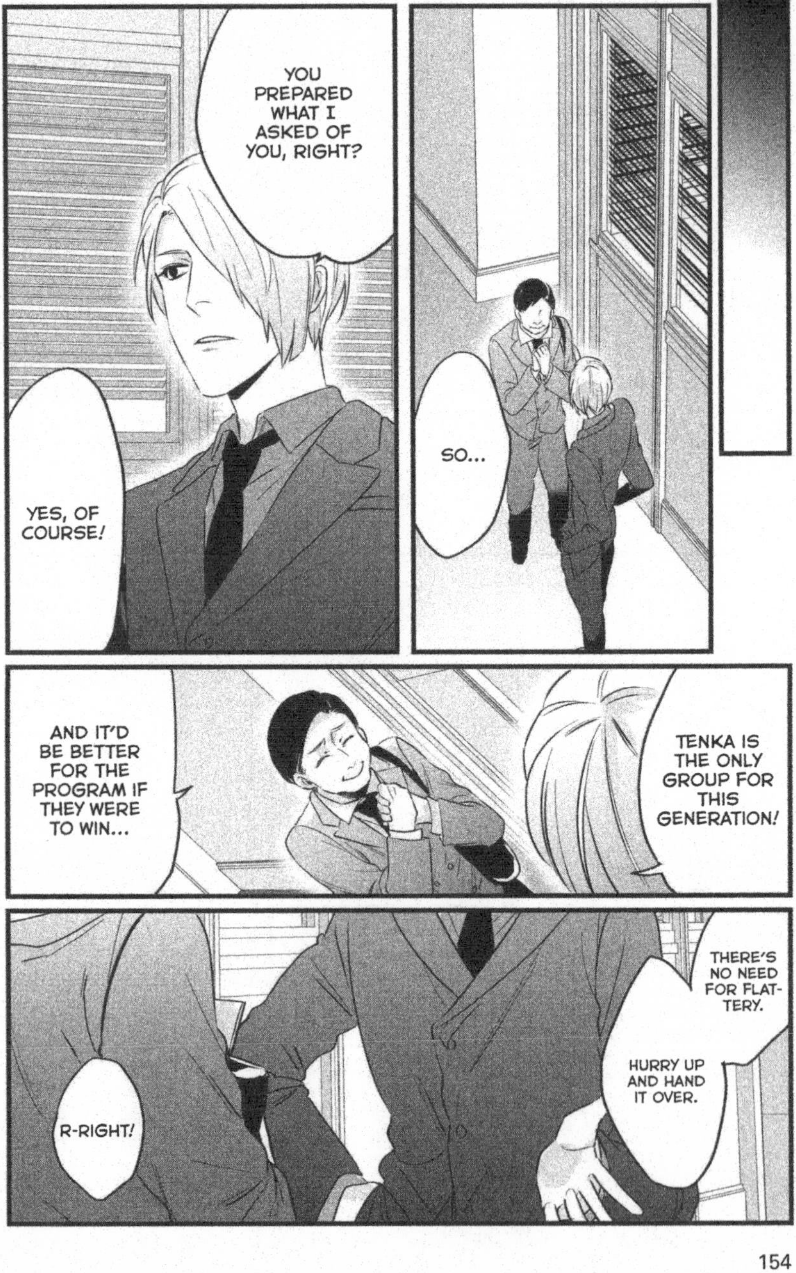
SO...
YOU PREPARED WHAT I ASKED OF YOU, RIGHT?
YES, OF COURSE!
TENKA IS THE ONLY GROUP FOR THIS GENERATION!
AND IT'D BE BETTER FOR THE PROGRAM IF THEY WERE TO WIN...
THERE'S NO NEED FOR FLATTERY.
HURRY UP AND HAND IT OVER.
R-RIGHT!

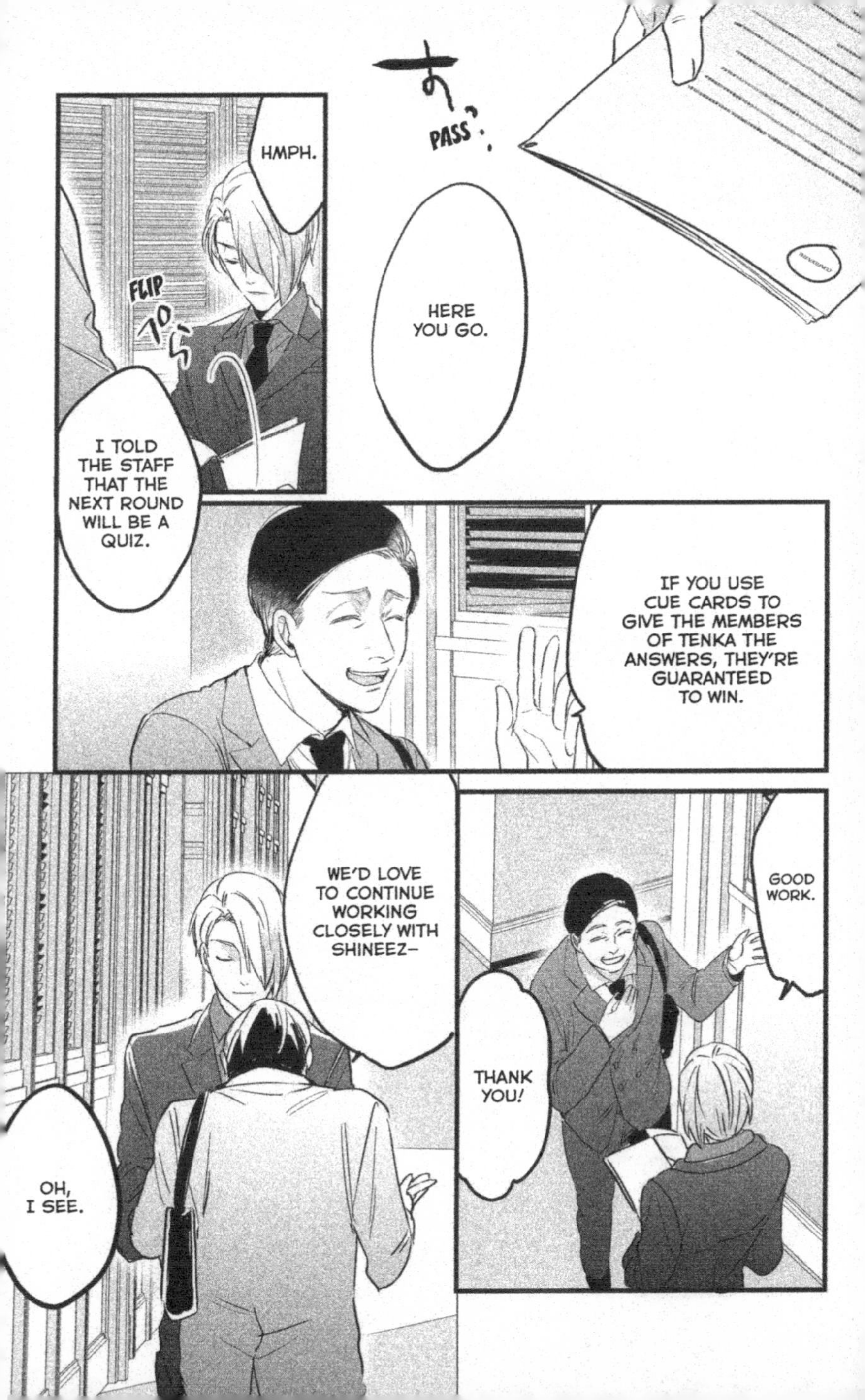
PASS
HERE YOU GO.
HMPH.
FLIP
I TOLD THE STAFF THAT THE NEXT ROUND WILL BE A QUIZ.
IF YOU USE CUE CARDS TO GIVE THE MEMBERS OF TENKA THE ANSWERS, THEY'RE GUARANTEED TO WIN.
GOOD WORK.
THANK YOU!
WE'D LOVE TO CONTINUE WORKING CLOSELY WITH SHINEEZ–
OH, I SEE.

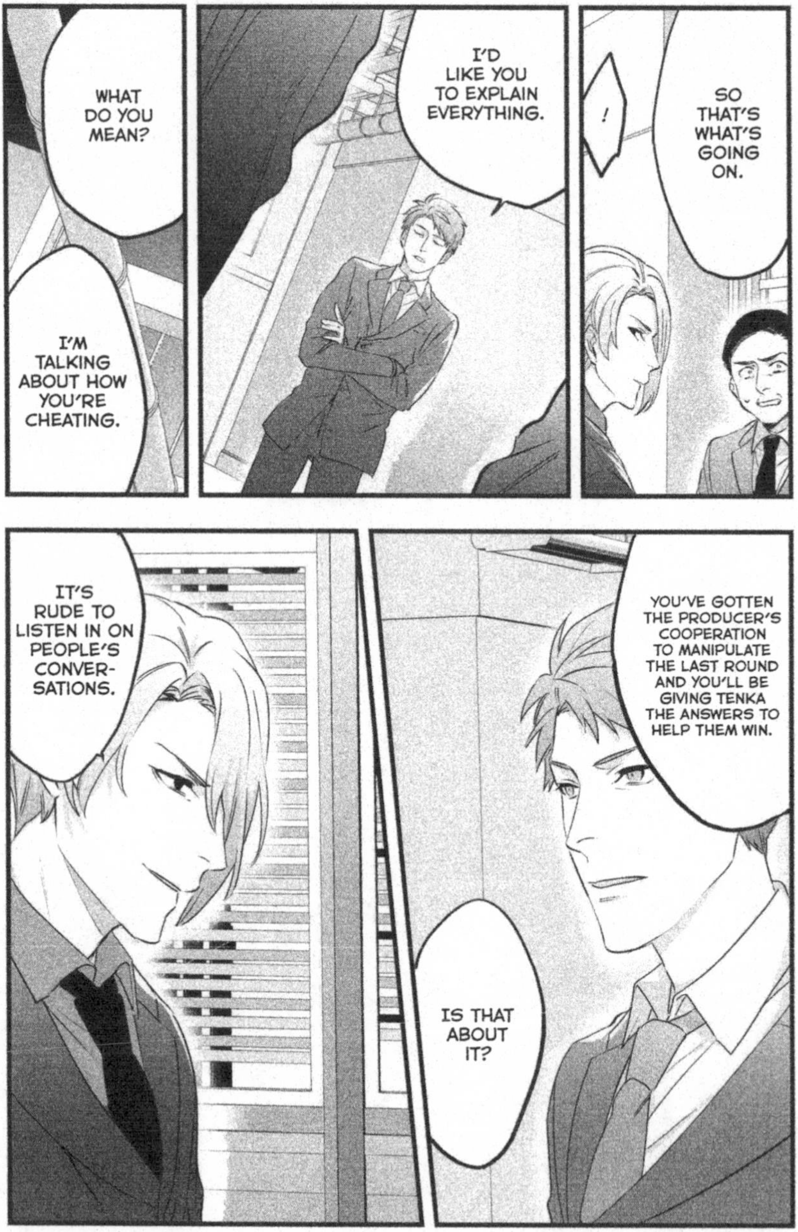
SO THAT'S WHAT'S GOING ON.
!
I'D LIKE YOU TO EXPLAIN EVERYTHING.
WHAT DO YOU MEAN?
I'M TALKING ABOUT HOW YOU'RE CHEATING.
YOU'VE GOTTEN THE PRODUCER'S COOPERATION TO MANIPULATE THE LAST ROUND AND YOU'LL BE GIVING TENKA THE ANSWERS TO HELP THEM WIN.
IS THAT ABOUT IT?
IT'S RUDE TO LISTEN IN ON PEOPLE'S CONVER-SATIONS.

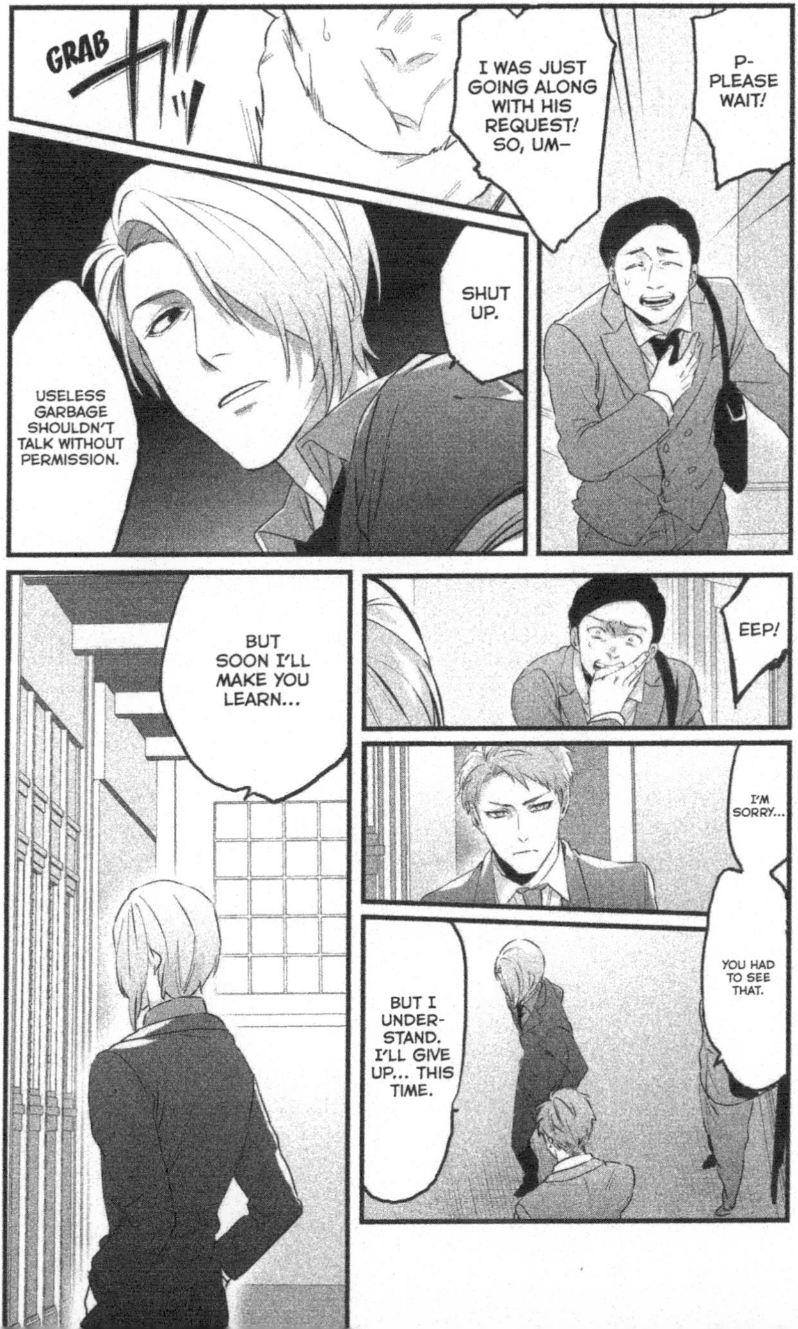
P-
PLEASE WAIT!
I WAS JUST GOING ALONG WITH HIS REQUEST! SO, UM–
GRAB
SHUT UP.
USELESS GARBAGE SHOULDN'T TALK WITHOUT PERMISSION.
EEP!
I'M SORRY...
YOU HAD TO SEE THAT.
BUT I UNDER-STAND. I'LL GIVE UP... THIS TIME.
BUT SOON I'LL MAKE YOU LEARN...

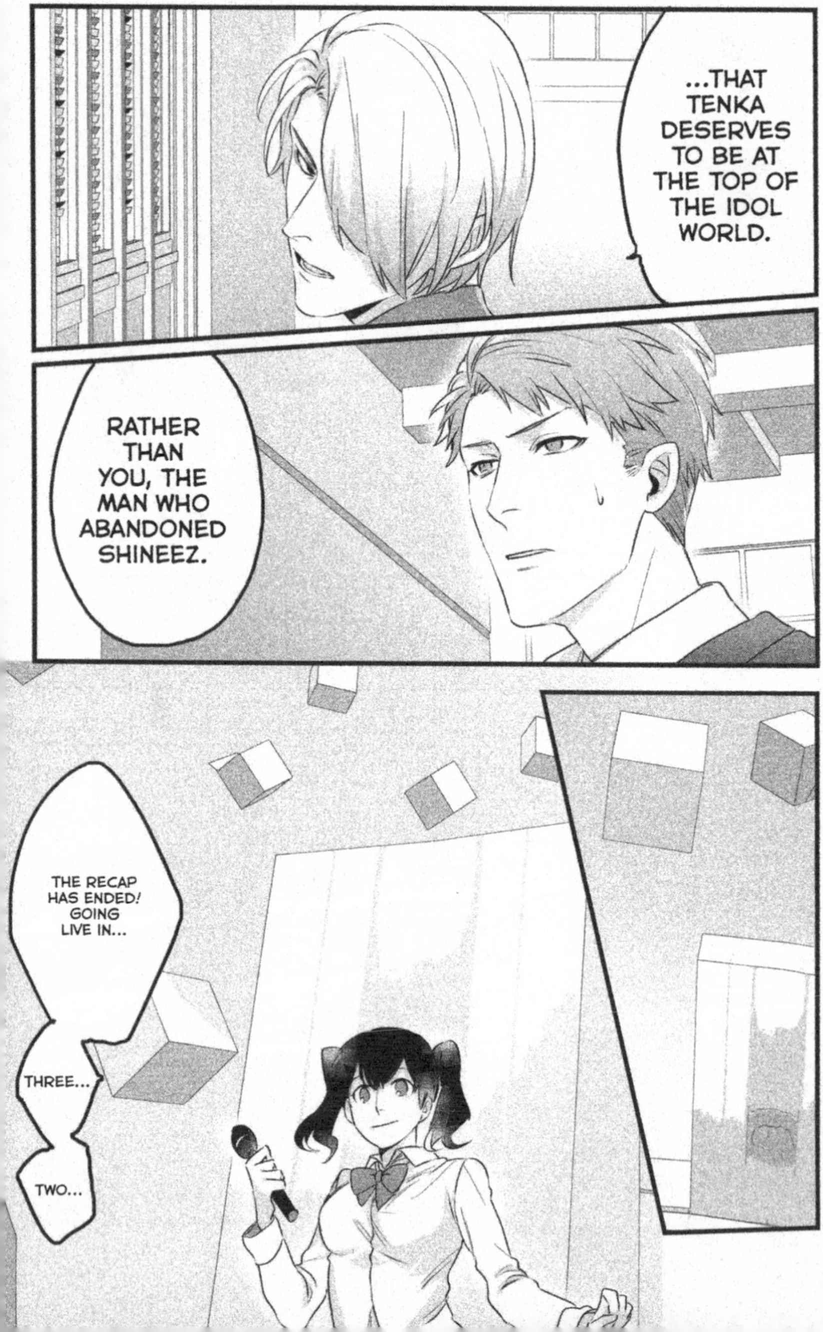
...THAT TENKA DESERVES TO BE AT THE TOP OF THE IDOL WORLD.
RATHER THAN YOU, THE MAN WHO ABANDONED SHINEEZ.
THE RECAP HAS ENDED! GOING LIVE IN...
THREE...
TWO...

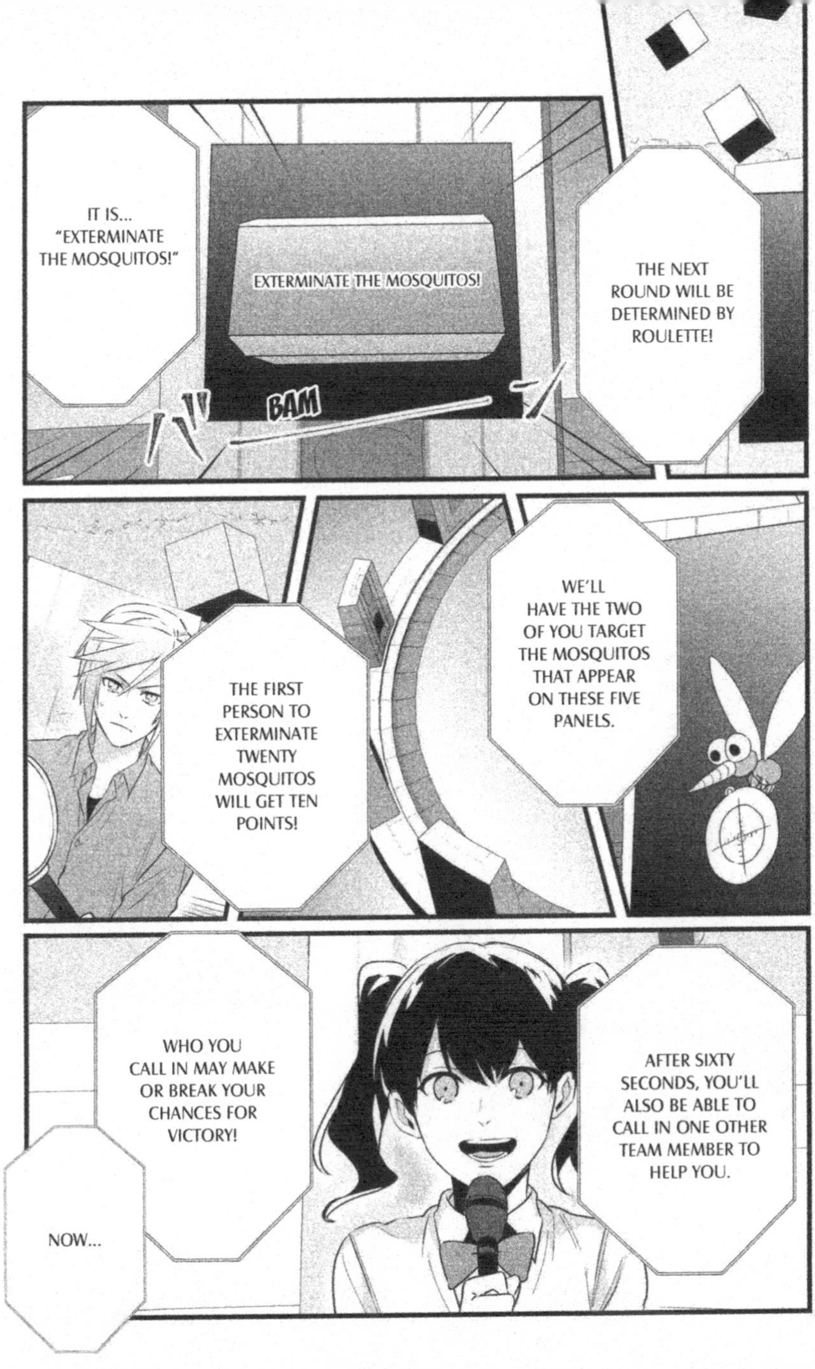
THE NEXT ROUND WILL BE DETERMINED BY ROULETTE!
EXTERMINATE THE MOSQUITOS!
BAM
IT IS... "EXTERMINATE THE MOSQUITOS!"
WE'LL HAVE THE TWO OF YOU TARGET THE MOSQUITOS THAT APPEAR ON THESE FIVE PANELS.
THE FIRST PERSON TO EXTERMINATE TWENTY MOSQUITOS WILL GET TEN POINTS!
AFTER SIXTY SECONDS, YOU'LL ALSO BE ABLE TO CALL IN ONE OTHER TEAM MEMBER TO HELP YOU.
WHO YOU CALL IN MAY MAKE OR BREAK YOUR CHANCES FOR VICTORY!
NOW...

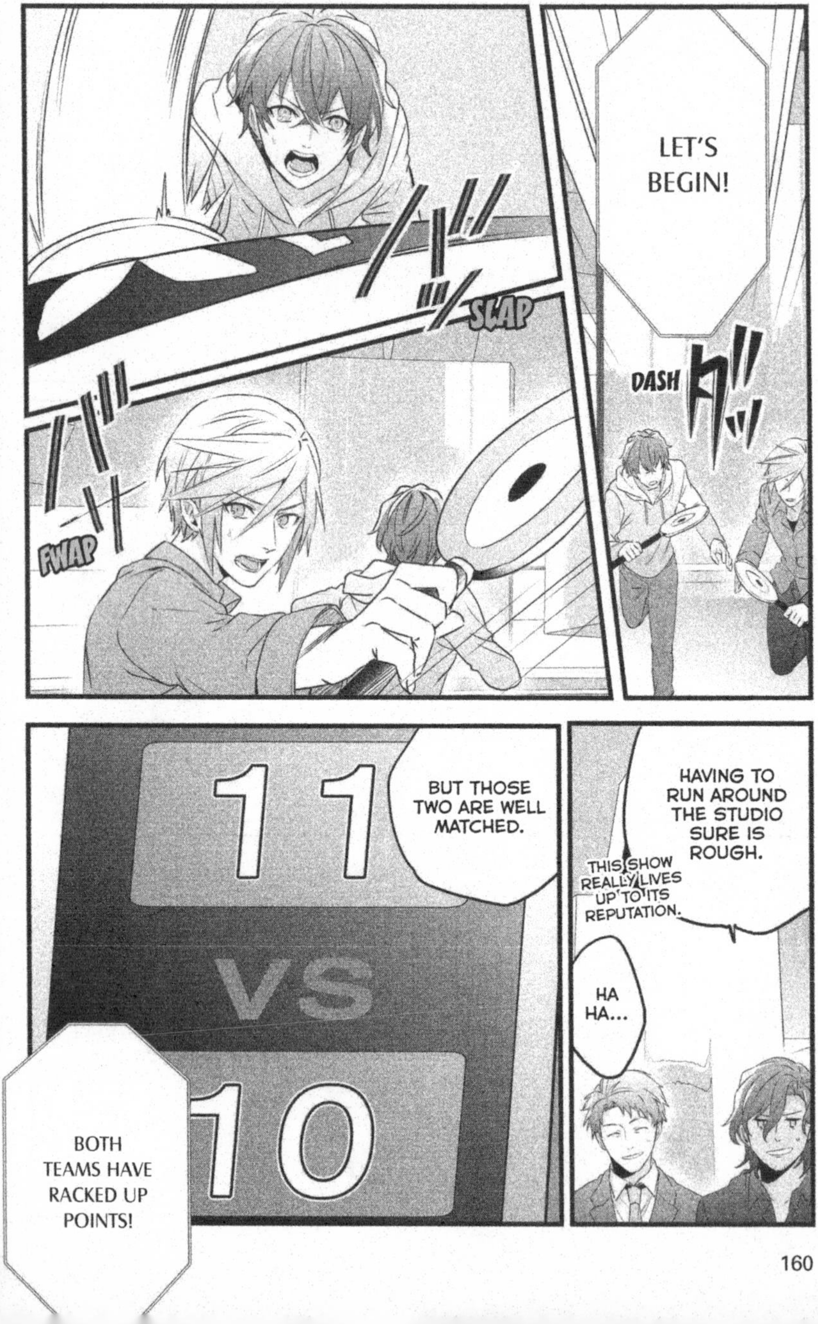
LET'S BEGIN!
DASH
SLAP
FWAP
HAVING TO RUN AROUND THE STUDIO SURE IS ROUGH.
THIS SHOW REALLY LIVES UP TO ITS REPUTATION.
HA HA...
BUT THOSE TWO ARE WELL MATCHED.
11
VS
10
BOTH TEAMS HAVE RACKED UP POINTS!

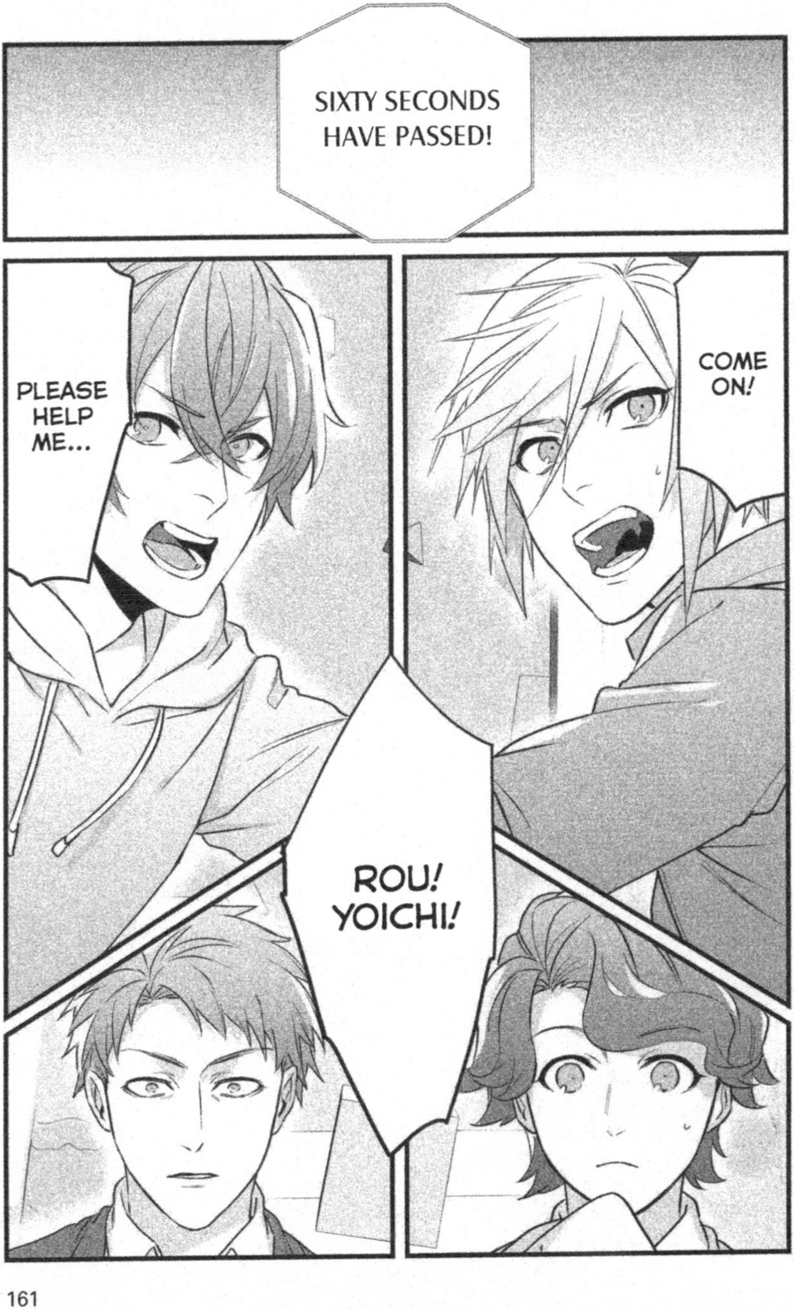
SIXTY SECONDS HAVE PASSED!
COME ON!
PLEASE HELP ME...
ROU! YOICHI!

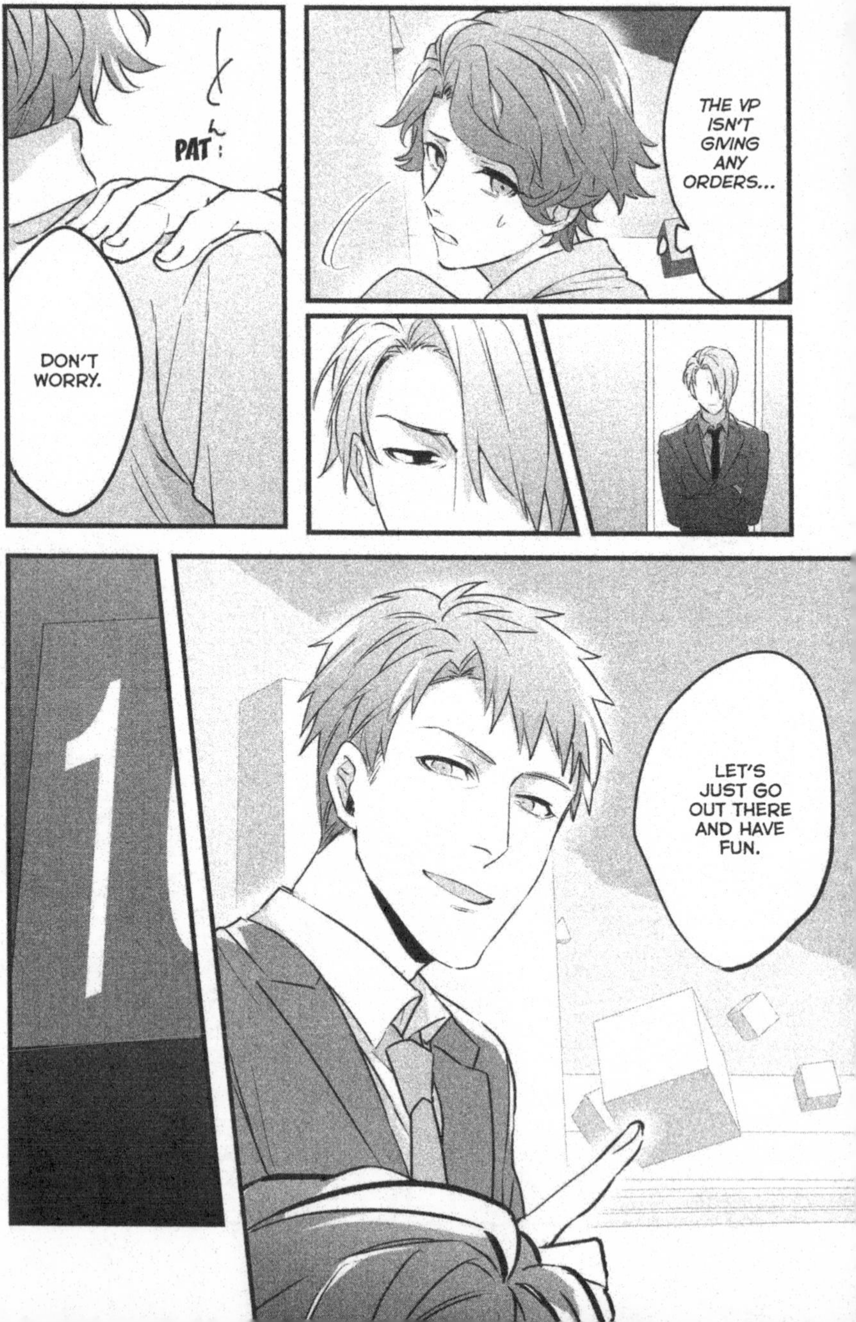
THE VP ISN'T GIVING ANY ORDERS...
とん
PAT
DON'T WORRY.
LET'S JUST GO OUT THERE AND HAVE FUN.

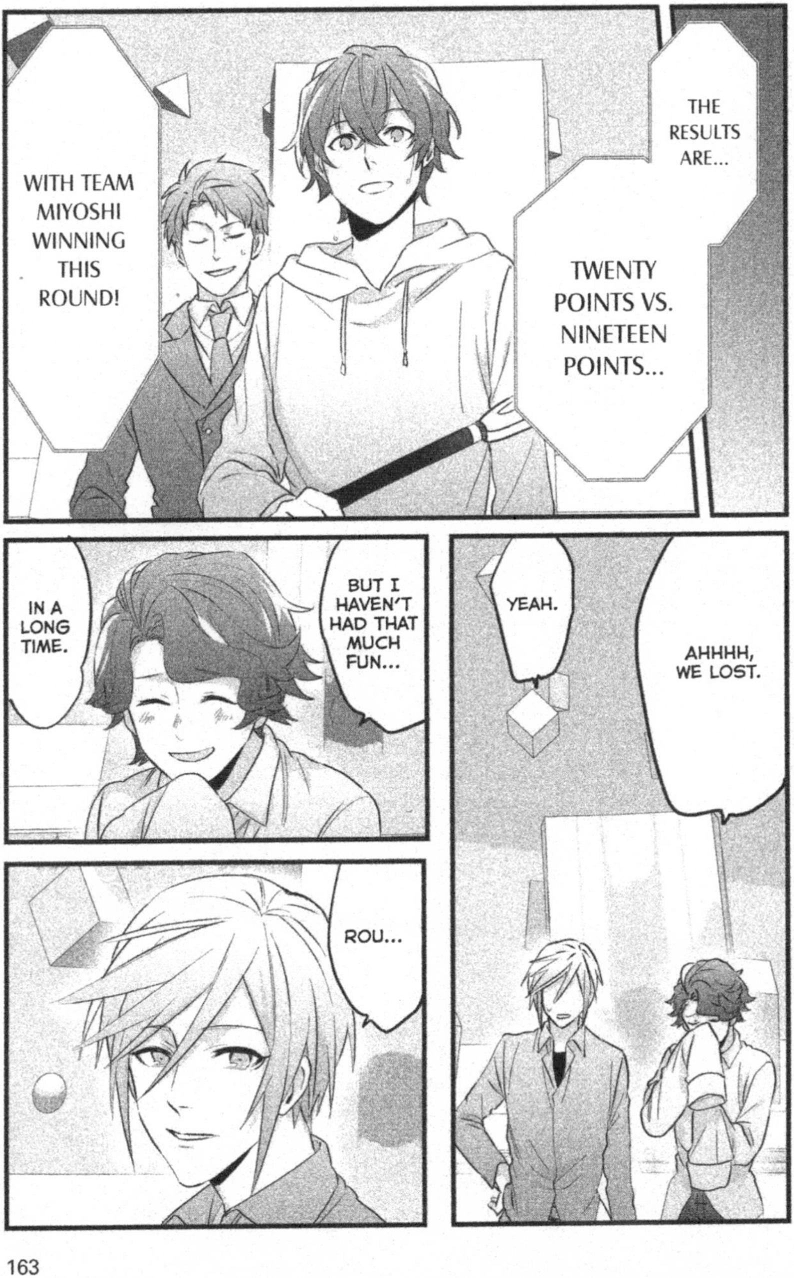
THE RESULTS ARE...
TWENTY POINTS VS. NINETEEN POINTS...
WITH TEAM MIYOSHI WINNING THIS ROUND!
AHHHH, WE LOST.
YEAH.
BUT I HAVEN'T HAD THAT MUCH FUN...
IN A LONG TIME.
ROU...

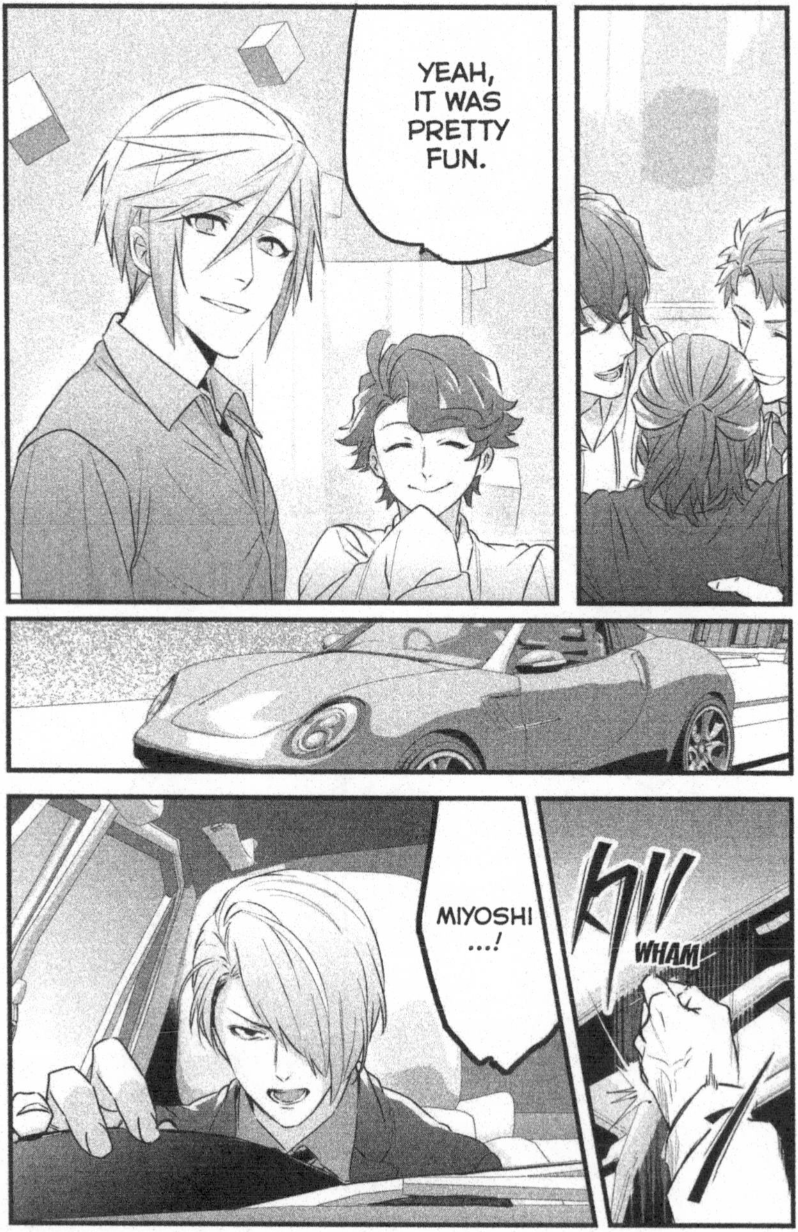
YEAH, IT WAS PRETTY FUN.
WHAM
MIYOSHI ...!

OSSAN IDOL!

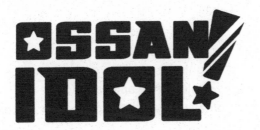

The Idols Play With a Fortune-Telling App
by Mochiko Mochida

Miroku had just finished a photoshoot as a model for a magazine and was stopping by the agency's office to let everyone know he was done. He could have just sent a message, but he was secretly hoping to see his beloved Fumi, the group's manager. However, he didn't let even a sliver of his ulterior motives show on his face—as expected of a pro!

"I'm back!"

"Welcome back, Miroku. Good work today."

"'Sup, Miroku?"

Yoichi and Shiju were the only ones in the office to greet him. Seeing the dejection on the youngest idol's face, Yoichi gave him a wry smile.

"Fumi will be back in a little bit."

"How could you care more about a woman than us? Where is your love for your fellow group members?!"

"That's not true! I love both of you too!"

Miroku bathed the two in the brightness of his largest and most charming smile, but Shiju only scolded him and said, "Save it for your fans!" It was an everyday scene for the three idols.

Then Shiju picked up a tablet and started to tap on its screen.

"What is that?"

"We're supposed to give our thoughts on this fortune-telling app."

"The tech team created it as a game app. It's going to be introduced in a magazine, so you should try it out too, Miroku."

"Wow, the tech team is working on so much stuff."

The fortune-telling app worked by asking the user a few questions, then giving a result based on the answers. Apparently, the paid version gave out even more detailed responses.

Miroku watched as Shiju gave the screen a few disinterested taps.

"The questions are so detailed…"

"You can just choose the answers randomly," suggested Shiju.

"Shiju, if you do that, you'll get a result that says your life is messy."

"I don't think I would… Would I?" The words The Fool popped up on the tablet in Shiju's hands. "Let's see, it says… 'As a proper adult, you should refrain from acting carelessly.' Boooo!"

Next, he read out the 'Advice' section of his result: "The card with advice to overcome your situation is The Empress and it says, 'Someone with deep affection and motherly instincts is the key. Be sure not to let them slip through your grasp.' Heh, that sounds about right."

"...Shut up." Miroku's lips pursed as a certain person came to mind.

Next, it was Yoichi's turn to use the app.

"Wow, that's amazing!" exclaimed Shiju. "You got The Emperor card and it says, 'It may be said that you have gained personal and social success, but you're working too hard. It's better to rest!' Even a fortune-telling app is worried about your health. Seriously, ossan, take a break..."

When he checked the next part of Yoichi's result, Shiju laughed. "Ha ha ha... The advice card is The Wheel of Fortune. It says, 'You've already met your fated person. This is your last chance with them, so do your best!' I see... This app really is accurate."

Miroku's lips pursed once again as yet another person who fit that description came to mind.

After shaking off those thoughts, Miroku answered the questions and hung his head dejectedly when he got his own results.

"Let's see what you got... Heh heh, Miroku got The Hermit card, which says, 'You want to connect with someone, but for some reason your shut-in mindset keeps taking over!' Holy crap, just how hopeless are you?! Pfft!"

"Shut up! I can't help being a shut-in otaku at heart!"

"Now, now, Miroku… Let's look at your advice," continued Shiju. "The Sun card says, 'You'll surely meet a bright, carefree person similar to the sun, so do your best to go outside!' That's good, isn't it?"

"I guess…"

The corners of Miroku's mouth turned up into the tiniest smile as he thought of a certain someone. Of course, it was easy to guess who.

At that moment, the three were greeted with a bright "Hello!"

"Fumi! Welcome back!"

"Thank you, Miroku. Oh, how is that app?"

"Oh! Um… I guess it's pretty fun."

Fumi tilted her head at the three ossans' complex expressions.

"Mr. Tapioca said the app doesn't give out results that say bad things. Was he wrong? Mine was normal."

"Huh? You already played, Fumi?"

Miroku leaned forward, his eyes sparkling as he asked his question. Fumi immediately took a step back.

"Um, I got The Strength card, which said something like, 'You are strong-willed and quick to act.'"

"Huh. What did your advice card say?"

"If I remember right, it was The Chariot and it said, 'If you keep moving forward with your passionate, fast pace, you'll become the strongest!' So I thought it best to continue focusing on giving my all to my work!"

Yoichi and Shiju trembled as they considered the mental image of a roaring lion and a chariot behind Fumi, smiling and posing proudly.

"W-well, don't work yourself too hard."

"Don't be silly, Yoichi! I have to put all my energy into it!"

"Ossan doesn't have enough time off as it is. His body's sending out emergency flags, saying he's overworked. Come on, Miroku, we have to do something!"

Shiju fearfully turned around looking for assistance, but Miroku was smiling bewitchingly and laying on the charm.

"Fumi is so cute…"

"This is no good!"

"Ha ha ha, Miroku thinks everything Fumi does is cute."

"Not everything! Probably… Right, Fumi? Fumi?!"

"Guh…"

Fumi was faced by an unexpected blast of Miroku's pheromones, caused by a seemingly harmless fortune-telling app.

"…Guh."

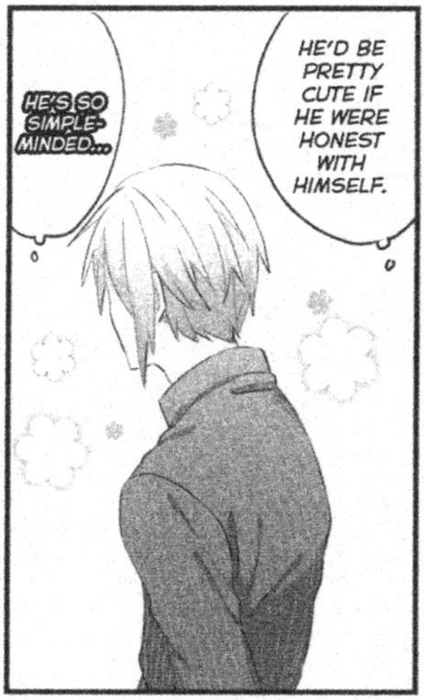
HE'D BE PRETTY CUTE IF HE WERE HONEST WITH HIMSELF.
HE'S SO SIMPLE-MINDED...

Original Excerpt
The 3 Members of TENKA (Part 2)

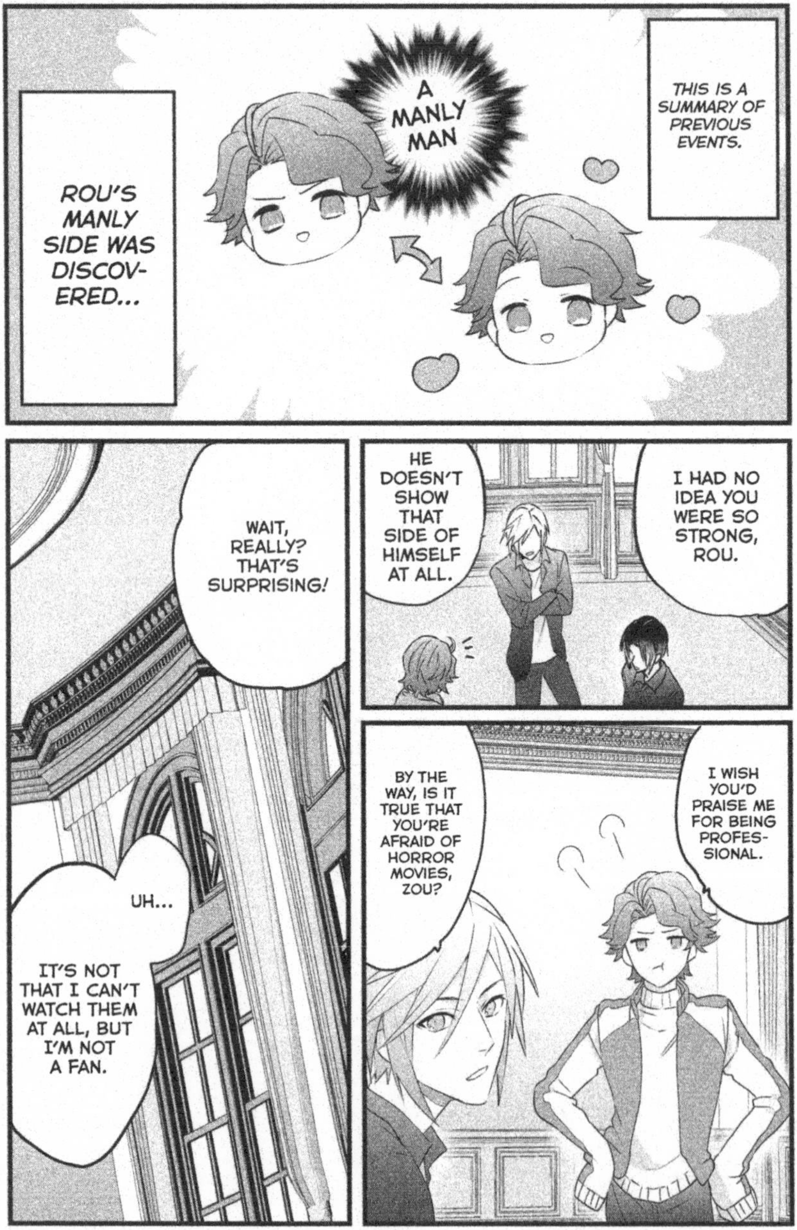
THIS IS A SUMMARY OF PREVIOUS EVENTS.
A MANLY MAN
ROU'S MANLY SIDE WAS DISCOV-ERED...
I HAD NO IDEA YOU WERE SO STRONG, ROU.
HE DOESN'T SHOW THAT SIDE OF HIMSELF AT ALL.
I WISH YOU'D PRAISE ME FOR BEING PROFES-SIONAL.
BY THE WAY, IS IT TRUE THAT YOU'RE AFRAID OF HORROR MOVIES, ZOU?
WAIT, REALLY? THAT'S SURPRISING!
UH...
IT'S NOT THAT I CAN'T WATCH THEM AT ALL, BUT I'M NOT A FAN.

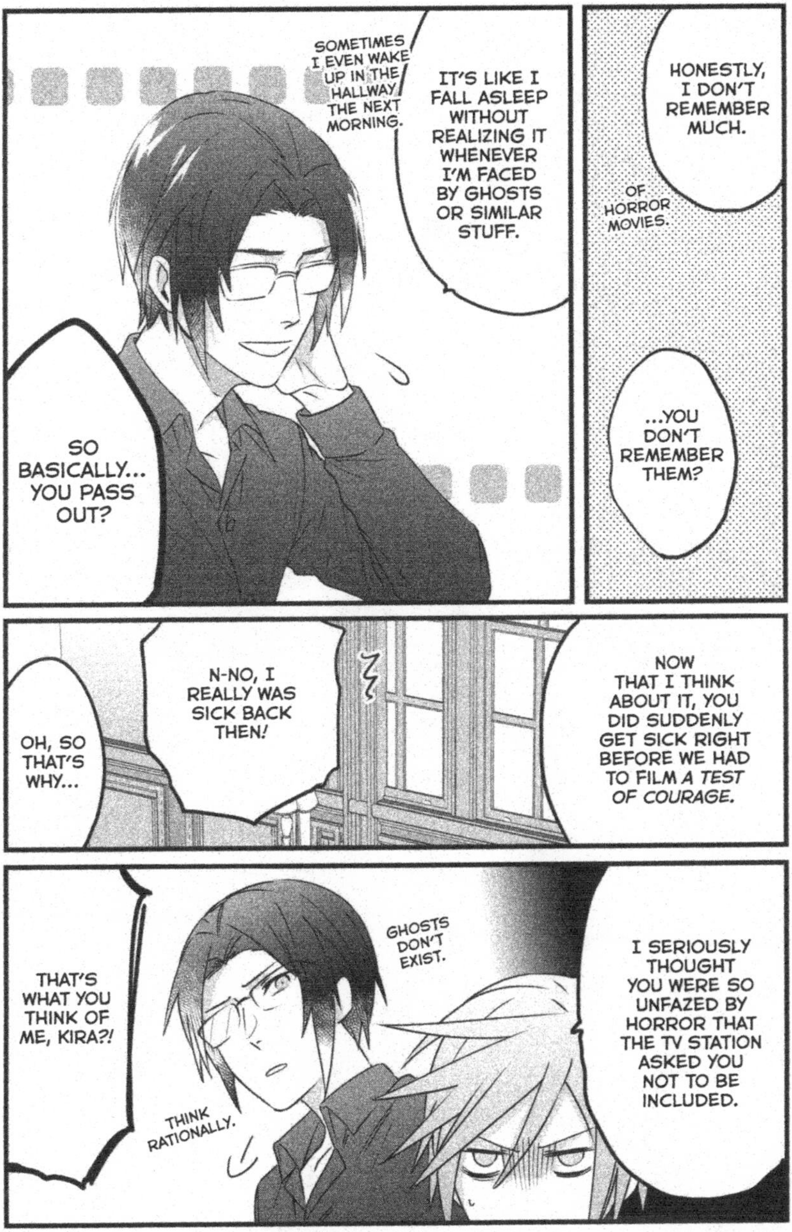
HONESTLY, I DON'T REMEMBER MUCH.
OF HORROR MOVIES.
...YOU DON'T REMEMBER THEM?
IT'S LIKE I FALL ASLEEP WITHOUT REALIZING IT WHENEVER I'M FACED BY GHOSTS OR SIMILAR STUFF.
SOMETIMES I EVEN WAKE UP IN THE HALLWAY THE NEXT MORNING.
SO BASICALLY... YOU PASS OUT?
NOW THAT I THINK ABOUT IT, YOU DID SUDDENLY GET SICK RIGHT BEFORE WE HAD TO FILM *A TEST OF COURAGE*.
N-NO, I REALLY WAS SICK BACK THEN!
OH, SO THAT'S WHY...
I SERIOUSLY THOUGHT YOU WERE SO UNFAZED BY HORROR THAT THE TV STATION ASKED YOU NOT TO BE INCLUDED.
GHOSTS DON'T EXIST.
THINK RATIONALLY.
THAT'S WHAT YOU THINK OF ME, KIRA?!

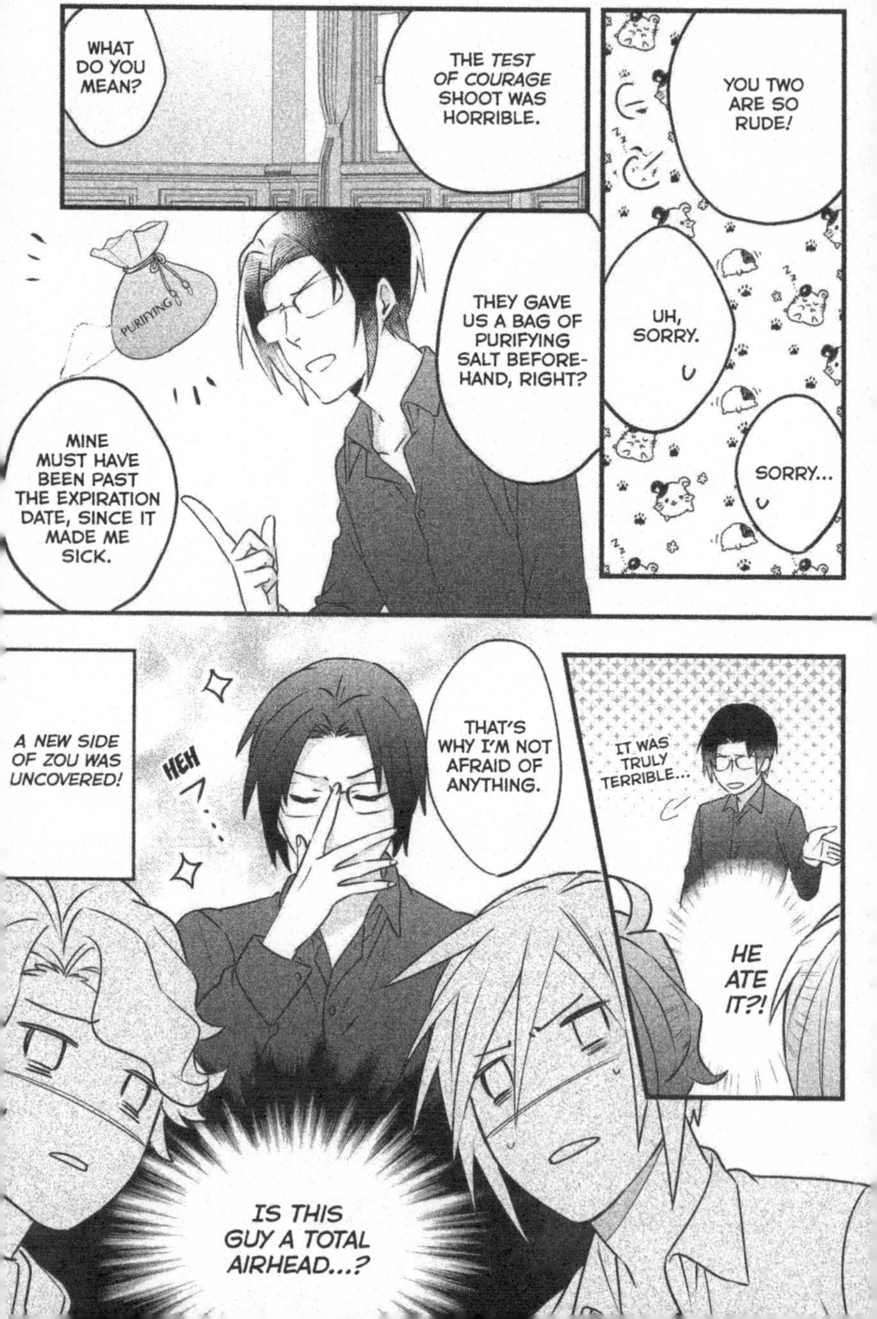
YOU TWO ARE SO RUDE!
UH, SORRY.
SORRY...
THE TEST OF COURAGE SHOOT WAS HORRIBLE.
WHAT DO YOU MEAN?
THEY GAVE US A BAG OF PURIFYING SALT BEFORE-HAND, RIGHT?
PURIFYING
MINE MUST HAVE BEEN PAST THE EXPIRATION DATE, SINCE IT MADE ME SICK.
IT WAS TRULY TERRIBLE...
HE ATE IT?!
THAT'S WHY I'M NOT AFRAID OF ANYTHING.
HEH
A NEW SIDE OF ZOU WAS UNCOVERED!
IS THIS GUY A TOTAL AIRHEAD...?

OSSAN IDOL!

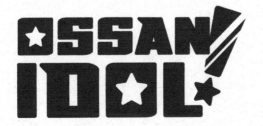

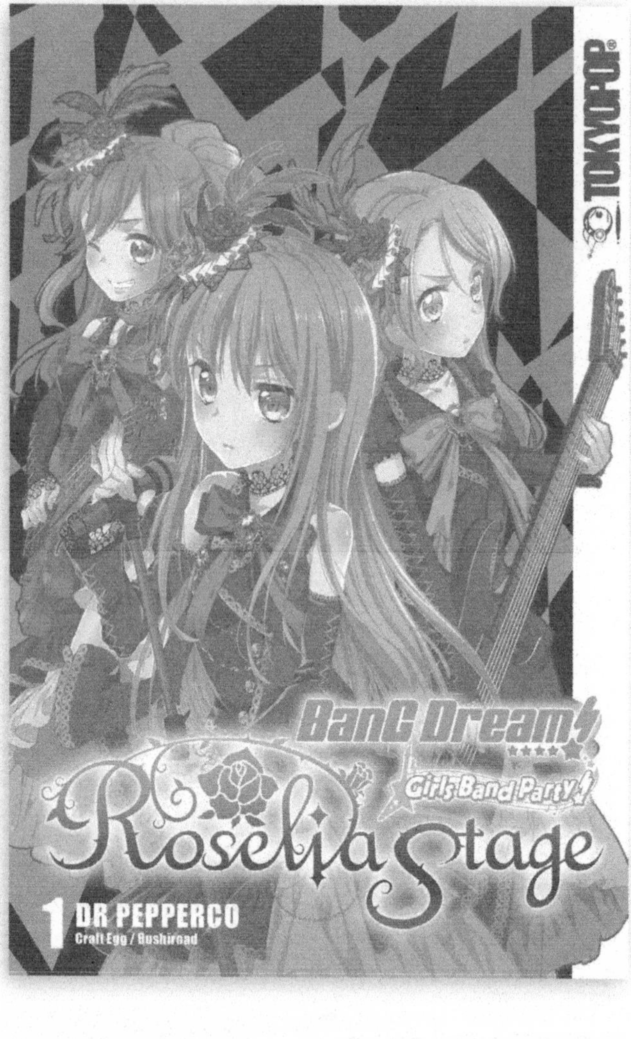
TOKYOPOP
BanG Dream!
Girls Band Party!
Roselia Stage
1 DR PEPPERCO
Craft Egg / Bushiroad

BANG DREAM! GIRLS BAND PARTY! ROSELIA STAGE, VOLUME 1

Dr pepperco

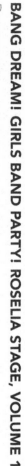

IDOL

After her father's dreams of making it big in the music industry crumble beneath the strain of trying to appease both his managers and his fans, singer Yukina Minato is determined to make him proud by forming the "perfect band" of her own. But first, she'll have to find all the right members. They'll need unparalleled skill, passion and drive if they're going to succeed as a J-rock band in such a crowded scene! Future World Fes is the biggest music event of the year, a world-famous spectacular that showcases only the best of the best. Do five high school girls have what it takes to rock their competition and secure a spot on the main stage?

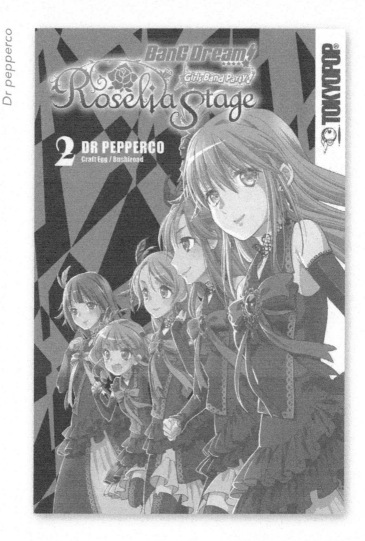

IDOL

What are the bonds that form a real band? As the contest to perform at Future World Fes draws near, pressure mounts from all sides for the members of Roselia — the rigorous practice they need to do every day to stay sharp, family tensions running high, and on top of everything else, a shocking development for Yukina.

When a professional record label approaches her to sign a solo deal, Yukina finds herself facing an impossibly heavy choice. Should she take the shortest path to achieving her dreams, even if it means leaving her band members in the dust? Or should she risk it all, staking her future on the ragtag group of amateur musicians she might actually be willing to call her friends?

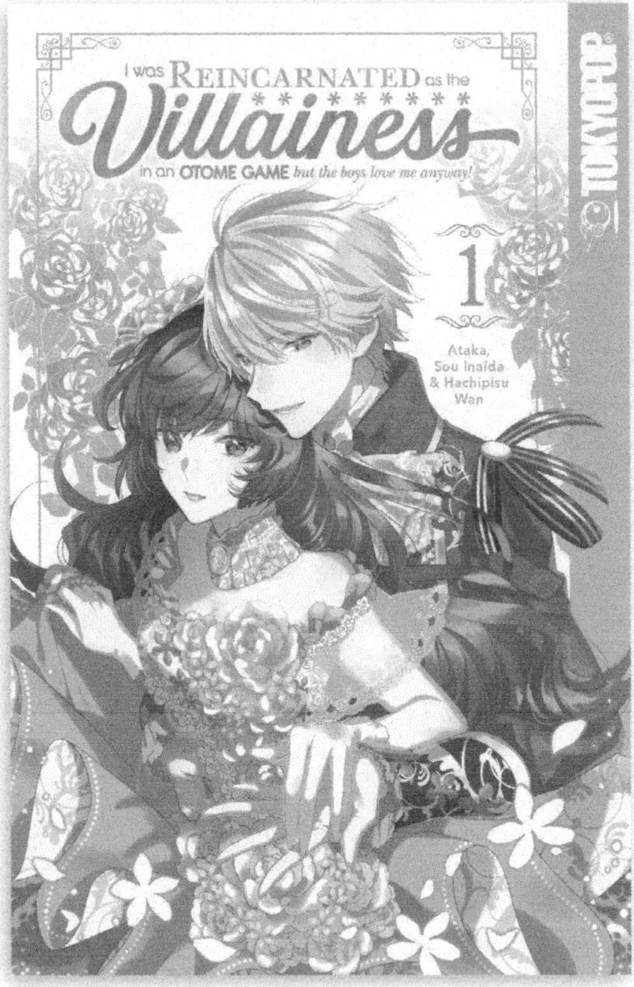
I was REINCARNATED as the
Villainess
in an OTOME GAME but the boys love me anyway!
1
Ataka,
Sou Inaida
& Hachipisu
Wan
TOKYOPOP

I WAS REINCARNATED AS THE VILLAINESS IN AN OTOME GAME BUT THE BOYS LOVE ME ANYWAY!, VOLUME 1

Ataka, Sou Inaida & Hachipisu Wan

LOVE-x-LOVE

Fated to die as the villainess of an otome game, Mystia sets out to change her own unhappy ending! Mystia Aren is the daughter of a noble family, and she just started high school. She's surrounded by a group of adoring classmates and her charming fiancé. Everything seems perfect. Except that this world is actually a dating sim called Kyun-Love, and Mystia knows she's been reincarnated into the role of the main character's evil rival! Mystia is determined to do everything she can to avoid her fate, but it's not as easy as it sounds. Especially when all the boys keep falling in love with her!

TOKYOPOP

♀LOVE-×-LOVE♂

Arika is what you could charitably call a vampire "enthusiast." When she stumbles across the beautiful and mysterious vampire Divo however, her excitement quickly turns to disappointment as she discovers he's not exactly like the seductive, manipulative villains in her stories. His looks win first place, but his head's a space case. Armed with her extensive knowledge of vampire lore, Arika downgrades Divo to a beta vampire and begins their long, long... long journey to educate him in the ways of the undead.

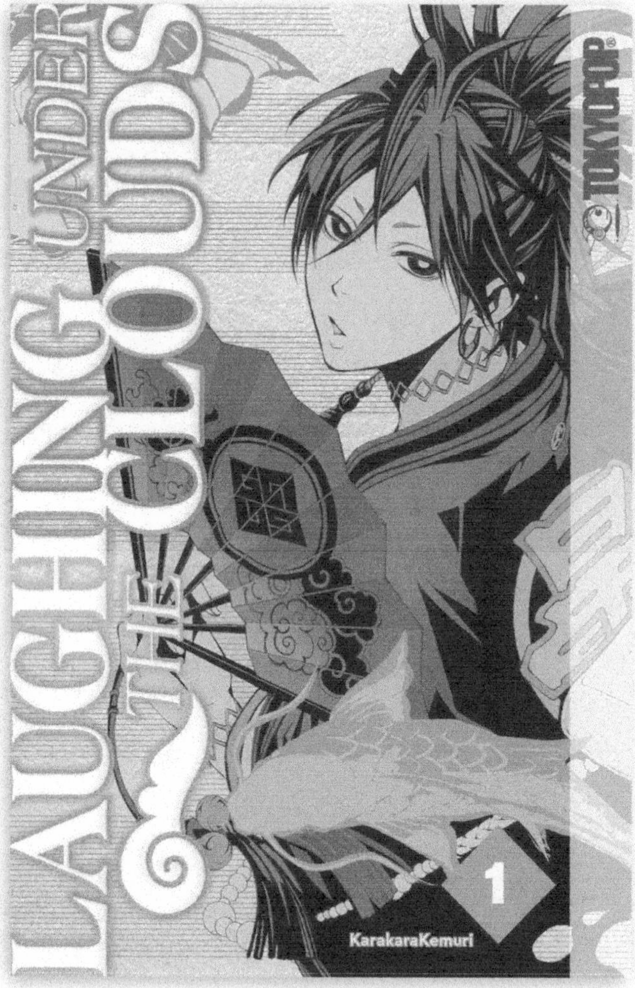
LAUGHING UNDER THE CLOUDS
TOKYOPOP
1
KarakaraKemuri

LAUGHING UNDER THE CLOUDS, VOLUME 1

KarakaraKemuri

FANTASY

Under the curse of Orochi, the great demon serpent reborn every 300 years, Japan has been shrouded in clouds for as long as anyone can remember... The era of the samurai is at an end, and carrying swords has been outlawed. To combat the rising crime rates, an inescapable prison was built in the middle of Lake Biwa. When brothers Tenka, Soramaru and Chutaro Kumo are hired to capture and transport offenders to their final lodgings in this prison, they unexpectedly find themselves faced with a greater destiny than any of them could have imagined.

TOKYOPOP

LAUGHING UNDER THE CLOUDS, VOLUME 2

KarakaraKemuri

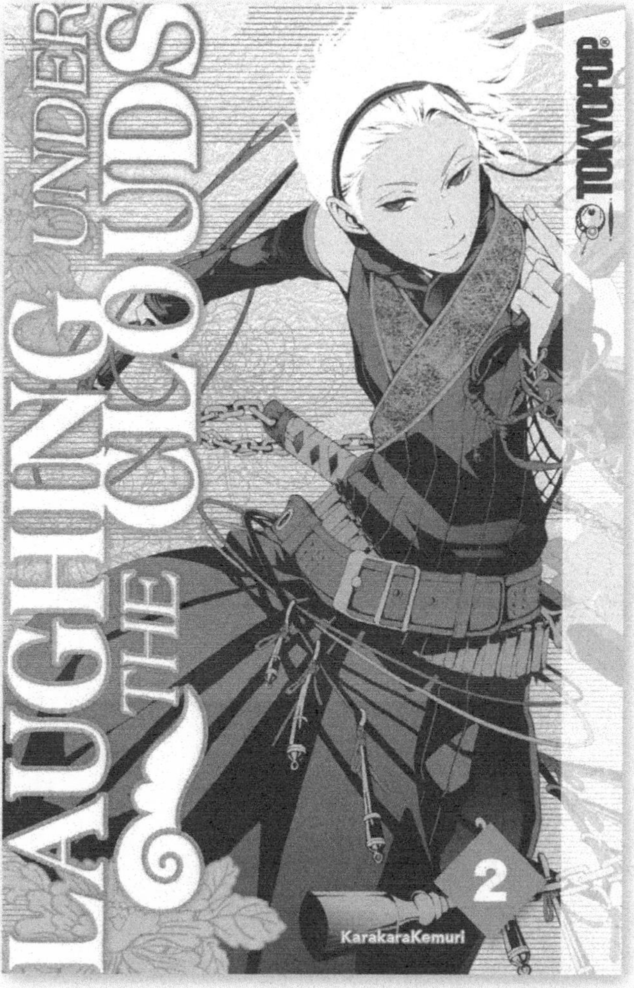
LAUGHING UNDER THE CLOUDS
TOKYOPOP
2
KarakaraKemuri

FANTASY

In the early Meiji era, against civil unrest and the end of the samurai way of life, Japan's crime rate skyrocketed. As prisons overflow, the government has no choice but to build a new, inescapable prison. This prison is Gokumonjo, located in the center of Lake Biwa, which means it relies on the three sons of the Kumo family to transport criminals to it. But is Gokumonjo truly just a prison for petty criminals? A dreaded murderer intrudes on the Kumo family's peace and brings with him news of an ancient calamity: Orochi. As Soramaru realizes his elder brother Tenka has been hiding things from him, he begins to look to outside sources to help him become stronger. At the same time, still other outside forces begin to reach out to Tenka for his knowledge of this ancient evil. The race to find and control Orochi's vessel begins!

BL FANS LOVE MY BROTHER?!

Mimu Oyamada

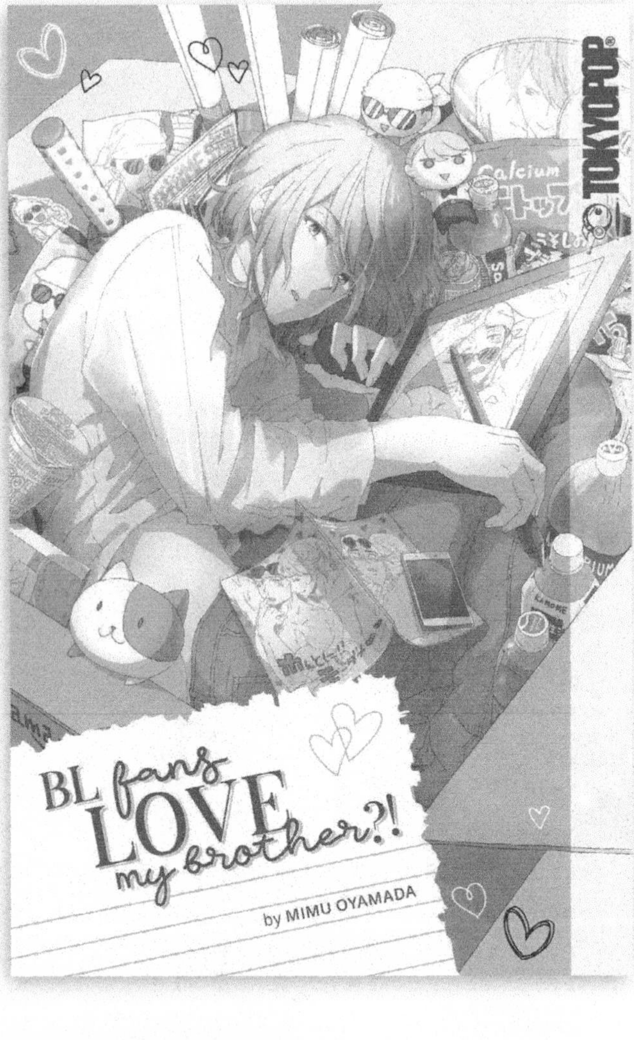

TOKYOPOP
BL fans LOVE my brother?!
by MIMU OYAMADA

COMEDY

Kirika Amano is just an unassuming college freshman, but her shut-in big brother, Teruo, is about to turn her life upside down... Even though he's barely left their family home in four years, Teruo has a big secret: he's been living a double life online as the boys love artist sensation Amaterasu! With his popularity online growing more and more, Teruo begs Kirika to pose as Amaterasu in the real world, throwing her right into the deep end of doujinshi conventions, hot and sweaty fan comics, and adoring fans who want to worship Teruo—and now Kirika—as a god! As Kirika begins to crack under the pressure, she relies on Teruo's knowledge to guide her through this new world of conventions, followers, and her own budding love for her big brother's OTP, just as Teruo needs his little sister to help him come out of his shell and explore the real world. And as each new event pushes them further into the limelight, can they find a way to keep the secret of Amaterasu's identity and also have room to be themselves?

TOKYOPOP

DRAMACON
Svetlana Chmakova

CLASSICS

Relive Christie's three-year adventure at the Yatta Anime Convention with this 15th-anniversary edition of Svetlana Chmakova's debut series: Dramacon. This special edition includes all three volumes in one gorgeous book!

When amateur writer Christie settles in the artist alley of her first-ever anime convention, she sees it as an opportunity to promote the manga she had started with her artist boyfriend. But when she unexpectedly falls for a mysterious cosplayer, things become complicated. What do you do when you love someone who is going miles away from you in just a couple of days?!

THE TREASURE OF THE KING AND THE CAT

You Kajika

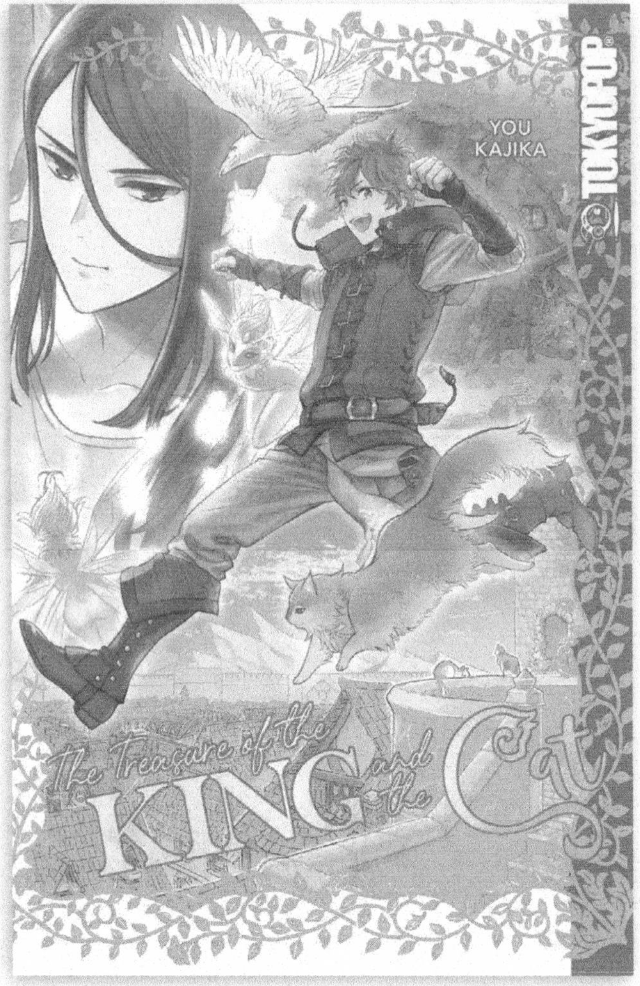
YOU KAJIKA
TOKYOPOP
The Treasure of the KING and the Cat

LOVE-x-LOVE

One day, a large number of people suddenly disappeared in the royal capital. When young King Castio goes out to investigate this occurrence, he comes across the culprit... but the criminal puts a spell on him! To help him out, the king calls the wizard O'Feuille to his castle, along with Prince Volks and his loyal retainer Nios. Together, they're determined to solve this strange, fluffy mystery full of cats, swords and magic!

TOKYOPOP

GRIMMS MANGA TALES

Ishiyama, Kei

TOKYOPOP
GRIMMS
manga Tales
Kei Ishiyama

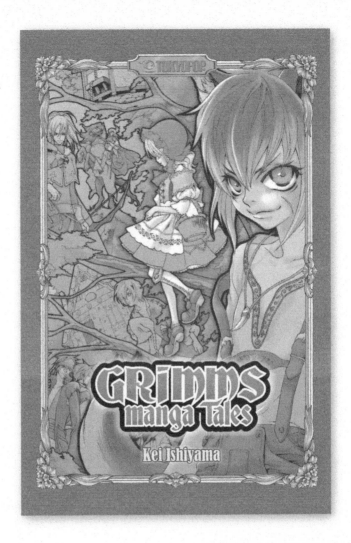

FANTASY

In this classic manga version of the Brothers Grimm fairy tales, Kei Ishiyama puts her own creative spin on these beloved stories. Featuring Little Red Riding Hood, Rapunzel, Hansel and Gretel, The Two Brothers, The Twelve Hunters, Snow White, The Frog King, Puss in Boots, and The Singing Springing Larck, this fantasy manga retells these timeless tales... but with a twist of originality!

TOKYOPOP

KONOHANA KITAN, VOLUME 3

Sakuya Amano

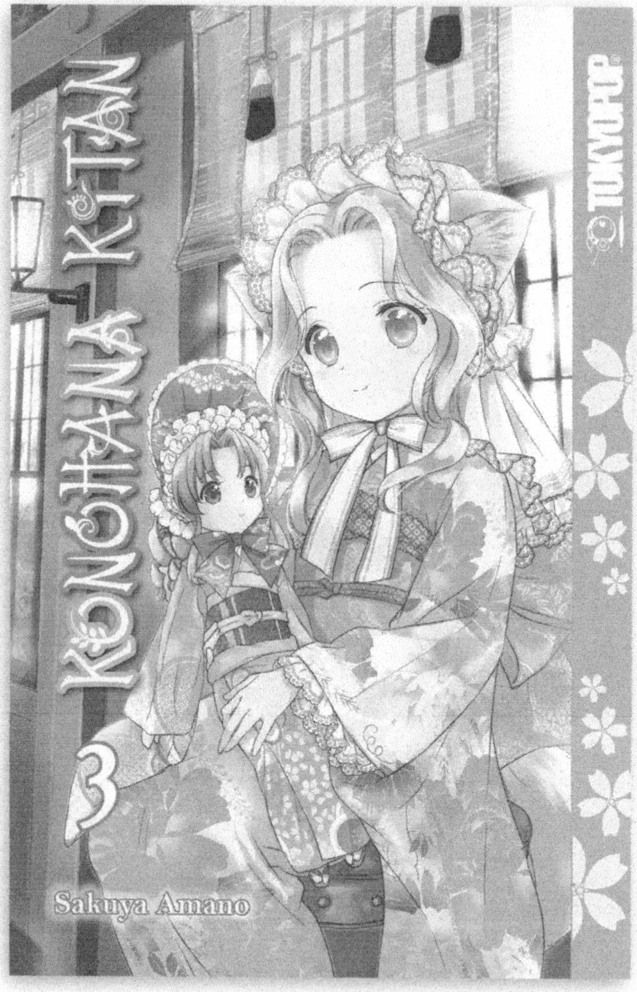
KONOHANA KITAN
3
Sakuya Amano
TOKYOPOP

FANTASY

It's wintertime at Konohanatei, which means all the foxes at the inn are getting ready to celebrate the New Year holiday together! But when Yuzu accidentally gets separated from Satsuki and her other friends on the way to the shrine, she finds herself somewhere completely different... and surrounded by strange foxes! Are these the foxes who take care of New Year's wishes? Making new friends is great, but there has to be a way back home... right?

TOKYOPOP

KONOHANA KITAN, VOLUME 4

Sakuya Amano

Every day, the foxes who staff Konohanatei work hard to make sure each of their guests is taken care of, but the healing power of the legendary inn that sits between worlds affects not only its guests but its workers as well! Take a stroll down memory lane with Kiri, who has been working there as an attendant since she was young, and who currently acts as a supervisor and mentor to Yuzu, Satsuki, Natsume, Ren, and Sakura. A glimpse of Kiri's past reveals what her first days at Konohanatei were like, and how working at the inn changed her destiny—and brought her together with one very special person.

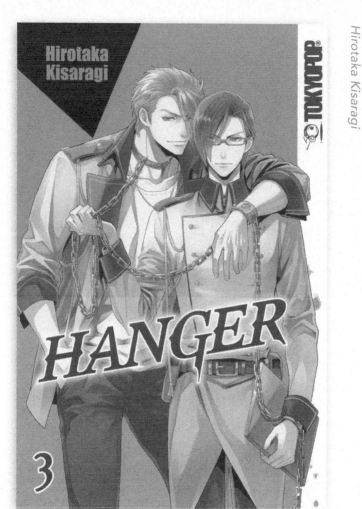

Hirotaka
Kisaragi

HANGER

3

Hirotaka Kisaragi

HANGER, VOLUME 3

δLOVE-x-LOVEδ

In a futuristic Neo-Tokyo, crime is rising rapidly in the wake of a new generation of super-drugs capable of enhancing the user's physical and mental abilities. Hajime Tsukomo is a new recruit on a federal task force trained to go after these powered-up criminals. Now he must team up with Zeroichi, a so-called Hanger looking to reduce his own jail sentence in exchange for helping to take down these chemically-boosted bad guys. With Neo-Tokyo's most wanted criminal organization — Nine-Tails — on the loose and active once again, everyone in the Security Service is on high alert. The Hanger program has always been met with some distrust from other law enforcement teams, but as tensions rise in the wake of Nine-Tails' destructive terrorism, Squad 4's Hangers and Keepers will have to work harder than ever to maintain the trust between them... and each other.

TOKYOPOP

A GENTLE NOBLE'S VACATION RECOMMENDATION, VOLUME 3

Misaki, Momochi & Sando

A Gentle Noble's
VACATION
RECOMMENDATION
MISAKI • MOMOCHI • SANDO
3
TOKYOPOP

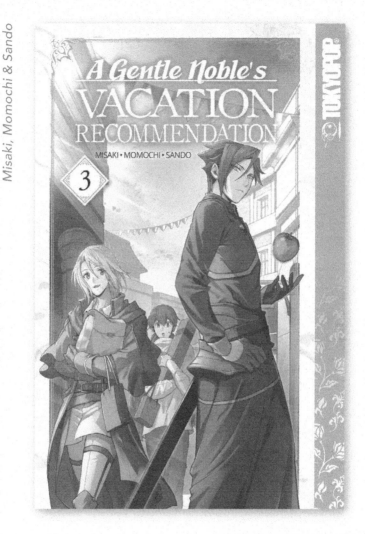

ISEKAI

After defeating the underground dragon and finishing up their business in the mercantile city of Marcade, Lizel and Gil resume their journey, having promised Judge's grandfather to protect Judge along the way. But danger soon catches up to them when a strange group of bandits called the Forky Gang attacks in the middle of the night! It quickly becomes clear that someone is targeting Lizel... but who could it be, and for what reason? As always, former noble and current adventurer Lizel takes all new developments in stride in his usual, laid-back fashion. He's celebrating his promotion from a simple E-rank to a D-rank adventurer — and setting his sights on ranking up again soon!

TOKYOPOP

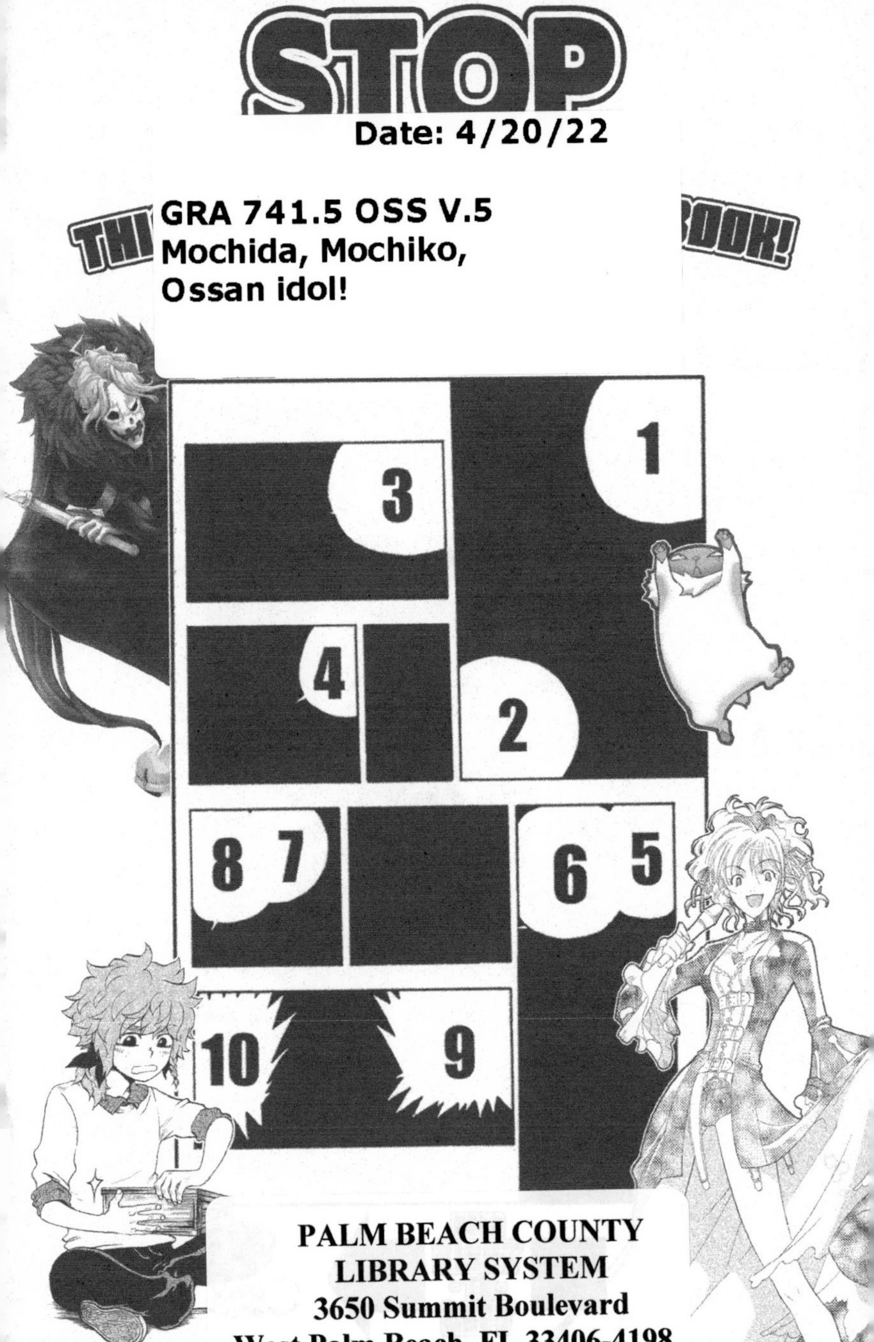
STOP
1
2
3
4
5
6
7
8
9
10

Crimson from *Kamo* / Fai...
Morrey from *Goldfisch* / Pr...

Ossan Idol, Volume 5

Manga by Ichika Kino

Original story by Mochiko Mochida

Editor - Lena Atanassova
Translator - Katie Kimura
Quality Check - Shingo Nemoto
Proofreader - Caroline Wong
Copyeditor - M. Cara Carper
Editorial Associate - Janae Young
Marketing Associate - Kae Winters
Cover Design - Sol DeLeo
Retouching and Lettering - Vibrraant Publishing Studio
Licensing Specialist - Arika Yanaka
Editor-in-Chief & Publisher - Stu Levy

A TOKYOPOP® Manga

TOKYOPOP Inc.
5200 W. Century Blvd. Suite 705
Los Angeles, 90045

E-mail: info@TOKYOPOP.com
Come visit us online at www.TOKYOPOP.com

www.facebook.com/TOKYOPOP
www.twitter.com/TOKYOPOP
www.instagram.com/TOKYOPOP

First published in Japan in 2020 by Shufu To Seikatsu Sha Co., Ltd.
English translation rights reserved by TOKYOPOP. under the license from Shufu To Seikatsu Sha Co., Ltd.

ISBN: 978-1-4278-6867-1

First TOKYOPOP Printing: September 2021